Caring for America

Caring for America

HOME HEALTH WORKERS IN THE SHADOW OF THE WELFARE STATE

EILEEN BORIS AND JENNIFER KLEIN

Oxford University Press, Inc., publishes works that further
Oxford University's objective of excellence
in research, scholarship, and education.

Oxford New York
Auckland Cape Town Dar es Salaam Hong Kong Karachi
Kuala Lumpur Madrid Melbourne Mexico City Nairobi
New Delhi Shanghai Taipei Toronto

With offices in
Argentina Austria Brazil Chile Czech Republic France Greece
Guatemala Hungary Italy Japan Poland Portugal Singapore
South Korea Switzerland Thailand Turkey Ukraine Vietnam

First issued as an Oxford University Press paperback, 2015

Published by Oxford University Press, Inc.
198 Madison Avenue, New York, New York 10016

www.oup.com

Library of Congress Cataloging-in-Publication Data
Boris, Eileen, 1948–
Caring for America : home health workers in the shadow of the welfare state / Eileen Boris and Jennifer Klein.
p. cm.
Includes bibliographical references and index.
ISBN 978-0-19-532911-7 (cloth); 978-0-19-937858-6 (pbk)
1. Home health aides—United States. 2. Home health aides—Labor unions—United States.
I. Klein, Jennifer, 1967- II. Title. III. Title: Home health workers in the shadow of the welfare state.
RA645.35.B67 2012
362.14—dc23 2011034402

9 8 7 6 5 4 3 2 1

Printed in the United States of America
on acid-free paper

For Nelson and Daniel,
In Love and Hope
—EB

In Memory of Theodore Klein
—JK

Table of Contents

Illustrations

Preface

The Personal Is Prologue

In March 2003, as the Bush administration launched its attack on Iraq, we came together to hammer out a conference paper on the role of public policy in shaping America's long-term care system. Our collaboration clicked, but how we each came to write this book illustrates the ways that personal narrative intersects with scholarship. It's not just that the past is prologue, as the very stonework of the National Archives in Washington, D.C., declares—so is the personal. Here are our stories.

Eileen's Story

Barely settled in California in June 2001, I responded to a call from the United Domestic Workers of America to testify before the Santa Barbara County Board of Supervisors. The year before, the state legislature had mandated that all counties become, for collective bargaining purposes, the employer of In-Home Supportive Services (IHSS) workers. I was to use my position as a professor to argue for the creation of a public authority to set standards and provide training for personal attendants and other home aides. It wasn't my explanation of how the care we applaud as a labor of love deserves living wages and benefits that led the supervisors to pass enabling legislation. I'd like to think that it was the testimony of the givers and receivers of care, and their daily struggles for dignity, that convinced the elected officials that care work is worthy of compensation. Probably the county supervisors looked at the budget and figured that because home care, with its low-wage workforce, is cheaper than institutionalization, they'd rather cut a deal with the union than lose state funding.

Having spent a good many years investigating the global movement of home workers for "dignity and daily bread," and thinking about the home as a workplace, I became intrigued—and then excited over the interpretative and theoretical dimensions encapsulated in this local deal. The state was paying some women to care for their own family members. I asked myself, could this transaction be used to argue for revaluing care work, despite the minimum wages that seem to reinforce its degradation? I soon discovered a vibrant group of social science researchers, based at the UCLA Labor Center and funded by the all UC Institute for Labor and Employment, who had joined with trade unionists to investigate conditions in state-funded home care. They were conducting focus groups, providing occupational training, and analyzing state data to argue for higher wages, health benefits, and unionization. But, all their work revolved around the present, with some nod to the organizing efforts of the 1990s. I became determined to give home care a history, to contextualize the wages of care by recovering its past.

Then the health of my 85-year-old mother, who lived across the country in northern Virginia, began deteriorating. Tending to her was becoming too much of a strain on my sister. We began interviewing home care aides referred to us by Jewish Family Services, a nonprofit social welfare agency. We would pay $15 an hour, but the aide would receive less than $12. Medicare and health insurance would pick up some of this cost, but only after a hospital stay and doctor's orders justifying the need. Mom entered the hospital for medical tests but died there a week later, and so we never hired the young woman from Ghana whose experience in providing comfort to the ill had so impressed us. Still, I had become acquainted and frustrated with the world of eligibility, certification, home health providers, and the private market in care as it had developed over the last two decades. We needed to write that history.

Jennifer's Story

I began thinking about home care while a fellow in health policy with the Robert Wood Johnson Foundation. Along with fellows in the fields of political science and economics, we began a reading group, surveying literature on long-term care from the social sciences and medicine. Strikingly, the discussion of care was so lopsided: care was something one received, not what people provided to others. I decided to bring the perspective of a labor historian to what, in policy circles, seemed predominantly defined as a consumers' issue. I was intrigued by the question of how the state itself created a particular low-wage labor market, all the while denying that the home was in fact a workplace. In my previous work, I had investigated the blurring of public and private realms—of state, market, communal institutions. I had written about workers organizing to gain power and security. What would it take for these particular workers to win dignity, security, and income? From whom would they demand it? And what would it mean for those taking care of loved ones?

I also had my personal interaction with home care—through my grandmother, Sara Klein, who during this period was a very alert woman in her nineties. She continued to live in her own apartment up to the very end of her life at age 99. What made her "independence" possible, of course, was the daily, and eventually nightly, care provided by two home attendants, Maria and Yvonne. They were immigrants from Central America and the Caribbean, caring for a woman who herself had arrived as an immigrant half a century earlier. Up until she was 98, they accompanied her on shopping trips, doctors' appointments, family visits, walks, and meals out; in her final year, they stayed with her at home. Sara was funny and charming but watched everything and everyone like a hawk. She defined herself by her strength and stubbornness, even in her waning years. During one hurricane season, when her area was ordered evacuated, she refused. "I survived the Nazis, I survived the war, I survived coming to America. What's a little wind going to do to me?" she said hanging up the phone on my dad. Maria and Yvonne had to put up with one very tough woman. "I'm made from iron," she used to say. It enabled her to get through a lot of what she faced in life but did not necessarily make for an easy working relationship!

When Sara passed away in 2008, about 100 people attended a public funeral service. Only the immediate family went on to the cemetery, and Maria and Yvonne. Like each family member, they placed dirt on her casket. Maria stood at the gravesite and cried heavily. They had spent the most time with her and now they had lost a friend. And now, somehow, their work would have to start all over again with someone else. How many jobs end, repeatedly, with such an emotional toll? There is a lot to this labor we have yet to understand, making it all the more imperative that we write about it.

Why We Should Care about Home Care

Like most Americans, then, we have an immediate and personal connection with the problem of providing care for family. Our loved ones were relatively fortunate because they had some resources—a patchwork of insurance, Medicare, savings, and income—that could secure and pay for care. Such periods of illness or family crisis are widely shared and difficult, emotionally, physically, and financially. But this book doesn't provide advice on how to obtain a home care worker for a member of your family or how to treat them over the weeks and months to come. We've told these personal stories because we've learned that public policies over the last 70 years or so created, funded, and shaped home care. To figure out why it is so difficult, even for people with resources, to obtain care, we have to look at how this system developed. How did we arrive at this point that the labor necessary to sustain life became invisible, under-compensated, and defined as not really work?

For decades, as the American population, like that of Western Europe and Japan, has aged and baby boomers have moved toward retirement, the U.S. Congress failed to enact a genuine long-term care policy. In the absence of guaranteed social insurance, the default has been to use public assistance and Medicaid. In this book, we will primarily be discussing services funded through various public programs. They are not unconnected, however, to the allegedly "private market" wherein middle-class families purchase care for their loved ones. The U.S. reliance primarily on means-tested social services available only to the poorest people fundamentally shaped the entire labor market for care. The claim of the Supreme Court in sustaining the exclusion of home care workers from the nation's wage and hour law exemplifies the fear that only through cheap labor can we provide long-term care.[1] Our book argues that we all have a stake in rethinking that assumption.

Acknowledgments

What a journey this has been! We each began working on the subject as separate, individual projects. Upon discovering that we were looking at the same group of workers, we thought, why not write an article together? We were amazed at how much untapped material we found and further at how our different methodological approaches and specialties became so complimentary. We were excited by the connections we were able to make together that we would have missed with each working on her own through a singular lens. Soon we had a book project that extended back to the 1930s and spanned the country. Alas, the idea that having two authors would speed up the process turned out to be far from true. As the decade wore on and the political sands shifted, we discovered in some ways that we had taken on more than we bargained for. So, most of all, we thank each other for an amazing time—and for pushing on even when other professional and personal events had to take precedence.

All books are collective efforts and this one is no different, though we take full responsibility for its outcome. We have accumulated a long list of debts. First, we thank the numerous archivists who guided our way through manifold unprocessed as well as fully indexed collections, including those at Barbara Bates Center for the Study of the History of Nursing, University of Pennsylvania School of Nursing; The Bancroft Library, University of California, Berkeley; McMillan Library, New York Human Resources Administration; The National Archives for Black Women's History (Mary McLeod Bethune Council House); The Ronald Reagan Presidential Archives; Sophia Smith Collection, Smith College; Wisconsin Historical Society; and Tamiment Library, New York University. Special appreciation goes to Louis Jones at the Walter P. Reuther Library for Labor and Urban Affairs, Wayne State University; Tab Lewis and Eugene Morris, the National Archives and Records Administration, College Park, Maryland; Catherine Powell, the Labor Archives & Research Center, San Francisco State University; Arlene Shaner, New York Academy of Medicine;

Lucy Barber, then at the California State Archives; and Barbara Bair, the Library of Congress.

Second, we couldn't have written this book without the willingness of those who made this history to answer our questions and offer their perceptions. Karen Zullo Sherr, Janet Heinritz-Canterbury, and Barbara Shulman shared personal papers and experiences. We also thank John Borsos, Donna Calame, Leon Chow, Steve Elias, Mary Ruth Gross, Lea Grundy, Hadley Hall, Catherine Jermany, Sue Kern, Paul Kumar, David Novogrodsky, Karen Orlando, Laura Reif, David Rolf, David Shapiro, Loretta Stevens, Catherine Sullivan, and Steven Ward. We especially thank Keith Kelleher for letting us read and quote from his unpublished memoir. Craig Becker kept us abreast of legal developments. We are grateful to the rank and file workers who told us their stories and to all the other union and independent living activists from whom we've learned.

Eileen would also like to thank Marcos Vargas, Das Williams, Harley Agustino and all the activists at CAUSE and PUEBLO, who first introduced her to the world of IHSS. Jennifer thanks colleagues at Yale for their support, including Laura Engelstein, Paul Freedman, Beverly Gage, Joanne Meyerowitz, and Stephen Pitti. Eileen acknowledges the support of her colleagues in the Department of Feminist Studies and the Department of History at UCSB, especially those in the Comparative Gender History Program and the Policy History Program. A number of former students assisted with this project over the years. Jennifer thanks student research assistants Matthew Bloom, Paige Austin, Jay Driskell, and Suzanne Kahn. Eileen thanks Elizabeth Shermer, Leandra Zarnow, Heather Berg, and, especially, Jill Jensen.

Third, we appreciate the willingness of others to share their unpublished and published work, including Mark Neal Aaronson, Linda Delp, Steve Early, Candance Howes, Patrice Mareschal, Vanessa May, Katie Quan, Lynn Rivas, and Peggie R. Smith. We benefited enormously from feedback at numerous conferences, talks, and seminars and from comments by and advice from other scholars, including Graham Cassano, Dorothy Sue Cobble, Leon Fink, Donna Haverty-Stacke, Alison Kafer, Alice Kessler-Harris, Felicia Kornbluh, Nancy MacLean, Sonya Michel, Premilla Nadasen, Annelise Orleck, Rhacel Parreñas, Claire Potter, Robert Self, Vicki Schultz, Mark Schlesinger, Danny Walkowitz, Barbara Welke, Joan Williams, Carol Wolkowitz, Carol Zabin and anonymous reviewers for Oxford University Press. A special thanks to Karen Balcom, Merlin Chowkwanyun, Wyatt Closs, Lola Cuevas, Erika Gottfried, Vanessa May, Julie Monroe, David Sachs, Judy Scott, and Karen Zullo Sherr for help securing illustrations. David McBride proved to be a knowledgeable, hands-on editor, and we have greatly appreciated his engagement with the book. We also thank his able assistants, especially Caelyn Cobb and the entire team at Oxford University Press. Sherri Barnes brought her talents to the index.

Fourth, grants and university funds facilitated this project. Eileen would like to acknowledge support from the Academic Senate and ISBER, UCSB; the UC Labor and Employment Research and Education Fund; the National Endowment for the Humanities; and Blair Hull, for endowing the chair she holds. Jennifer received support from the Robert Wood Johnson Foundation, a Morse Fellowship and Yale Senior Leave. We both thank the Rockefeller Foundation, Bellagio Center, for making possible a wonderful month of writing looking down on Lake Como.

Most important was the support that came via the home front.

For Eileen, the transformations in the political economy impacted our labor historian household. I used to work on garments and Nelson Lichtenstein used to work on autos. Now he writes on retail and I, on health and welfare. In 1999, Nelson published an op-ed on the Los Angeles home care victory. Little did we realize that just a couple of years later, I would be the one to probe the larger historical meaning and political significance of home care. There's no better wordsmith than Nelson and I can't imagine a world without his hard-hitting analysis, keen historical sense, fierce politics, and tender love. And he does more than half of the home labors. Our son Daniel's own union and community organizing, and studies in public health, proved inspirational, giving hope that the next generation can carry it on.

For Jennifer, it's hard to believe life could have changed so much in the course of one book project. When I started the reading for it, I had a different job, no permanent home, no children, and family members who are now gone. I never could have imagined my father, Ted Klein, would not be alive to see this book come to fruition. After his devastating illness and death, I thank his many friends for reminding us that Ted was a beloved person of great integrity, wit, judiciousness, and generous mentoring. He is dearly missed. The circle of life turned again when the following year two beautiful daughters were born, Hannah Lily and Teya Samara. Sara Klein, the eldest surviving twin sister in our family, lived just long enough to see and hold them. Now four years old, they already have Ted and Sara's wit—and silliness. Leslie Klein has always been the strong feminist who raised me to write a book like this one. Through it all Jim Berger has been there with wholehearted and calming support, great love, and a persistent editing pen. He illuminates the big picture—in terms of the book and life.

Credits

Material in the Introduction, Chapter 5, and Chapter 7 is adapted from Eileen Boris and Jennifer Klein, "'We Were the Invisible Workforce': Unionizing Home Care," from *The Sex of Class: Women Transforming American Labor*, edited by

Dorothy Sue Cobble. Copyright © 2007 by Cornell University. Used by permission of the publisher, Cornell University Press.

Material in Chapter 3 and Chapter 7 is adapted from Eileen Boris and Jennifer Klein, "Organizing Home Care: Low Waged Workers in the Welfare State," in *Politics and Society* 34:1 (March 2006), 81–108, by SAGE Publications Ltd./ SAGE Publications, Inc., at http://pas.sagepub.com/content/34/1/81. All rights reserved. ©

Material in Chapter 6 is adapted from Eileen Boris and Jennifer Klein, "Organizing the Carework Economy: When the Private Becomes Public," from *Rethinking U.S. Labor History: Essays on the Working-Class Experience, 1756–2009,* edited by Donna T. Haverty-Stacke and Daniel J. Walkowitz (New York: Continuum Books, 2010), 192–216. Used by permission from the publisher, Continuum Books.

Material in the Epilogue is adapted from Eileen Boris and Jennifer Klein, "Making Home Care," from *Intimate Labors: Cultures, Technologies, and the Politics of Care,* edited by Eileen Boris and Rhacel Salazar Parreñas. Copyright © 2010 by the Board of Trustees of the Leland Stanford Jr. University. All rights reserved. Used with the permission of Stanford University Press, www.sup.org.

Material in the Epilogue also is adapted from Eileen Boris and Jennifer Klein, "Labor on the Home Front," *New Labor Forum* (Spring 2008), 32–41. Used with permission of the publisher, *New Labor Forum,* Center for Labor, Community and Policy Studies, Joseph S. Murphy Institute, CUNY.

Abbreviations

ADC	Aid to Dependent Children
AFDC	Aid to Families with Dependent Children
AFSCME	American Federation of State, County, and Municipal Employees
AHA	American Hospital Association
AJPH	*The American Journal of Public Health*
AJN	*The American Journal of Nursing*
AN	*Amsterdam News*
ANA	American Nurses Association
APHA	American Public Health Association
APTD	Aid to the Permanently and Totally Disabled
APWA	American Public Welfare Association
BANC	The Bancroft Library, University of California, Berkeley, CA
Bethune	National Archives for Black Women's History, Mary McLeod Bethune Council House, Washington, DC
CB	Children's Bureau
CF	Central Files, U.S. Children's Bureau Records, NARA
CHA	California Homemakers Association
CIL	Center for Independent Living
CIL Records	Records of Center for Independent Living, BANC
CORE	Congress on Racial Equality
CRLA	California Rural Legal Assistance
CSA	California State Archives, Sacramento, CA
CWRO	California Welfare Rights Organization
DOL	Department of Labor
DORS	Illinois Department of Rehabilitative Services
FOIA	Freedom of Information Act

FLSA	Fair Labor Standards Act
HEW	U.S. Department of Health, Education, and Welfare
HIP	Health Insurance Plan of New York
HRA	Human Resources Administration, New York
HSS	Henry Street Settlement Records, SWHA
IDOA	Illinois Department of Aging
IHSS	In-Home Supportive Services
IS	Division of Information, Information Service, File 1936–1942, WPA Records, NARA
Jarrett Papers	Mary C. Jarrett Papers, Sophia Smith Collection, Smith College, Northampton, MA
JLP	Mayor John Lindsay Papers, MA
LAT	*Los Angeles Times*
LC	Library of Congress, Washington, DC
MA	Municipal Archives, New York, NY
MAA	Medical Assistance for the Aged
MDTA	Manpower Development and Training Act
MFY	Mobilization For Youth
NAACP	Records of the National Association for the Advancement of Colored People, LC
NARA	National Archives and Records Administration, College Park, MD
NCHE	National Committee on Household Employment
NCHE Records	Records of the National Committee on Household Employment, Bethune
NCHHAS	National Council for Homemaker–Home Health Aide Services, Inc.
NHA	Barbara Bates Center for the Study of the History of Nursing, University of Pennsylvania School of Nursing, Philadelphia, PA
NNC	Records of the National Negro Congress, microfilm edition
NUL	Records of the National Urban League, LC
NWRO	National Welfare Rights Organization
NYAM	The New York Academy of Medicine
NYAMR	The New York Academy of Medicine Records, Historical Collections, New York, NY
NYT	*New York Times*
OAA	Old Age Assistance
OEO	Office of Economic Opportunity
PWN	*Public Welfare News*, North Carolina

PHS	Public Health Service
Posner Papers	Seymour Posner Papers, Collection 70, Wagner Archives, Tamiment Library, New York University, New York, NY
PSP	Division of Professional and Service Projects, 1935–1941, WPA
RG 47	Records of Social Security Administration/Federal Security Agency, NARA
RG 69	Records of the Work Projects Administration, NARA
RG 102	Records of the U.S. Children's Bureau, NARA
RG 235	Records of HEW, NARA
RG 363	Records of Social and Rehabilitation Services [SRS], HEW, NARA
Roberts Papers	Edward V. Roberts Papers, BANC
RRL	Records of Governor Ronald Reagan, Ronald Reagan Presidential Library, Simi Valley, CA
Sampson Papers	Timothy Sampson Papers, SFSU-LA
SB	*The Sacramento Bee*
SEIU	Service Employees International Union
SFC	*San Francisco Chronicle*
SFNLA	San Francisco Neighborhood Legal Assistance Foundation
SFSU-LA	San Francisco State University, Labor Archives & Research Center, San Francisco, CA
SPFSR	Division of Service Projects, February 1942–June 1943, Final State Reports, WPA, NARA
SSA	Social Security Administration
SSI	Supplemental Security Income
SSEU	Social Service Employees Union
SWHA	Social Welfare History Archives, University of Minnesota, Minneapolis, MN
TNAHR	*The Trained Nurse and Hospital Review*
Trager Papers	Brahna Trager Papers, LC
UDWA	United Domestic Workers of America
UHW	United Health Workers West
USES	United States Employment Service
UW Records	Union Wage Records, SFSU-LA
Wagner Archives	Robert F. Wagner Labor Archives, Tamiment Library & Robert F. Wagner Labor Archives, New York University, New York, NY
WHS	Wisconsin Historical Society, Madison, WI
WID	World Institute on Disability
WID Records	Records of World Institute on Disability, BANC

WPA	Works Progress Administration
WP	*Washington Post*
WPP	Division of Women and Professional Projects, WPA
WPR	Walter P. Reuther Library of Labor and Urban Affairs, Wayne State University, Detroit, MI
WRO	Welfare Rights Organization
Zukas Papers	Hale Zukas Papers, BANC

Caring for America

"Two Women," original drawing 8.5 by 11 pencil and wash on watercolor paper, from Karen Zullo Sherr, *Beatrice and Lucia: A Book of Drawings* (San Francisco: Planning for Elders in the Central City, 2002) Copyright © 2002 by Karen Zullo Sherr.

Introduction

Making the Private Public

These are the faces of home care. For 47 years, single mother Evelyn Hawks looked after her developmentally disabled daughter, Hester Brown. A former data entry operator, Hawks, an African American, was paid to care for her daughter through California's In-Home Supportive Services program. The work was hard, the income just enough to rent a tiny one-bedroom apartment in central Los Angeles. But Hawks judged the sacrifice to be worth keeping her daughter out of an institution. Shortly after taking office in 2003, Governor Arnold Schwarzenegger sought to eliminate personal attendant services for children like Hester when a parent performs the labor of care. A coalition of disability rights activists, organized seniors, and trade unionists beat back his assault.[1]

After bathing, shaving, and cooking for Hector Bertull for seven hours a day in San Ysidro, California, 62-year-old Mexican American Rosa Perez went home. But she treated the 93-year-old as if he were a member of her own family: "I've grown so attached to him that I sometimes take him home with me." Bertull returned the affection: "I love Rosa . . . like I loved my own mother." Such attachments blur the boundaries between family and work.[2]

On the tenth anniversary of "welfare reform" in August 2006, Philadelphian Mysheda Autry, a 25-year-old African American high school dropout, faced the loss of her welfare benefits. "Sooner or later she'll have to get a job," admitted the head of the social service agency whose help Autry sought. The administrator pointed her to work as a home health aide.[3]

Evelyn Coke, a 73-year-old Jamaican immigrant from Queens, had spent 20 years cooking for, cleaning up after, and bathing clients on Long Island, sometimes working 24-hour shifts, though she was rarely paid for overtime. Infirm from a car accident and undergoing kidney dialysis, she relied on her computer technician son for personal assistance. "I loved my work, but the money was not good at all," she recalled. "The job didn't even give us health insurance."[4] She became the plaintiff in a high-profile lawsuit demanding overtime compensation for all those extra hours of work, but in June 2007, the Supreme Court ruled that Coke and 1.4 million other aides at the time fell outside the Fair Labor Standards Act, even when employed by a for-profit agency.[5]

Women like Hawks, Perez, Autry, and Coke perform intimate daily tasks—such as bathing bodies, brushing teeth, and putting on clothes—that enable people to live decent lives at home. They labor in private spaces meeting individual and family needs. But how they do their jobs is anything but private: theirs is a story of political economy, one that reflects the major shifts in work and welfare that define contemporary America. Home care aides compose a vast workforce—much larger than that of the iconic auto and steel industries. Their lives tell us much about the shifting relations between home and market, state and family. Their fate links together some of our most challenging social issues: an aging society and an inadequate national long-term care policy, the rise of a vast medical-industrial complex, the neoliberal restructuring of public services, the need for disability rights, the crisis of domestic labor and decline of family income, new immigration and systemic racial inequality, the expansion of the service economy, and the precariousness of the American labor movement.

For decades they labored in the shadow of a welfare state that shaped the very conditions of their occupation. They rarely earned a living wage. But during the last third of the twentieth century, these previously invisible workers, disproportionately women of color, organized to demand rights and recognition. They surged into unions, making claims on the state despite a market fundamentalism that sought to deny any right to care; over 400,000 had joined unions by 2010. They made unions relevant by defending and valorizing relations of dependence and interdependence. Still, their modest gains and continual struggles also underscored the formidable obstacles to social justice with the unraveling of the New Deal order.

This book gives home care a history. We address the development of long-term care and the intertwined efforts of workers and clients to win dignity, self-determination, security, and personal and social worth. We rethink the history of the American welfare state from the perspective of care work. Social policies are not just income transfer programs. They also depend on a particular configuration of labor that facilitates support on a daily basis. Government has had a central role in creating labor markets in human and social services. Broad trends in U.S. social policy over the latter half of the twentieth century fostered the creation of new occupations, funded by the state, and actively channeled particular workers into these jobs, especially poor and minority women, deploying and perpetuating gender and racial inequality.

The term "home care" includes a variety of skills and occupations, ranging from visiting nurse to physical therapist to housekeeper. This study focuses on personal attendants, in-home support workers, homemaker-housekeepers, and home health aides. Though not officially classified as health workers, they are part of health systems and health care unions and have taken to calling themselves "home health workers." These essential workers are America's front-line caregivers. More than social workers or nurses, they enable people to remain home by providing personal care and maintaining a safe and clean environment. They earn average hourly wages lower than that of all other jobs in health care and historically have labored without security of employment, social benefits, or even workers' compensation.[6]

Once considered economically marginal, home care has moved to the center of the economy. By the end of the twentieth century, it was among the fastest growing occupations. While manufacturing shed jobs, long-term care and the "health care support" sector added hundreds of thousands of positions at a steady clip.[7] Not only did the number of jobs increase, but the percentage of the nation's workforce employed in these fields rose. At the start of the Great Recession in 2008, over 1.7 million people across the nation worked as home health or personal care aides. Nor did the U.S. Department of Labor expect the recession to reverse this trend. Citing technological advances and the growing number of older people, the Bureau of Labor Statistics projected rapid employment growth in home health aide jobs, second only to registered nurses.[8]

This statistical story points to fundamental changes over the last few decades. Low-waged workers stand at the core of a new care work economy, defined, on the one hand, through the long shift of household labor into commercialized and public service sectors and the now permanent participation of married white women in the workforce. Families increasingly sought other women to take up the slack. They hired immigrant and U.S.-born women of color not only to clean their houses and care for children but to assist elderly and ill people, tasks associated with the unpaid labor of mothers and wives within families. On the other hand, with the development of more outpatient services, the rapid discharge of sicker patients from hospitals, and the increasing emphasis on deinstitutionalization in the last quarter of the twentieth century, care work also began to move back into the home. The workers, as well as their patients, clients, or consumers (names variously used to refer to recipients of care), also traveled a continuum between care in nursing homes, hospitals, and homes. The care work economy includes a host of other jobs: child care providers, preschool teachers, school lunchroom and teacher's aides, mental health and substance abuse counselors, social and human services assistants and specialists, and occupational therapists. Under an entirely separate job category, "personal care" occupations, the Department of Labor registers an additional 3.5 million workers.[9]

Such numbers signal the reason that these jobs define the future: they cannot be offshored. Wherever capital may migrate globally to produce goods or provide technical services, care work stays home. Moreover, as had been the case with manufacturing a century earlier, waves of new immigrants continually replenish these workforces. The demographics reflect the migrant flows of this era's global economy: home care aides are Latin American, Chinese, Vietnamese, Hmong, Eastern European, African, and Caribbean. As a *New York Times* journalist observed, "Home care aides are the garment workers of the modern New York economy"—immigrants caught in a new sweating system. Nonetheless, among those counted in this workforce by the U.S. Department of Labor, blacks still represent over a third of the workforce, with "Hispanics" hovering around 15 percent.[10]

Consequently, women's labors—once considered outside the market or at the periphery of economic life—have now become the strategic sites for worker struggle and the direction and character of the American labor movement. For nearly 40 years, the real growth in organized labor has been in health care, public employment, food service and hotels, and education. These workers joined the Service Employees International Union (SEIU), American Federation of State, County, and Municipal Employees (AFSCME), National Education Association, American Federation of Teachers, Hotel Employees and Restaurant Employees Union, and California Nurses Association. In the late twentieth century, SEIU claimed the place that the United Automobile Workers occupied during the mid-twentieth century as the major organizing and political force among wage earners. These new union members also shifted the profile of organized labor. At the end of the first decade of the twenty-first century, when only one in ten labored in manufacturing and about half were in the public sector, women composed 45 percent of unionized workers. The percentage of Latinos in the unionized workforce had more than doubled. One in eight union workers was an immigrant.[11]

In turn, these workers transformed organizing strategy, union demands, and the very nature of collective bargaining. Home care became a pivotal sector in which unions experimented with new tactics. Since the job stood outside New Deal labor laws, unionization ultimately had to take shape apart from that framework. Just as industrial unionism emerged in the 1930s as the structural response to mass production, an expanding care work economy compelled a reawakening labor movement to reconsider questions of strategy and structure, "industry" and the state, labor value, and the employment relation. Organizing low-waged workers in dispersed locations, many of whom lacked the legal status of employee, required unions to think outside the box of the National Labor Relations Act—with its format of signing up members, holding an election for representation, gaining certification, and then bargaining with an employer. Furthermore, the location of home care, straddled between welfare and a state-subsidized medical sector, forced unions like SEIU to confront a fundamental strategic question: how to build a labor movement of poor people in a service so dependent on state funding. As workers and their organizations reformulated who constituted their movement, they also had to take account of the complex interpersonal relations essential to care work. They had to enter into alliances with the receivers of care.

To understand the struggles of home care workers, then, we must reflect on the nature of care and its place within the welfare state. For some feminist ethicists, the notion of a care work economy represents an oxymoron. Care and market just don't mix; just like love and money, they exist apart in hostile worlds. Caring for dependents, usually defined as the frail, ill, and young, should defy the cash nexus. Caring represents a special kind of work involving personal relationship and emotional attachment so that, as economist Susan Himmelweit has claimed, "much of the quality of our lives would be lost if the imposition of inappropriate forms of market rationality turned such work into mere labor."[12] In the popular imagination as well, care stands in its own special place. It is only most genuine—that is, caring—if undertaken freely, not for pecuniary reward. Such assumptions repackage the ideology of separate spheres: women give care, men earn money.[13]

Care work as employment, in contrast, no longer appears as a labor of love, but becomes unskilled work that allegedly any woman could perform. Cleaning bodies as well as rooms, home care workers engage in intimate labor, a kind of toil that is at once essential and highly stigmatized, as if the mere touching of dirt or bodily fluids degrades the handler. This devaluation thesis assumes the unworthiness of the labor because of the race, class, and gender of the workers. Black, immigrant, and poor white women long have undertaken these jobs; indeed, men who engage in them usually earn less than other men, experiencing the costs of racialized feminization.[14] This labor is devalued, however, not just because of its ascribed racial or gendered meanings but because of the way the state chooses to structure it. This outcome, we show, is historical rather than epiphenomenal; devaluation is not only structural and ideological, but a product of conflict and accommodation between experts, state authorities, workers, care receivers, and institutions since the New Deal.

Care also has been low paid because it is justified in terms of the paramount needs of the recipients: they need care no matter what. That is, our society thinks about care in terms of its consumers and their condition rather than the providers of care, the workers. In response to Evelyn Coke's appeal, Supreme Court Justice Stephen Breyer insisted that millions of people would not be able to afford home care if they had to abide by the nation's wage and hour law, so government was acting in the public interest by divorcing such workers from the larger fair labor standards regime.[15] This understanding grants additional moral license to expropriate their labor on the cheap. It implies that denial and self-sacrifice are essential to the "ethic of care." Hence, instead of regarding this work as a form of paid employment, some name it "caregiving." These formulations further mystify the relations of class exploitation.

Policy analyst Deborah Stone suggests that the rules and regulations of caring in the public or commercial sphere "promote disengagement, distance, and impartiality," discounting the love, partiality, and attachment that many develop toward those cared for. Most caregivers, she concludes, feel demeaned by the label "worker," for that implies managed, bureaucratic concepts in contrast to their own "relational and personal concepts of care."[16] Indeed, home care workers describe themselves as caregivers and view "their work more as service than as employment," a calling infused with spirituality.[17] They end up working longer than scheduled, even weekends without pay, because clients need them.[18] Their sense of vocation tells them that this is right. At the same time, philosopher Eva Kittay argues that if care for dependents is to be valued at all, providers of care must themselves be cared for—valued—in material ways.[19]

Home care workers may not always regard themselves as workers, but their labor power is being extracted nevertheless. Within the larger system, the labor power of each individual worker is interchangeable; it is commodified. In order to control public budgets and intensify the labor, social workers and agency supervisors have tried to reduce the job to household maintenance and bodily care, in contrast to intangibles, like keeping company or chatting together about family and friends, which aides constantly remark as essential to work well done. To reduce what the state pays out, administrators have measured the work by tasks accomplished, creating Taylorized schedules: 15 minutes to move someone out of bed, 20 minutes to shower or bathe them, an hour for breakfast. If a person is in pain on a particular day or disoriented, none of these tasks may be completed within budgetary allotments. But workers will have to get the job done, even during the time when they are not being paid for the task.[20]

The very nature of the job, therefore, generates conflict and self-exploitation. Each client has his or her own unique needs. In spite of the commodification of the carer, the actual labor process is relational, creating interdependence. Essential to the job is emotional labor, affection, and building trust. The worker must make her own decisions, based on judgment and feeling. The expectation of the job is that one puts his or her personal, emotional self into it.[21] Workers do not simply go on strike and abandon clients who are unable to get out of bed. Because the work consists of more than tasks completed, because it doesn't produce something that can be quantitatively measured, or easily represented in the GNP, part of these workers' struggle involves establishing the legitimacy of what they "produce": human care and kindness, which itself defies our most taken-for-granted definitions of work as production.

The intimacy of the work and its home location therefore have posed unique hurdles for its rationalization and regulation, not to mention the possibility of unionization. These factors obscure care work as labor in multiple ways: through ideological and discursive dismissal of such labors as real or worthy work;

through the service ethos of some care workers, which leads them to work beyond hours paid; and historically through legal classification that refuses to recognize the home as a workplace and the care worker as a worker. More ominously, those who have favored omitting these workers from labor standards present this exclusion as a positive good because recipients can then stretch their benefits to afford more hours of care.[22] How did this situation arise? How have home care aides come to define themselves as workers and articulate, from their perspective, what constitutes rewarding labor?

Public policy and professional expertise shaped home care as an occupation, thus setting the framework through which families could obtain help for their loved ones and unions would seek to organize this workforce. Care work resembles service labor, like restaurant work and retailing, because it involves what labor scholars call a third party—that is, the client or customer—in addition to the relationship between employer and employee.[23] But the employment relation of home care is even more complicated, since fourth and fifth parties are central to the care work transaction as well: family members who hire and supervise the worker, and the state (represented by agencies, administrators, social workers, and others), which determines eligibility, cuts the check, and oversees care services either directly or through private agencies. Unions, worker centers, and other advocates have sought to change the terms of these interactions and the balance of power therein. While clients have chosen to call themselves consumers, they are not quite the same as customers. Rather than free market agents defined by an ability to pay, clients, constrained by meager finances and impaired or not yet developed capacities, do differ from shoppers of other goods. At times, we use the term "consumer"—instead of client or recipient—when discussing the independent living movement to reflect its self-identification and political impact, as seen in the social services concept of "consumer-directed" care and the adoption of this designation by policy makers in the last quarter of the twentieth century. Yet we also remain alert to the ways in which consumer terminology obfuscates political concepts of rights, obligations, and the ethics of human interconnectedness.[24]

Government social policies directly shaped the development of home care. By the 1990s, Medicaid made up over half of all monies for it. A decade later, Medicaid was the primary funding source for home health aide jobs.[25] The beneficiaries of the service, the structure of the industry, and the terms and conditions of the labor all were products of state intervention. As public work performed in private homes, home care illuminates the public-private configuration of the American welfare state, the workings of federalism, and the twisted logic of welfare reform. When taxpayers felt that the undeserving, or nonproductive, received special services, they sought to cut funding for care labors; when politicians needed to balance a budget, they eliminated services for those with less power. We cannot therefore discuss home care without the state; low pay for care workers is integrally bound up with anxiety about public budgets.

Precisely because home health care unites public assistance with labor, old age, and disability policy, and because its value reflects the privileged position of medical models of care, it offers an opportunity to rethink the growth and devolution of the U.S. welfare state. This story complicates the narratives of America's divided welfare state by challenging the separation of state, markets, and families and by shifting the emphasis from distinctions between different social programs to their connections. To understand both the political economy of home care and organizing by workers, we begin with home care's hybrid structure: part domestic service, part health care. Though federal policies shaped its contours, implementation occurred on the local level and in light of state governments and their budget allocations. Given the workings of federalism, then, a national overview is not enough to understand home care. To chart this history, we therefore focus on those places with robust or illustrative programs—New York, Illinois, Oregon, and California—where organized groups of workers and recipients additionally played a determining role. Moreover, multiple arenas—the public hospital, the social welfare agency, and the market for domestic service—created this political economy of home care.

Home care as a distinct occupation emerged in the crisis of the Great Depression to meet both welfare and health imperatives. Through the New Deal's Works Progress Administration (WPA), state funding began to formulate a new occupation that helped poor families and individuals facing medical emergencies, chronic illness, and old age, while curtailing the costs of institutionalization. One strand—the subject of chapter one—took shape as work relief for unemployed black women who had previously labored in domestic service. State and local governments would provide aid to one group of needy Americans—women with children—through employing another needy group—poor, unemployed women, a majority of whom were African American—as "substitute mothers." Such origins distinguished home care, no matter who actually did the work; haunting this history was the legacy of slavery and segregation that racialized the labor and defined it as low paid and unskilled—as fitting work for black women.

Relieving public hospitals of long-term chronically ill and elderly patients became the other origin of state-supported home-based care. The WPA initiated programs to move such people out of the hospital and give them the necessary assistance to become "independent" at home. These programs often called the workers "housekeepers," reflecting the non-medical designation of manual labor in hospital settings. In either case, social workers within welfare agencies oversaw the provision of care as a service for indigents.

Following World War II, we show in chapter two, private family agencies led by women social workers and aided by the U.S. Children's Bureau attempted to turn homemaker services into a good job for older women. Over the next decade, a mixture of public welfare departments and private agencies established visiting homemaker and boarding programs to maintain aged and disabled people in the community rather than in more expensive hospitals and nursing facilities. Rather than a universal benefit, homemaker service was meant for those living on very low incomes.

At the same time, hospitals began their own physician-supervised home care programs in order to discharge chronically ill and impoverished patients more quickly. Home care would be one element in a far-reaching medical-institutional complex. Chapter two therefore charts the emergence of a postwar medical model for home care that contested the professional authority of social welfare caseworkers. Whether provided through the medical model of hospital-based programs or the social assistance model of private or public agencies, the clash of professional expertise left the home attendant in occupational limbo, expected to perform the auxiliary labor of social or physical rehabilitation and to provide home comforts—still cast as neither nurse nor maid.

The history of home care further allows for a more expansive understanding of the significance of the Social Security Act in the development of the U.S. welfare state, as traced in the first three chapters. Most scholars, like policy makers, have focused on old age insurance, unemployment insurance, and Aid to Families with Dependent Children (AFDC).[26] Yet, by considering the less visible titles of Social Security—those set up for child welfare, adult categorical aid (for age, blindness, and disability), and social services—another portrait emerges. A network of social welfare advocates used these subsidiary health and public assistance provisions as channels for publicly subsidized, non-medical care at home. Through the U.S. Children's Bureau and voluntary, private family agencies, this network of dedicated women (and a few good men) relied upon incremental means, including legislative amendments and administrative rulings. They could never elevate home care to the status of an entitlement; they usually had to attach it to some other benefit or program as a subsidiary service. Thus, even when support for social services for the needy (especially those that would allegedly end welfare dependency) gained ideological and political credence, home care programs remained small, without institutional capacity, prestige, or political clout. Although home-based care would eventually become crucial to the medical system, these programs stayed within the stigmatized realm of welfare policy.

When we look at the provision of such services and the accompanying ideologies of rehabilitation, it appears that the "deserving" clients of social assistance—elderly, chronically ill, and disabled persons—depended on the "undeserving" recipients of AFDC. From the 1930s on, each generation of government officials and public welfare professionals clung to the premise that poor single mothers could end their own dependency on welfare by maintaining the independence of those incapacitated through no fault of their own—that is, by performing care work. They could become rehabilitated in the process of rehabilitating others. The deserving and undeserving, like the public and private sectors, stood interconnected rather than apart.

Policies that would expand the rights of seniors had a coercive edge when applied to poor single mothers, who found themselves channeled into a low-wage, part-time occupation. The War on Poverty in the 1960s provided new vehicles for the state to expand the home care labor market. Once again, this time under the umbrella of anti-poverty policy, the state set terms that maintained a racialized, gendered occupation. The 1962 Public Welfare Amendments to the Social Security Act asked public welfare departments to identify services that would "restore families and individuals to self-support" and "help the aged, blind, or seriously disabled to take care of themselves."[27] This emphasis on services and self-support required a labor force that could undertake such tasks. "Manpower development" policy, first under John F. Kennedy and then Lyndon B. Johnson, would direct poor recipients of public assistance along this track. The new Office of Economic Opportunity in 1964 created programs for AFDC recipients to meet the labor shortage in service occupations, especially health and child aides, home attendants, and homemaker aides, programs classified by the U.S. Department of Labor as similar to domestic service.[28] Chapter three revisits the War on Poverty with a new emphasis on how its administrators clearly saw service sector jobs as the wave of the future and used various anti-poverty programs to train poor women to enter that sector at the bottom rungs, as if they hadn't been there before.

Yet there remained an irony. Whether under the rubric of rehabilitation, manpower development, or welfare reform, such social services risked reinforcing racial and gender inequalities. Poor women's path to independence depended on the very household labor that reduced them to the social status of servants.[29] Impoverishment and marginalization were only further reinforced in the mid-1970s, when new amendments to the Fair Labor Standards Act (FLSA) extended labor law protection to domestic workers but specifically excluded elder care aides. Law, social policies, and professionals' use of rehabilitation ideology developed home care as a stigmatized and low-paying hands-on job in an expanding health care industry.

Throughout this period, as chapters two through four demonstrate, the state did not and could not act alone; it facilitated private long-term assistance. Scholars now commonly refer to the American state as mixed, hybrid, hidden, divided, residual, and public-private. The particular strategy of governance that emerged from the use of private or quasi-governmental entities to fulfill public purposes expanded state power in hidden, disguised, and often unaccountable ways.[30] Home care reveals the manner in which the distribution of public welfare depends on both public and private entities, which developed in tandem. Most federal welfare policies require implementation at the state, county, and local level. While we tend to think of these as "public programs," each level of government has relied on private charities, nonprofit agencies, proprietary vendors, and workers to carry out its dictates. The private sector was not initially intended to displace the state. From the 1930s through the 1960s, welfare advocates, case workers, and various federal government officials believed that privately sponsored demonstration projects and public subsidy of family service agencies would further stimulate welfare support and services in the public sector. Starting in the 1970s, through Medicare and Medicaid rules, state subsidies, federal social service grants, job training funds, and vendor contracts, governments boosted a for-profit industry in home care services, opening new conflicts over public funding and the responsibility of the state.

Consequently, this study of intimate labor exposes the inner workings of American federalism. Federalism often is presented as a fixed set of structural constraints. Different levels of government, however, often have competed with each other, sought to outmaneuver the others, or secure more or less power, responsibility, and money. Whether responding to injections of federal funding in the 1950s and 1960s or contractions in social welfare spending in the 1970s and 1980s, states and localities perpetually attempted cost shifting to other levels of government and used various tactics of privatization, including contracting out to nongovernmental entities, through a complicated set of strategic moves. Given public ambivalence over paying for social services for the poor and people of color, especially for labor that many believed should be freely given by wives, mothers, and daughters, home care illuminates the continual renegotiation of the terms, funding, and institutional structures of federal governance.

While the expanding welfare state helped to create this particular low-wage labor market, national budget politics and retrenchment further casualized the job. Under the banner of market reform and deficit reduction, the federal government reined in social welfare spending in the 1970s and 1980s; states and localities desperately coped through privatization of services and "flexible" labor policies. Highlighting New York and California, the states that received the bulk of federal funds, chapters four and five show how states used the politics of budgetary crisis to restructure the labor market for care and the nature of the job. Through their own routes and under different pressures, these states turned more to outsourcing and the reclassification of attendants as independent providers. Over the years the work became harder, but fiscal pressures squeezed the workforce. The subcontracting system, abetted by Medicare and Medicaid, turned home care into a sweated industry, compounding the consequences of worker exclusion from the nation's wage and hour law.[31] The ever expanding use of independent contractor designations and a casualized employment relation had broader implications; within a generation, these practices spread throughout the American economy, affecting workers in fields as wide-ranging as retail, financial services, university teaching, journalism, television entertainment, and transport. Home care's past prefigured the future.

The second half of the book is a story of social movements. Even as the welfare state location of the labor devalued the workforce, it opened up a new site of social and political struggle. With the structure of home care, it was never enough just to win collective bargaining rights with individual vendor agencies. To make economic gains, unions had to go to government. Political brokering with the state thus became an important part of home care unionism.

The state may have organized home care, but it did not do so without contestation and confrontation. Chapters four through seven turn to social movements that erupted within the welfare state. Senior citizens, disabled people, domestic workers, welfare recipients, and aides each shaped the home care system. In the political cauldron of the 1960s and 1970s, they formed militant civil rights movements of their own. Organizing in the streets, welfare offices, campuses, and state capitols, they pushed forward their own definitions of independence, dignity, access to public services and housing, and rights to support. We bring a range of actors into the welfare wars that ignited in the 1960s and spilled into the 1970s: the Rolling Quads on the Berkeley campus, radical social workers, independent living centers, the National Committee for Household Employment, the California Welfare Rights Organization, the Grey Panthers, the Older Women's League, and the United Labor Unions (ULU). The ULU activists, especially in Chicago, were true innovators, former SEIU President Andy Stern has admitted; they "created a belief that there was actually something that could be done with an incredibly invisible workforce."[32]

How did each of these movements reshape the state and its programs? Their goals and claims overlapped but could be contradictory. Under what conditions were they allies? How did confrontational politicians, like California's Governor Ronald Reagan, unite or divide them? Who would speak for those who labored? Did the culture and structure of unionism and collective bargaining clash with the goals of other stakeholders? Social conflicts within the welfare state and among its recipients forged the terrain upon which unionization took off.

State policies created the possibility of a new political unionism that in the last decades of the twentieth century brought together workers, consumers, and voters to demand better wages and better care. Victories in the 1990s and the early years of the twenty-first century did not just happen; they were the culmination of a 35-year struggle that began with the surge in public sector unionism in the mid-1960s. Home care unionism benefited from an effervescence of organizing among poor, black, Latina, and immigrant women. It originated in movements of domestic workers in New York and San Diego; farm worker unionism in California; public sector militancy bound up with political struggle around state budgets in many cities; and the community organizing of groups like ACORN (Association of Community Organizations for Reform Now), most successfully in Chicago. Mirroring home care's hybrid origins, home care unionism had roots in the welfare rights movement and the dynamic growth in hospital and health care unionism in the latter decades of the twentieth century. Chapters five through seven reveal the dramatic struggles in these different paths toward unionization, as well as their implications for the American labor movement as a whole.

These movements not only reached out to workers in casual or service sectors; they experimented with new structures of representation and distinct forms of unionism. They had to devise legal and political strategies for a neoliberal era in which governments denied that they were the employer responsible for poverty wage rates or 12-hour shifts, the National Labor Relations Board (NLRB) election too often was a dead-end, and even courts refused coverage under the FLSA. Before caregivers were even able to bargain for better conditions, they had to see themselves as workers and fight for such recognition by the public, the state, and the very users of their services. They had to seek the right to organize in the first place—and as they did so, they came to understand themselves as wage earners, as workers in a class relation to the state, agencies, or, in some cases, the consumers for whom they cared. They had to gain visibility and dignity, two key phrases in both self and media representation of home care providers. With consumer allies, they had to challenge representations of self-sacrificing workers and helpless recipients, as well as the stigmatization of dependency, whether on other human beings or the state.

The organizing of home care calls into question the standard categories of unionization. We are accustomed to thinking of unionism in the United States as taking distinct forms relating to the character of the industry: craft, industrial, public employee, health, or service sector. Despite often-conflicting assumptions about the nature of work, the definition of the worker, and the relationship to the employer, these types of unions have drawn upon similar tactics and aspirations, depending on the historical moment. Though we associate particular unions with workplace-specific strategies, in fact they have deployed electoral politics and lobbying, community mobilization, consumer alliances, and social services provision as tools to win improvements for workers and sometimes broader social change. Because the arrangements for home care have varied by time and place, no single term captures the full range of organizing strategies for this workforce. These unions engaged in political unionism, because they had to influence the state; social movement unionism, because they depended on mobilizing clients and communities; and service sector unionism, because they helped create this new epicenter of organized labor. As a whole, it is perhaps most constructive to see these new trends as "care worker unionism": a solidaristic attempt to move the labor of care away from its marginalized status to recognize its centrality to the contemporary political economy.

The final chapters trace the story of how disparate movements finally came together at the end of the century and saw conditions of labor linked with conditions of care. Seniors, disabled people, and families had to accept aides as workers with needs independent of their own. In turn, home care unionism had to plead for larger social goods, advocating better care in order to obtain better jobs for union members.

Whether the process of struggle has provided greater recognition of the value of care labor has remained an open question. Would, for example, the emotional content of the labor achieve legitimacy through unionization? Could real gains in wages, public resources, and quality of care be sustained amid the deep economic and fiscal crisis that erupted in the final days of the Bush era? As the epilogue suggests, this history helps to explain the devastating impact of neoliberal restructuring of the welfare state on the livelihood of home care workers, the quality of available long-term care, and the fate of democratic unionism. With the new round of fiscal crisis for states since 2008, governors and legislatures turned to pitting "taxpayers" against public workers. And yet plenty of the former will soon be elders in need of care. Longer life expectancy means that more of us live with chronic illness. A majority of Americans, across the spectrum of class and ethnicity, will at some point depend on a caretaker, often one who has long labored in poverty and struggled mightily to balance her own and others' social needs. The macroeconomic structuring of the occupation, as well as its interpersonal challenges, heighten the stresses of an already emotionally and psychologically intense and economically precarious job. Workers, family members, state administrators, and policy makers all wring their hands in frustration over the undependability of home care services; for the former, there aren't enough steady hours; for the latter, there never seem to be enough trustworthy workers. Although the assumption has long held that only through low-waged labor could we provide long-term care, perhaps it is time to reframe the question. Can we really afford to maintain a system that impoverishes workers and stigmatizes both the recipients and providers of care?

Home care has existed in a clouded nether world between public and private, employment and family care. It was possible because of the devaluation of not only women's work but the stigmatization attached to the labor of poor women of color. The epilogue further considers the degree to which we have met the challenge of balancing respect, dignity, and social rights for recipients *and* providers. The continuing struggle for good care and worthy work makes this an ongoing story, propelled by political confrontations and upheaval within the trade union movement, state capitols, and the halls of Congress, and the inevitable dependency that is the human condition.

1

Neither Nurses nor Maids

One year after the inauguration of New York City's Housekeeping Service for Chronic Patients in 1936, beneficiaries expressed gratitude for the in-home care and support they received through this Works Progress Administration (WPA) program. Cardiac patient Mrs. A. L. confessed, "I really would not have known what to do if it were not for the aid of my housekeeper. . . ." She both kept "the house tidy" and, as "a cheerful soul," made "me happy in many ways." Another recipient praised "the housekeeper . . . [who] has been most kind to me. She goes back and forth to the hospital with me, she also does all my housework . . . she has washed my woodwork, furniture covers, and put up my curtains making my little home very comfortable for my little boy and my husband."[1] Program administrators reprinted these thank-you notes in 1936 to show that home care was more than simple domestic service. The visiting housekeeper was to be "a companion as well as a coworker in the treatment of a case . . . confidante and servant, mother confessor and maid of all work."[2]

The New Deal extended the boundaries of public employment and public service. It brought the labors of care under its aegis yet incorporated the tensions within the social divisions of care work. The chief purpose of the visiting housekeeper program was, as Maud Morlock of the U.S. Children's Bureau explained, to employ needy women. Housekeepers were to "offer free assistance in housework and/or care of children in the homes of the needy." Although new types of health care jobs were emerging within an expanding medical sector, visiting housekeepers were, according to all involved, "not nurses" but also "not maids."[3] Neither were they social workers or home economists. They were auxiliary workers under registered nurses (RNs) and caseworkers. But most of them were African American, and they performed laborious household tasks as part of ministering to the ill—thus the image of maid or domestic stuck. A murky line separated visiting housekeeper from domestic servant, despite the best efforts of New Dealers and their social welfare allies to establish a good job for older women without "professional skills."[4] Through the agencies and networks of the

New Deal, we see how the state became embedded in the seemingly private worlds of family, medical care, employment, and charitable support.

Before the Welfare State

For most of the nation's history, the household served as the locus of care. We have depended on domestic labor to maintain families, communities, and society. Wives, daughters, sisters, and female servants tended and comforted the sick, but this work was not necessarily private, in the sense of involving only kin or benefiting individuals. Domestic labor directly served public ends. In the seventeenth century, the town of Plymouth, Massachusetts, for example, organized care by placing unattached men and orphaned children within families. The Southern plantation appropriated the labor of enslaved African women, but white mistresses often ministered to illness and infirmity in the slave quarters as well as the big house, with only an occasional visit from a physician. Frontier societies also relied upon home units, bringing in strangers to heal.[5]

Households were rarely isolated. Care existed in and through communities, with the midwife traveling from place to place. Across ethnic and racial groups, nineteenth-century women entered the homes of their neighbors to fight disease, sit with the dead, help with childbirth, or aid in the myriad tasks of daily life. Urban ethnic enclaves similarly engaged in sharing resources and watching over incapacitated people. Mutuality characterized care work among rural African Americans and in the Pueblo villages of the Southwest. Well into the twentieth century, working-class families exchanged care, along with goods and cash, through a gendered reciprocity in which friends, kin, and neighbors helped each other.[6] Such extended homes—and the labor of their female inhabitants—anticipated the use of nongovernmental agencies to deliver care.

With the growing nineteenth-century emphasis on indoor relief, state-run and private institutions housed afflicted and needy people, but whether inmates received physical and emotional attention varied tremendously. Both chronically and acutely ill people were shut off from the larger society in an effort to control disease. For the kinless poor, the almshouse functioned as an old-age home, orphanage, sick house, and asylum rolled into one. Over the course of the nineteenth century, specialized institutions for dependent care siphoned off each population, so that by the turn of the century the elderly were the almshouse's main residents. Ethnic and religious charities developed in urban areas; funded by congregants and landsmen, these orphanages, hospitals, and elder homes sometimes received public funds. In New York City, for example, Tammany Hall funneled monies to Catholic charities, sustaining group care by nuns. Protestant charities, in contrast, sought to place children in foster families or to rehabilitate the households of the poor, encouraging individualized rather than collective care work.[7]

By the late nineteenth century, competing medical and social work models of home care began to emerge. Spurred by the organization of medicine as a profession, the hospital evolved from the pest house to become a place for curing or, in the case of chronic illness, confinement. Institutionalization hardly relieved families of work, as women had to provide clothes, bedding, and other necessities to those in sanatoriums or hospitals. Families with means hired practical, private duty, or attendant nurses to sit and comfort loved ones at home as well as in hospitals. They would ask African American nurses to perform additional domestic tasks. Charity organizations created visiting nurse services as a new form of public health delivery, but some doctors, those with the Boston Dispensary, for example, already replaced trained nurses with "attendants" for those with chronic illnesses. (This same venerable institution had treated the poor in their own homes as early as 1796.) The users of services paid when they could. The Metropolitan Life Insurance Company instigated visiting nurses for policy holders. Although the program operated under the auspices of a private company, Met Life understood its nursing program as a form of public health. Otherwise, volunteer agencies organized much of this work, with local governments establishing public facilities during the first decades of the twentieth century.[8]

Assessing the deservedness of the distressed justified the intervention of social workers in the organization of care. At the turn of the twentieth century, social settlements and urban charities, along with nurse associations, initiated the first homemaker services. They sent helpers into immigrant neighborhoods to substitute for the sick mother. These efforts combined a number of functions: short-term child care, instruction in home economics, and domestic labor. New York's Association for the Improvement of the Condition of the Poor supplemented the work of visiting nurses with visiting cleaners. Lillian Wald of the Nurses' Settlement also deployed housekeepers to clean patients' living quarters. Some, like the Associated Charities in Detroit, stressed the Americanization of diet, hygiene, and housekeeping. A unique experiment in Brattleboro, Vermont, dispatched "home helps" to the poor as a substitute for nursing. Over the next three decades, private family agencies continued on a limited scale a practice of reverse foster care, sending substitute mothers into the home rather than taking children away from distressed families.[9]

The Great Depression swept away what little security families had, ushering in a crisis of care along with economic hardship. Private family agencies lacked the financial and organizational capacity to cope with soaring caseloads; they turned to government to relieve mounting need. Public hospitals overflowed their capacity as rising numbers of chronically ill patients lingered in the wards. States had to invent new mechanisms of aid, especially when more people became classified as "medically indigent." Worried that cash handouts threatened prolonged dependency, state and federal officials turned to work relief. The WPA visiting housekeeper program emerged as a public extension of homemaker services that had been pioneered by settlements and charity organizations.

Two New York City projects illuminate the curious tangle that distinguished New Deal approaches to the crisis of care.[10] The first offered an employment alternative to the infamous "Bronx slave market" where African American women stood on street corners to be picked up for a day's work, enduring personal indignities and heavy labor, often only to discover that they barely made carfare home.[11] The second pioneered in the medical management of chronically ill and aged individuals through housekeeping and attendant services. The employment of low-waged women of color came to distinguish home care as an occupation; so would close cooperation between private organizations and government agencies. From the start, gender and racial divisions of labor, as well as government funding and client poverty, shaped the home care project.

The New Deal and the Rehabilitation of Work

In his first inaugural address, President Franklin Roosevelt announced: "Our greatest primary task is to put people to work."[12] Work meant independence, not dependency, a condition associated with unemployables—the helpless and derelict, the young and old, and the wife and mother. The right to live meant the right to earn, which government, perhaps for the first time, embraced as its duty by assuring that people—particularly white men—could work and that work would pay. Over the decade, Congress funded a series of job programs to reinforce this work ethic. Means-tested need determined eligibility, but federal rules required public jobs programs to pay real wages at a fair rate. The WPA's more generous compensation led the unemployed to view themselves as workers, not welfare recipients.[13] Housekeeping programs under the WPA met the test, substituting work relief for "the dole."

Though not the first New Deal public works program, work relief broadened under the WPA. Initially, during the Depression Winter of 1933–1934, only 3 percent of funding went to public health and welfare employment programs. Then, in the spring of 1935, the newly created WPA shifted money to arenas beyond visible, large-scale construction projects. The Women's Division under Ellen S. Woodward, a savvy Democratic Women's Committee member from Mississippi, established projects specifically for women, like sewing rooms, nursing services, school lunch matrons, household training, and housekeeping aides, which tapped into existing labor market configurations.[14] The WPA actually spent more money on home-based care projects than on public health and hospital work. Before it disbanded in 1942, some 38,000 housekeeping aides in 45 states and the District of Columbia assisted the needy.[15] Still, this investment in social services paled in comparison to funding for physical infrastructure, as highway construction alone absorbed nearly 40 percent of available resources.[16]

Across the nation, the Visiting Housekeeping Program represented a major form of work assistance for black women, even though the number of African Americans on work relief was disproportionately low.[17] Southern employers responded by complaining that the wages of relief, which were higher than those in textiles or agriculture, caused labor shortages, undermining the racial caste system.[18] To the contrary, New Deal relief projects accepted existing divisions of labor. Like other locally administered policies, they reflected and reproduced the dominant racial and gender order. In Southwestern states, for example, Mexican American citizens obtained housekeeping aide positions, while African Americans only received instruction in domestic service.[19] At its height, between 300,000 and 400,000 women worked for the WPA, some 20 percent of its labor force.[20]

Despite the presence of racial liberals and activist women within the New Deal, policies reinforced the existing order in other ways. The male breadwinner ideal, which envisioned a lone man supporting the family, shaped eligibility for work relief. So the WPA limited jobs to one household member, usually the male head. Uneasiness over maternal employment persisted within the women's reform network itself, with some lobbying for paying women to care for their own children instead of sending them out as housekeepers to tend to those of other people.[21] Such scruples usually disappeared when it came to black women, about a third of whom headed households. Since slavery, employers disregarded their motherhood when other women's homes needed labor.[22]

New York's Housekeeping Aide Project, organized in 1934, solved the mounting problem of developing work relief for unemployed domestics, whom federal officials disparaged as a group with limited skills.[23] In cooperation with the city's Home Relief Bureau and the Henry Street Visiting Nurse Service, the Brooklyn and New York Urban Leagues ran the project, mostly serving families with acute rather than chronic illnesses. Since 1910, the National Urban League had sought to improve the conditions of black migrants from the South, to advance black employment, and to mediate labor relations. Focused on social investigation rather than individualized casework, it protested discrimination not only by private businesses but also within the civil service and the New Deal itself.[24] In Brooklyn, the Urban League helped to organize both the distribution of cash relief and an employment bureau where it encountered domestics seeking help.[25] With household workers composing nearly 85 percent of the borough's black women wage earners, their joblessness brought distress to the entire community.[26]

In cities like New York, household employment maintained its association with servitude. Five or six dollars a week was "good pay." During the Depression, some middle-class families dropped domestics as expendable luxuries, while others sought to procure help at rock-bottom prices, offering payment as low as four dollars for a 40-hour week, and piling on additional tasks, like upper-window washing, laundry, and child care. Unpredictable assignments, unregulated hours and wages, and social stigma continued to cast the work as undesirable.[27]

After WPA rules required that public agencies coordinate projects, Housekeeping Aides came under the New York City Department of Welfare and the mayor's office. Though sometimes sharing training facilities, WPA Visiting Housekeeping differed from household-worker demonstration projects that existed to increase the supply of domestic servants. They also stood apart from WPA public health projects that provided jobs in hospitals, clinics, and schools for unemployed skilled professionals, who were mostly white and middle class.[28] Home economists, public health nurses, and social workers trained and supervised housekeepers according to the imperatives of their fields.[29] Between February 1934 and July 1935, 200 black women cared for 2,056 Manhattan and Brooklyn families, with 6,610 children. As of 1937, 53 black men also labored as supervisors, clerical workers, and timekeepers, earning more than the women. By 1938, the number of housekeepers reached nearly 1,800.[30]

Yet while New Deal work relief created paid caregiving positions, New Deal labor law ignored the resulting workforce. The labor rights of the New Deal—old age insurance, unemployment benefits, collective bargaining, minimum wages, and maximum hours—excluded domestic workers. This exclusion reflected both political realities—especially the Southern hold on Congress—and the persistent prejudice that those who labored at home were not real workers. In 1940, the Fair Labor Standards Act categorized nurse-companions and other in-home care workers hired directly by clients as domestic servants. New Deal labor laws also omitted employees of nonprofit organizations. Since most hospitals and visiting nurse organizations were nonprofit, health workers therefore stood outside the law as well.[31] As the New Deal made work the entrée to a host of new social benefits, domestic work suffered further marginalization.

The demographics of home care linked the job to domestic service. African American women dominated the visiting housekeeping projects, though not to the same extent that they did domestic service. In the Housekeeping Service for Chronic Patients, four of every five aides in 1938 were African American; 67 percent of them had previously worked in domestic and personal service. Most were between the ages of 25 and 44. The overwhelming majority were or had been married and cared for and supported dependents. For this reason, program administrators judged such women experienced, especially those who both had "handl[ed] things on her own initiative under economic conditions resembling those in the patients' households" and had labored "under somebody else's initiative" as a domestic. In addition, housekeepers had to be able to undertake strenuous labor, be in good health, and be free from both contagious and organic diseases, like syphilis and heart problems. The New Deal compelled domestics alone to submit to syphilis testing. Not only did such requirements express the lingering association of black women with sexual contagion, but they also demonstrated official concern with protection of the white household.[32]

Welfare officials expected the ideal aide to be like the ideal servant: cooperative, optimistic, cheerful, flexible, and "well-balanced," able to restrain emotions and maintain "some insulation from the intimacies of the family life."[33] Government evaluators claimed black women to be more suitable for this work, as if personal care and household labor came naturally to them, but still insisted that they needed training in homemaking. Classes offered instruction in all aspects of the job, such as "simple care of the sick, infant care, laundry, home management and care, personal hygiene and safety," covered in a four-day week, with once-a-week follow-up every 11 weeks. For most workers, training more aptly consisted of a re-training in familiar housekeeping skills. Project leaders, however, claimed that housekeepers improved personal appearance and "poise," along with developing self-confidence from "the thought that the job they do is one that has its own technique, requiring study, like other skilled jobs." Skills that would be useful for the improvement of their own homes and communities would serve as an added benefit from training.[34]

Throughout the North, WPA administrators actively fought against the maid designation. Clients often treated the aide with "utmost contempt, taking it for granted that they have a perfect right to order her around as if she were a personal servant paid with funds taken from the family income."[35] White former factory workers initially felt "humiliated" or "disgraced" by what they perceived as servile labor. The WPA countered with two arguments: that housekeeping labor, "with its variety of situations and problems and its requirements of skill," was "more interesting than the monotony of factory work"—an old claim of middle-class reformers—and that it resulted in social good. Housekeeping programs attempted to dignify the job by addressing the aide by "the more formal 'Miss'" rather than by the first name commonly used with servants; introducing, at least in the Housekeeping Service for Chronic Patients, a uniform with a WPA label to distinguish her from a maid; and reducing personalism by prohibiting the acceptance of gifts from clients.[36] With the hospital, family welfare association, and visiting nurse or community health agency assigning clients, housekeepers could not, by definition, be maids—unless one traveled South. In Louisiana, with 250 black housekeepers, the service was known as the "maids project."[37]

Black representatives made their concerns known. One African American organization in mid-1936 apparently "asked for discontinuation of the projects because they were listed as being 'for colored housekeepers' and this was 'rank racial discrimination.'"[38] Winning a small victory, applications for new projects no longer designated the race of preferred workers, but WPA press releases and reports still emphasized the overwhelming presence of black women.[39]

By limiting chores unrelated to care and prohibiting labor in homes with contagious diseases, the WPA sought to professionalize the occupation.[40] New York City's Women's and Professional Division began a course of instruction in 1938 to instill "the sole objective and principal aim of the Project work—that of *unstinted service,*" while teaching "the utter fallacy of unsound methods, lost motion, and inefficiency."[41] Within two years, the first of four housekeeping aide training schools opened.[42] Countering notions that household work was unskilled labor, the WPA joined with the National Committee on Household Employment, the National Urban League, and the U.S. Women's Bureau to emphasize the composite skills required, sharpened through training like any other craft.[43] In this context, detailed guides on how to make proper beds or prepare nutritious foods on a relief budget signified the worth of the labor and stood not merely as mechanisms to discipline poor black women.

Nonetheless, project evaluations thinly masked the repeated fear that black women working in the WPA would be spoiled for private household employment. One WPA investigator worried that those earning $60.50 a month "are not interested in preparing for household employment which pays $45 to $60 for competent workers."[44] As her concern suggests, conflicting agendas swirled around a project that originated in relief but was to uplift its participants and advance the goals of social work, medical care, and home economics. The WPA did little to improve the compensation or working conditions of private household employment. It promoted the image of the happy, self-sacrificing home aide, who displayed her "fine spirit and interest . . . not only in working overtime" but in finishing her tasks "before thinking of picking up her own wages."[45]

Being a WPA aide undoubtedly was a better deal than private household employment. The work required initiative and it paid more. Interviewed decades later, former aides ranked the job "a step above domestic work, though much of their job description meant 'running errands for the sick or invalids, straightening up clothes and housekeeping.'"[46] Aides and black supervisors resisted transfer to WPA domestic service assignments.[47] While a small number of domestic servants sought to unionize—such as Harlem workers who joined the Domestic Workers Union (an early local of the Building Service Employees International Union, a predecessor to SEIU)—we could find no evidence that housekeeping aides turned to unionization in this period.[48]

"In Patients' Own Homes"[49]

In New York City, as elsewhere, the Great Depression underscored the inadequacy of social and medical services for the indigent chronically ill. During the Depression, public hospitals were expected to take in every New Yorker who arrived on their doorsteps. As private voluntary hospitals limited admissions and closed ward beds, ever more desperate and destitute patients turned to the public ones. Hence, by the mid-1930s, these hospitals were intolerably overcrowded and financially precarious. Federal monies alone could facilitate an amalgam of private and public initiatives to meet the crisis.

For 40 years, visiting nurses had tended the homebound, but with the economic collapse, they lacked adequate resources to meet patient demand.[50] In 1933, the eight-year-old Welfare Council of New York, an umbrella group of private and public agencies with close to a thousand affiliates, formed the Committee on Chronic Illness. It promoted an appropriate and efficient use of hospitalization, boarding (which became the nursing home), and home care for those requiring long-term treatment. Mary C. Jarrett led this effort. A founder of Smith College's School of Social Work, Jarrett innovated in applying medical, especially psychiatric, casework to public health. She would serve as the technical advisor to the experimental WPA project that developed from her investigations. Jarrett believed that chronic illness was "a community responsibility just as much as slum clearance, relief for the impoverished and the unemployed and other undertakings which are generally conceded to be matters of public conscience."[51]

In 1934, Jarrett (aided by the State Department of Social Welfare) led a vast survey of chronic illness in the city, which "made us all conscious for the first time of the magnitude of the problem and the inadequate provision." She found that, of those receiving old age assistance from the city, 75 percent suffered from some disability, and nearly a quarter were homebound. The final report, endorsed by the New York Academy of Medicine and the United Hospital Fund of New York, recommended "a municipal system of home care integrated with institutional care for the chronically ill." Physicians under New York Heart Association chairman Dr. Ernst P. Boas went a step further, suggesting that judicious amounts of home care could eliminate expensive institutionalization.[52]

In pursuit of this mission, the Welfare Council endorsed yet another WPA project, proposed by Ruth Hill, the city's Deputy Commissioner responsible for the Division of Old Age Assistance: Home Care for the Aged on Public Assistance. This project began operating in late 1935, but six months later, the question arose of whether it was merely assisting in the administration of Social Security or was "supplementary and extra-ordinary," as Commissioner Hill defended it to

Ellen Woodward. WPA appropriations could not go to "direct relief, or to supplement the work of the government being done in the field of Old Age Security which is financed by [a] separate appropriation." So Hill stressed the role of professional medical personnel, classifying the project as a research demonstration to gain "a closer picture of the dependency of our more feeble and unprotected recipients." Protesting to WPA officials in Washington, Jarrett and the Welfare Council claimed the project as essential for devising "an intelligent program for the home care of the aged." In emphasizing technical expertise, they distinguished this effort from that of the Housekeeping Aides. The old age project resembled those of charitable family agencies, which focused on the recipient rather than the provider of care.[53]

Home Care for the Aged aimed to prevent recurrent hospital admissions. Organized to "determine whether it is better for the client and cheaper for the city to care for the dependent aged in their homes than in institutions," it included physicians who undertook initial examinations. Aides received training in meal planning for low-income invalids in the kitchen of the city's welfare department. While men and women equally were on assistance, the project served double the number of women since more elderly women lived alone. "Without housekeeping aid," the WPA concluded, "they would have had to give up their independence to live with relatives or go to an institution." Family members praised the service: "When Miss S. came I was on the verge of a nervous breakdown because of attempting to properly take charge of my household duties during the day after sitting up with my mother at night," a typical confession claimed. The visiting housekeepers also freed this daughter and other family caregivers to go about their business. Images of cleanliness, order, and brightness replaced discourses of dirt, disorder, and gloom in WPA press releases, shaping a narrative of the home care worker as savior and provider of relief.[54]

The fieldwork of the Committee on Chronic Illness spurred New York City's Department of Hospitals to focus seriously on what to do about chronic patients. The Department estimated that elders and adults with chronic disease occupied approximately half of its 20,000 hospital beds. Many others were sent to the city's long-term institution on Blackwell's Island, which included a former prison infirmary. Hospitals Commissioner Dr. S. S. Goldwater acknowledged that chronic patients and the institutions dedicated to them were usually "the neglected stepchildren . . . of organized medicine." Instead, "for many chronic invalids care at home is the happiest solution"—and such care would reduce the use of hospitalization as a refuge for the impoverished sick. Thanking Jarrett for outlining an approach for the Department of Hospitals, Goldwater concluded, "The problem is so vast that nothing less than a government-sponsored program will suffice."[55]

The mayor's office and the Department of Health therefore agreed to sponsor with the Department of Hospitals a new home care service under WPA auspices.

This housekeeping project was distinct from others because it involved medical social workers, visiting nurses, and doctors. The Committee on Chronic Illness provided technical direction, supplemented by an advisory committee that was an A-list roster of New York religious and secular charities.[56] After a year of operation, the project employed 100 housekeeping aides who cared for about 200 chronic patients.[57] It merged with Home Care for the Aged in June 1938. The payroll and client list steadily grew, with city hospitals and private agencies making referrals: in nine years, housekeepers made well over a million visits to over 60,000 households.[58]

During its operation from February 1934 to April 1943, the service retained its own supervisory staff and training program.[59] This layer of social supervision distinguished it from Housekeeping Aides, a program that Jarrett judged "as being on the whole very unsatisfactory."[60] In July 1940, the WPA placed the larger black-run program under the chief medical social worker of the Housekeeping Service for Chronic Patients, presumably to save administrative costs but perhaps also to mark the authority of a medical mission over domestic service.[61] This chronic patients project, federally funded but locally administered, showed the feasibility of personal attendants to enhance well-being, promote efficient use of hospitalization, and maintain the independence of those able to remain home with assistance.[62]

While the Welfare Council certainly welcomed the idea of a new program, it did not want to cede authority to medical professionals. The Hospital Council of Greater New York, a similar umbrella organization representing private and public hospitals, competed with welfare administrators to shape the tenets of the new program and to advance its own institutional prerogatives. Although New York State's Public Welfare Law clearly designated medical care for the poor as the duty of the Department of Social Welfare, the Hospital Council and physicians of the New York Academy of Medicine argued strenuously for shifting this responsibility to the Department of Hospitals and "competent medical authority."[63] Medical professionals formulated two political arguments that they would use for the rest of the century: continuity of care, that is, "medical and social care carried out without interruption over a period of time," and centralized decision making.[64]

This contestation also reflected gendered assumptions about expertise—a conflict that would emerge with greater consequences after World War II. The physicians who sat on Hospital Council and Academy of Medicine committees were all male. Many key representatives from the Welfare Council were women. Physicians claimed a monopoly over the expertise of care, and attempted to convince New York State authorities that Home Care for the Aged should be placed within the Health Department, particularly since the Welfare Department lacked "professional opinion and knowledge."[65] Such framing threatened middle-class women who had gained political power within the state and control of public resources precisely through their claim to expertise over family, welfare, and domestic issues. It potentially discredited state support for care that was not explicitly medicalized.

These tensions played out within the WPA Housekeeping Service for Chronic Patients. Medical professionals sought to assert authority over the service, yet social welfare criteria were integral to the process. A staff physician and visiting nurse recommended home care on the basis of "medical diagnosis, the degree of disability, and the ability to participate in household work"[66]—the latter, a social, indeed gendered, criterion. The composition of the household was as significant a factor as the medical diagnosis, with the incapacitated mother of small children the ideal candidate to avoid more expensive institutionalization and foster care of children.[67] Conflicts between medical institutions and the Department of Welfare reflected the hybrid nature of the work, which offered care and comfort as well as housecleaning. In practice, welfare professionals touted housekeeping as a form of care, easing worries and offering a more conducive environment for comfort, if not recovery.[68]

Doctors, nurses, and hospitals had to operate within confines set by social welfare. Whatever the medical diagnosis, Housekeeping Service for Chronic Patients only provided a care worker for those on public assistance. Only the Department of Welfare could therefore approve the referral for home care service. Adhering to a casework approach, the Housekeeping Service assumed that welfare caseworkers could best judge the suitability of the home and—of utmost importance for the economics and politics of relief—determine just how truly destitute the person was. They were the gatekeepers for designating worthiness for care.[69]

Not Nurses, but Aides

At the same time that welfare administrators sought to place the visiting housekeeper above the servant, promoters faced resolute nurses determined to restrict any encroachment upon their responsibilities. Nursing was in the process of establishing its professional credentials. States, led by New York in 1935, sought mandatory licensing, a certification needing approval by national nursing associations.[70] A new generation of graduate or trained nurses saw themselves moving up the medical ladder, subsuming tasks performed by physicians as doctoring also became redefined. "I see no possibility of public health nursing organizations, either public or private, sending graduate nurses into the home," proclaimed one nurse advocate in 1934, "to get Dad's breakfast, send Johnny off to school with a clean face and Mary in a clean dress, and give nursing care to the sick mother. *That is not the graduate nurse's job.*"[71] A delegate to a 1938 nurses' convention argued that such work ought to "be labeled 'maid service' so that there would be no confusion in the public mind," although others felt that such a designation would repel the "more refined, more acceptable person" from desiring "to work with ill patients."[72] Nurse associations more than ever sought to distinguish themselves from the "undereducated, unprepared," presumably from less desirable social backgrounds, whom they feared would degrade the work, lower wage rates, and lessen status.[73]

Against skepticism from the nursing associations, the WPA took every opportunity to note in press releases and communications that the housekeepers were not nurses.[74] Woodward told the Red Cross, "It is not the object of the WPA to furnish 'Practical Nurses' to needy homes through housekeeping aide projects"[75] and explained to Jarrett that "most housekeeping aides come within the classification of unskilled workers and we do not feel that they should be allowed to care for sick persons, unless they are working under close medical supervision."[76] Over the years, WPA officials vigilantly watched local classifications of the aides, holding up projects that listed them as "student nurses."[77]

Nurses and doctors soon left their mark on the shape of home care by limiting the housekeeper's repertoire of tasks. Instructions went to the patient, who assumed responsibility, rather than to the housekeeper. The Subcommittee on Medical and Nursing Relations of the Housekeeping Service, along with the State Nurses Association and the Board of Nurse Examiners, drew the line where "simple home care" ended and nursing began. It approved of "helping patient with daily personal care, giving bed pan and care of it, filling of hot water bottle, preparing and serving meals for patient, and helping patient to take simple medicine." Excluded were "installation of nasal or eye drops, applications of dressings, bandages or poultices, . . . electric lamps, heating pads, simple types of massage, preparation of infants' formulas, helping the patient apply a brace, hypodermic injection of insulin, and administration of enemata and douches"—all procedures that the Subcommittee thought possible but the nurses rejected as belonging to the practical nurse, not a housekeeping service. The Department of Hospitals made clear that the extensively trained visiting nurse was "too valuable to be absorbed by household services."[78] Such restriction of tasks reinforced classification of home aides as unskilled, akin to domestic servants. A survey of chronic project housekeeper duties found that cleaning consumed more hours than any other chore, with the bedridden requiring the most personal care. "The field supervisors watch constantly to see that aides are not used exclusively as laundresses, which could easily occur," it noted.[79]

Despite pressure from nurses, however, the WPA held fast to the sickroom duties of the aides. When, in June 1937, the American Nurses' Association urged

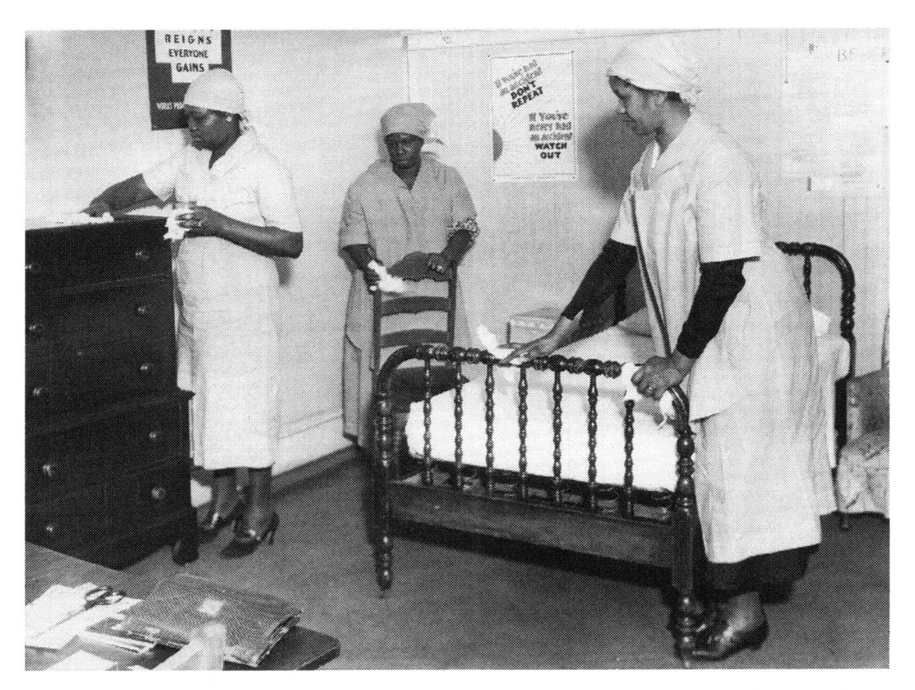

Figure 1.1 Housekeeping Aides in Training. Welfare Council of the City of New York, 38 Rockwell Pl., December 2, 1937. Training Center, Brooklyn, New York, 1940. Photographer/creator: unknown. Copyright: unknown [probably WPA]. Mary C. Jarrett Papers, Sophia Smith Collection, Smith College.

"removal of all references to nursing or care of sick" from the WPA handbook on housekeeping aides, Woodward explained, "to delete all reference to care of the sick in the home . . . would handicap the service which the workers can render." Yet even in defending her program, Woodward differentiated between nursing and housekeeping services that merely made the home sanitary. Aides would work under the close supervision of medical professionals.[80] "The Housekeeper Code of Conduct" confirmed their status as "wholesome and trained" assistants. "The Aides' Pledge" reiterated their position: "Knowing that I am not a doctor, nurse or social worker, I shall not attempt to prescribe for ailment, diagnose illnesses or make social adjustments in the family. Such difficulties I shall report to my supervisors."[81]

Other practices established a class relation within the home. In disciplining the housekeeper as a worker, various requirements undermined the portrait of the aide as substitute mother or good neighbor. Housekeepers were enjoined from accepting anything from the families, taking lunch during a time that would conflict with that of the client, or from smoking or chewing gum while on the job. They were urged to "work cheerfully and efficiently," "use a quiet tone of voice," and "never borrow from a neighbor." They were to follow the directions

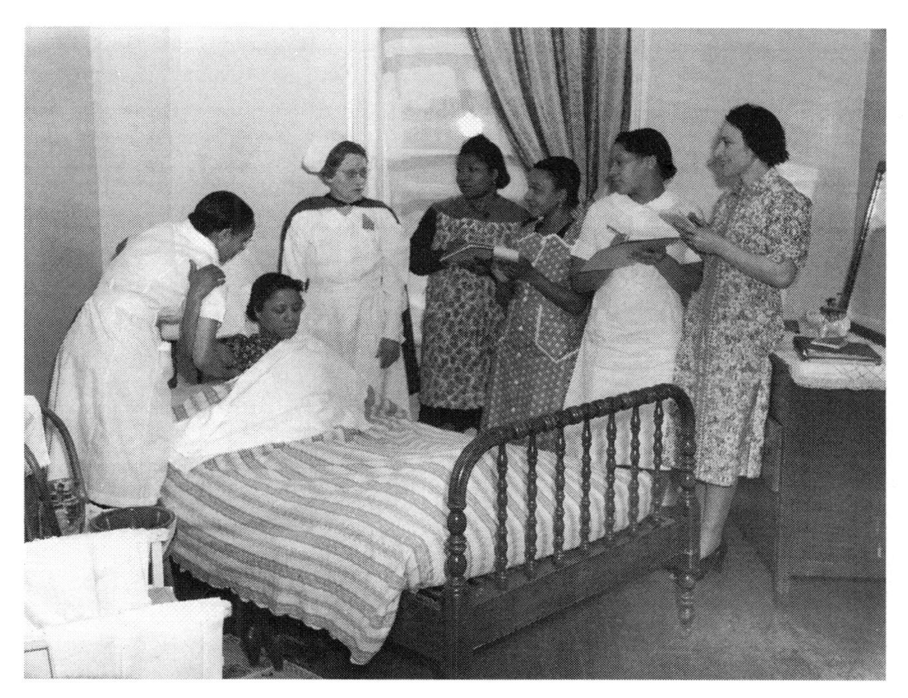

Figure 1.2 Housekeeping Aides training session at 3375 Reservoir Oval, Bronx, New York, February 5, 1941. Photographer: "Rose," New York City WPA Art Project Photography Division, 110 King Street. Credit: New York City WPA Art Project. Mary C. Jarrett Papers, Sophia Smith Collection, Smith College.

of supervisors. That meant making no personal arrangements with clients in terms of work schedules.[82] Given the absence of supervisors at work sites, though, precise instructions in household labor represented a means of labor control. Administrators were well aware that most of the housekeepers had long done domestic work. Nonetheless, they issued detailed "how-to-dos." The compilation of such manuals not only provided unemployed home economists with WPA jobs, but the manuals themselves served to codify the right method against the customary.[83]

Regulations further required "immaculate cleanliness of person and clothing," extending the program's authority deep into the personal lives of workers. The WPA issued direct instructions on what to do in their own homes: regular baths, shampooing, teeth brushing, change of underclothing, use of deodorant, as well as proper laundering of uniforms. They called for light makeup and clean, short fingernails.[84] Guides dictated exactly the type of clothing to be worn, including stipulations that no pins should fasten clothes; nor should jewelry, fancy belts, bedroom slippers, or high heels be worn. Stockings had to be "businesslike." Foundation garments (girdle and brassiere) were to "support the body and help to keep the worker from tiring."[85] Such strictures marked the aide's difference. "Nurses' uniforms are usually white, blue, or gray, consequently much confusion on the part of the general public may be avoided if some color other than these is used."[86]

Refashioning the body fed into a larger "rehabilitation" effort. New Dealers understood rehabilitation as more than physical regeneration and occupational therapy for the wounded, associated with the term since World War I.[87] Woven through many New Deal programs was an idea of social rehabilitation linked to economic modernization. New Deal farm programs aimed at rural rehabilitation, which would help farmers to become self-sufficient; rural electrification, public health, medical care, and migrant camps would rehabilitate the social environment. Rehabilitation was more personal with poor women, improving their very womanhood. New York City officials presented their case for restoring outdoor relief through home care by claiming that welfare officials would be "providing medical treatment for the purposes of social rehabilitation." Home care combined work relief and services to end dependency and to inculcate the deficient in the work ethic, female "respectability," and the domestic ideal.[88]

Visiting housekeeping would transform the worker as well as her client. "Besides making it possible for them to earn a living," claimed Ellen Woodward, "the projects are giving them practice training which enable them to care better for their own homes and families, and also for the homes of others when opportunities for private employment arise."[89] While race neutral, such talk belonged to a discourse of uplift surrounding African American women since emancipation. Rehabilitation was a class as well as a race project; a similar rhetoric toward the poor persisted even where provider and recipient were white. Thus the *Oklahoma City Times* explained in 1941, "The WPA calls it service. Beneficiaries of the program are quick to call it 'home rehabilitation.'"[90]

Newspaper articles, government reports, and other portrayals of the aides reflected the Depression era's more positive attitude toward poor women than would be the case in the 1960s and 1970s, when the press and politicians excoriated African American women as welfare queens.[91] The Welfare Council applauded those "who are anxious to rehabilitate themselves through the new job." Jarrett spoke of "intelligent and forceful women," lauding the understanding housekeeper who showed "calm but firm control." A 1939 article in *The Trained Nurse and Hospital Review*, for example, constructed the image of the competent worker, whose efforts kept families together, brought "order out of chaos," and became the ailing mother's "right hand." But racial stereotypes also permeated such discourse. So Sadie became "a comely Negro woman, neat, energetic and bustling," who steps out the door with a "yo' Mama can let yo-all know if she wants somethin' extra," and an unnamed woman became "a light-hearted little Irish girl."[92]

Housekeepers resented being classed as servants, so trainers lectured on "the difference between servitude and service," asking them to take satisfaction in ministering relief to the distressed.[93] Notions of sacrifice and service pervaded official talk. The Los Angeles District Health Officer embraced the ideology of rehabilitation: "Because of the double service rendered in each case, there is none of the demoralizing and pauperizing effect that occurs so often where the employment given is not definitely useful or constructive."[94] The California's Women's and Professional Projects director explained, "What cannot be seen or measured is the high spirit of service which animates the workers, or the gratitude of the persons they serve."[95] The hand of the WPA Division of Information only generated some of this praise, for testimonials also came from recipients and community leaders.[96]

Worker thoughts mostly survive through mediated sources, through stories crafted by the WPA Information Division or in official reports, which sought approval from WPA administrators and local sponsors of projects.[97] According to a Los Angeles study, "What My Job Means to Me," housekeepers expressed satisfaction. African American Valera Fuller saw "an opportunity to fulfill the ultimate destiny of man: that of service to humanity." Self-reminders when "dealing with my clients"—like "don't gossip"—reflected maxims stressed in WPA manuals, rules that she may have learned during training sessions. Other aides reiterated official policy. Delma Floyd, identified as "white," believed, "this work will in time, if continued, save the country a great deal of expense." Others offered additional evidence of their rehabilitation, especially regarding ways in which the work both prepared them for future employment and improved their own family labor. A "Mexican" woman called the job "a haven for me, giving social and economic security to my family and myself . . ." Only one—a white, probably Jewish, housekeeper—spoke the language of class, referring to "human needs of our great working masses." The confession of an unidentified worker especially illustrates the heady combination of care work and a service ethic that obscured the wages of care: "If it seems necessary to work overtime, I tell my client we can chalk that up to neighborliness. I am getting something more lasting than money out of my W.P.A. work."[98]

The association of home care with unpaid maternal work and despised and exploited servants stacked the decks against high wages and prestige for a job readily classified as subsidiary to medical treatment.[99] Under the WPA, though, home care was a "good enough" job. At a time when the minimum wage was 30 cents an hour and domestics and laundry workers earned even less, the housekeeping aides worked 30 hours a week, with assignments of either a whole or half day, for a monthly stipend of $52.80.[100] WPA rules and regulations, which limited individuals to 18 months of work relief, generated the most turnover. Researchers on New York's project for chronic patients increasingly attributed "favorable reasons, such as qualification for a better position and private employment" as explaining why women left. Following WPA layoffs after a budget cut in July 1941, many took attendant jobs in the city's hospitals, meeting a newly emerging wartime labor need.[101]

Public and Private: The Hybrid State in the New Deal Era

Despite the success of the WPA projects, prominent New York social workers worried over the dependence of home care on federal relief. Since the late 1920s, Manhattan and Brooklyn Jewish welfare agencies had deployed older Jewish women as "substitute mothers" for crisis-stricken co-religionists. In 1933, the New York Junior League established a small homemaker program with the Children's Aid Society that catered to Catholic and Protestant, black as well as white, families. By 1935, these private agencies used 50 housekeepers, reaching 300 households, when the city's WPA projects were sending nearly 1,400 visiting housekeepers into the homes of some 5,000 families.[102] At its peak, the WPA projects employed over 2,000 aides and another 400 staff. Given sudden shifts in federal allocations for work relief, agency social workers feared that the WPA units could close with little warning. They thus turned to the U.S. Children's Bureau, as had countless other nonprofits and individuals over the previous two decades, to undertake research on home care, with the goal of defining fundamental principles and advancing the service.[103]

In November 1937, the Children's Bureau brought into dialogue private and public social welfare agencies and national associations of public health nurses, public welfare administrators, home economists, and child welfare advocates. Representatives from the WPA, Social Security Board, Women's Bureau, Division of Home Economics, Farm Security Administration, and Public Health Service joined the conversation in recognition of the multiple components of health, education, work, and welfare that were involved. These leading experts considered situations in which homemaker service helped families and compared experiences with and the duties of various types of workers: homemakers (deemed "substitute mothers"), housekeeping aides (judged as domestics), and visiting housekeepers (connected to home demonstration)—distinctions that often hid the similarity of tasks performed. More than differentiating one worker from another, these titles enhanced the separate professional expertise of those formulating them. In calling for standardization and job analysis, the Children's Bureau gathering sought power through the production of expertise rather than control of funding alone. It concluded that recruitment depended "upon making such work a clearly defined occupation having definite functions, opportunities for training and development . . . and compensation commensurate with the service given."[104]

Two years later, the Bureau spearheaded the creation of the Committee on Supervised Homemaker-Housekeeper Service, named to enhance the status of the "visiting housekeeper" through a designation that linked the job with the performance of casework by a private social welfare or family agency.[105] An informal organization, with rotating officers mostly from member agencies of the Family Welfare Association of America and the Child Welfare League of America, the Committee met twice a year, once with the National Conference of Social Work. Its presidents came from private nonprofit agencies in Cleveland, New York, Boston, Pittsburgh, and Chicago.[106]

Maud Morlock of the Bureau's Social Service Division advised this growing movement. She was an experienced social worker, trained during the Progressive Era. Like many of her generation, she cultivated a strong network of sister practitioners; letters with Committee members seamlessly moved from strategizing over funding to talk of vacations. Certainly her tireless correspondence, circulation of pamphlets, and site visits linked a generation of social workers who connected a maternalistic past to a scientific future. A 1911 graduate of Oberlin College, with a master's degree from the University of Chicago, Morlock attended the London School of Civics and Philanthropy, where in the early 1920s she first encountered "home helps." She taught at Case Western University and practiced social work at the United Charities of Chicago before coming to the Bureau in 1936. Her fields included unwed mothers, adoption, and maternity homes; she became the expert on homemaker services in Europe as well as in the United States. Through her efforts, the small and underfunded Children's Bureau coordinated a campaign over the next 20 years with the committee that it organized for the use of "substitute mothers" as a tool for individual and family rehabilitation.[107]

World War II and the New Deal Legacy

The approach of war further justified the use of housekeepers. As one Los Angeles WPA official proclaimed: "Our first responsibility in home defense is the care of our own families." Housekeepers advanced "the Government's Home Defense program." The training especially would enhance home life through "more efficient housecleaning" and "more nutritious meals built from surplus commodities."[108] Other reasoning drew the WPA closer to the maternalist goals of the Children's Bureau's network. Speaking in 1940 on "WPA's Part in National Defense," Florence Kerr, the new head of the Women's and Professional Projects, explained that housekeeping aides could provide day nursery service for children of working mothers. A year later, Children's Bureau Director Katherine Lenroot pushed this option at the Conference on Day Care, reminding that "when the house is clean and the meals are prepared, obviously members of the family are going to be happier about it."[109]

Such deployment shifted the mission of the housekeepers, but few wage-earning mothers took advantage of the service, even on an emergency basis. More often, homemakers aided pregnant wives of soldiers covered by the federal Emergency Medical and Infant Care Program. Since homemakers were not nurses, however, they could not be paid directly through the program; instead, their payment came from voluntary organizations, like the Red Cross. But in suggesting that "with a small amount of training by Public Health Departments, housekeeping aides would be equipped to do practical nursing," Kerr blurred the distinctions that the WPA previously had accepted.[110]

In the early 1940s, the Children's Bureau and its national network reiterated that the WPA projects met "a very real need . . . that private agencies are not equipped to give either because of lack of funds or of staff." With Congress about to eliminate the WPA, other federal officials argued that the aide projects were never intended to continue indefinitely, but were demonstration projects that local public and private agencies were to absorb. With the actual dissolution of the WPA in 1943, advocates pleaded for continuing the homemakers.[111] Black and white women, though, were rejecting household labor for any job in the war economy.[112] Unable to offer competitive wages, the private agencies witnessed homemakers quitting for more lucrative employment.[113] The WPA projects ended without real plans or resources to continue the service through other means.

As a leader of the Committee on Chronic Illness, Mary Jarrett noted the wartime shift in emphasis of housekeeper service toward child care with some concern, worried that it might displace home care as a viable alternative to institutionalization. With medical personnel leaving for military service, the Department of Hospitals, desperately short-staffed, put planning for home care on hold during the war. The Committee on Chronic Illness moved toward investigating nursing homes for elderly and chronic patients discharged from municipal hospitals. Within two years, the Welfare Council observed that the end of the WPA project left a large gap in community resources and again made necessary the use of institutional beds for those who did not need such a level of confinement. Advocates like Jarrett feared that the value of the housekeeping aide in the prevention and care of illness might be lost amid the makeshift adaptations of the war.[114]

In 1938, *The New Republic* declared, "There is no reason why a civilized society . . . should not get to regard the work of cleaning floors and making beds and cooking dinners as exactly on a par with any other work. When that happens women will be no more reluctant to enter domestic service than they are now to take up nursing as a career."[115] But equation with domestic service was precisely what nurses wished to avoid by restricting the activities of housekeeping aides to household labor. As much as supervisors "appeal[ed] that it is a privilege to be of such a service in their community," housekeepers still were relief recipients, better off than maids but confused with them precisely because they performed the same tasks and the same women worked at these jobs.

The WPA housekeeping aide program put women to work without competing with any organized group of employers, countering the charge that the WPA engaged in make-work devised only to compensate relief recipients. The housekeepers undertook useful labor, performing a community service that, as Woodward explained, "existing agencies long realized underprivileged families needed, but which the agencies were not able to give before the inauguration of WPA projects."[116] It was "one of the best methods of getting the most for the money," exclaimed an Iowa administrator.[117] Hospital social workers further emphasized how home aides reduced expensive stays and facilitated convalescence, while public health officials equally heralded the assistance.

Not everyone applauded the service. The politics of race and class appropriateness played out on the local level. In Iowa, the WPA tried to keep the program out of the news for fear of an adverse public reaction over providing help to the poor.[118] Scattered letters to the WPA requested maids and grumbled about the difficulty of hiring personal attendants now that they all worked for the WPA.[119] Placing Anglo women, who complained of dirty and exhausting labor, in private homes as aides drew fire from the conservative Texas Protective League, which protested "that the aides were no more than slaves sent to work in the homes of the affluent."[120] Entrenched attitudes toward the privileges of class and race fueled such criticisms.

The New Deal left a threefold legacy, which persisted through the rest of the century. First, although tied to the medical sector, states would pay for home-based care through welfare agencies but often with federal funds. Second, policy experts and welfare administrators saw female public assistance recipients as a ready supply of labor for home care. And, third, the exclusion of home attendants from the national wage and hour law remained in place for the next seven decades. Though first focused on families with children, with the growth of Social Security after World War II, homemaker services eventually came to prioritize support for the elderly, a group of voters privileged by the American welfare state over other recipients of social assistance. A new emphasis on chronic illness and an aging population after the war would channel home care through alternative routes, especially as hospitals, buoyed by massive infusions of public investment and private insurance, jumped aggressively into long-standing debates over the definition of care and the deservedness of those in need of support.

2

Rehabilitative Missions

In spring 1949, a newly formed Commission on Chronic Illness convened its first conference to address challenges of illness, aging, and dependency. The Commission represented a promising collaboration between four national professional organizations—the American Public Welfare Association, American Hospital Association, American Medical Association, and American Public Health Association. Opening the meeting was New Jersey's Ellen Potter, Deputy Commissioner of Welfare from the first state that would locate homemaker services in a public health department. She explained that "whereas the major welfare problem of the 30's grew out of unemployment, the major cause of economic dependency in the 40's arises from chronic illness and old age."[1] Potter was a physician who advocated a medical solution to what she judged as the curse of welfare dependency.

Following World War II, local public welfare agencies continued homemaker/housekeeper services for families with young children. In seeking to extend the program to adults, administrators discovered that they had to confront chronic illness. They held fast to the belief that the New Deal created a right to public support, but joined income maintenance with social services, the field that the Children's Bureau long sought to foster through public-private collaborations. Federal, county, and municipal welfare officials pushed to expand the state's role in sustaining families and ending dependency. Joining them was a range of charitable agencies, which continued to develop homemaker initiatives, often as small demonstration projects whose usefulness, they envisioned, would convince the community to fund centralized public services. Most social welfare advocates felt that the future belonged to public programs that would serve all economic groups.[2]

Public and private agencies aspired to work together. They shared an emphasis on casework and, through mutual cooperation, expected to broaden the meaning of "public." So if a public department could not supply homemakers, government would purchase the service from private agencies.[3] Relying on a dense network of social workers, home economists, and public health nurses, welfare proponents attempted to subject the private realm of the home to the rehabilitating effects of government. In the process, they created and defined a new occupation for women, especially poor ones—a job that took place in the home but performed care work for the welfare state.

In the wake of the New Deal, private agencies redefined their role. If government now provided income support and relief, charities and voluntary social agencies would present something else: what they called advanced, professionalized social services. Considering themselves the therapeutic avant garde, they offered psychiatric understandings and assessments of social problems, approaches that gained heightened legitimacy with wartime studies of trauma, battle fatigue, and neurosis. As the ideology of rehabilitation became ever more prevalent, public welfare policy makers and administrators thought that they should mirror the approach of the private agencies. Homemaker services became part of a battery of casework supports for individuals and families to adjust to personal mishap and social stress.[4] Social workers embraced the home as a central building block of society, and homemakers therefore promised to strengthen family life by maintaining domestic space.[5] Like an earlier generation of child savers, agencies dispatched homemakers to the burdened mother and the "disorganized home," teaching better methods of care in the process of relieving immediate distress.[6]

In a parallel development, the rapidly expanding postwar medical system sought its own strategies for aiding chronically ill and disabled persons. Hospitals and physicians had constructed a heroic narrative in which hospital-affiliated doctors conquered contagious disease. Now health experts contended that it was time to take on chronic conditions through scientific research, clinical studies, and centers for rehabilitation.[7] Home care would become one element in a far-reaching medical institutional complex extending outward from the hospital.

World War II further propelled disability into public view as a new medical challenge. Physicians asserted that their professional definitions, diagnoses, and treatment should frame rehabilitation, a field previously left to the relatively subordinate area of vocational education. Like caseworkers, these physicians relied on public programs and federal money, no matter whether operating through public or private facilities.[8]

Welfare and medical initiatives shared an emphasis on dependency, defined in social, psychological, physical, and gendered terms. Professionals in each realm agreed that large numbers of relief recipients suffered from chronic illness or impairments. With the right intervention—or *care*—a significant percentage of such individuals should and could be moved off public assistance, the categorical programs for the elderly, disabled, and children. Each group deployed notions of rehabilitation toward the goal of ending dependency, believing that it could help patients or clients achieve some final state of independence.

The promotion of home care in the two decades after World War II demonstrates how competing definitions of care—particularly the labor of

Figure 2.1 Maud Morlock, U.S. Children's Bureau. US National Archives. 235-N-CB228-3.

care—fundamentally shaped old age, disability, and welfare policy; job training; and an emerging labor market. Welfare, health, and medical professionals held contrasting views on the location of care; they also had distinct ideas about who should perform the valorized or menial aspects of such labor. Gendered and racialized understandings of care work, home life, and institutional authority initially led home care down two developmental tracks. Throughout this process, social workers sought to maintain some control over a new occupation in the face of rising medical authority.

Defining Home Care

In the early postwar period, the significance of homemaker/housekeeping services came not from numbers of workers, but from efforts to bring an occupation into being. The availability of home care was uneven, concentrated in major metropolitan areas and a few rural counties. In 1949, 66 private agencies and a handful of public welfare departments offered services.[9] By 1958, 32 states and the District of Columbia provided homemakers, but coverage remained uneven.

Figure 2.2 Martin Cherkasky, 1950s. Photographer: Fabian Bachrach ©, Courtesy of Montefiore Medical Center.

Public and private entities employed fewer than 2,000 workers, mostly clustered in ones and twos.[10]

After World War II, the Committee on Supervised Homemaker-Housekeeper Service struggled with naming this new occupation.[11] Increasingly, family welfare experts feared that the designation "substitute mother" not only offended some clients but also had damaging psychological consequences. Nor did it apply to the care of adults.[12] The Committee substituted "homemaker" for "housekeeper," the WPA title, to stress the responsibility of caring for children as well as doing housework, and renamed itself the National Committee on Homemaker Service.[13] Still, "homemaker" did not necessarily capture the work, either. The quip of a rehabilitative clinic organizer expressed one stream of objections. Arguing for the addition of "aide" to emphasize the proxy nature of the service, she exclaimed, "NO woman who comes in to my house to replace me is the Homemaker—any more than she is the children's mother or my husband's wife (she may become any of these—but it will be over my dead body—)."[14] Other individuals and organizations continued to refer to homemakers as housekeepers.[15]

This definitional struggle occurred in a shifting labor market, one in which service jobs outside the home grew, private household service declined, and white-collar retail and clerical work became the major realms of employment for women. Despite a resurgent ideology of domesticity, a quarter of all married women were in the labor force by 1950, and increasing numbers of mothers sought part-time work.[16] Policy makers noticed problems faced by women over age 40 seeking gainful employment. Government agencies and the popular press alike worried whether women could combine wage earning and caregiving.[17] Home help promised to relieve the employed women from family care while providing other women with jobs.

During the late 1940s, social work advocates crafted a standard description of the occupation. Maud Morlock, of the Children's Bureau, wrote an entry on "Homemaker Service" for an authority they controlled, the *Social Work Year Book,* issued by the Russell Sage Foundation. Honing previous definitions, she spoke of "supervised placement by a casework agency of a woman, chosen for her skills and her ability to get along with people, in a home where her services are requested and needed to maintain and preserve the home as a unit." This social work context separated homemaker service from other household labor.[18]

The New York Welfare Council further proposed a definition for the *Dictionary of Occupational Titles,* the job classification scheme of the United States Employment Service.[19] The 1949 second edition of this reference guide first contained an entry for "Homemaker": "Under supervision of a welfare agency maintains homes of families disrupted by absence or incapacitation of housewife. Cares for children and ill or elderly members of family. Prepares reports required by agency." The homemaker clearly substituted for the unpaid labor of wives and mothers. The U.S. Employment Service, however, undermined the distinction cultivated by social workers by listing "homemaker" as part of domestic and personal service.[20] Such classification—along with the home location and tasks performed—cemented a status outside the labor law.

The specter of servile labor continued to haunt this new category of worker. "The difference between a nurse and a homemaker is obvious," the Jewish Family Service of New York City noted in 1950, "but there continues to be confusion regarding domestic service." Families would call agencies looking for a domestic; other times, though asking for a homemaker, they really needed either a domestic or a nurse.[21] Some agencies countered these assumptions directly, telling their predominantly African American workforce "that they are staff members and not maids."[22] Even if aged clients demanded performance of spring-cleaning or heavy laundry, these and other onerous tasks overstepped allowable work.[23] In contrast to the domestic servant, homemakers were to help the elderly client "with his real needs and yet preserve fully his capacity for self-maintenance" and instruct "how to manage" when alone. The homemaker engaged in emotional work; she had to "maintain a sympathetic, warm, and objective attitude."[24]

Advocates faced a dilemma in determining an appropriate salary. In numerous consultations, Morlock insisted on greater compensation than that for domestics in order to attract and retain the right kind of woman. Reliant on local community chest drives and private philanthropy, however, agencies usually could afford only the going rate for domestic service.[25] Demand for household labor therefore influenced wages. When asked whether it paid a living wage, the head of a Houston agency responded, "barely".[26] New York's Welfare Council took the lead in devising wage rates based on practical nursing and domestic service, the very occupations from which it sought to distance homemakers.[27]

The Council urged the private welfare and family agencies to hire homemakers as staff and to offer uniform benefits to all employees. Recommendations for generous vacation and sick leave recognized the hazards of working with the ill and the stress of long hours. Yet the Council accepted policies that they considered "realistic for the agencies" and appropriate for the specialized requirements of the job. Agencies might pick up limited transportation, telephone, and meal expenses. They could demand that homemakers undergo examination for physical and moral fitness, much in keeping with New Deal treatment of domestic servants but not with requirements for other employees.[28]

Over the next decade, agencies attempted to adhere to Council standards with mixed results. Wages and salaries depended more on regional location than on the size or type of organization. Half of the agencies placed all their homemakers on salary, while a fifth employed only hourly workers. Half offered no wage steps. Workers might be on call for a 24-hour shift but, at most, were paid only for 10 to 16 hours. Vacation with pay after a year's work was common and, while about two-thirds provided sick leave, few offered health insurance. Salaried employees received retirement benefits at two-thirds of public agencies, but at less than half of the private ones.[29]

Homemakers themselves had little direct say in standardization efforts. The Community Service Society of New York organized a Homemakers' Club, an attempt to generate loyalty and facilitate *esprit de corps* among women located in isolated worksites—rather than prepare them for collective action.[30] While those employed by public welfare came under civil service or some kind of defined personnel system, few were unionized. Social worker unionization itself was scattered, concentrated in cities like New York and Chicago that had vigorous radical movements and strong labor unions. Such white-collar and service sector organizing soon would become a victim of postwar anti-Communism, especially after the CIO expelled Left-led unions like the United Public Workers.[31]

Enabling the Public Sector: The Postwar New Deal

After the war, New York, Cleveland, Chicago, Washington, D.C., Milwaukee, and Denver continued WPA programs. These cities had large populations, well-developed women's social welfare networks, umbrella organizations that brought together public and private agencies, and chapters of national organizations, like the American Public Welfare Association and the Family Service Association. As the nation turned from war to peace, homemaker programs under public auspices existed in such varied places as Jacksonville, Denver, Puerto Rico, Cincinnati, and Worcester. Mississippi and North Carolina drew upon federal child welfare funds for limited efforts.[32] The Department of Welfare in New York City became the most successful model of a public agency that directly employed homemakers, worked closely with private agencies, secured federal funds, and expanded services from child welfare to elder care.

When World War II ended, New Yorkers were ready to reenergize the New Deal. In the city's unique social democratic culture, trade unionists, public officials, workers, political groups, and neighborhood associations built a remarkable array of public institutions, including health clinics, cooperative housing, cultural centers, and medical insurance programs. The broad orientation of the city's unions created a social infrastructure that reached New Yorkers well beyond organized labor's ranks. This local welfare state blended government and private resources.[33] Other postwar cities also hired thousands of new workers in the departments of education, police, fire, highways, and parks, but in New York, half of its burgeoning public workforce labored in social welfare: hospitals, housing, higher education, mass transit, and social assistance.[34]

Beginning in August 1945, the Homemaker Service became a permanent part of New York City government, with its own staff. For the next three decades, homemakers belonged to a booming public sector, though their actual workplace was client homes. Even amid the postwar economic boom, New York's welfare administrators assumed that the problem of dependency would persist. Still, they felt confident that home care offered an effective solution. Gertrude Bolden, a training supervisor with the Department of Welfare, specifically linked the goals of the postwar program with the "eminently satisfactory" experience of the WPA. In seeking the assistance of the Children's Bureau, Bolden explained that the department had maintained its project both to train women receiving public assistance in homemaking skills and to serve other recipient families.

When the city launched the Homemaker Service, it began modestly, with 15 homemakers assigned to families on home relief or Aid to Dependent Children (ADC).[35]

Confusion over the nature of the work persisted. Its child welfare focus led the city to classify workers under the civil service as "mother's aides." This job title dated from the war, when Mayor Fiorello La Guardia established the designation to ensure services for children.[36] Subsequently, the Children's Bureau and the National Committee on Homemaker Service urged the new title of "homemaker," both to clarify the service being offered and to expand its future potential. The Commissioner of Welfare concurred, although the designation "mother's aide" remained in place until the next round of Social Security amendments expanded services to seniors and disabled people.[37] Other welfare departments were not as fortunate in placing homemakers or housekeepers on the payroll as home care workers. Cuyahoga County's welfare department, which covered Cleveland, had to circumvent official classifications by listing them as "charwomen to clean the office," even though they actually went into homes.[38]

Soon after launching the new program, New York turned to win direct federal support. Previously advocates had to appeal for subsidization through the smaller welfare titles of Social Security. The Bureau of Public Assistance, the federal unit with direct jurisdiction over ADC, helped the city make the case for accessing this relatively larger pot of funds.[39] Bureau staff argued that homemaker service, rather than merely supplying housekeeping, directly met the purpose of the Social Security Act to provide individuals with "economic support and services . . . for health and development." It allowed the needy to live with their families. In February 1947, the Commissioner of Social Security approved New York's petition for ADC coverage.[40] Social workers and the federal women's network had achieved one of their most important goals, tightening the connections between the private home and the public welfare state.

For the welfare network of the Children's Bureau, the location of homemakers in the non-competitive class of civil service turned New York into a model. With that classification, homemakers were eligible for pensions, health insurance, sick leave, and vacation days.[41] Like other public employees, and unlike the typical domestic, city homemakers officially worked a 45-hour week. They could obtain overtime from Sunday and holiday work. Advancement in annual salary was possible within a narrow range.[42] New York's social democratic public culture led to a more generous construction of the job. Within a few years, its program expanded. Homemaker Service employed 63 workers, 55 of whom were African American; by 1951, the total number reached 95, primarily middle-aged women; many were former WPA housekeepers.[43]

As with Jewish social agencies and Catholic religious orders, New York's Department of Welfare sought to match the ethnicity, religion, or race of the homemaker with that of the client. The Department of Welfare hired Spanish-speaking homemakers, since a growing number of clients were Puerto Rican.[44] It looked for women familiar with "foreign cookery," including kosher food and Spanish and Italian dishes. Nonetheless, the Homemaker Service typically sent black women into white homes. New York's Children's Aid Society was unusual in servicing families from all major religious groups, with employees evenly divided between blacks and whites.[45]

While African Americans dominated the workforce in most places, the racial dynamics of an area, as well as its overall demography, determined placements. Houston hired four black, one or two Latin American, and one or two white homemakers.[46] North Carolina's experimental project replicated the Jim Crow system by having whites serve only whites. Boston reflected race and class divisions. The city made it explicit policy never to assign white homemakers to African American homes, claiming "Negroes would not find white women acceptable." While most whites in Boston accepted black homemakers, the Irish often refused, leading to a workforce disproportionately Irish and Catholic. Class also shaped interactions between providers and receivers of care. African American homemakers resisted placement with better-off black families, claiming they were more "likely to be treated as a servant."[47] By the end of the 1950s, with more than 80 percent of recipients across the nation labeled white, African American and, to a lesser extent, Latina women yet again found themselves engaged in manual labor in white homes.[48]

Many families were extremely destitute. In 1958 more than half of the clients nationally were on public assistance or at the poverty line.[49] Some families in New York lacked basic household appliances and utilities, so that "when electricity and gas were turned off, the homemaker had to improvise cooking and lighting facilities while the caseworkers negotiated with the utility company." These families, noted caseworkers, "lived in buildings that were in a state of extreme deterioration and neglect" and "rooms that constituted a gross violation of the Board of Health standards."[50] In multiple ways, homemaker service opened up the home to inspection by the state.

In order to classify the labor as a professional social service, New York's Department of Welfare promoted training. It located its new Homemaking Center in the building of the Welfare Training Institute, which had a model kitchen and other facilities for professional instruction. A home economist taught household skills, while Bureau of Child Welfare staff lectured on child development. As with the WPA, workers learned how to manage households with meager resources. The welfare department claimed to be creating professionals: once the trainee qualified for a regular assignment, it announced, "these homemakers take great pride in their attainment to staff and justifiably so, since the required standards of performance are high."[51] After a six-month probationary period, homemakers received full civil service status. As early as 1949, the Homemaker Center boasted: "There might have been 541 homes broken up in New York City . . . had it not been for our Homemaking Service."[52]

Though not required to wear a uniform, many homemakers in New York and elsewhere had emblems "to give the homemaker a sense of identity and make . . . public recognition easier." One Chicago agency preferred that symbol of cleanliness, "a white house dress." Agency supervisors claimed that the uniform and insignia boosted the homemaker's pride in her job and displayed to other community members the caring role of the state. Yet precisely because they could be visibly identified, New York's Jewish Family Service rejected uniforms for breaching family privacy by revealing the homemaker's presence to neighbors.[53]

Saving one set of families was not enough. The Rehabilitation and Service Training Program, established by the Homemaking Center in 1953, continued the dual project of the WPA: African American and poor women would be rehabilitated through new jobs in domestic labor. Homemaker services recruited directly from public assistance rolls.[54] Cities aimed to put women on welfare to work, while private agencies turned to the same labor force. The Chicago Department of Welfare initially hired most staff homemakers through referrals from caseworkers, who recommended women currently or recently on public relief. All but two of its homemakers were African Americans. Southern migrants, who had labored for as little as $5 a week, found public housekeeping to be a step up.[55] Half of Cleveland's housekeepers were former ADC recipients. Its family agency sought part-time, temporary workers among older women no longer eligible for ADC; these workers acted as floaters or substitutes for full-timers.[56] Homemaker advocates described the ideal worker as "a member of a minority racial group with no employment opportunities except domestic service although she knows herself to be capable of more than that and longs for status."[57] New York officials expected the Service Training Program to ready welfare recipients for various types of household employment. After a mere 14 months, the Homemaking Center claimed in 1954 to have moved recipients "from the relief rolls to payrolls."[58]

Evolving into Long-Term Care

New York's private agencies laid the groundwork for expanding homemaker service to elderly and chronically ill persons through demonstration projects in the late 1940s. Religious and ethnic family agencies faced the challenges of aging populations, especially as overcrowded hospitals and nursing homes began turning away medical referrals. In some cases, disease-specific charities or service organizations, such as the New York Cancer Committee, sent homemakers to assist those suffering from a designated malady. In 1948, New York's Jewish Family Services pioneered the use of homemakers for elder care through a year-long demonstration project, funded by the Federation of Jewish Philanthropies and supervised by the Home for Aged and Infirm Hebrews. Those selected for this service were considered physically and emotionally able to remain safely at home.[59] Such demonstration projects aimed at making the case for some blend of public and private funding, if not a shift to state-provided services.

The prospects for this outcome seemed a bit brighter in 1950 when Congress passed the first major amendments to Social Security since 1939. Best known for extending the reach of social insurance pensions, the 1950 Amendments opened a different door for home care support by expanding public assistance titles, or what were called categorical aid, confining home care firmly within the realm of "welfare." The Social Security Amendments of 1950 made it possible for adult caretakers of children, including those other than the biological mother, to receive income support through ADC. They added an entirely new category, Aid to the Permanently and Totally Disabled. Rather than a social insurance program, Congress established disability support as a state-run public assistance program for the needy.[60] For states prepared to take advantage of disability support, the provision opened new funding for public assistance; by mid-1951, 31 states covered nearly 100,000 individuals, a fifth of them homebound. Such support especially helped states seeking remedies for long-term care.[61] Social Security now had four categorical aid components: programs for the children of poor single mothers, for permanently disabled workers, for the blind, and for the poor elderly.

Illinois moved first to have homemaker service covered by all of the categorical aid programs, thereby connecting federal aid to state and local support. The Chicago Department of Welfare started a homemaker program for recipients of state general assistance in the summer of 1942, just before the WPA project ended. The 1950 Amendments prompted Illinois to seek federal funds, and to go beyond New York's application for federal participation under ADC. In early 1951, Illinois submitted a request for coverage under all four federal programs; New York subsequently joined the petition.[62]

The Bureau of Public Assistance now generalized the maintenance role of homemakers, advancing a new interpretation of the Social Security Act. Seeking a definitive ruling from the Commissioner of Social Security, Bureau Director Jane Hoey argued that such an extension meshed with the goals of social security "to help needy individuals through assistance and other welfare services to remain in and maintain their own homes." Finally, Social Security Commissioner Arthur Altmeyer in 1952 allowed federal participation in the administrative costs of long-term homemaker service in all federal welfare programs, but required that states obtain advance approval.[63] With these small, incremental extensions, the women's network sustained modest amounts of long-term care in the era before Medicare and Medicaid.

As a result, New York City formally extended Homemaker Service in 1952 to elderly recipients of public assistance who, because of either illness or just "the infirmities of age," could not perform all household or personal care tasks. By the end of the decade, the caseload of aged or ill adults grew at a faster pace than the overall program, moving from only a few cases to a third of the total.[64] With older people living at 40 percent of the city's median income, the number of elderly receiving old age and other forms of public assistance rose steadily during the 1950s, numbering 45,000 in 1959. Nearly 44 percent of all adult public assistance recipients suffered from some chronic illness or disability. Assignment of a homemaker, however, was hardly automatic. In the casework tradition, the welfare department conducted home visits to determine whether friends, relatives, or neighbors could care for the client instead.[65]

Administrators of New York's Homemaking Center now called for continued expansion of homemaker service as a more cost-efficient and humane alternative to institutionalization. Proponents simultaneously invoked the language of independence and protection. "The homemaker's supportive role," they argued, "has been found to have sound psychological values for the older person in increasing his security and his ability to do things for himself." Homemakers further would provide "protective services." Hoey repeatedly insisted that welfare clients should have the freedom of choice to accept or reject home rehabilitation. States were not to impose the service, but rather guarantee recipients "unhampered use of the money payment." The goal was to be protected, but independent.[66]

These interpretations circumscribed the payment mechanisms that voluntary agencies could use. So they devised a dual check made out to the client and the agency or homemaker. In Massachusetts, the state refused to approve direct payment to agencies on the basis that the service was not medical care. So the Boston Provident Association relied on such dual checks, which the client had to endorse before the agency could pay the homemaker. Elsewhere, the client paid the homemaker directly.[67] This practice would become the basis for considering the client both as a consumer and an employer, with profound consequences for the ability of workers to bargain with the state. It became one of the critical means for masking the employment and class relations of the system.

More generally, service became central to new conceptions of public welfare. Homemaker Service in New York was part of the Bureau of Special Services.[68] The Bureau provided enabling or restorative services, such as homemakers, protective living arrangements, and job placement to enhance self-sufficiency or encourage self-support by making employment possible—the imperatives that had infused WPA programs.[69] These forms of self-support clearly belonged to the same project for ending dependency and meeting long-standing goals of the American welfare state.

Within the postwar welfare state, New York now offered homemaking jobs regarded as permanent, resulting in little turnover. In 1959, the welfare department honored 37 women who had been city homemakers for over 10 years. Such recognition ceremonies occurred regularly over the next decade. By October 1963, after increased federal funding, 263 women worked as full-time homemakers, covered by a union collective bargaining contract with the American Federation of State, County, and Municipal Employees (AFSCME).[70]

Private agencies followed the city's lead. The Catholic Charities of the Archdiocese of New York, for example, added both full- and part-time homemakers to its staff. Some went further, matching the type of benefits offered in standard private employment. In the late 1950s, the Children's Aid Society paid for major medical insurance as well as life insurance and retirement for full-time homemakers, while Jewish Family Service gave both medical insurance and Blue Cross Hospitalization. A few private agency programs began to raise salaries.[71]

Even as public funding and programs grew, the city's welfare department deepened its association with private family agencies throughout the 1950s. As envisioned by the Welfare Council a decade earlier, public-private cooperation had become essential to state provision of services. For example, civil service rules prohibited public welfare homemakers to work as live-in caretakers on 24-hour call. After the State approved the purchase of homemaking assistance for aged and disabled people from charitable agencies in 1958, the department contracted out round-the-clock service to such groups. It subsequently worked with approximately 50 agencies concerned with client rehabilitation and employment. While the private agencies had fewer homemakers, they could be more flexible—which often meant underpayment for over-night shifts, when the worker was on call but perhaps not persistently engaged in tasks.[72] The Federation of Protestant Welfare Agencies at this time organized the Association for Homemakers Service, subsidized by a large philanthropic grant, specifically to tend families and ailing elderly persons for the Department of Welfare.[73]

Enhancing the turn to services was an increased awareness of the impact of illness and other forms of disability on dependency.[74] Social workers and public welfare administrators remained committed to the idea of an entitlement to income support, although they began to interpret monetary assistance as a legacy of Depression-era unemployment. In this new environment, they embraced the words of national public welfare leader Elizabeth Wickenden, who insisted that "an organized system of social service" best could express "the ultimate concern of government for the well-being of its individual members."[75] The American Public Welfare Association confirmed this position in 1955, holding that public welfare departments had "an obligation to assure essential rehabilitation services for their clients."[76]

Amendments to Social Security in 1956 promised a means to accomplish that task. They authorized demonstration projects, again with the goal of helping to "restore public assistance recipients more quickly to their maximum economic and personal independence."[77] Advancing the social rehabilitation agenda, the 1956 Amendments proposed to refashion ADC around public services to reduce dependency and encourage self-support, while still protecting a mother's right to cash assistance.[78] In reality, such a shift remained aspirational because Congress did not provide sufficient funds to match state spending on such services.[79] As public welfare departments struggled with meagerly funded, ad hoc adaptations, welfare professionals like Maud Morlock feared that medical authorities and public health departments would take over, especially with their soaring public funding and enhanced social authority.[80]

In-Home Support and the International Development of Postwar Welfare States

The United States was not alone in developing homemaker services during these years. European states, as well as Canada, New Zealand, and Australia, initiated home assistance or home helps for similar reasons: to address the crisis in family welfare during the 1930s, uplift the homemaking of the poor, aid ill and elderly people, and relieve wartime shortages of domestic labor. They too created mixed systems that were public and private, national and local. Some countries, like Sweden, constructed a floating boundary between the voluntary sector and municipalities, while others, like Switzerland, depended upon the private initiative of welfare societies, religious congregations, and women's groups. Sweden began government subsidies to local governments and private agencies in 1943 and expanded the service to elderly people in 1950.[81]

Many nations insisted on standardized and regularized working conditions, treating home helps like other public employees. That intent coexisted with pegging wages and labor standards to those of "institutional domestic workers," as was the case with the British program, which relied on women whose main qualification was a lifetime of housewifery. Throughout war-ravaged Central Europe, "many married women are very glad they are working, as they have a different position in the family," reported the head of Frankfurt's Centrale Für Private Fürsorge in 1952. Only Sweden had an association charged with monitoring worker rights and promoting proper enthusiasm for the job.[82]

To be sure, the organization of visiting housekeepers and homemakers through public agencies, social insurance programs, and health departments reflected distinctions within welfare states, which were undergoing economic and political reconstitution following World War II. Indicative of its developing corporatist system, Japan relied on private companies to offer "Home-Help Service within Industry."[83] Great Britain placed its program under the National Health Service, implemented by local authorities. Substituting for an absent relative, the home help made it possible for the doctor and district nurse to carry out their duties, while easing hospital overcrowding. The service in Ontario, Canada, functioned as a low-cost substitute for hospital care of indigents, though advocates envisioned a broad-based community health system to maintain elders at home. Associated with poor relief, it belonged to the arena of social work and public health, especially after being excluded from both federal and provincial hospital insurance. Into the 1970s, Canada resembled the United States more than Western Europe, with a low-paid casual workforce, a bias toward institutionalization, the pursuit of cost efficiency through privatization, and an ascendant medical model of care. Only with the fruition of its universal national health insurance system did provision of home care begin to change.[84]

Municipal homemaking promised an alternative form of organization. Home helps were often civil servants in Sweden.[85] In still agrarian Finland, municipal homemaking initially targeted rural families: the housekeeper would milk cows as well as cook and clean for the confined mother in an attempt to stem demographic decline. In the 1960s, with the explosive growth of women's wage-earning, the elderly turned into the chief beneficiary of Finnish services, much like the United States and other nations faced with aging populations. Here the state formed a professional social welfare occupation for women and the homemaker became "an ally for poor women," feminist scholar Leila Simonen has noted. In advancing a woman-friendly welfare state and offering a universal service, Finland enacted the dream of U.S. advocates like Maud Morlock, who kept in close touch with their European counterparts through various international meetings. After a series of exchanges during the 1950s, 20 nations, mostly European, founded the International Council of Home Help Services in 1959, with the National Committee of Homemaker Service as the U.S. representative and Grace Bell of the Bureau of Family Services as a member of the central committee.[86] In contrast to the United States, then, European social democracies began to regard care work and women administrators as essential components of the welfare state. Domestic labor done by women was not inherently exploitive; recognition of its value depended on the ways in which states organized care.

Public Health: Between Welfare and Medicine

One of the major challenges that U.S. welfare advocates faced as they tried to bring care within the welfare state was the widening gulf between welfare and an increasingly profit-driven medical sector. Public health departments institutionally straddled welfare and medical networks. Their staff included physicians, nurses, sanitarians, engineers, biostatisticians, and nutritionists. By necessity, public health agencies supplied services for poor and working-class populations since they focused on sanitation, infant health and mortality, and contagious diseases, like tuberculosis. Some urban health departments had legal responsibility for providing medical care to the poor and medically indigent.[87]

When social workers established homemaker programs at the end of World War II, they were aware that there might be a role for public health agencies, but they were ambivalent. During most of the 1940s, the central players active in the National Committee on Homemaker Service held health agencies at arm's length.[88] A few welfare professionals, however, sought a strategic alliance with medical and health officials. Having discovered the role of chronic illness among assistance recipients, welfare administrators recognized that they lacked enough resources to tackle this problem. In 1947, they initiated a joint attempt with physicians and public health practitioners to address the growing issue of chronic illness, urging the importance of homemakers in enabling chronic patients to remain at home or in the community.[89]

Few public health departments responded. They generally focused on statistical surveying and institutional care—nursing homes, rehabilitation centers, and hospital outpatient services. In scattered places, county or state departments organized homemaker service, but more often public health facilitated public reliance on private agencies. When New Jersey, for example, passed the Prevention of Chronic Illness Act in 1952, the Department of Health became a statewide coordinator of private agency housekeeping aides. It took responsibility for training courses, grants-in-aid for county-level demonstration projects, and distribution of educational materials.[90]

Home care was not a priority either for the American Public Health Association (APHA), but public health offered a bridge between social welfare administrators and medical professionals. Public health officials potentially had a direct line of influence with hospitals, since the U.S. Public Health Service had been granted jurisdiction over the massive amount of newly available federal funds for hospital construction. So when social workers approached the APHA about the issue of care for the chronically ill, public health professionals immediately argued that no progress could be made without including physicians. The APHA viewed itself as a connecter, explaining that its medical care subcommittee could bring the American Medical Association on board. Out of these discussions came the Commission on Chronic Illness in 1949.[91]

While ostensibly a partnership between medicine and welfare, physicians and hospital administrators dominated the Commission's board. Women from the Children's Bureau were not represented; neither were those from the Bureau of Family Services. Almost all of the technical advisers were physicians, giving the commission a distinctly medical cast. As Dr. Ernst Boas, long active in New York health and welfare circles, put it, "We cannot dissociate the care of the chronically ill from the general problem of medical care." Physicians like Boas staked out a heroic and curative mission "to bring these diseases under control as we have brought the infectious diseases under control in the past generation." The Public Health Service just had established a Division of Chronic Disease to supplement the work of national institutes on mental health, cancer, and heart diseases.[92] Key hospitals in large urban areas appeared ready to act on the Commission's agenda, including the provision of home care for chronically ill and disabled individuals.

Hospital and Home: The Medical Model of Home Care

American hospitals emerged from the war in an enviable position; they managed to benefit from government funding of expansion yet avoid state regulation, New Deal labor standards, and subordination to organized doctors. With the growth of Blue Cross, a type of prepaid hospital insurance, hospitals developed an institutional structure that would assure them growing numbers of paying patients.[93] Congress enacted the Hill-Burton Hospital Survey and Construction Act in 1946, creating a massive federal program to finance expansion of the entire medical infrastructure, including medical and nursing schools, public health centers, and outpatient and skilled nursing facilities. Bowing to the traditions of federalism, Hill-Burton left discretion to the states, which had to supply matching funds. Such immense public investment stimulated so much growth that, by the mid-1950s, hospitals ranked as the fifth-largest industry in the nation.[94]

Hospitals seemed to embody the hopes of postwar America, and high-tech services came to exemplify better care, promising miraculous cures. Through self-promotion and cultural perception, hospitals represented scientific progress, prosperity, and the fruits of public investment. More than ever, they defined themselves as the leading producers and promoters of medical technology and scientific research. They aimed to attract medical school affiliations by offering more exciting research challenges than the treatment of older, chronic diseases, like tuberculosis. The technological model of hospital care balanced uneasily with a model of these institutions as monuments to charitable giving, community service, and altruism.[95] The question of what to do with increasing numbers of chronically ill and aged patients stood at the heart of this tension.

Home care offered a possible remedy for problems of overcrowding and patient priority driven by budget concerns. Voluntary and public hospitals sought a way to rid themselves of the cost of chronically ill, often impoverished, patients—without abandoning them. Postwar hospitals had decided to concentrate on acute care and thus wanted patients who were as curable as possible. Private hospitals converted many wards into semi-private rooms for middle-class, paying patients, sending more chronically ill and disabled people into public institutions. Meanwhile, budget reorganizing encouraged the concentration of resources in areas, like surgery, that generated maximum income.[96]

Although the New York City Department of Hospitals had discussed home medical care since the 1930s, a demonstration program by a Jewish voluntary hospital first showed the feasibility of hospital-provided home care. In early 1947, Montefiore Hospital in the Bronx began its home care project for advanced cancer patients with grants from two private charities. Montefiore expected to save one-third to one-half of the cost of comparable care in the hospital and to open beds for early-stage cancer patients. Medical services included physician checkups, physical therapy, and occupational therapy. Its program also supplied limited weekly housekeeping. Montefiore contracted with the Visiting Nurse Service to furnish in-home nursing and to instruct family members in daily care. It soon extended the program to patients from the Bronx and upper Manhattan with any long-term, non-acute illness.[97]

Dr. E. M. Bluestone, the director of Montefiore, and Dr. Martin Cherkasky, the director of Home Care, emphasized the scientific professionalism and expertise of their program. The son of an immigrant rabbi, who had led a strike during his intern days, Cherkasky would transform Montefiore into a modern teaching hospital—and would break ranks to recognize the hospital workers' union in 1958.[98] In the late 1940s, he promoted home care through a series of speeches and articles in national publications. "In Home Care," Cherkasky boasted, "we have provided the best of scientific medicine and the best in environment."[99]

As a member of the Federation of Jewish Philanthropies, Montefiore also belonged to the world of New York charity. The Federation eventually financed 90 percent of the home care program.[100] Montefiore's directors understood home care as a social service, one that necessitated "an understanding of sick human beings as social human beings." Since it served indigents, the program clearly drew on welfare agency traditions for implementation, such as the home visit, or what Cherkasky called the "social service work up." The social worker who cared for the patient on the ward would follow the patient through home care and would work with the family.[101] By intent, the boundaries between public and private dissolved. The program attempted to remove home care from the domain of welfare and charity and to situate it within the medical world. According to Bluestone, the project sought "to extend the hospital's facilities into the community and to take the home under its wing."[102]

New York City's public system soon followed this private pioneer. Throughout the 1940s, its hospitals continued to receive far more patients than they had beds or personnel to accommodate.[103] Blaming high occupancy rates on the long-term chronically ill, Commissioner Dr. Edward Bernecker sought to reduce the burdens that the intertwined forces of old age, financial dependency, and medical indigency placed on the system by providing alternative custodial and nursing care for the aged sick.[104] In 1948, the Department of Hospitals initiated "a revolutionary step," he recalled. Beginning with five general hospitals, it established Home Care, a program that rapidly expanded to 16 municipal hospitals by 1950.[105] Within a few years, the average occupancy in public hospitals dropped below 100 percent for the first time since the onset of the Great Depression. "No doubt," claimed hospital officials, "home care has been the principal factor in the improved occupancy rate."[106]

In discussing home care, the Hospital Council of Greater New York deployed a set of long-standing rhetorical constructions centered on selection, supervision, continuity of care, and integration of hospital and home care.[107] These carefully crafted arguments justified the removal of poor people from hospitals, while at the same time expanding the realm of medical authority. Hospitals did not want to appear as though they were callously tossing poor or sick patients into the street, or neglecting their duty. Hence the commissioner of hospitals repeatedly stressed that candidates for home care were "carefully selected," based on definite medical diagnoses by physicians, who would then prescribe home care as a course of treatment.[108]

Nor would the patient be sent home alone. Everything that the hospital had to offer would accompany her. The commissioner of hospitals assured the mayor that "the patient's hospital record will be continued as if he were still on the wards of the hospital and regular visits will be made to the home by physicians on the staff of the hospital." The first annual report on Home Care presented an ideal version in which "patients are visited by the same member of the resident staff who had contact with the patient on the ward."[109] Continuity of care arguments enabled hospital administrators to relocate the patient's body, without ceding authority, and reassign bed space in the hospital. Indeed, they invoked "continuity of care" whenever social welfare authorities asserted competing claims over indigent clients and their home care.

Hospital leaders imagined the home easily transformed into a medical space. The "sick room" of the patient would be "supplied with the appurtenances necessary for hospital care." Whenever physicians and hospital officials depicted their version of home medical care, it included technological equipment, appliances, wheelchairs, syringes, needles, dressings, and charts. Home patients would receive injections, physiotherapy, electrocardiography, and blood work.[110] Such representations not only enabled medical professionals to define home care as medicalized care, but they also buttressed the notion of the hospital spreading the benefits of advanced medicine throughout the community.[111]

Eligibility for home care went almost entirely to patients from the wards. Although not exclusively a program for the aged, many were elderly. The majority were women, who lived longer but suffered from more chronic ailments than men. Over a quarter of them were also on public assistance; the rest lived meagerly on Social Security, pensions, and help from family.[112] In this respect, New York sat squarely within national trends. Women comprised 62 percent of federal Old Age Assistance recipients in the early 1950s, at a time when this welfare program under Social Security encompassed 2.5 million persons.[113]

Not everyone had a home to return to or a family to watch over them. While the Social Security Act displaced the old almshouse with cash payments, new institutions, characterized as "between home and hospital," proliferated in the 1940s. These "sheltered care" facilities included convalescent homes, public and private nursing homes, foster care, small proprietary hospitals, and boarding homes. Licensing developed to reassure families that they could safely place their relatives in such "homes." Public health advocates redefined the nursing home from a place of last resort to a modern site of "nursing care under medical supervision." Family agencies saw adult foster care homes as a substitute "type of family living for the older person in which his physical needs are met, he has . . . companionship . . . and can remain part of the community." Only those on public assistance initially could take advantage of such boarding arrangements. In succeeding decades, the nursing home mushroomed to become the alternative to home care for the middle class, especially among those who associated homemaker services with welfare or had insurance that only would pay for institutional care.[114]

The Commission on Chronic Illness promoted the hospital model of long-term care. As of 1950, 30 hospital-based home care programs existed, some private and others public, often in the same cities that had developed homemaker service through social welfare networks. In New York, four voluntary hospitals ran home care programs in the 1950s. Around the nation, university teaching hospitals specifically used home care as field training for medical students and residents.[115] The Richmond Department of Public Health contracted with the Medical College of Virginia for medical service, prescription medications, and diagnostic and laboratory testing and, with the Instructive Visiting Nurse Association, for home nursing service.[116] In 1953, Los Angeles County started a home care plan but delegated the administration of it to Rancho Los Amigos Hospital. This plan served a very specific population—indigent polio survivors who needed mechanical respiratory aids—so it never was very large. Similar to other hospitals, it described the program as "an extension of the hospital into the home."[117] Like homemaker service, hospital-based home care was small during these years, but the ambiguities of divided authority and the contestation over what constituted care entrenched legacies that would long persist.

The actual extent of programs hardly stopped medical professionals from developing a specialized definition of home care around the notion of a patient-physician relationship, with medical supervision as the essential element. Medical and health institutions assumed that a central institution would serve as a gatekeeper, determining the distribution and the allocation of resources, personnel, and clients. The Public Health Service designated only programs that coordinated multiple services, including "medical, nursing, and social services, essential drugs, and supplies" as a "home care program." In the early 1950s, state public health departments, visiting nurse associations, and national organizations of doctors, hospitals, and nurses adopted this definition.[118]

Not only did the Hill-Burton Act promote the hospital base for home care, but the amendments to Social Security in 1950 and 1956 offered financing for indigent medical care. States, counties, and localities previously paid for medical and hospital care for the poor from their own revenues, folding an amount for medical care into the client's monthly grant. The 1950 amendments permitted states to pool money from Old Age Assistance into a general medical fund for elderly recipients. Six years later, amendments allowed states to offer medical benefits through any of the categorical aid programs, after gaining federal approval. Most participating states relied on direct payments to vendors (not individuals), which meant that the funds went overwhelmingly to hospitals and physicians. Only Oregon included home housekeeping and nursing services in lieu of nursing home care in a special direct payment to the needy person.[119]

Federal disability policies further privileged the medical direction of home care. Programs administered by the Office of Vocational Rehabilitation always had reemployment as their focus. Doctors in the postwar years inserted their authority into the field, determining disability status and thus access to benefits. Treating returning veterans, physicians and hospital administrators recast rehabilitation as the "third phase of medical care" that "takes the patient from the bed to the job."[120] With the Vocational Rehabilitation Act of 1954, federal support went to rehabilitation facilities operated "in connection with a hospital . . . prescribed by or under the general direction of persons licensed to practice medicine." Two years later, the 1956 amendments to Social Security, which added disability pensions for the permanently disabled, codified disability as a social status requiring medical certification.[121]

Rehabilitation propped up dominant social assumptions about family as well as employment. Hospital home care programs, boasted their proponents, could restore gender order within the family. Like social welfare advocates, hospitals fed popular magazines with triumphant personal stories. *Woman's Home Companion* told of Harry Robinson, a middle-aged bookkeeper with advanced diabetes. The Robinson family lived on a small disability allowance and a part-time salary while Harry spent four years in various hospitals. Montefiore's

Home Care program enabled him to return home with medical assistance, taught his wife to administer medicine and cook a special diet, and got his disturbed son psychiatric help and vocational schooling. "No longer working at cross-purposes, the family seemed to draw together again. After six weeks, Robinson felt well enough to find an easy clerical job that once again made him the major breadwinner." As Harry explained his triumph over dependency, "At least now I'm really the head of the family instead of a half-dead body occupying an endowed bed in a ward."[122]

Women could regain their proper place, too. When Mrs. Closier, who suffered from a debilitating bone disease, returned home in 1948, Montefiore made it possible for her to resume all of the family chores, despite the presence of a husband and "two strapping sons." She received a special wheelchair for getting around the house "that was just the right height for cooking and putting things into a washing machine. She could hang clothing out in the back yard with a grocery clerk's pronged pole, which she also used for fetching cans of food from upper pantry shelves. In a month, she was filling her old role of mother and housekeeper for the family with the assistance of a Home Care housekeeper." This assistance hardly improved her health, since Mrs. Closier died soon afterward.[123] Though claiming to be a scientific alternative, hospital programs carried ideological presumptions long rooted in public and private welfare. They reproduced gendered class processes within the household.[124]

The medical model also promoted "teamwork." All hospital medical programs asserted that home care depended on the cooperative interaction of physicians, nurses, various kinds of therapists, and sometimes medical social workers and vocational rehabilitation counselors. The Hospital Council of Greater New York embedded this view in its 1956 comprehensive survey of city home care programs. The study showed that hospital personnel or visiting nurses—the team players—provided all medical services. Much to the chagrin of the women's welfare network, the hospital social worker just hired "any individual she deemed suitable to perform housekeeping duties," including relatives and friends. Whereas welfare administrators repeatedly stressed the professional character and training of public homemakers, hospital programs presumed the opposite. Marginalized as those who simply provided domestic labor rather than care, hospitals omitted these workers from the team.[125] The Children's Bureau had attempted to convince hospitals to use the term "homemaker" in order to avoid confusing these workers with maids and practical nurses, but Montefiore, along with other hospitals around the country, ignored this appeal and instead insisted on their own term, "housekeeper aide."[126]

Indeed, the Hospital Council barely noticed housekeepers or home aides. Although their visits were far more regular than those of the rest of the team, their labor went unrecognized. Like other forms of domestic work, the Hospital

Council treated this labor as informal, voluntary, and open-ended. Neighbors, it thought, would take up the slack. As was often expected of domestic workers, medical staff assumed "the housekeeper was usually available to provide extra assistance in the event of emergency."[127] For the Hospital Council, care referred to nursing and doctor's work.

The ideal of home care deviated significantly from the actual provision of care. During the first decade of Home Care, each of New York's Commissioners of Hospitals spoke of the significant opportunities offered for physicians interested in chronic disease, rehabilitation, and cancer. Montefiore's director described the program as a fertile field for doctors. The Commission on Chronic Illness imagined medical school curricula for specialists in chronic illness also addressing home care.[128] But within the exciting, highly remunerative world of postwar scientific medicine, few physicians had any intention of moving from the high-status, high-tech world of the hospital into the home. Only four or five years into its program, New York City hospitals were struggling to find enough doctors to carry it out. Some hospitals ended up rotating all residents to home care duties; others placed temporary caps on the number of patients accepted. Although the city's hospital department considered physician visits essential to the service, a continuing shortage of participants hindered its growth.[129]

The spread of private health insurance coverage drove the tremendous growth of medical and hospital care; yet this very same engine stymied medical home care. In the 1950s, nonprofit prepaid health plans, such as the Health Insurance Plan of New York and Group Health Insurance, started covering visiting nurse and physician-ordered home medical care following hospitalization. Commercial insurers also considered the potential market for home care. The Health Insurance Association of America sought to determine whether home care involved domestic or medical-professional service. Its director of research acknowledged that homemaker service was undoubtedly essential for an incapacitated person to avoid institutionalization. Nonetheless, the association concluded that such auxiliary care could never be included in an insurance contract "because of the absence of licensure, standards, or other clear definition as differentiated from generally available domestic service."[130] That a relative or persons living with the patient could undertake these tasks most definitely rendered them not health care. Thus insurers determined in 1959 that "there is little need or opportunity for voluntary health insurance mechanisms to provide, or consider providing, coverage designed to meet the costs of this form of care."[131] From their point of view, whether procured by a hospital or a public agency, housekeeping and personal care were indistinguishable from domestic labor.

Consequently, nurses were not eager to return home, either. The home represented a workspace without standards, guidelines, routine hours, or even regular work.[132] Prior to World War II, well over half of nurses worked in private duty, the low end of the profession. Often laboring 12- to 24-hour shifts, these women found family members requesting that they perform maid's work. Nurses with more elite training fled from the home, entering public health and institutional settings. During the 1940s, especially after wartime service, graduate nurses pressed hospitals to create full-time, regular staff jobs. With nurses spending more time supervising, coordinating patient activities, handling medication, and organizing a complex staff, those lower down on the hierarchy, the practical nurses and aides, took over the body work—the laying on of hands involved with changing dressings, feeding, bathing, making beds, or taking vital signs.[133] When home care came along, nurses hardly jumped at the opportunity.

Indeed, the American Nurses Association (ANA) initiated a major postwar push to improve labor standards for registered nurses, whose wages and working conditions lagged behind other professionalizing occupations. In 1946 the ANA House of Delegates passed an "Economic Security Plan," a demand for justice that would include them in New Deal labor and social security rights. The hospital became the major worksite for this struggle, which required lobbying to end the exemption of nonprofit hospitals from collective bargaining and the Fair Labor Standards Act. The ANA combined a traditional obligation to care with a new worker consciousness that justified group advancement as essential to the expansion of health services. "We can't just 'want economic security' any more than we can just 'want the patient to get well,'" explained one RN in 1952. "We have to work at it. That's our professional responsibility."[134] The struggle for this economic security platform persisted into the next decade, but only with the upsurge of feminist consciousness and new workplace pressures in the hospitals did unionization grow among nurses.[135]

For the most part, registered nurses expected that practical nurses would meet the shortage of home care, especially for chronic patients. In 1949, the ANA drafted a definition of practical nursing for state legislatures to use for professional licensing: "a person . . . who performs such duties as are required in the physical care of a convalescent, a chronically ill, or an aged or infirm patient."[136] Nurses pushed for these "nurse practice acts" in order to bring newly emerging categories of auxiliary workers within a nursing hierarchy controlled by their professional organizations. The functions assigned to the practical nurse were remarkably similar to those undertaken by the social welfare homemaker: "providing for the emotional and physical comfort and safety of patients," cooking meals, and light housekeeping.[137]

One group of public health nurses continued to provide care in the home. All hospital programs depended on contracts with a visiting nurse service, but nurses were careful to delineate their responsibilities as medical, not custodial. Visiting nurses viewed themselves as caring for acute patients, setting up specialized equipment, and supervising auxiliary workers. Visiting nurse associations, such as those in Philadelphia and Detroit, initiated housekeeper services to relieve their own nurses from household tasks. Beginning in 1955, Detroit's Visiting Nurse Association employed its own home aides, the majority of whom were Southern-born, married African Americans, for limited family washing, shopping, food preparation, and care of children. Within five years, the number of aides nearly doubled, while the nursing staff levels remained the same. Smaller communities like Madison, Wisconsin, and Monroe County, New York, created similar programs.[138]

Rhetoric aside, visiting nurses delegated most home care labor to others. The first nurse visit to the homebound was often the last. In 1951, for example, 21 percent of Montefiore Home Care patients received only an initial visit after discharge. For another 8 percent, the visiting nurse instructed family members on needed procedures before the patient returned home. Most patients had intermittent contact with professional nurses, who spent on average only 47 minutes with them.[139] At the end of the 1950s, the Public Health Service found that three-fourths of families with ill or disabled persons in all types of home care programs received no professional nursing. Instead, "a family member, the homemaker, or some other person assisting in the home" undertook care.[140]

To its surprise then, New York's hospital department discovered that housekeepers were doing valuable work. Twenty percent of clients in hospital home care programs received housekeeping service. During the late 1950s, administrators began talking far less about physicians following patients into the home and more often about "the housekeeping service without which many patients could not have been discharged." They now expressed concern that they had treated the service too casually, assuming it was easily available labor, just like that of the unpaid housewife, mother, and neighbor. The commissioner of hospitals signaled this new awareness in naming housekeeping "an essential feature of the home care program" and admitting that it had not been utilized to its full potential. With the workforce coming from relatives and friends, he acknowledged the desirability of more effective control and spoke of the need for training, supervision, and overall direction. In 1961 the Department of Hospitals connected the necessity of creating a more dependable pool of labor to both the financial savings of home care and the development of a supervised job with civil service status.[141] The next year, it followed the city's welfare department in contracting with private social welfare agencies for homemaker service.[142]

Just as the hospitals finally recognized that home care's real contribution was assisting with the daily tasks of living, new federal legislation forced them back into a medical model. The Kerr-Mills Act of 1960 established medical assistance to the needy elderly through federal grants to states. After New York established its matching program, hospitals were eager to gain state reimbursement for home care. Yet securing reimbursement required "standards of care." Hospitals had to show that home care was a medical service delivered by medically trained staff. Consequently, the hospital department recommitted itself to recruiting qualified physicians, nurses, and paramedical staff for its home care program. Hospitals had to appoint a medical coordinator to prove that home care was integrated with other medical services and to oversee relations between the hospital, social agencies, welfare recipients, and the state.[143]

State supervision of Blue Cross also reinforced the privileging of medical supervision. Throughout the 1950s, Blue Cross faced unprecedented surges in hospital utilization and costs, especially from aging subscribers. By the late 1950s, Blue Cross in New York sought to use home health care to control inflationary pressure on premiums and hospital charges. State law, however, confined Blue Cross payments strictly to services performed in and through hospitals. If Blue Cross wanted to add a home care benefit to its standard coverage, it had to apply for approval from state authorities.[144] The resulting authorization defined the possible range of reimbursement narrowly: it applied only to professional nursing, medical equipment, medicines, or particular services provided in hospitals.[145] Blue Cross would not be allowed to pay for assistance with routine activities of daily living. This medicalized definition, later codified in Medicare, limited the insured middle class person's access to home care, leaving them with nursing homes, domestic help, or family labor. This outcome was not inevitable, but it reflected the growing power of medical authorities in policy and politics and the waning influence of the Children's Bureau's welfare network.

The Structural Divide

Given the strands of home care provision that emerged in the 1950s, professionals asked, "Are we heading toward the development of specialized homemaker or health aide services for different ages, illness, or problem situations?" They wondered, "If we are not careful we may be in the position of providing the patient with *two* kinds of sustaining personnel: the aide who washes his face and the homemaker who washes the kitchen sink."[146] The differentiation in occupational title reflected a proliferation of sponsoring programs and funding sources. With this expansion came confusion over what the provider of home care actually did. No longer the substitute mother, never the nurse, was she more than a maid? Could the labor of care be transformed into stable employment that might redefine work in a newly emerging service-sector economy?

As the dominant focus of homemaker service shifted from mothers with young children to elderly and disabled adults, the job began to change. When agencies had assigned a homemaker to care for children and the household during a mother's illness, the homemaker worked with that family all day for several weeks or months. Agencies perceived adult clients' needs differently. The worker might go in just for a couple of hours to help with morning tasks and then move on to another client. This type of structure increasingly lent itself to part-time assignments and a fragmented work week. With the new division of labor, private agencies clearly saw home care workers as a contingent labor force. Social welfare advocates noted this trend toward part-time, casual employment with dismay.[147] With the service gravitating more toward health sector resources and authority, the Children's Bureau network seemed to be losing out on its vision of home care as a full-time occupation, with agency employees covered by labor law.

The retirement of Maud Morlock in 1959 symbolized the displacement of the Children's Bureau by other federal agencies as the focal point within the state. The Public Health Service and the Bureau of Family Services now would compile the Directory of Homemaker Services.[148] In 1960 the American Medical Association, through its Council on Medical Services, became the publisher of a national newsletter on home-based long-term care. The National Committee on Homemaker Service, a legacy of the New Deal–era Children's Bureau, in 1962 became the National Council for Homemaker Services, revived by joint efforts of social workers, public health officials, and physicians.[149] From then on, social workers sought to hitch their agenda to the institutional resources and prestige of health care, with varying success, as their subsequent involvement in the War on Poverty would demonstrate.

Through patchwork means and back-door channels, social workers and welfare advocates transformed a program originally intended for children into a long-term care system. That it took shape as a welfare service would have ramifications well into the future—for policy makers, consumers, workers, and the American labor movement. For in the years after World War II, the major expansions of the U.S. welfare state occurred through the Hill-Burton Act, which funneled money into hospital development, and social insurance. Advocates for home care never had access to those more generous components of the American welfare state. This outcome was partially due to their location within the state: the administrative agencies where these women had authority and control were small and underfunded. Their limits also derived from the devaluation placed on the predominantly African American workforce and the type of labor that home care entailed: bodily and household maintenance. Although advocates tried to use their expertise to promote better jobs for female breadwinners, they could not overcome the ideological constructions of reproductive labor as unskilled and economically marginal, especially once the growing power of hospitals and medical professionals reinforced such assumptions.

Home care's hybrid structure—part domestic service, part health care—persisted for the rest of the century. The War on Poverty in the 1960s would continue a welfare approach to long-term care. The Great Society's new national health care programs—Medicare and Medicaid—incorporated this split and its accompanying tensions right into the heart of the most important additions to Social Security in a generation. These programs aimed to establish some minimal right to health care, but they carried forward stigmas about dependency, ideologies about independence, and notions about rehabilitation that undercut their full potential. The unresolved divide of the postwar years created frustrating obstacles to security for those seeking care and those providing it. Despite entering, or being forced into, the waged workforce, home care workers found that economic security or independence remained elusive. Their position—straddling medical care and welfare, public and private, family and the state—would shape future struggles.

3

Caring for the Great Society

One day in 1976, Ruth Molendyke, a New Jersey widow with four children, found her mother lying on the floor when she arrived with a midday meal. Not able to leave her alone, Molendyke quit work. She was able to secure some publicly funded homemaker services, but not enough to resume employment. She couldn't afford to pay an aide $5 an hour for an eight-hour day. Two years later, she confessed, "I will have no money [soon] and my mother and I will have to live on the $284 per month she receives from social security and veterans benefits. I don't know how we will get along. I cannot put her in a nursing home, and I pray every night that she will pass in her sleep."[1] A decade after a vigorous senior citizens movement, the tying of elder care to the War on Poverty left the middle class with impossible choices: institutionalize their parents or become impoverished. It wasn't supposed to be like that.

Elder care had moved from "merely a private concern" to an issue that "vitally involves the welfare and well-being of our whole society," the *New York Times* announced in 1960.[2] Organizing among retirees and older citizens created a new political opening. During the late 1950s and 1960s, senior activists and their advocates demanded increased state support, eventually gaining an annual platform for their issues at the White House and, by the mid-1960s, significant legislative victories. Signing both Medicare and the Older Americans Act into law in the summer of 1965, Lyndon Johnson promised "a real new day for older Americans in this country." Ideologically and politically, Johnson elevated their citizenship claims as hard-won justice for "those who have given a lifetime of service and wisdom and labor to the progress of this progressive country."[3] To build his Great Society, governments at all levels initiated new programs, including publicly supported medical care, elder housing, home-delivered meals, jobs, and legal assistance.

Several rounds of welfare reform during the Kennedy and Johnson years cast public assistance recipients in a different light. A major struggle emerged in the early 1960s over the rights, obligations, and worthiness of those receiving government welfare checks. Clashing concepts of dependence and independence meant that not all rights would gain equal recognition. As more African

Americans in Northern cities became eligible for public assistance, critics of the program defined welfare as a dirty word and scorned recipients as lazy and immoral. Although social scientists and policy makers continued to fret over the impact of maternal employment on children, they judged black women as bad mothers if they were not in the paid workforce.[4] Legislators, Department of Health, Education, and Welfare (HEW) officials, welfare administrators, and social work leaders fused medical, psychological, and economic meanings of dependency. Within government, even advocates for the poor began to speak of them as "tax-eaters" who needed to be transformed into "taxpayers."[5]

The expectation that non-elderly welfare recipients should seek wage work became hitched to the demands of older Americans for care and social services. The 1962 Public Welfare Amendments, "manpower" training, and the War on Poverty built the bridge between these groups. Once again, policy makers and welfare administrators assumed that the job of home care aide perfectly served the demands of dual rehabilitation.[6] To be sure, some disagreed on the saliency of work goals for mothers on public assistance, and advocates for homemaker services feared stigmatization of the program, but turning welfare recipients into home aides offered a fix: poor mothers could become rehabilitated by caring for other poor, dependent, or incapacitated people. The remaking of poor women into caregivers became a nationally articulated goal when the War on Poverty set its sights on the creation of "paraprofessional" service jobs, particularly through the public sector.

Yet the War on Poverty also aimed to satisfy the rising expectations and demands of African Americans, especially in the cities that formed the national Democratic Party's base. The War on Poverty both responded to and stimulated vocal and militant organizing.[7] Welfare politics was never just an institutional clash among professionals. Civil rights, senior, public sector worker, and welfare rights activists now challenged the state over the nature and extent of social assistance. Their struggles would reshape home care again, this time through confrontations between state governors and county welfare offices; public sector unions and government employers; welfare mothers, lawyers, and mayors. In these clashes, an emphasis on training—embedded in gendered and racialized assumptions about who works where—would eclipse the goal of a meaningful standard of income and security.[8] Even amid the aspirations of the Great Society, home care became a jobs program on the cheap.

Care and Old-Age Politics

Since the end of World War II, the Children's Bureau and its network of women social workers had relied on comparatively meager funding to develop home care services as an occupation for older women. They found their efforts constrained by the limited budgets of child welfare services, public assistance, and indigent medical care in the 1950s, as well as by the professional exclusivity of nursing and medicine. Yet once John Kennedy entered the White House, social workers brimmed with optimism. Kennedy created a new Welfare Administration within the federal government and appointed their own experts to key leadership positions. He initiated an active manpower policy, later elevated by Lyndon Johnson to the center of the War on Poverty, which promised to train the home care labor force. An activist state would implement their proposals.

In actuality, the Kennedy administration's initial stabs at health policy further undermined social worker control over home care. During Kennedy's first year, Congress passed the Community Health Services and Facilities Act specifically to address the mounting challenges of caring for chronically ill and elderly people. Of 17 million persons 65 years of age and over, 11 million had some type of chronic health problem, and over 6 million were limited in their daily activities of living as a result. Placed under the jurisdiction of the Public Health Service, the act boosted federal matching grants to state health departments, which they in turn could grant to public and private nonprofit agencies to develop home care and other services. While privileging the medical perspective, the Public Health Service shared one essential premise with social worker predecessors: "Homemaker service can markedly improve the employment opportunities for middle-aged and older women." Still, the act's real emphasis was on nursing homes, for which it appropriated twice the money.[9]

There remained the question of how an elderly or chronically ill person would purchase services provided by the evolving smorgasbord of local and state, public and private programs. Insurance, firmly tied to full-time employment, had by now become the mainstream means of accessing and paying for health care, shutting out the aged. It was also clear by this time that private insurance would not pick up those considered higher risk. When Kennedy emerged as the Democratic presidential candidate, senior citizens, as they called themselves, launched a concerted effort to pressure the Massachusetts senator to include government health provision for the aged in his platform.

In 1957, the Forand Bill had sparked a nationwide senior citizens movement. An ally of organized labor, Rhode Island Congressman Aime Forand proposed a new social insurance program under Social Security: hospital insurance and short-term nursing home care for Americans over 65. From that moment on, leaders of the newly merged AFL-CIO and union retirees, along with grassroots and national organizations of seniors, committed themselves to the struggle for elder health insurance.[10] The Golden Ring Clubs of Senior Citizens, the National League of Senior Citizens, Social Security Clubs of America, and the AFL-CIO's National Council of Senior Citizens sponsored rallies and picnics, organized petition drives, testified at hearings, and followed candidates to various campaign appearances. In a 1958 declaration passed at Carnegie Hall and submitted to the House of Representatives, the Assembly of Senior Citizens celebrated themselves as the New Deal generation, who "brought a measure of order to an economic jungle. We brought a measure of security to the people. . . . Care of the work-injured, control of hours, minimum wages, guarantee of workers' rights, all these we fashioned in our generation. We preserved and extended the liberties of our democracy. . . ." And now the assembled seniors announced, "We want to live in pride and dignity."[11]

These groups became so active and visible during the 1960 presidential campaign that they made medical care for the aged "the most potent political issue in domestic politics."[12] A massive rally in Madison Square Garden that May "celebrate[d] the 25th anniversary of the Social Security program by urging another candle on the cake: the Forand Bill for health insurance." More than 15,000 senior citizens listened to liberal luminaries, such as FDR's labor secretary Frances Perkins, Mayor Robert Wagner, and labor leaders Walter Reuther and David Dubinsky. Enormous rallies and picnics continued through the summer.[13] In California, the National League of Senior Citizens ran their lead organizer for governor on an expanded Social Security platform; he received more than 600,000 votes during the June primary. Proclaiming, "The old folks are on the march again," the *New York Times* compared their level of mobilization and influence to the turbulent 1930s.[14] Eager to capture the seniors' votes, Senator Kennedy endorsed the Forand Bill, organized Senior Citizens for Kennedy, and made a special pilgrimage to Hyde Park on the anniversary of the Social Security Act to obtain the blessing of Eleanor Roosevelt.[15]

The prospect of a major expansion of Social Security raised serious alarm among Southern Democrats and conservative Republicans. The House Ways and Means Committee instead steered a deceptive alternative to a vote: means-tested medical assistance for a restricted number of the elderly poor to be administered by the states. By the end of the summer, Eisenhower signed the Kerr-Mills Act into law as the presidential campaign moved into high gear. The Republicans now had a campaign issue, and the states had another categorical public assistance title for the needy.[16]

Kerr-Mills provided aid to medically indigent elders. Medical Assistance for the Aged (MAA) made medical benefits available to a new group of citizens not currently on relief. States could use federal matching grants for hospitalization, nursing homes, or home health care. The state would have to contract through an agency; a beneficiary could not simply use a grant check to hire a home attendant or pay a relative for assistance.[17] Thus Kerr-Mills reinforced earlier precedents of contracting out to vendors to provide public welfare benefits. It also suggested that this program provided a service, not income support.

The states treated Medical Assistance for the Aged as a welfare program with very limited benefits, no guarantee of quality of care, minimal reimbursements for contractors, and punitive terms. They created restrictions that made the pool of eligible and actual recipients exceedingly small. Through "family responsibility" provisions, a dozen states imposed means tests directly on relatives of the aged, deterring many potential recipients from even applying for support. While many states never allotted adequate, or any, funding, the wealthier among them quickly substituted more lucrative federal monies for services that, for the most part, they already paid for. In a pattern that would repeat itself, Massachusetts and New York immediately shifted their old-age assistance caseloads onto this new funding stream to receive the better federal match.[18] Ninety percent of all payments went to only four states.[19]

While ultimately short-lived, Kerr-Mills underscored the underlying conflict between welfare jurisdiction and medical authority. Organized medicine opposed this legislation, just as they had every expansion of Social Security involving hospital and medical care. Once passed, physicians quickly tried to assert control. New York located MAA within the welfare department as a form of categorical assistance. The New York Academy of Medicine turned to a tactical language used in previous struggles: continuity of care. "If home care is an equivalent or parallel kind of program to hospital care," asked Dr. George M. Warner of the New York State Department of Hospitals, "should not home care programs also be administered by agencies that are led by medical directors?" Only then would "high standards" of care result. New York's Commissioner of Social Welfare firmly countered that it was "the duty of public welfare officials . . . to provide adequately for those unable to maintain themselves."[20] The central issue was dependency, not consistency of care, and therefore welfare agencies became the gatekeepers.

Senior activists and advocates, and even the Senate Committee on Aging, resented the stigmatized taint surrounding MAA. Protesting its passage, Senior Citizens for Kennedy paraded with banners proclaiming, "Care With Dignity, Not Charity," and "We Want Dignity, Not Paupers' Oaths." The laborite National Council of Senior Citizens and the Golden Rings Clubs kept up mass rallies, letter-writing campaigns, petitions, and appearances at hearings throughout the Kennedy years.[21]

Seniors formally expressed their discontent with the Kerr-Mills approach at the 1961 White House Conference on Aging, just before Kennedy took office. Attending the conference were members of Congress, HEW staff, social security and welfare experts, and activists. The assemblage not only demanded genuine social insurance for elder medical care, but also called for a federal grants-in-aid program to provide rehabilitative services. Invoking the goals of "self-care" and "self-help," a final report noted that many elders are dependent on others, but with "modern rehabilitative services, many could once again learn to live their lives of independence." Home care and homemaker services could facilitate dependency's end.[22]

Emerging from the White House Conference was a comprehensive agenda. Mobilized supporters also were in place to pressure the new president. The Senate, in turn, constituted a Special Committee on Aging. Eventually, Kennedy responded to the conference by proposing a program of categorical grants for elder services, a precursor to the 1965 Older Americans Act.[23]

Self-Care and Self-Support: Welfare Reform in the Early 1960s

Before President Kennedy could act on the seniors' agenda, welfare reform took priority. It was not just the welfare approach to elder medical care that generated political heat in the early 1960s. Welfare in general came under a critical magnifying glass. Critics of Aid to Dependent Children (ADC) became more vocal and demanding. Congressional conservatives targeted ADC as wasteful and bloated, especially as more African American women gained access, and immediately pressed Kennedy's new Secretary of HEW, Abraham Ribicoff, for changes. At the same time, defenders of welfare hoped that Kennedy's HEW appointments would showcase the latest research and thinking from social casework. The Public Welfare Amendments of 1962 tried to appease both sides.[24]

Ribicoff promised Congress a systematic review of federal welfare programs and a comprehensive package of reforms. Ribicoff and Wilbur Cohen, his assistant secretary, assembled the Ad Hoc Committee on Public Welfare for advice on new proposals with two objectives: "to promote rehabilitation services" and "to develop a constructive new approach aimed at getting people off relief and back into useful employment."[25] Ribicoff, Cohen, and the Ad Hoc Committee believed that they could disarm attempts to isolate and discredit ADC by prioritizing rehabilitation, services, and "prevention" across categorical aid programs.[26]

Under the rubric of containing the growth of welfare, HEW actually expanded the bureaucracy of the federal government and its ability to intervene in state matters. Cohen instructed public welfare bureaus to train and deploy a workforce "who will energetically and aggressively work with the states in the development of services."[27] Without much clarity or distinction, Cohen, Ribicoff, and others drafting the welfare amendments repeatedly invoked training as a key element in their plans. Yet they often seemed carelessly to blur who and what the training was for, referring to community work-training programs, reemployment and retraining of ADC recipients, or training of employees. Training functioned as a slogan more than as actual policy. President Kennedy publicized HEW's legislative agenda in his 1962 State of the Union address in which he called for a shift in public welfare to emphasize "services instead of support, rehabilitation instead of relief and training for useful work instead of prolonged dependency." The "talk of services," welfare consultant Charles Gilbert observed a few years later, "distracted attention from inadequacy of grants."[28]

The mantra of training complemented the macro-economic approach of Kennedy's economic advisors, particularly what came to be known as "manpower" policy. Kennedy took office amid a recession, and although the economy picked up again during his first year in office, unemployment remained over 6 percent in 1962. Slow growth and high aggregate unemployment, his economic team argued, were the sources of poverty. They offered two key remedies: tax cuts to spur growth and the Manpower Development and Training Act (MDTA). Drawing on human capital theory, which stressed the role of personal characteristics, individual behavior, and rational choice in overall employment, Kennedy liberals embraced the notion that poverty and unemployment could be overcome through expanding individual opportunity without substantial redistribution.[29] If public policies could modify individual behavior and skills, then poor people would be prepared to take advantage of labor market opportunities. Manpower training programs were to supplant welfare by setting recipients on the road to self-sufficiency.[30]

Several months later, Congress passed major public welfare amendments that attempted to reconcile these critiques of poverty and welfare. Providing a substantial boost in funds aimed at "ending dependency," the federal contribution to states rose to 75 percent of the cost of services for welfare recipients and 50 percent of the administrative expense. Congress did not specify the services eligible for matching funds, instead charging public welfare departments with the ambiguous task of identifying ones that would "restore families and individuals to self-support" and "help the aged, blind, or seriously disabled to take care of themselves." ADC was renamed AFDC, Aid to Families with Dependent Children. These directives also meant that agencies would have to expand their staffs dramatically. Legislators concerned about rising welfare numbers thought that a modest increase in administrative costs could reduce public assistance rolls.[31]

To this end, the federal government allowed use of its matching funds for vocational training, which long had emphasized work-related independence. Now states had an additional incentive to link rehabilitation to training and to moving public assistance recipients into work.[32] The National Council for Homemaker Services (in 1971 renamed the National Council for Homemaker-Home Health Aide Services) predicted that "ample womanpower" would be available for care work jobs if MDTA channeled funds in its direction.[33] By 1965, the handful of homemaker service programs in public welfare agencies more than doubled.[34]

Rehabilitation also justified work and training programs for unemployed parents receiving AFDC, including fathers or other relatives, although liberals remained divided on the implications. Ribicoff proposed that recipients participate in work training and labor on public jobs, compensated only by their public assistance benefits. Advocates within the main welfare organizations saw this approach as compromising a fundamental right to cash support. African American leaders, such as the Urban League's Whitney Young, particularly objected to work relief, especially as a condition for receiving benefits. As a compromise, AFDC would combine income support with work requirements, reclassifying poor mothers as "employables." This designation as "employable" would take on heightened importance in coming years, when Congress enacted more punitive workfare measures.[35]

Wilbur Cohen, a key author of the amendments, articulated these connections in racialized terms. "The Public Welfare Amendments of 1962 contain a number of provisions which should materially enhance the prospects of employment by Negro workers," he explained. Expansion of homemaker services "should directly utilize significant numbers of Negro women as trained homemakers," while subsequent need for caseworkers would mean "employment of substantial numbers of additional Negro staff in public welfare agencies."[36] Once again, policy makers assumed, tending to others would rehabilitate black women.

Meanwhile, Kennedy facilitated the institutional linkages among clients of the welfare state by consolidating the Children's Bureau, the Bureau of Family Services, the Office of Aging, and the Office of Juvenile Delinquency and Youth Development into a new Welfare Administration. The post of Commissioner of Welfare went to Ellen Winston, ideally suited to mesh the interests of the aged and chronically ill with new directions in public welfare. Commissioner of Public Welfare in North Carolina since 1944, Winston was an integral part of the Children's Bureau network and a leading figure in the national homemaker movement. She had presided over the American Public Welfare Association in the late 1950s, participated as a member of numerous state and federal committees on aging, and served on the board of the National Council for Homemaker Services. The *Washington Post* endorsed her appointment enthusiastically, remarking, "Mrs. Winston knows that needy families can achieve self-support because she has operated statewide welfare programs which focus on protective, preventive and rehabilitative services for the destitute." She had shown that the "cycle of dependency can be broken."[37]

Coming out of the New Deal, Winston gained a national reputation as a welfare proponent and innovator. With a doctorate in sociology, she worked as a social economist in various New Deal agencies and, during World War II, for the technical committee for work and relief policies of the National Resources Planning Board. She also chaired the Department of Sociology and Economics at Meredith College. A native of western North Carolina, this Southern liberal believed in "federal responsibility . . . to help the states provide a decent level of living below which no one need fall," that is, a universal right to public assistance.

Winston represented a coercive side of liberalism too, as a member of the North Carolina Eugenics Board, a state-run program that relied on sterilization to reduce illegitimacy, poverty, and dependency. While aimed broadly at lowering the number of children born to poor women, the eugenics program increasingly targeted African Americans in the late 1950s and 1960s.[38]

Winston had long-standing experience with home and community-based care. Soon after taking office in North Carolina, she promoted deinstitutionalization, beginning with a 1945 state law that enabled the Board of Public Welfare to license boarding homes for seniors and chronically ill adults. She hoped to enable long-term residents of state hospitals to return home. Homemaker Service began in 1947 in a few counties and grew over the next 15 years. By embracing the use of homemakers, she argued, the state could expand welfare services while phasing out county poorhouses and creating community-based alternatives for elderly and chronically ill individuals. Both of these initiatives were implemented in accordance with racial segregation. For Winston's staff, deinstitutionalization and community and home-based alternatives best fulfilled "our responsibility for social rehabilitation."[39] Cohen, Ribicoff, and Kennedy placed the development of homemaker services as a good job for black women in the hands of a proponent of eugenics who, like other Southern New Dealers, determined the problem of public assistance was "not difference on racial basis but rather the inadequate financing of the total program."[40] To her credit, Winston integrated her own staff meetings in North Carolina and upheld the right of black women to receive adequate public assistance.

Winston remained a New Deal liberal who defended rights to security as well as public services. While leader of the new U.S. Welfare Administration, she instructed staff and bureau chiefs to "not forget the basic purpose of providing money support for the economically deprived." Everyone had a right to "some basic floor of economic security, underpinning all persons in this country." When she got to Washington, Winston pressed beyond the New Deal by insisting that welfare support, especially services, "should be available on an equitable basis to all persons without regard to residence, settlement, citizenship requirements, or circumstances of birth."[41] She supported AFDC recipients. An expanded program of social services, though, required a workforce to deliver the meals, counsel troubled families, attend to the elderly, assist disabled people, care for children, and train job seekers.

"On the Outskirts of Hope": The War on Poverty

Lyndon Johnson's Great Society—the boldest comprehensive liberal agenda since the New Deal—absorbed each of these smaller initiatives. In his State of the Union address following Kennedy's death, Johnson, a Texas-born Southerner and ardent

New Dealer, laid out an eloquent vision of hope and inclusion, recommending "the most Federal support in history for education, for health, for retraining the unemployed, and for helping the economically and the physically handicapped." These objectives could not be achieved, Johnson emphatically declared, without a simultaneous commitment to end racial discrimination.[42] In contrast to the 1930s, this new round of liberal reform explicitly aimed to include—and enfranchise—African Americans, Latinos, the poor, seniors, immigrants, and farm workers.

Yet a different understanding of poverty and its remedies informed the policy makers of the 1960s. For the president's Council of Economic Advisers, government should not take a direct role in creating jobs; instead, it could address poverty through tax-cut induced faster growth, without any need for structural measures to combat unemployment and poverty. Opponents of the "simple solvent of growth" offered a contrasting view of poverty that put inequality at the center of their analysis. In their view, general economic growth policies always left behind "those structurally disadvantaged by age, geography, racial discrimination, and family structure." The structuralist school had different strains, but the dominant one emphasized the social and psychological isolation of the poor, their "deviant characteristics," and a self-perpetuating cycle of deprivation. Government therefore should aim to correct these deficiencies.[43] Johnson's policies straddled both schools of thought, and the fate of home care reflected the tensions between them.

The centerpiece of the War on Poverty, the Economic Opportunity Act of 1964, addressed the supply of labor by offering education, training, and jobs. Directed by a new Office of Economic Opportunity (OEO), it initiated a group of programs based on manpower premises: Job Corps, Neighborhood Youth Corps, Adult Education Program, Volunteers in Service to America (VISTA), and Work Experience. The anti-poverty warriors had faith that public policies could modify individual behavior and develop skills: poor people would then be prepared to take advantage of emerging labor market opportunities.

The segment of the low-end labor market with the most growth potential was the service sector. The rate of job increase there rose 40 percent between 1957 and 1963, especially in "personal services" provided through health, education, and welfare institutions. Unemployment and anti-poverty policy would have to take account of this "manpower revolution."[44] For women, however, manpower training meant placement in an expanding service economy as orderlies, attendants, and laboratory aides for hospitals and nursing homes; commercial and dietary kitchen workers; homemakers; and day-care and teacher assistants. That is, skill-building and job placement efforts directed women to the low paid equivalents of unpaid care, reinforcing the racialized and gendered segmentation of the labor market, much as New Deal work relief had done 30 years before.

Under Work Experience, OEO funded "on-the-job training in constructive work." It pointed with pride to the first 164 local projects that trained beneficiaries to meet labor shortages in service jobs, including health and child aides, home attendants, and homemakers. "Many formerly unemployed, disheartened fathers and mothers are demonstrating that they are finely tuned to the problems of other needy or sick people, and they are performing their vitally needed services with empathy and understanding," OEO reported in 1965.[45] Those who "had lacked all the qualifications for decent employment—good work habits, skills, motivation, and education," it boasted, now had decent work.[46]

Commissioner Winston told the Senate Special Committee on Aging that her department quickly had established a working partnership with OEO for services to the elderly on public assistance. Her staff prioritized projects in communities where there were OEO Community Action Programs.[47] County welfare departments with projects begun under the 1962 Public Welfare Amendments could now expand these operations with OEO funding.[48] Dispensing training grants, the Vocational Rehabilitation Administration also participated in this general effort to develop community services, including home care as both a service and a rehabilitating job.[49] These efforts seemed destined to alleviate "the culture of poverty." The *New York Times*, for example, portrayed homemaker services as a poverty-fighting measure that could help maintain "strong family life."[50] Since home care advocates had spent years associating it with social as well as physical rehabilitation, Winston could confidently tell Congress, "In the 'war on poverty,' homemakers have a crucial role."[51]

Communities around the country applied for these modest monies to run homemaker programs. Los Angeles, for one, asked for MDTA funds to train home health aides to "free" visiting nurses for more skilled care.[52] The Bureau of Family Services approved state projects in Mississippi, South Carolina, Georgia, Alaska, New Mexico, Wisconsin, and Kansas, including two on Native American reservations.[53] Demonstration projects provided welfare funding for locales, like rural Troup County, Georgia, desperate for resources to supplement casework.[54] On the Menominee Reservation in Wisconsin, another project provided transportation and personal care to isolated elders—and served as a means to educate the community about Great Society resources.[55] The one at Bernalillo County, New Mexico—which represented its program with a line drawing of an adobe house cradled by the protective palm of a woman's hand—proved that home care saved money.[56]

Washington officials did all they could to boost the meager wages of homemakers. Troup County paid slightly above the federal minimum wage as a condition for receiving funds.[57] Explained welfare specialist Winifred Bell, later known for her pioneering analysis of AFDC, only better pay and employee benefits—the same packages recommended some 15 years before by the New York Welfare Council—could prevent rapid turnover. "Such security would have a marked effect on the caliber of person applying for a homemaker position and would be a real stimulus to the qualified public welfare recipient."[58] Demonstration projects promoted Maud Morlock's earlier vision of a corps of mature women raising the status of homemaking "to the level of a skilled and much-sought-after service."[59]

Welfare reform never really provided the necessary support to fulfill this vision. After additional public welfare amendments in 1967 authorized the Work Incentive Program, states could end assistance to parents and children over the age of 16 if they refused participation in training or work programs. In 1971, Congress mandated the employment of mothers with children older than six, encouraging states to establish their own programs. The numbers forced to work or thrown off welfare remained small because child care funds proved inadequate, and most states accepted that mothers of young children had a good cause for staying home. Nonetheless, the Work Incentive Program laid one of the cornerstones for workfare, promoting the goal of welfare policy as ending dependency through wage labor, no matter how inadequate the compensation.[60]

The 1967 Amendments also opened the door to a new form of federal spending that would grow substantially over the next decade. The Administration on Aging, the Welfare Administration (including the Children's Bureau), and Vocational Rehabilitation moved into a new agency, Social and Rehabilitation Services. Beginning in 1968, the new agency granted funds to states for a much wider range of activities. Within the next four years, its social services grants quadrupled. Over a quarter of all such grants went to California.[61] While small, these social services grants could proliferate without the need for new congressional legislation, eventually fueling the ire of conservatives in the 1970s.

No matter the funding source, most of these projects failed to employ any significant number of women on AFDC. This outcome reinforced the observations of home care specialist Brahna Trager that mothers on public assistance, juggling the needs of their own households, "cannot be expected to assume comfortably the responsibilities required," especially "by pressing this type of training and employment on them."[62] Moreover, Trager, the former director of a San Francisco care agency, argued that the casualized labor of day work for the aged or disabled does "not compete successfully with Public Assistance which *does* at least offer the minimum guarantee of continuity and a practical approach to subsistence needs."[63] To substitute for AFDC, home care jobs had to become decent work.

The War on Welfare and the War on Poverty in New York

New York City became an epicenter of 1960s confrontations over welfare, attacked from all sides: opponents, recipients, and public workers. New York was both a laboratory for the War on Poverty—home to Mobilization for Youth

(MFY), the model for OEO's Community Action program—and a target of outrage over alleged fraud, corruption, and waste. Just outside New York City, the town of Newburgh gained national attention in 1961 for opening a war against local welfare recipients, pressuring national Democrats to accede to national-level welfare reform. Within New York, protests over racial discrimination and rights spiraled into a broader insurgency and gave birth to a militant welfare rights movement. Originating as a juvenile delinquency prevention program, Mobilization for Youth broadened its mission in 1963 to fight poverty by becoming a militant advocate for those denied welfare support and by organizing poor people for much more confrontational political action.[64]

From 1963 on, New Yorkers created and lived through protest and tumult. Organized rent strikes swept through the city in 1963, eventually winning action from the mayor, and 1964 proved to be even more turbulent. Confrontations over urban renewal and affordable housing escalated. African Americans and Latinos staged a massive boycott of city schools to protest segregation. Protests and civil disobedience marked the opening of the 1964 World's Fair. Riots exploded in Harlem and Bedford-Stuyvesant that summer, the first major urban riots of the 1960s.[65]

Amid this cauldron of protest, tenants' rights groups and other community organizations took shape, especially with the help of government-funded projects. MFY and community groups in Brooklyn founded a Welfare Recipients League; chapters soon formed in other neighborhoods, tapping years of frustration and humiliation with the welfare system. Beulah Sanders, a federally supported "community worker," began organizing welfare recipients in 1964. When her organization, the Westside Welfare Recipients League, hooked up with MFY and Brooklyn groups, they formed the People's War Council Against Poverty in early 1966. They criticized the welfare system for its punitive surveillance and denial of privacy, as well as paltry, or nonexistent, support for school clothes, household necessities, and food. Yet they also became more vocal about their lack of real opportunities and child care for those who sought decent work.[66]

By 1965, not only were neighborhood residents, tenants, and welfare recipients in revolt, so were many city workers, especially those of the Department of Welfare. The rapid rise in caseloads had intensified work levels well above legal limits. Working conditions and pay deteriorated, falling well below those of private agencies. At the same time, caseworkers saw welfare grants as inadequate for any family's needs. The city's social workers had a history of militant and independent unionism, which the state legislature tried to crush during the early Cold War years, when it passed the punitive Condon-Wadlin Act. This law outlawed strikes by state and local government employees. In the mid-1960s, with the growth of public sector employment, worker militancy erupted in a wave of organizing and strikes that matched the era of the Great

Depression. Many new human service workers came with backgrounds in civil rights or the student Left, bringing a more systemic critique of the politics of exclusion and poverty. In October 1964, those in the Department of Welfare joined the independent Social Service Employees Union (SSEU), rather than a staid local of the American Federation of State, County, and Municipal Employees (AFSCME). When the city refused to bargain over working conditions, such as a cap on caseloads and improved training opportunities, 8,000 welfare employees went on strike in January 1965. The strike forced the city to close two-thirds of its welfare centers.[67]

Strikes against the Department of Welfare hit New York City hard. Not only social workers walked out; children's counselors and homemakers also signed up with the militant SSEU. AFCSME members joined the strike. Civil rights groups like CORE provided active support, as they had for unionizing municipal hospital workers. The strike turned contentious when the city, under the no-strike law, obtained an injunction and jailed worker leaders. A month later, a settlement favored the union with substantial wage increases, full city payment of health insurance, caps on caseloads, and new hiring.[68] This settlement did not

Figure 3.1 Members of the Social Service Employees Union demonstrate outside New York City Welfare Commission, January 4, 1965. Photo Credit: Ed Giorandino, New York *Daily News*. © Daily News L.P.

end SSEU's militancy. These unionists, their clients, and MFY picketed together, exposing the gap between state-mandated standards and what the city actually gave in welfare support.

The city government was not unresponsive; it had applied for OEO funding for anti-poverty projects. Yet it also sought to defuse the political militancy of MFY and the Welfare Recipients Leagues by promoting Work Experience programs, run through its own agencies, which would be less volatile than Community Action. For men, work training and remedial education projects aimed to place them "in competitive industry at a higher level of skill that they would have otherwise achieved." Counselors directed female recipients of AFDC into a new Home Helper Project, which sought to provide supervised part-time work experience that would not interfere with household responsibilities. Within six months, the welfare department lauded this part-time, neighborhood-based program as fulfilling Work Experience goals through placement in the apparently interchangeable sites of "homes for the aged, nursing homes, the Division of Homemaker Service, and the Bureau of Child Welfare."[69] By 1967, the program had mutated into TEMPO, Training and Employment for Mothers in Part-Time Employment, which accepted referrals from welfare centers in Brooklyn, the Bronx, and Manhattan.[70] These programs could appear to meet some of the planks of the civil rights movement, as well as welfare mothers' demands for jobs. Still, burdened by long-standing gendered assumptions about work, they reinforced the limited opportunities that had perpetually left such women poor.

Welfare administrators expressed great satisfaction with this gender-targeted strategy. Of the over 900 recipients in "work-experience assignments," they claimed, numerous women gained part-time or full-time employment by the end of 1966. Even those who remained unemployed received "important psychological benefits." Plus, TEMPO had allegedly brought financial savings to the city, reducing welfare payments. Rehabilitation apparently did not depend on real or living wage jobs, since most placements were in the low-wage service sector.[71]

An interconnected dual agenda—preservation of family life and improved prospects for employment—stood at the center of another local War on Poverty program, a Housekeeping Aide Project begun in August 1964. With the goal of molding AFDC recipients into better mothers and leading them to "economic independence," this update of WPA housekeeping offered manpower training for the home, teaching laundry and cooking, budget management, shopping, home sanitation, care of both children and the aged, with demonstrations in feeding, bathing, moving the patient, and checking vital signs. Training occurred in model public housing apartments. The hope remained that women would deploy these skills not only in the paid labor market but also in their own homes. Those who completed the training were regularly sent not for job interviews but to TEMPO and related projects for work experience.[72]

The welfare department used the housekeepers to tend to elderly or disabled persons. *Housekeepers* provided chore services—cleaning, shopping, and laundering—supposedly distinct from the work of *homemakers*, who focused on families with children and remained city employees. In contrast, housekeepers were independent contractors or contingent workers for voluntary agencies. Thus women on welfare were now trained for positions that might have even less compensation and job security and fewer regular hours than that of homemaker. Such classification obscured who was responsible for proper payment, Social Security deductions, or workers' compensation. In 1969, the State Department of Social Services realized that housekeepers (and a still newer job category, the home attendant) received none of these benefits and ruled that the city could not keep these workers in employment limbo. To continue the program, the city would have to find some other means of employing them.[73]

Community-based anti-poverty groups, focused on expanding the right to public assistance, had more direct ties to the poor. They also turned to homemaker services as a way to employ needy people within their own neighborhoods. Even the now-radical MFY employed 64 visiting homemakers, claiming that their new workers viewed the low yearly salary of $4,000 "an economic step up." Serving clients in their own building or neighborhood, they considered missing work a failure of personal obligation; their relationship with clients "resembled that of friends." MFY anti-poverty activists argued that these jobs promoted empowerment. Women developed job skills but they also learned about other state benefits, how to help clients establish eligibility for public assistance, social services, or public housing, and how to utilize community resources.[74]

The activism triggered by community action, groups like MFY, and welfare rights mobilization put so much pressure on urban mayors and Democratic administrations that the latter furiously went back to President Johnson for relief. Following yet another summer of urban riots, Congress had to act. Consequently, it renewed the Economic Opportunity Act in October 1966 with a greater emphasis on job training but reductions for community action. In an attempt to earmark OEO money for something less controversial, the new bill approved up to $70 million to train low-income or unemployed individuals as "paraprofessionals" or sub-professionals in "human service fields," a program called New Careers. The federal government would pay up to 90 percent of the cost for jobs that included on-the-job training and credentialing for auxiliary aides in teaching, nursing, social work, mental health, and home care, jobs that would allegedly offer career ladders and a shot at upward mobility. Congress was also responding to liberal concern that, owing to other Great Society programs, the need for workers in human services was growing faster than the supply. Automation of manufacturing, on the one hand, and massive investment in the public sector, on the other, had generated this "manpower" need.[75] Along with police, welfare, and recreation aides, homemakers were among the 5 million human service jobs called for by Americans for Democratic Action in 1966.[76]

The philosophy behind New Careers meshed with the multiple goals of the War on Poverty. Activist social scientists Arthur Pearl and Frank Riessman had introduced this approach in their 1965 book, *New Careers for the Poor*. A writer on educational and political issues, Pearl was associated with the Center for the Study of Youth and the Community at Howard University. Riessman, a social psychologist, belonged to a group of New York anti-poverty academics involved with MFY and the welfare rights movement, including Richard Cloward and Frances Fox Piven. Aided by federal funds, he soon would direct the New Careers Development Center at New York University that used job training in social work, health care, and education to create a pathway out of poverty.[77] According to Pearl and Riessman, such welfare-state jobs could fulfill one of the War on Poverty's mandates, "maximum feasible participation" of the poor in anti-poverty programs and services. Simultaneously, these new welfare state workers would act as a bridge between public agencies and the community, interpreting client needs to the professionals and enabling more low-income residents to access public services. New Careers depended on an expanding welfare state in two senses: both job training and jobs themselves rested on the flow of money into health, education, public recreation, and community service centers. It channeled resources and energy into a program more palatable than community action.

The New Careers idea presented genuinely new possibilities, and a range of liberal activists and labor groups endorsed it. It respected the knowledge that women had of their community. It potentially met civil rights demands for good employment as essential to full inclusion.[78] In the right setting, an individual could start in a low-level service job, be subsidized for further education, and eventually become a social worker, teacher, or nurse. Unions such as the Hospital Workers Local 1199 and the American Federation of Teachers could negotiate career ladders, better pay, upgrading, and release time for education. Riessman certainly believed that unionization would play a critical role in enhancing the status, value, and compensation of paraprofessional jobs.[79] For women who "would have been reluctant to work directly for the client as domestics or as cleaning women," becoming homemakers under the auspices of an agency, "which guaranteed regular pay checks and limited the type of service the client could require," had advantages. Dressed in uniforms with an identification pin, they "saw themselves as sub-professionals, combining some of the skills of social workers and nurses," noted one program administrator, reiterating yet again the distinction between homemaker and cleaning lady. "In short, they had status, which is missing in the role of the domestic."[80]

For those directed into jobs associated with domestic work or family care, however, the new service sector career actually turned out to be a lot like the old one. With wage rates hovering close to the poverty level, investigators discovered instances in which trainees made more money before than after placement. Sub-professional programs enlisted the aide for jobs that "are generally limited to the homemaker assistant, child care aide, or other low level and peripheral functions," noted anti-poverty advocates—jobs with no real entry onto professional ladders.[81] In such positions, they ran the risk of being confused with a maid, as MFY reported about their visiting homemakers.[82] While the Great Society also included Health Manpower and Nurse Training Acts, these supported college-educated professionals and the skilled end of the medical field. The job of aide, attendant, and caretaker belonged to anti-poverty policy, still separated from health policy.[83]

As the War on Poverty played out, training and jobs became ends in themselves—and sometimes served as punishment for those who needed income assistance. Initially, welfare officials like Winston could imagine that rights to income and equity would accompany the expansion of services. The activists on the ground sought greater income, too, but also an explicit acknowledgment of rights and the opportunities American life had to offer. Over the course of the decade, welfare recipients and their allies won exhilarating victories from local welfare offices, mayors, and courts. Still, with federal policy makers unwilling to tackle the gender and racial segmentation of the labor market or to seriously upgrade the standards and compensation of service work, they remained trapped in a cycle of economic dependency. Policy makers eagerly followed the path laid by their predecessors: accepting the promise that home care jobs would end women's poverty without any demonstrable proof that the change had yet happened. While these longer term battles would stretch beyond the Johnson presidency into the Nixon years, the Great Society made good on key promises to the elderly when it enacted both national health insurance for Americans over age 65 and the Older Americans Act. Care, or at least medical care, would become an entitlement of the elderly.

The Great Society's Rights for the Elderly

Senior citizens and organized labor won one of the monumental achievements of the Great Society: passage of Medicare. After 1935, liberals had regarded health insurance as the "next step in social security." Roosevelt subsequently included it in his Economic Bill of Rights.[84] Throughout the 1940s, New Dealers and their heirs sought comprehensive national health insurance for all, but in the mid-1950s they regrouped around a more circumscribed proposal: insurance for the elderly. When Johnson signed the Medicare Bill in Independence, Missouri, in July 1965, at the side of Harry Truman, a long campaign finally achieved a victory.

Health care, indeed, had been one of the three main planks of the Great Society, along with education and job opportunity. This landmark legislation, however, further perpetuated the split between health policy and welfare, distinguishing between entitled "beneficiaries" and means-tested "recipients," by establishing a companion program for the poor—Medicaid. Given its previous history, from New Deal chronic illness programs through Kerr-Mills, long-term care ended up on the welfare side of the equation. While Medicare was considered the crowning achievement, Medicaid evolved into America's long-term care program. This outcome thrust recipients, family members, and care workers into a persistent battle against the stigmatization and insecurity of welfare.[85]

With its emphasis on medical treatment, Medicare provided the elderly with hospital and voluntary, but subsidized, coverage for physicians. Physicians could authorize home care as a supplemental support. Under Part A, Medicare would pay for in-home "professional" services, such as skilled nursing or physical therapy, up to 100 visits within a year following discharge from a hospital or nursing home. A further 100 visits became available under the Part B insurance plan for those who purchased this coverage. A physician had to order and a registered nurse or therapist supervise any in-home health care, always of limited duration. Homemaker-type services lasted only as long as the patient primarily needed skilled medical care and were provided only for those classified as "homebound."[86] By establishing a particularly medicalized definition of the care worthy of state reimbursement, Medicare reinforced the devaluation of household and bodily care.

Medicaid, also known as Title XIX of the Social Security Act, continued the traditions of poor law and charity care, and for this reason, labor and senior activists were initially quite opposed to it. It established a joint federal-state program for poor people's care and committed federal matching funds to states that chose to create a program. Moreover, state welfare departments supervised eligibility and enrollment. The law explicitly referred to potential enrollees as "recipients," while calling those in Medicare "beneficiaries."[87] For those identified as "functionally disabled elderly individuals," Medicaid offered medical assistance through community health or welfare agencies. Physicians could prescribe in-home health services under Medicaid to any person who would be eligible for a nursing home. Unlike Medicare, no need existed for prior hospitalization. Soon Medicaid became the main funding source for nursing home care, but it also offered a vehicle through which states could finance in-home support for indigent elders and people with disabilities.[88] It freed welfare administrators from having to piece together meager funding for home care from child welfare, OEO, manpower, vocational education, and other small grants. Together with Medicare, it offered an opportunity for procuring a more robust right to care within the welfare state.

Both programs set in motion an important reorganization of home and community-based long-term care. Whether under Medicare or Medicaid, only a new entity, the "licensed home health agency," could deliver in-home health services. The availability of public reimbursement funds quickly led to the formation of local home health agencies—as outgrowths of public welfare or health departments, nonprofit agencies, or a handful of for-profit businesses—which could carry out the new social service mandates of the welfare state. Within a decade, an entire industry developed. Despite the concerns of traditional visiting nurse associations, for example, California quickly chose to license proprietary firms, which by 1971 represented a fifth of all agencies in the state. After 1979, across the board, proprietary, for-profit agencies increasingly delivered home health services.[89]

Which services, and thus jobs, actually qualified for Medicare reimbursement was initially unclear. It took three years before administrators clarified terms like "reasonable costs," "custodial care," and "skilled nursing care."[90] To be certified as a Medicare or Medicaid provider, a home care agency had to have skilled nurses and therapists on staff for acute medically related care. The significant boom in labor demand, however, was for custodial and daily support workers whose labors enabled patients to remain at home; indeed, their numbers quadrupled between 1966 and 1972.[91] But because of Medicare and Medicaid's medical definitions, certified home health agencies treated attendants as contingent and casual workers, called up on short notice for a few hours, or for overnight work, often not deployed for days at a time. The separation of personal care from housekeeping, however, became extremely difficult to apply. These were not going to be the good public jobs that OEO and New Careers advocates had imagined.[92]

The attitude of medical professionals and Social Security Administration proxies undercut the expressed goals of War on Poverty jobs programs, like New Careers, that sought to use job training as a ticket to better employment and economic independence. Medical professionals continued to regard the home care aide as unskilled. Educational requirements, a spokesman for local health officials told the California legislature, were "the least important for home health aides. Rather, what is needed is persons who have native ability to learn to help . . . I don't think it takes a tenth grade education." Ironically revealing the multiple meanings of "care," he warned that "care should be exercised that we don't try to over-qualify people who are trying to help other people in their homes."[93] While anti-poverty warriors claimed that these jobs would provide new skills to lift women out of poverty, health policy experts, it seemed, wanted the ideal worker to remain the essentialized woman whose life experiences as housewife and mother provided "basic training."[94]

Medicaid, nonetheless, offered major relief to states with large social welfare expenses. New York again is instructive. In 1965, the Empire state spent

$449 million on medical care for poor families and individuals; thus it especially applauded the expanded federal responsibility for medical care as long overdue. To comply with Title XIX, New York enacted Medical Assistance for Needy Persons in 1966, which included not just public assistance recipients but also the "self-supporting" who were "unable to cope with rising hospital and medical costs and the crushing burdens of chronic or catastrophic illness." Under this program, local welfare departments would issue direct payments to physicians, hospitals, or other service providers. New York's Medicaid program became the most expansive and generous in the nation—far more inclusive than federal law required.[95]

As with Kerr-Mills, Medicaid categorized and administered medical reimbursement as "welfare." Governor Rockefeller therefore designated the State Department of Social Welfare as the single state agency responsible for overseeing the program—appeasing the private social welfare establishment.[96] Doctors once again expressed indignant opposition, insisting that medical programs "should be transferred to health departments or state agencies for medical care in which physicians would be in authority and control." Private family agencies and physicians continued to tussle over this issue, even after the program began. Eventually, New York settled on a compromise. The state hospital department would supervise medical and health-related services, but the welfare department would determine eligibility and compensation.[97] Deeply held suspicions of indigency and dependency continued to overshadow health policy.

To access Medicaid funds for elder care, New York City devised a new vehicle for providing home care: *home attendant services*. Aiming to meet the medical requirements of Medicaid, a new Home Attendant Service would serve more severely functionally limited, usually older, clients requiring greater personal care for more hours each week. As part of its cost-shifting goal, the city cast loose these workers, treating them instead as independent contractors. Thus it turned to the tactic previously tried out on housekeepers: the "two-party check." The client received her grant as a check made out in the names of the client and the home attendant. This mechanism allowed the city to claim that the client was the employer and that the family or client recruited, hired, supervised, and fired the worker. Wherever possible, the family of the client was expected to oversee the care, eliminating the need for continued oversight by caseworkers as well. The city merely maintained a Home Attendant Roster with a list of names for individuals in need of an attendant. By the end of the decade, New York's long-term care agenda was no longer in sync with the ambitions of the War on Poverty. Instead, municipal officials clearly sought to expand home care through means that would minimize their labor costs.

The elderly also won their own declaration of rights during these years, with the passage of the Older Americans Act in 1965; at the same time, it became yet another source of funding for the anti-poverty strategy that turned poor women into caregivers. This act belonged to the War on Poverty's overall redefinition of "independence" through access to community services, rather than income or economic security. Offering a formal declaration of the new rights and deservedness of seniors, the Older Americans Act rested on rhetorical and ideological premises similar to the Economic Opportunity Act and the 1964 Civil Rights Act: the state's responsibility for enabling elderly Americans to "secure equal opportunity to the full and free enjoyment" of everything from decent housing and employment to health services. It created an Administration on Aging to distribute grants for planning and demonstration projects to develop community-based services for the elderly. Units on Aging, with community involvement, would coordinate state-level activities.[98] By 1971, the total appropriation under this act had grown to $27 million but the strategy reached only about one million elders, or 3 percent of the older population.[99] Similar to the community action program, the Older Americans Act offered the possibility for social justice and senior engagement and empowerment, but it did so without requiring major government investment or redistribution of income. What it did do is encourage the privatization of home care by handing out monies to nongovernmental agencies to run services.[100] Again, improvement in the lives of seniors rested on minimal investment in the care workforce.

Turmoil Within New York's Public Sector: Rising Militancy Within the Welfare State

New York City government had a political, as well as fiscal, reason for moving toward an independent contractor model for home care services: unionization. The welfare department's homemakers developed an extensive bargaining agenda through SSEU Local 371. They sought competitive civil service status, based on an exam that would be "practical and oral," time-and-a-half pay for overtime work, and a detailed list of employment conditions that would make care work in people's homes formalized, regular employment. Each of their demands concentrated on reducing the arbitrariness of domestic work.[101] In late 1966, welfare department unionists took to the streets to protest an impasse in negotiations. Commissioner of Welfare Mitchell Ginsberg, a former consultant to the Community Action Program of the OEO and Columbia University social work professor, argued that while the department shared many of the "social goals of the union," these were ultimately "policy matters," hence outside collective bargaining. SSEU, which represented over 7,000 workers, again walked out in January 1967, followed by a six-week strike that summer. Both sides justified their actions in terms of better service for clients. As the city was uncomfortably finding, in the public work of the welfare state, labor issues were integrally connected with social policy.[102]

These strikes occurred as the welfare rights movement forced more fundamental changes in welfare policy. Welfare activists flooded the city with petitions and appeals for fair hearings for recipients. Already swamped beyond its capacity to conduct so many hearings, and pay for the staff and space to hold them after regular business hours, the Department found itself in 1967 and 1968 offering settlements that often exceeded the petitioner's request. These settlements only emboldened the movement, raising its political profile. Abetted by a shrewd litigation strategy, welfare rights activism pushed the city to turn to the state and federal governments for relief.[103]

Union militancy and pressure also seeped through the porous boundaries between public and private welfare. AFSCME Local 1701, the Community and Social Agency Employees Union, set out to organize homemakers in the private agencies that contracted with New York City's Department of Welfare. The struggle to unionize 160 homemakers who worked for the Association for Homemakers Service became a highly visible test over definitions of public and private employment involving public spending. Both city officials and labor

Figure 3.2 Welfare workers on strike, New York City, 1965. Social Service Employees Union Photographs Collection, Robert F. Wagner Labor Archives, Tamiment Library, New York University.

leaders understood what was at stake. Most of the homemakers were African American women making the state minimum wage.[104] Although the union represented a majority in the spring of 1967, the Association for Homemakers Service refused to recognize or bargain with it. Because the Association held a substantial contract with the Department of Welfare, the union turned to the city and, using the threat of a strike, demanded intervention. This AFSCME local took work done in homes, run by a private agency, and recast it as public. Claiming that 45 percent of the Association's budget came from public welfare funds, Harry Van Arsdale, head of the Central Labor Council, cogently summed up the union's claim: "We consider it untenable that public funds are used for organizations that are anti-union." With that, Welfare Commissioner Ginsberg stepped in. He conducted what he called "a clarifying" discussion with the private agency's board members, among whom were leaders of the National Council for Homemaker Services, urging them to "reconsider their position." One week later, the Association for Homemakers Service recognized the union.[105] The union used the welfare state location of home care as an arena of struggle to transform the conditions and status of the work. Ultimately, this victory was short-lived. The administration of welfare itself would undergo a major reorganization in which the contracting out of home care would recast social provision, generating new battlegrounds between workers and the state.[106]

By 1968, the official War on Poverty was in retreat, its defenders embattled and exhausted. The attention and resources of the Johnson administration had shifted decisively toward the war in Vietnam. In turn, Congress exerted greater targeted control over OEO disbursements. It handed community action programs over to the very local officials that the programs had been designed to pressure or circumvent. OEO would no longer be "an action agency."[107]

The policy and social struggles of the 1960s hinged on the questions of what it meant and what it took to gain full standing as citizens in the United States. Who would get to live in the Great Society? The decade opened with recognition that it was not acceptable to have mass poverty amid plenty. The explosion of the civil rights movement heightened the urgency of dealing with those left on the margins of American prosperity, "the outskirts of hope." During this era, the issues of low-wage workers and low-income families received serious national public attention, the last such time in twentieth-century America.

Self-sufficiency, however, rested on more than a right to work; it also required an adequate income. Poor women's rights to work and to independence were quickly shading into an obligation to labor—at low wages, serving others. The welfare rights movement therefore also sought the right to reject the opportunity to work if that employment fell short of providing sufficient income and dignity.[108] In the 1960s, black women were seeking genuine alternatives to personal service; few wanted to be pushed back into "a white woman's kitchen." With passage of Title VII of the 1964 Civil Rights Act, other jobs began to open up.[109] Wage work held out the promise of a higher standard of living and the standing crucial for citizenship. But some groups of poor women found themselves tracked into jobs—for the sake of jobs—that couldn't possibly fulfill that promise, especially when these jobs were tied to public budgets that over the next two decades came under vociferous attack. The late 1960s by no means would mark the end of the welfare wars.

The Social Security Act remained the main instrument for addressing economic insecurity. Prior to this period, the largest single group of poor Americans was the elderly. Because the Great Society tackled one of their most pressing economic problems through Social Security, their poverty rate began to decline. Congress also raised pension benefits three times between 1969 and 1972, including those for widows, and finally indexed benefits to inflation in 1972.[110] Seniors could rely on Medicare to cover acute illness but not daily in-home assistance in the case of chronic conditions. In the mid-1970s, a bipartisan group in Congress, led by the liberal House Select Committee on Aging and Representative Claude Pepper (D-Florida), introduced a half dozen bills to expand Medicare to cover home care for elders living above the poverty line with their employed children.[111] Such measures might have relieved women like Ruth Molendyke, but the new tidal wave of political conservatism soon overrode them.

Rather than turning into a middle-class entitlement, long-term care became more tightly identified with welfare. Despite claims by some Medicare champions that a public assistance program like Medicaid would eventually fade away as unnecessary, Medicaid grew into an essential, core program in its own right. It became the predominant means for long-term care. By the early twenty-first century, elderly and disabled people consumed 70 percent of its expenditures.[112] Medicaid and Medicare thereby fueled the rapid, vast growth of new labor markets: millions of jobs in hospitals, nursing homes, community health centers, licensed home health agencies, and nonprofits. Over the next 20 years, the health care sector became one of the largest employers of women, in both the public institutions and private enterprises through which Medicare and Medicaid money flowed.

At first, it seemed that home care aides would share in the new wave of unionization that swept through the public sector in the 1960s. As unionism became more contentious and successful, city or county governments increasingly looked to minimize its costs. They could take advantage of various ambiguities of home care—its history of provision through private charities, private agencies, or hospitals; its association with the social rehabilitation of the welfare poor; and its location in the home—to block that path to better working conditions and security. Instead, as the homemaker/housekeeper mutated into the home health aide or personal attendant, she increasingly worked in the shadows of the welfare state.

Their fates intertwined by the same programs, would the activism of senior citizens, or other constituents of the welfare state, ever align with those who provided their care? Could rehabilitation and rights coexist? Could the presumed objects of rehabilitation have some control over their care or labor? As the War on Poverty became a war on welfare, resistance did not recede, but rather exploded into new forms of coalition politics.

4

Welfare Wars, Seventies Style

"I want the right to earn a living, the right to fulfill my potential and, if need be, the right to fail," proclaimed 29-year-old disability rights activist Connie Panzarino in 1977. Three years before, she quit her job as a caseworker assistant because she earned too much to qualify for state funding but too little to pay for the full-time aide necessary for her survival. Born with a neuromuscular disease, Panzarino had always been in a wheelchair and relied on what she called "total care"—a full-time aide whom she needed "to eat, dress, bathe, brush her teach, get in and out of bed and travel." Turning frustration into political activism, Panzarino explained, "They said I was eligible financially because I didn't have enough income to pay an attendant but by law, if I was working full-time, I was not disabled, so I was not eligible" for home care subsidy. Neither local nor federal officials could resolve her dilemma. Then she found a supporter in Bronx Democratic Congressman Mario Biaggi, one of a group of liberal House representatives pushing for Social Security reforms that would expand access to home care. Assisted by her aide, Panzarino went to Washington to lobby for her civil rights, including the legislation that Biaggi proposed to remedy the "catch-22" in which she found herself.[1]

The case of Connie Panzarino provided Biaggi with an example of the dysfunctional regulations that hampered the delivery of home care. As a leader on the House Select Committee on Aging, he convened hearings on "New York Home Care Abuse" in February 1978. New York City officials calculated that quadriplegics and other "functionally handicapped" people made up only 2 percent of home attendant users, but they were "extremely active and extremely vociferous;" their protests had paid off with an ever "larger political voice in this city." Their activism contrasted with the alleged passivity of the majority of home care recipients, poor elderly women, whom newly elected Mayor Edward Koch and his recently appointed welfare commissioner Blanche Bernstein represented as victims of fraud and theft by corrupt care providers. While Biaggi also sought answers to numerous grievances of the workers—the home aides—Mayor Koch had no sympathy, seething, "They are jackals feeding on the health, safety, and the very lives of people who need our help the most." In the racially charged atmosphere of late 1970s New York City, Koch and Bernstein depicted such breach of trust as symptomatic of the War on Poverty run amok.[2]

By the mid-1970s, New York, California, and other states faced a crisis in the long-term care of elderly and disabled people.[3] Nursing home scandals exposed deep and systemic abuse and neglect, forcing cities, states, and even Congress to authorize investigations, convene hearings, and close facilities. Home care had expanded over the previous decade as the humane alternative to nursing homes, but it too appeared out of control, with confused regulations, spiraling costs, charges of fraud, and a poorly paid, untrained, and unsupervised workforce.[4] Although public anger over nursing homes rose and Congress sought alternatives to institutionalization, Medicare and Medicaid could not accommodate these demands; the initial legislation had left significant gaps. Starting in 1973, liberals in the Senate and the House introduced bills to amend these programs in piecemeal fashion to provide greater support for in-home services. In 1977, with a Democrat in the White House and a large Democratic majority in Congress, Claude Pepper (D-FL), chair of the House Select Committee on Aging, and Biaggi introduced a more ambitious proposal: a National Home Care Bill. Expanding social rights, it included unlimited home health visits, ended the requirement of prior hospitalization, and eliminated deductibles. They saw the bill as completing the project of the Great Society's promises to the aged. At the same time, it responded to the needs of the disability rights movement.

The political moment of the late 1970s, however, was a long way from the heady days of the Great Society. In 1974, the U.S. economy had slid into recession with the rest of the industrialized world. It turned out to be prolonged and unprecedented—the worst downturn yet of the post–World War II era. Americans experienced a new phenomenon, stagflation: high unemployment accompanied by untamed inflation that reached almost 13 percent by decade's end. Conservative business leaders blamed economic stagnation on unions, the welfare state, taxes, and government regulation. Along with emboldened conservative political organizations and think tanks, business organized as a class to stop any further expansion of government. This rightward turn popularized the idea that New Deal liberalism could no longer solve the problems that the nation faced—an analysis that became very persuasive as a number of states and cities dealt with fiscal crisis in the 1970s.[5]

The War on Poverty was over, but welfare politics became even more contentious. Just as recipients were determined to change the terms under which they received benefits, they also struggled for some control over how or whether they entered the paid labor force. In the early 1970s, welfare rights organizing converged with the turbulence of public sector unionism and a militant disability rights movement to press forward a broad set of demands for dignity and income. Republican governors and mayors responded to social upheaval and fiscal crisis by blaming public aid recipients; as the hard-pressed 1970s dragged on, Democratic mayors soon followed them. When conflicts over public benefits burst into the open, some unlikely alliances became possible—until other changes in social policy shattered common bases for mobilization.

As the ground that held up postwar politics shifted, the commitment to Keynesian liberalism dropped away. New Democrats—distant from labor, urban voters, and the poor—joined Republicans in launching a long-term restructuring of the American welfare state. They began shifting more authority from the national welfare state to local and state governments and private enterprises. Government at all levels sought to cut expenses, lighten welfare, and cap surging home care costs.[6] Yet cities were expected to pick up greater costs at a moment when they were overwhelmed by structural change. Deindustrialization, surging oil prices, and suburbanization not only drained tax revenue but population, voters, and congressional support. Under the sway of a sour new populism, a rightward-drifting nation embraced the politics and culture of punitive anti-welfarism and tax revolts. Public-sector unions responded with renewed militancy. Urban Democrats, like Koch and Bernstein, turned away from newly politicized social groups in the national party's coalition and opened their arms to the agenda of business, privatization, and neoliberalism. In California, these conflicts played out on the state level, where groups of disabled people, welfare recipients, and public workers clashed with the rising conservative leader, Governor Ronald Reagan.[7]

The welfare wars that rocked the late 1960s and early 1970s generated not only California's independent provider system but also solidified the vendor agency model in New York, in which governments transferred employer responsibility by contracting the work to private enterprises. This fragmented and more conservative context did much to frame the organization of home care that unions and other advocates would have to confront for the rest of the century. Neither governments nor unions had a free hand in these matters. Just as organized seniors had a decisive impact on elder policy in the 1960s, so the emerging political voice of disabled people in the early 1970s pushed home care in a new, consumer-oriented direction, particularly in California, where a vigorous independent living movement took root.

Amid the fiscal crisis, economic restructuring, and changing political culture of the 1970s, the possibilities for making home care a good job faced new challenges. The National Council for Homemaker–Home Health Aide Services, the legacy of the Children's Bureau women's network, long argued for raising the standards of home care and providing workers with job security. But in the climate of the time, home care went in a decidedly different direction. Instead, two soon-to-be dominant forms of delivery emerged—the independent contractor and the private vendor—seemingly pushing workers to the margins of the welfare state. In California and New York, local and state governments turned to contracting home care to private agencies or designating care workers as "independent contractors" without benefits or job security. By distancing such workers from public employment, states denied responsibility for the working conditions of an occupation whose contours government policies had done so much to set during the previous quarter century.[8] Privatization derailed the public sector organizing that was initially pursued by the American Federation of State, County and Municipal Employees (AFSCME) in New York, but it would mesh with the demands of the most vocal users of support services, college-educated wheelchair users. When it came to home care, privatization meant that a low-wage minority workforce, laboring in the shadows, would carry forth state policy in the most intimate matters of health and welfare.

Disability Rights, Welfare Rights, and the Political Struggle for Independence

California's home care system emerged out of the battle between Governor Ronald Reagan and the social movements that responded to his onslaught in the courts, legislature, media, and streets. It also took form as a result of prior policy decisions that distinguished its program from most other states, where home care stemmed from homemaker services. California, in contrast, extended an attendant care program that allowed severely disabled individuals to avoid institutionalization. This legacy positioned the rising independent living movement to have a significant impact on the shape of In-Home Supportive Services (IHSS), the state system legislated in 1973. Consumers won "choice," which meant that they could select, hire, fire, and supervise attendants, who became independent providers. Such classification absolved county administrators of responsibility for working conditions, even though they authorized client hours, set the wage rate, supervised the care, and financed the service. There was an irony to this outcome: fighting conservative politicians who would defund attendant services, militant disability activists demanded greater social assistance on the basis of "choice" and "independence," key tenets of the neoliberalism that would come to dominate policy circles.

In the early 1950s, California's liberal Republican Governor Earl Warren promoted enhanced Social Security, only to be rebuffed by a rural-dominated legislature more willing to spend for civil defense than for welfare. In 1957, lawmakers finally authorized California to participate in the disability provisions of Social Security, known as Aid to the Permanently and Totally Disabled. Two years later, they established the attendant care program in response to lobbying by respirator-using post-polio quadriplegics. These men and women turned to the state after a strapped March of Dimes no longer could pay for the personal care that allowed them to live outside institutions. As disability aid recipients, the polio generation became eligible for supplemental monies for attendant care, but medical verification of applicants made the category of "totally disabled" initially more restrictive than other forms of social assistance.[9]

Following the election of Democrat Edmund "Pat" Brown in 1958, the state Social Welfare Board embraced the concept of "preventive and rehabilitative welfare."[10] The most prominent member of the Social Welfare Board, appointed in 1950 at the age of 39 and elevated to its chair by Pat Brown, was Berkeley professor Jacobus tenBroek. After losing his eyesight during childhood, tenBroek attended the pioneering California School for the Blind, received a law degree, and then forged a distinguished career in constitutional law and social welfare. He founded and presided over the National Federation of the Blind. TenBroek was an integrationist, or "mainstreamer." He argued for self-support and self-care, goals that the Great Society also aimed to incorporate into social welfare policy.[11] His foundational legal writings linked disability with the right to welfare, arguing on the basis of the Fourteenth Amendment that public aid should be a right, not "an alms-taking privilege."[12]

Under tenBroek's leadership, the Social Welfare Board took an openly liberal turn, promoting services for poor single mothers, seniors, and disabled people to encourage independent living and thus the ability to participate in society.[13] The state loosened requirements for disability coverage, upped the income limit so that more of the elderly could qualify for home help, and in 1962 eliminated citizenship as a precondition for social assistance—catching up to New York and other industrial states.[14] The organization of care through county government, though, inhibited the growth of services for aged and disabled people. Despite the availability of money under Kerr-Mills and other federal grants, the state provided no administrative funding, and thus few counties opted for such programs.[15] Finally, in 1966, California established Medi-Cal as the state's version of Medicaid, which would become the major source of home care financing.[16]

TenBroek's influence spread more broadly as he helped form the California Welfare Rights Organization (CWRO) out of more than 20 individual groups in 1966.[17] Since the late 1950s, African American and Latina mothers throughout the state had created community organizations that confronted local welfare departments. In 1961, poor women formed the Los Angeles County WRO, which generated activists, like Johnnie Tillmon and Catherine Jermany, who would lead the national movement. These welfare rights militants demanded income as well as training, respect as well as relief from poverty. They protested midnight raids that looked for a man in the house, whom officials assumed should support the children, whether or not he was the father. They objected to stringent means tests that forced recipients to own practically nothing in order to receive assistance. They resented social worker interference with their consumer as well as reproductive choices. And, contrary to stereotypes of the welfare queen, they sought to leave welfare for real jobs, work that paid enough to live on. "We want to be self-supporting and productive—and I don't mean producing children," one activist declared.[18]

With its low wages, home care did not quite fit the bill. Welfare rights activists understood the labor as another form of "maid work," recalled Jermany, rather than a stepping-stone to higher wages and professional status available through paraprofessional training in law or nursing. Nevertheless, they also realized the potential of home care as a form of social support that could bring additional resources into their families. Organizers learned that women preferred to qualify for public assistance on the basis of "the incapacity of the mother, rather than the absence of the father," since being disabled bore less stigma than being on AFDC. So they arranged visits to doctors who would diagnose poor women as unable to work. Those certified as disabled could obtain monies for home attendants. If they hired friends or relatives, they not only gained help with daily activities but also increased the flow of cash within the community, putting other poor women to work.[19] What appeared as gaming the system to opponents of welfare allowed poor families to make ends meet. In a sense, this strategy echoed an aspect of the New Careers concept. But in the growing backlash against women on welfare, such use of public assistance fueled calls for eliminating welfare fraud and curtailing such supports.[20]

Los Angeles WRO therefore learned to engage in coalition politics.[21] With "a cry to organize the poor under the slogan of 'welfare power,'" in 1966 it joined with unionized social workers, religious social action committees, War on Poverty centers, the United Automobile Workers, and the California Council of the Blind to form the Citizens Committee for a Decent Welfare System. David Novogrodsky, the Los Angeles executive director of the Social Workers Union, Local 535 of the Service Employees International Union (SEIU), especially embraced their cause. "Administrators," he complained, were "'gutless wonders unwilling to defend the inadequate public assistance programs or take steps essential to properly run the programs'" because welfare had become "a political and racial scapegoat."[22]

Founded in 1964, Local 535 spanned 11 county welfare departments, growing from 2,600 in 1968 to 5,000 members two years later. It was a militant union, conducting yearly strikes, with one in Sacramento lasting nearly all of 1967. Confronted with daily pickets at the state capitol, the legislature passed a collective bargaining law for government workers, the Meyers-Milias-Brown Act. Like radical social workers in New York, Local 535 protested not only low salaries and understaffing, but also the organization of welfare itself.[23] Against its own "anti-union and anti-poor" supervisors, Local 535 found common ground with clients, each joining the other's demonstrations.[24] It facilitated the creation of the Committee for Rights of the Disabled, which in demanding that "'this welfare system—the whole bag of worms—[be] opened up,'" expressed a frustration that welfare recipients of all sorts and their caseworkers shared.[25]

The victory of faded movie star and corporate spokesman Ronald Reagan over Pat Brown in the 1966 gubernatorial elections alarmed these newly mobilized welfare rights activists. Reagan rode to political prominence in the wake of the Watts rebellion and the student Free Speech Movement by promising law and order. He would "clean up the mess at Berkeley" and ensure that Southern blacks didn't migrate to California to take advantage of the state's generous public assistance. Fanning resentment through the line that "the working man and woman has [*sic*] discovered that they are not the beneficiaries of the 'Great Society'—they are only paying for it," Reagan crafted an anti-welfare framework that associated social expenditure with misused government and higher taxes. He positioned himself as the champion of the traditional values of family, work, and nation, against which the poor single mother stood as an antithesis.[26] He vowed to "squeeze and cut and trim until we reduce the cost of government."[27] Such rationales undergirded Reagan's support of home care as a cheaper alternative to hospital and institutional care.

But Reagan operated in the liberal political order of the 1960s, in which Democrats wielded power in Sacramento and the public approved of an activist state that provided accessible, quality services ranging from higher education to highways. Rhetoric aside, Reagan signed a large tax increase, liberalized abortion laws, and let state spending jump more than twofold to $10.2 billion before leaving office in 1975. With recession hitting the state more severely than elsewhere in the late 1960s, he saddled California with a huge budget deficit. At the same time, property values kept soaring, pushing home owners into higher tax brackets. The clash of "bracket creep" and the state's continual need for money would generate what journalist Robert Kuttner has labeled "the revolt of the haves." This protest culminated with Proposition 13 in 1978, which, by reducing property taxes and requiring a two-thirds vote in the legislature for budgetary measures, put a brake on government in ways that Reagan never could. The infamous Prop 13 helped ignite the nationwide tax revolts of the late twentieth century.[28]

Welfare spending also increased under Reagan, even while he fought to change how and to whom the state delivered assistance. The century-old distinction between the deserving and undeserving poor guided his pronouncements. Reagan embraced "our obligation to help the aged, disabled and those unfortunates, who through no fault of their own, must depend on their fellow man," while simultaneously pursuing "reforms which, wherever possible, will change relief checks to paychecks" for those who were making welfare into a way of life.[29] Indeed, California spent three times as much as did New York on impoverished disabled and elderly people.[30] Reagan simultaneously consolidated all adult aid programs, ostensibly to save paperwork and lessen costs, but actually to reduce the number and discretion of social workers, who mobilized clients against cutbacks. He would replace caseworkers with intake clerks, who merely applied recently tightened eligibility formulas.[31] He promoted workfare and "birth control training" and refused to implement federal directives, including those promulgated under fellow Republican Richard Nixon.[32] Finally, despite Reagan's constant disdain for Washington, California still behaved like other states and eagerly took advantage of any opportunity to shift the cost of welfare to the national government; during his first term, the state would receive almost a third of all federal social service grants.[33]

Subsequently, in 1968, the governor and the legislature agreed to require all counties to replace attendant care programs, paid for by the state, with homemaker services, for which the federal government picked up most of the tab.[34] For Reagan, homemaker services had additional advantages. Counties could contract out the program to nongovernmental groups, including for-profit agencies, thus encouraging private enterprise. Contracting out took more power away from government social workers, who would be replaced by agency employees. But disability rights activists, we shall see, objected to having their control over attendants pass to private agencies; they opened a long-term fight against this mandate.[35] In-home care, which touted the independence he so much admired, began as the exception that legitimized Reagan's war on welfare.

During his 1970 reelection campaign, though, the governor wielded his budget knife capriciously, seeking to slash attendant care for the previously designated deserving poor. In early July, Reagan ordered a $10 million cut as an emergency budget measure to cap the growth of welfare, even though home care constituted merely a ½ percent of all public assistance. This directive triggered an automatic drop in federal and county matching funds, potentially affecting some 55,000 aged, disabled, and blind users. In response, the state welfare department halved the maximum allowance and ended supplemental grants for shopping and housekeeping services.[36]

Reagan tarred elderly and disabled recipients with charges of abuse previously hurled only at poor single mothers. He accused attendants of "simply stealing the money," because "[r]elatives and friends and neighbors who have been doing favors for a neighbor, disabled, for some time, suddenly find out they can be paid for this."[37] Love, family duty, or friendship, not money, should motivate such labor. Reagan later admitted, "the intended targets" of his attacks "were families where one relative was caring for another and was receiving governmental remuneration."[38]

No one outside the administration defended the cuts, which many claimed would force attendants and homemakers to apply for welfare themselves. The counties particularly objected to Reagan's directive. "'Are we supposed to balance the state welfare budget by ignoring the bedridden?'" the chair of the Los Angeles County Supervisors questioned. "'Are you going to let them lie in bed and feed themselves?'"[39] Across the state, letters to editors castigated the governor for his "cruel and discriminatory" order, "lack of heart," and "denial of human rights." As taxpayers, veterans, and compassionate citizens, writers legitimatized their right to be heard, warning, as did one from the Sacramento area, "that before your own deaths, you may be grateful for assistance from these same welfare funds."[40]

This struggle marked the first coordinated effort of an emerging independent living movement. The majority of program users were elderly, but "many of the older folks were not used to speaking up and complaining," consumer lobbyist Emma Gunterman remembered.[41] Reagan's reduction of the attendant care budget galvanized a new generation of physically disabled but politically active young adults centered in Berkeley. While the organizational acumen of the blind community earlier had led to higher benefits and special services and the deaf community long had its own schools and programs, by 1970, Berkeley students had obtained federal and state rehabilitation grants to establish the Physically Disabled Students' Program.[42]

Leading the group was Edward V. Roberts, a post-polio respiratory quadriplegic, who had paved the way for others with severe disabilities to attend the University of California when he became the first student resident of Cowell Hospital in 1962. An innovator, Roberts organized service, political, and research institutions, notably the service-oriented Center for Independent Living in 1972. Three years later, under Governor Jerry Brown, Roberts would head the Department of Rehabilitative Services, an agency that originally had doubted the worth of a university education for someone with his condition.[43]

In Berkeley's social movement milieu—surrounded by civil rights, black power, and women's liberation—and in the midst of student rebellions against received authority and the Vietnam War, relatively advantaged white men like Roberts forged a new disabled manhood with the aid of motorized wheelchairs and an identity as disabled people who advocated for their own rights. They were no longer the "crippled." In rejecting the medical model of rehabilitation, they redefined independent living from "tasks one could perform without assistance" to "the quality of one's life with help." The disabled themselves, they argued, best understood their needs and how to meet them. They built the independent living movement on three tenets: self-determination; comprehensive programs with many different services; and integration as fully as possible into their community.[44] In a system where health professionals claimed sole authority to irrigate catheters and suction lungs, but the attendant performed intimate labors, like bowel and bladder care, independent living activists wanted to employ and train attendants of their own choice.[45]

Figure 4.1 "The Rolling Quads": Edward V. Roberts, Hale Zukas, and Herbert Willsmore, Berkeley, California, early 1970s, Courtesy of Bancroft Library.

The battle over attendant services was among the threats in the early 1970s "that stirred us up and really made us political," remembered Herbert Willsmore, who joined Roberts as one of Berkeley's Rolling Quads. "We were kind of working on behalf of all the disabled communities, but it was very personal too."[46] With other disabled people and their supporters, he wrote to his state assemblyman. The proposed reduction, Willsmore argued, would make it impossible for him to meet the cost of daily living care—forcing him to stop "the educational training which would normally lead to employment" and return home to a family unprepared to handle his care. He could end up in a more expensive, custodial institution.[47]

The Berkeley students formed a statewide network with counterparts in Long Beach, Chico, Sacramento, and Davis. Rejecting media visions of incapacitation and representations of victimhood, they organized disability rights groups to lobby the legislature. They compiled a fact sheet based on their experiences as quadriplegics, emphasizing the unsavory alternatives of returning to aging parents, living in a nursing home with inappropriate facilities and staffing (with aides incapable of lifting them), or entering very expensive hospitals. The sight of the Rolling Quads wheeling through the capitol made onlookers take notice.[48]

Along with other Democratic liberals, Willsmore's Assemblyman John T. Dunlap of Napa championed the students' cause. At a July 21, 1970, news conference, surrounded by a dozen wheelchair-using supporters, he announced the introduction of a resolution to restore attendant monies. "People are being made scapegoats," Dunlap charged. "Why is it all right for millionaires to hire tax attorneys to look for loopholes in paying their taxes but illegal and a disgrace for poor people to seek every available dollar they can get on welfare?" His resolution failed to pass, but the confrontation did not end there.[49]

San Francisco Neighborhood Legal Assistance (SFNLA) stepped in to challenge Reagan's ultimatum. SFNLA, a Legal Aid agency, filed a lawsuit in Sacramento. An institutional legacy of the War on Poverty, Legal Aid not only provided low-income individuals with lawyers but also engaged in impact litigation, using class action lawsuits to force more fundamental social change. By challenging regulations and delays of welfare checks, it fought poverty through the law and with government money.[50] Under Peter E. Sitkin, and then Ralph Abascal, it became the main defender of welfare rights in California. As Sitkin explained, "Most of the plaintiffs in our cases came from legal services offices and from the California and local welfare rights organizations. Some came from social workers who were outraged by the treatment welfare recipients received during the Reagan years."[51] In a tactical move, SFNLA filed for a temporary restraining order on the basis of statutory and procedural violations of the welfare code. Reagan had failed to give notice or conduct a public hearing. Since the legislature had already "appropriated the funds for the very services he is eliminating," the lead attorney told the press at the time, "there is no emergency whatsoever" to justify gubernatorial action.[52]

The lawsuit certainly got the attention of top Reagan officials, who agreed to strike a deal. The governor would back down if the judge refused a temporary restraining order. Reagan restored attendant funding and hastily convened a press conference in order to take credit. Before the legal aid lawyers could announce victory, the governor was standing before reporters accusing social workers of distorting his intentions by using "'Nazi-like' scare tactics" to deny "essential services to those most in need."[53] A master at framing political discourse and translating defeats into ideological victories, Reagan pledged to protect "the handicapped who have been terrorized" and deployed as pawns by special interest groups, in this case, the "arrogant social workers who seem determined to use the poor as basis for creating a bureaucratic empire."[54]

This resolution by no means quelled the welfare wars. To block the social work professionals and defend the public, as he claimed, Reagan rededicated himself to overhauling the welfare system. To stop him, Local 535 and disability activists in wheelchairs staged protests across the state. Demonstrations became dramatic, including one at the capitol featuring a woman strapped to a wheelchair-like bed. Reagan would be back with new cuts, they predicted, but next time "he will go through standard procedures."[55]

Reagan indeed returned with a comprehensive proposal for welfare reform, which the legislature passed in a modified form the next year, hoping it would remove the issue from the political agenda. The governor portrayed himself as the slayer of the "welfare monster" by tightening eligibility, instituting workfare, restructuring MediCal, and increasing the financial obligation of children for their elderly parents and absent fathers for their children. Such provisions merely reinforced the dominant belief that family, no matter the circumstances, should care for its own without state aid. His budget continued to shrink state funding for attendants and homemakers, even though analysts recognized the possibility of poorer living conditions for aged and disabled people, increased institutionalization, and renewed protests and publicity. Every cut in service intentionally reduced the number of social workers.[56]

The poverty lawyers moved to challenge the most egregious aspects of the reform bill, although the political winds around them were rapidly changing. Legal aid lawyers sued the state over grant determinations and family responsibility requirements.[57] By the early 1970s, though, the judiciary was more willing to defer to legislative or administrative authority. In upholding a state's right to set maximum grants, the Supreme Court ruled in *Dandridge v. Williams* that the Fourteenth Amendment protected the right to fair procedures in applying for welfare but gave no right to receive aid.[58] The California lawyers lost their suit, but San Francisco's liberal representative John Burton subsequently managed to overturn some provisions through counter-legislation. Still, within a few years, welfare rights activists in California and elsewhere lost the ability to extract victories from politicians tired of urban disorder and increasingly swayed by appeals to fiscal crisis.[59]

At this juncture, congressional reorganization of aid programs at the national level sparked a new confrontation among Reagan, welfare advocates, and the disability rights movement that would lead to a permanent solution: the creation of In-Home Supportive Services (IHSS). In 1972, Congress merged public assistance to the blind, disabled, and aged into a single new program, Supplemental Security Income (SSI). While AFDC remained a federal-state partnership subject to widely divergent local standards and budgets, the federalization of the adult aid programs, administered by the Social Security Administration, elevated elderly and disabled people, who became "worthy" beneficiaries of Social Security. It also extended Medicaid coverage to disabled persons under 65. More generous states like California could supplement the basic federal grant to maintain previous higher benefit levels. Congress would pick up the administrative cost. All California had to do was pass enabling legislation before January 1974. Failure to do so meant loss of federal funding for MediCal.[60]

The governor and legislature deadlocked as 1973 drew to a close.[61] Reagan again maneuvered to cut the state's contribution by bypassing the legislature altogether and declaring new regulations on the basis of "potential severity of the situation" and conformity to federal law.[62] Legal Aid's Ralph Abascal responded, as one disability activist remembered, with "'Oh, no, you can't,'" and promptly filed a suit on behalf of nine senior, welfare, and disability rights groups to block the governor's unilateral action.[63] The Court of Appeals ruled against the governor's authority to act alone. Only a special session of the legislature could avert cuts.[64]

Disability rights groups urged such legislative action, and their mobilization significantly shaped the outcome, thwarting the changes Reagan had initiated a few years earlier. The Berkeley activists established the Disabled and Blind Action Committee of California as their political arm to work with a newly invigorated coalition of social justice clergy, lawyers, social workers, community organizers, other disability groups, and recipients themselves. Lawmakers asked what they wanted in a bill. Based on recent federal initiatives, including revenue sharing, the independent living promoters proposed legislation for direct payments to disabled people for attendant services.[65] They again called witness to their situation in Sacramento by forming a phalanx of wheelchairs in the rear of the chamber during the debate.[66]

All this agitation forced the legislature into a special session, in which the balance of power tipped away from Reagan in favor of the disability activists. The legislature enacted SSI authorization. While doing so, it reversed the earlier mandate for homemaker services modeled on subcontracted agencies and instead created IHSS, which enabled consumer-directed care. Within the IHSS system, workers—called personal attendants—would be classified as independent contractors. The legislation incorporated the demands of people with significant disabilities to allow a higher monthly maximum for attendant services and an option to employ their own attendants through a cash grant. Counties could now choose among three kinds of services—homemaker, chore/housekeeping, or attendant care—provided directly, through a subcontractor, or by way of a consumer-hired worker. The independent provider model, with its savings to counties, would eventually predominate.[67] Because the federal government did not yet cover personal care, the cost of the attendant program would be borne by the state treasury—a cost that escalated within a few years. Nonetheless, for recipients, these provisions opened new doors. "Five months after all this went into effect, I moved into my own apartment with [personal attendant] Eric Dibner," boasted activist Hale Zukas, who was born with cerebral palsy.[68]

Who won? Although politically outmaneuvered, the Reaganites saved face by claiming that the new arrangements were less expensive than earlier proposals, despite higher average grants than those previously voted by the legislature. The state promised to make up shortfalls for provisions falling outside federal funding. The National Senior Citizens Law Center subsequently monitored the statutory language. While conservatives warned of a "Geritol Gold Rush," John Burton echoed the senior activists of a decade before: "We have done something for poor people. We have given them a measure of economic security. . . ."[69] The biggest beneficiary was the independent living movement, which won consumer control of the process. Meanwhile, despite the political tussle, no one heard from the home care workers themselves. For the next 25 years, the IHSS independent provider model would pose a serious impediment to workers' attempts to organize for better pay, conditions, and rights.

The work of the recipient coalition continued after the state authorized SSI, but its reach began to narrow. At informational conferences in southern and northern California, social work activists briefed different groups of aid recipients and their advocates on the big changes ahead.[70] SSI, though, had attenuated the connections among these groups. With the shift of aid to the blind, the disabled, and the elderly to the federal government, AFDC alone remained subject to individual state determination. California WRO astutely predicted that its "recipients would . . . now be more than ever vulnerable to scapegoating and harassment." Indeed, soon after, California's welfare department was forcing poor single mothers into welfare-to-work programs that compelled poor women to work off their benefits but offered no path to higher paying jobs.[71] A new boundary between the deserving and the undeserving had emerged.

In the struggle against Reagan, the only workers heard from were the members of Local 535. Attendants supported the disability community, but being an attendant was not a worker identity among those hired by the Berkeley activists. The disabled students initially found their workforce among other students and wartime conscientious objectors, helpers who never envisioned attendant care as a long-term occupation or one that required any special training. The informality of student life spilled over to the use and treatment of attendants, who worked split shifts: they readied people in the morning, sometimes accompanying them to classes, and returned in the evening for personal care. They shared social life and apartments. Though the independent living proponents knew about plans to place welfare recipients in homemaker positions, these activists were more concerned with getting along with their attendant than with providing jobs. That the most outspoken were white reflected their relative race, class, and educational privilege: they possessed an ability to obtain the resources, including knowledge of social policy, necessary to avoid institutionalization.[72] The program that offered them the resources to move away from home allowed others to hire family members to keep the family together.

A conflict of interest existed between attendants and those they served. To better stretch assistance checks, some advocates offered strategies to avoid paying the social security of attendants. Berkeley radicals supported worker organization, but Zukas admitted to their dilemma. He confessed: "I want control over—I am jealous of my prerogative as an employer." Nearly a quarter of a century later, Kitty Cone, a Center for Independent Living staffer who had been with the Socialist Worker Party, explained, "The unspoken issue was the rights of the attendants or the personal assistants." Higher wages and benefits would balloon costs. "It was just something that you talked around."[73] Consequently, officials allowed recipients to choose relatives and friends and encouraged county governments to contract out housekeeping to private businesses.

In gaining control over attendants and taking charge over their training, the disability activists inadvertently reinforced the devaluation of the labor that their very survival and independence rested on. If any one could do the work, how could it be worth more than minimum wage? By hiring their own workers, disability rights activists further clouded the responsibility of the state as employer. The social welfare location of attendant care allowed consumers more freedom than a health or medical location, which would have displaced supervision to medical professionals. But there were hidden costs to the social services funding of IHSS: a period of budget deficits and tax revolts soon thrust the program into perpetual crisis. Under such precariousness, the actual administration of the program suffered tremendously, State Senator George R. Moscone (D-San Francisco) charged in 1974, with a bevy of regulations undermining any pretense at compassion.[74]

Beginning with funding shortfalls in 1974, a predictable consequence from Reagan's last gubernatorial budget, poor mothers began to enter the home care debate as workers and not only as clients of the welfare state. Some attendants joined the coalition of aged, blind, and disabled people and their advocates to protest reduction of IHSS services. At a December rally that year, African American domestic and home attendant Viola Mitchell, president of the small California Homemakers Association, marked the first time in which "workers and recipients here in Sacramento have united and are sitting across the bargaining table from County officials to demand decent care and a living wage." She reminded the crowd, "Only in Unity is there strength."[75] With the creation of IHSS, though, it would require not only a strengthened coalition but also a deep shift in labor organizing philosophy and new structures of governance before homemakers like Mitchell would win living wages and union recognition.

Contracting Out Services: New York's Agency Model

Developments in New York illuminate another, particularly gendered, trajectory of privatization and welfare state devolution. The privatization and obfuscation of home care as a welfare service began in New York several years before the infamous fiscal crisis of 1975–1976. Therefore, we cannot simply understand contracting out as a product of that particular moment and the imposition of austerity by financiers. Privatization was never a linear process or progression. It was a continually evolving political tactic, part of the politics of welfare, Medicaid, and elder care. It also was a specific response to militancy among poor women of color.

Labor activism of the late 1960s intensified pressure on the public budget, both because AFSCME and the Social Service Employees Union (SSEU) pushed up public workers' compensation and because they demanded greater investment in social services and welfare benefits. Unionism pried open greater pressure points within the state. By 1969, state and city officials were ready to launch a counterattack. It began as an assault on welfare. Because home care was so closely linked to welfare and welfare recipients, its fate became bound up with the ideological and fiscal revision of cash assistance programs. Yet, as the crisis of the needy elderly only burgeoned, New York City once again would try to serve that group by squeezing another—low-income women of color. The city took advantage of the racialized and gendered devaluation of care labor to balance its welfare books and to keep the costs of elderly programs at bay. It also benefited from the ambiguities of care work—particularly the emotional and psychological connections between workers and clients—to defray the real costs and build the program on a casualized, minimally-compensated workforce.

At the end of the 1960s, New York and the Department of Social Services (formerly the Department of Welfare) sought a reduction of its workforce to contain union militancy. The Department moved to accomplish that task through collective bargaining as well as through policy and programmatic changes. Beginning in 1969, the City reached an agreement with three welfare department unions to reduce social service personnel by 9,000 employees over two years. Employees from caseworkers to homemakers received immediate wage raises, while job eliminations decreased promotion opportunities. City and state officials also set out to strip caseworkers of recently won gains, such as union voice on caseloads and the right to strike. These changes accompanied a major reorganization of the whole department.[76] Referring to the 1969 contract as "slow death" and "taming of Welfare staff," one militant caucus within the SSEU exclaimed bitterly, "our entire Contract is based lock, stock and barrel on re-organization . . . a draconic [*sic*] program of cutting services to clients, increasing harassment, downgrading our wage structure, increasing caseloads." These militant unionists emphasized that case aides, homemakers, and home aides, "predominantly Black and Hispanic titles," were being treated as "second-class citizens."[77]

At the same time, with welfare and health costs rising, New York State and City began an intense struggle over the terms of social support—who would receive assistance and services, who would pay, and how much. By 1968, welfare had become the most expensive program in the city's operating budget, surpassing even education. For the next year, the city faced a 51 percent increase over the 1968 budget of $918 million, topping $1 billion. Commissioner Ginsberg pleaded with the state to take over the city's child welfare, relief, and Medicaid costs.[78] New York State, none too happy with its rising costs, had a different cost-shifting strategy, which had the added benefit of ending dependency: "welfare reform." The Republican-controlled legislature made its first move through Medicaid restrictions. In 1969, it tightened eligibility standards, dropping 75,000 from coverage in year one. Another 800,000 were to lose benefits because of increased co-payments. The state cut AFDC, shifting decisively to welfare-to-work requirements.[79]

SSEU militants perceived all of these moves as a joint assault on the gains of public workers and public aid recipients. They acknowledged that New York City and the state faced budget stress but criticized them for not focusing on the revenue problem. Instead, "Welfare clients and public workers have been the first targets."[80] Social welfare organizations turned to the courts. While they unsuccessfully filed suit against workfare, federal judges did block further cuts in Medicaid. Nonetheless, the new state restrictions significantly curtailed city efforts to support needy adults.[81]

Faced with an imperative to force welfare recipients into work, the drying up of federal anti-poverty funds, and rising demand, New York City chose a twofold strategy: moving their home care client load onto the federally subsidized Medicaid program and classifying the workers as independent contractors. As we have seen, the Home Attendant Program emerged after the labor troubles of the late 1960s as a separate service in order to access Medicaid funds. Social Services increasingly characterized it as medical, requiring applicants to obtain a plan of care prescribed by a physician. The agency contracted with two visiting nurse associations to provide medical evaluation and supervision. Finally, in 1973, the city obtained federal approval for Medicaid coverage of this program. Since Medicaid had no spending caps and paid 50 percent of the cost, the city began to transfer more and more of its elderly caseload to Home Attendant Service. To maintain that federal cost sharing, the city went to great lengths to insist that the job of home attendant was very different from that of a housekeeper—a fiction that workers themselves often refuted. As Brooklyn home care worker Elizabeth Johnson told Congressman Biaggi, "They say they have separate departments, one for home attendant and one for housekeeping, that they are different jobs, but that is not true because I am a home attendant and I do a housekeeper's job too."[82]

Simultaneously, New York City came up with a clever scheme to keep its War on Poverty initiatives on life support. It would transform anti-poverty community action agencies, stranded by Nixon's cuts of Office of Economic Opportunity (OEO) funding and loss of support for their original mission, into home care vendors. Taking advantage of connections to the unemployed and underemployed in New York's poor neighborhoods, the agencies would provide housekeepers for elderly and disabled public assistance recipients. They would form a new partnership with Social Services in the name of "economic development." Social Services would continue to certify eligibility, while the Housekeeper Vendor Program of the city assigned clients to vendors. In 1973, contracts went to nine vendors, who received hourly reimbursements (to cover overhead as well as wages) ranging between $3.12 and $7.50 at a time when it cost the city $8.72 an hour to provide its own homemakers. Community action agencies thereby became the new low-wage employers of women, particularly immigrants from the Caribbean, who did the work of the privatizing welfare state.[83]

The Nixon administration by now had shifted priorities decisively away from Great Society liberalism. With OEO already effectively strangled, it looked for other sources of federal welfare spending to end. Since executive reorganization of Health, Education, and Welfare (HEW), states and localities had drawn substantial increases in federal support through social services grants, funds with no mandated annual ceiling, which quadrupled between 1969 and 1972.[84] President Nixon moved to cap the open-ended federal match and place a tight ceiling on social service expenditures. As the politics of budget control hardened in the mid-1970s, the goal of ending dependency became explicitly hitched to cost cutting, budget control, and devolution. In September 1972, the Senate passed a $1.6 billion ceiling on such grants, panicking Mayor John Lindsay and his administrators, who had relied on these funds to pay for services for the elderly, but now faced at least $75 million less in reimbursement. The city could fund only services that directly supported "self-sufficiency," an imperative incorporated into Title XX of Social Security in 1974.[85] Thus, during the 1970s, when the city tried to move its long-term care burden to federal and state sources of payment, the federal and state governments constricted those funding streams and attempted to shift the responsibility for service provision back to localities. Each level of government relied on the casualization of service labor as a response to fiscal crisis.

Within these shifting political currents, Home Attendant Service became New York's major program for home care during the 1970s. The number of municipally employed homemakers, which peaked in 1972, began a precipitous drop, as the city assigned cases to Home Attendant Service or to the Housekeeping program instead. Home attendants did not have public employment; they were independent contractors. The Home Attendant caseload grew 231 percent between 1974 and 1978, when it stood at over 12,000 clients. Meanwhile, the market for vendor agencies and independent contractors expanded, and so too did complaints over inadequate housekeeping services.[86] Privatization actually was a strategic move by city government to expand a service by renaming and redefining it, thereby shifting costs to a new federal funding source, much as Reagan attempted in California.

In an effort to keep the workers at arms length as independent contractors or employees of vendors, Social Services refused to monitor the actual delivery of care. This strategy resulted in marked deterioration of both the conditions of labor and the care received. Clients found themselves with untrained, unprepared caretakers, who rapidly left. Abuse of workers, ranging from client demand to wash outside windows to physical harassment, followed from lack of precise job specifications. Neither the visiting nurses nor the city explained duties to attendants or clients. By design, home attendants received no employee benefits, workers' compensation, disability insurance, or unemployment insurance. There were no deductions for income tax or Social Security or payment for overtime.

Investigators repeatedly found that home attendants made less than the minimum wage. "The home attendant neither punches time clocks nor signs in," like the domestic of old.[87] No one knew how many hours the attendant worked because the client paid the worker from a check made out to both worker and client. If the patient was fully incapacitated, the worker could not cash such checks on her own. As Elizabeth Johnson explained, "There is one basic complaint that we keep saying over and over again and that is the two-party check system."[88]

Thousands of home attendants never even received their pay. The Home Attendant Program underwent several audits between 1974 and 1978, each of which discovered mounting, and often egregious, problems for both workers and clients. Every audit, whether conducted by a public or private agency, found numerous payment errors. Elderly and disabled clients dipped into their own SSI checks to help out attendants, who waited weeks or even months for their wages. Edna Walch, an immigrant from Guyana who cared for an elderly woman in Queens, received no pay for five months; nor was she an exception. Provision of carfare and meal money to home attendants was sporadic. Some attendants hid the fact that they had to apply for public assistance.[89] Attendant Maria Frederique explained her dilemma, testifying to Biaggi's Committee on Aging, "I wait for the check and the check no come . . . but I have to get paid. I have to take a bus, I have to take a train . . . I have my children. They have to eat. I have to pay rent. In a way, it is better to live on welfare. . . ."[90]

The Housekeeper vendors also took advantage of their reimbursements and the emotional ties of caring labor. As part of their deal with Social Services, the anti-poverty community agencies could use any surplus or profits made from the vendor contract for other "anti-poverty" programs in the neighborhood. These monies ended up going into everything from a fast food restaurant (to "provide jobs") to dinner dances and neighborhood Christmas parties. Meanwhile, sometimes housekeepers received no paychecks at all. Yet they were unwilling to abandon clients.[91] Mrs. Johnson reflected the sentiments of other women when she said that despite not receiving her wages, "I did continue to work because this lady needed this help. . . . I took care of my mother and so I know what agony that lady was going through."[92]

In this new climate of fiscal retrenchment, some of New York's older charitable agencies struggled to stay afloat and keep their services going—and to avoid doing so at the expense of care providers. Henry Street Settlement House, whose roots stretched back to the Progressive Era, represented one of the better vendors. Federal and state funds for job training and social services had allowed the venerable institution to adapt its mission to meet the needs of new groups settling on the Lower East Side.[93] Henry Street converted its Good Companion friendly visitor program into a Department of Social Services housekeeping aide project in which it hired, trained, and supervised workers on the basis of a set reimbursement. It became one of the first organizations to sign a contract with the city, specifying at least minimum wage plus carfare. Social Services' contract with the Settlement clearly stated that "such employees are not City staff nor do they any enjoy Civil Service status or protection." Henry Street therefore put housekeepers on its staff. As employees, they became eligible for Social Security, workers' compensation, and disability insurance.[94] Reflecting the Settlement's community action approach and links to Mobilization for Youth, manpower director Miguel Rios urged housekeepers, who numbered 200 by 1973, to organize and represent themselves.[95]

Soon they formed their own Association of Housekeepers in June 1973. "We organized because we want a pay increase, medical coverage, carfare, and other benefits," explained Florence Rivera, Sophie Feld, Priscilla Ramirez, Carmen Rodriquez, and Margarita Riveras. "We like Henry Street and we feel a loyalty to it. Some of us have been here many years and we feel close to the clients and the staff," they declared, but they were tempted to join others who had gone to work for vendor programs that provided desired benefits and monthly meetings to discuss problems.[96] Workers understood that higher wages depended on upping the reimbursement rate received from the city, and so they directed their pressure at the city government for an increased hourly rate. Within a year, they were not alone in this effort. The community agency vendors organized as the Association of Neighborhood Services Vendors. Although Henry Street did not join, it sent a representative to meetings and benefited from the Association gaining a better contract with the city in 1974.[97]

Settlement staff responded sympathetically to the Association of Housekeepers; they may have encouraged its efforts. By mid-decade, Henry Street managed to increase pay rates for more experienced workers, provide a job ladder, offer additional carfare, extend more generous benefits to workers with at least 20 hours a week, and protect the employment status of those who had to interrupt work due to illness.[98] The organization of care work through Henry Street, though, reflected its unique history: long-standing ties to New York labor, social democratic politics, and the War on Poverty's more participatory strains.

New York's disability rights movement also attempted to navigate the often opaque system of home care and, as in California, proffer a more consumer-responsive mode of organizing attendant services. Its disability activists gained national attention during a sit-in at Nixon's reelection headquarters to protest his veto of the 1972 Rehabilitation Act. Influenced by the civil rights and women's movements, savvy young adults formed Disabled in Action in the early 1970s to protest restrictions on their mobility and to join people with different disabilities into one activist organization. Although the presence in New York of strong national organizations, like the National Paraplegic Foundation, made the founding of disability centers less of a grassroots effort than in Berkeley, here too activists generated networks through college campuses.[99]

As students cohered into a disability community in the 1970s, they sought greater control over attendant services. They helped individuals manage interactions with both agencies and attendants, including sensitive issues, like the right of clients to have a sex life despite the presence of a 24-hour attendant.[100] They formed their own centers to provide referrals for home attendant/personal assistants "because in New York City, at that time, that was a mess," leading activist Patricio Figueroa remembered.[101] Some of the centers obtained contracts from the city. Denise McQuade, who went on to work for Independent Living for the Handicapped in Brooklyn, underscored the New York situation when she recalled that "there were some scandals with the home care program that the city was running. Also, the unions were trying to organize the workers. So, what they decided to do—the city, not to have them working directly for them—was to offer contracts to nonprofit agencies to run home care programs."[102] Not only did consumers and workers lack any control within the system; the city lost control over it as well.

By 1975–1976, the chaos of Home Attendant Service had become mired in the general fiscal crisis that shook the whole city of New York. With over $12 billion in debt, the private capital markets refused to lend New York any money in the spring of 1975. When city officials appealed to the federal government for aid, President Gerald Ford and his treasury secretary turned them down. The bankers and financial community pressed the mayor for a major austerity program and looked to the governor and state legislature to give them reins over the situation. Politicians obliged, creating the Municipal Assistance Corporation, known as "Big MAC," staffed by bankers, brokers, and business leaders. In return for lending the city money, MAC gained enormous leverage over city affairs. Under its pressure, Mayor Abe Beame implemented an austerity budget in the summer of 1975: wage freezes, layoffs, closing of hospitals and library branches, cutbacks in city services, and, for the first time, tuition at the City University of New York. The city reopened union contracts and scaled down wages. In the fall, the governor and his financial team went further, establishing an Emergency Financial Control Board (EFCB) that gained control over all city revenue and had broad powers to reject city spending and labor contracts.[103]

For the bankers and EFCB, the solution to New York's woes seemed simple and straightforward: reduce the municipal workforce and privatize city services. Masking the impact of risky lending practices on the fiscal crisis, bankers blamed it all on greedy unions and indulgent social policies. Cut those and New York City would be on its way to recovery. So the city laid off employees and shrunk agency budgets. Consequently, services only worsened, clearly apparent with the Home Attendant Program, which by the end of 1976 was a full-blown disaster. No one in the newly named Human Resources Administration (HRA) could even figure out how to get a handle on it. As the caseload ballooned during 1977, HRA slashed reimbursements, laid off caseworkers, and failed to pay thousands of home attendants. Attendants flooded HRA with complaints. Faced with eviction or utility shut off notices, increasingly desperate home attendants, some unpaid for two or three months, called the mayor's office. Yet when his office tried to find out what was happening over at HRA, "all inquiries are met with the response of 'inadequate staff.'" In short, "everyone passes the buck."[104]

Top HRA officials acknowledged lack of both staff and full-time management as part of the problem. Yet how the agency chose to run the program—with as little government responsibility as possible—worsened the situation. It added thousands of clients yearly, but without systematic planning or accountability. An HRA spokesman acknowledged that "the program grew faster than we expected." Officials were unsure how many home attendants worked for their clients, with one estimating 11,000–13,000 attendants, another reporting 14,000, while yet another claiming 20,000–22,000. Moreover, they rooted whatever haphazard monitoring there was in the racial stereotypes and gendered expectations of care work. Invoking the potential for fraud and abuse, HRA constantly compared the home attendant roster with public assistance rolls to make sure the women were not "welfare cheats." Inordinate check delays resulted from constant recertification of attendants each month. Admitted HRA: "We did not want people to use the program to get live-in maid service." Poor people obtained surveillance rather than entitlement to decent benefits.[105]

The Home Attendant Program expanded rapidly in part because nursing homes fell into disrepute. In early 1971, after closing 1,500 substandard nursing home beds, city administrators pushed home care "to insure the elderly can stay in their homes."[106] In the mid-1970s, despite public funding beyond $150 million a year, corruption and neglect stranded nursing home residents amid appalling conditions. Discrimination systematically placed black and poor people in homes with the worst conditions. After a *New York Times* investigative series exposed widespread horror in 1974, newly elected Governor Hugh Carey appointed a special investigative commission headed by future Governor Mario Cuomo. In January 1975, Cuomo recommended criminal prosecution of nursing home operators. Clearly, no one wanted to see their relatives placed in nursing homes; deinstitutionalization became a political imperative.[107]

New York's legislature responded to the crisis in long-term care with a home care mandate. In August 1977, it passed a home care services act, prioritizing the provision of quality home care as "a viable part of the health care system" and "an alternative to institutional care." A "certified home health agency" had to dispense the service.[108] The bill's sponsors insisted that home care would bring significant savings for the state and localities. They expected to cap monthly state expenditures at 75 percent of the average rate paid to nursing homes. Given that home care primarily consisted of labor costs, the resolution to the fiscal crisis and crisis of care would be ensured through state-enforced, low-wage labor.[109]

The home care mandate could not have come at a more difficult time for New York City. Newspaper, municipal, and congressional investigations already had targeted its home care programs. The State Assembly's Labor Committee and Secretary of State Mario Cuomo's office were taking a closer look. HRA responded by proposing vendorization of the home care program, which it believed would allow the city to relinquish administrative functions. Throughout 1977, HRA management consistently discussed vendorization beyond the community agencies, accompanied by Taylorization of the labor. At the same time, it remained dubious that vendorization actually saved any money. One internal study even found that per case expenses would almost double, increasing the cost of the total program by $40–$50 million. HRA noted with concern that it already lacked the staff or capacity to administer, monitor, and evaluate even the existing housekeeping contracts, of which its audits had found more than $1.5 million in misspent funds.[110] It had not paid some vendors for five months. HRA managers concluded, "Further expansion of vendorization will increase the severity of this problem."[111] Nor did contracting out to for-profit agencies translate into better outcomes, for after setting the rate, it found, "service levels would drop."[112] Still, with New York under siege by the financial community, further privatization of the service seemed to be the only remedy on the table—thus leading to further casualization of the labor. Reduction of home attendant hours was the other solution that HRA repeatedly offered: home attendants would just have to get more tasks of daily care done more efficiently in less time.[113]

Moreover, the new Koch administration, eager to prove its toughness on government waste and fraud, invoked a harsh anti-welfarism that steered the Democratic Party toward neoliberalism. Pepper and Biaggi's 1978 hearing was meant to uncover the problems in New York's program, so they could move forward with a more effective, universal entitlement at the national level. Instead, New York City officials pledged to end the era of "the rip-off": flush out the cheats, reduce eligibility for home care, implement "careful surveillance," and reduce the rates paid. When New York State officials urged the city to get its house in order by placing home care service and workers once again fully under public auspices, Koch and HRA Commissioner Bernstein looked the other way—toward privatization. Such political confrontations over care exposed the fissures in liberalism and the Democratic Party.[114]

"I Am Not a Slave": Workers' Response to Casualization

Despite these discussions, HRA did not move to vendorize the Home Attendant Program until workers started organizing and demanding union recognition. Privatization came not at the height of New York's fiscal crisis, but rather a few years later, in response to an uprising of poor black and Latina women. Tired of "working for slave wages" and being treated like servants, these women started to walk off the job and fight back.[115] Home care became embroiled in the racial politics of the city.

Fledgling union movements first began among housekeepers working for HRA vendor agencies. During August 1977, a grassroots organizing effort emerged in the South Bronx district of State Assemblyman Seymour Posner, a former social worker and AFSCME member, who had recently led the campaign to pass a collective bargaining law for household employees.[116] Disgruntled home care workers, unpaid for weeks, demanded restitution from the Morrisania Community Corporation, an anti-poverty agency turned vendor.[117] "A lot of times because you're peaceful they don't want to listen to you. So you have to do something in a demanding way to them [so they] know that we're serious. Because we're women don't mean that we shouldn't have rights and shouldn't fight for what we believe," recounted one of the housekeepers.[118] With guidance from La Raza Unida and its organizer Ramon Jimenez, a core group of African American, Afro-Caribbean, and Puerto Rican women, led by former clerical employee Alyssa Torrez, organized a union. Nearly the entire workforce of 217 turned in union pledge cards.[119]

Whether the exploitation originated with the city or the vendor, the housekeepers moved toward collective action. Elizabeth Johnson, who attended weekly meetings in her public housing complex with other home care workers, joined a group of women "trying to get some ladies together to get a union for us so that we can get benefits and have somebody to represent us." Together they went to HRA to complain about delayed payments, but only received "a big run around. . . ." As she recounted, they learned it was "a political baseball game" and therefore they'd have to take their fight to that terrain. Women holding their ground and remaining in the HRA offices became a common sight. Not only did workers journey there for fair hearings to recover money never received through bureaucratic snafus, but they increasingly came to protest.[120] Guards would physically remove them.[121] Finally, in October 1977, Morrisania housekeepers refused to leave a meeting with administrators until promised that they would receive earnings withheld by the community agency.[122]

The city certainly had mismanaged its home care programs, but scandal equally enveloped some of the vendors. Morrisania stood as a major culprit. The corporation, with 400 employees and a $3.7 million budget, faced a federal probe for improper use of its facilities for partisan political activities.[123] The feds investigated Chairman Hubert Irons Jr. for forcing staff to work on his failed bid for an Assembly seat, while an HRA audit found the corporation's real profit to be double its reported one.[124] Charges of corruption, especially use of monies for politics, long had plagued community development under the War on Poverty, with some activists caught appropriating government funding for other than designated purposes and even for personal gain. The consequence of opponents scrutinizing the books of anti-poverty agencies, however, was ideological as well as political: to undermine confidence in such agencies and discredit government assistance and black self-determination.[125] It also made it harder for Democratic liberals, like Pepper, Biaggi, and Maine's Edmund Muskie, to pursue legislation at the federal level.

To fight back, the Morrisania women accepted the help of the Teamsters, the union most visibly trying to unionize home care. Teamsters Local 854 began signing up home care workers in Queens and in June had organized 200 housekeepers with Social Concerns, Inc., another anti-poverty Community Development Agency, though they lost the NLRB election there.[126] On October 24, women started picketing Morrisania. They chanted, "We want equal rights! We want a union!" demanding to see Chairman Irons, who had refused to meet with them.[127] "My clients are in full support of this work stoppage," Francine Beale let one local reporter know. Because only poor elderly and disabled people were being inconvenienced, "the fact that 200 minority women went on strike instead of on welfare hasn't received much media attention," charged feminist writer Janice Prindle in the *Village Voice*. Indeed, the *New York Times* failed to carry any stories on the walkout.[128]

Prindle cast the strike as an "attack on antipoverty pimpdom," that is, the use of public monies by poverty administrators for personal gain. She further viewed the walkout through a feminist lens. The strike was demanding "that housework, the only job that has always been women's domain, must command wages and benefits comparable to those in equally unskilled but more physically demanding male occupations."[129] The phrase "antipoverty pimpdom," despite its use to distinguish housekeepers from those who profited from their labor, fed into the coded racism of opponents of African American political power. Thus the newly elected mayor Ed Koch would respond to "Home Care Abuse" by declaring, "we're not going to allow the poverty pimps to rip us off any more."[130] Indignantly, Irons dug in his heels, resisting the attacks from all sides.

When Morrisania continued to forestall unionization, the housekeepers took over the corporation offices on November 2, the night of the monthly board meeting, and addressed the full board for the first time. While the women and their allies waited outside the room, board members attacked their chairman for withholding information. "There's definitely an accountability factor," one board member told the press. "Most of the board comes from the community. While most sympathize with the demands, they also didn't want to face a lot of angry community women." Fearing a general community backlash, the board voted for an election to certify a union.[131]

Meanwhile, political leaders at every level of government looked into the situation. Assemblyman Posner, who chaired the Labor Committee, initiated an investigation into the financial practices of the vendors. He subpoenaed 23 vendors to hand over their records. Posner walked the picket line with the women. Secretary of State Cuomo pointed out the systemic issue that the home care agencies shared with the scandal-tarnished nursing homes: "The basic problems involve the concept of 'vendorization' of these programs and the lack of adequate controls and monitoring devices."[132]

Morrisania women won recognition after an eight-day strike, but the Teamsters' commitment to home care workers soon withered. Used to bullying private businesses, this unsavory union floundered when faced with state intransigence. The city made it clear that it would not release additional funds for any meaningful contract. Caught off guard by the difficulty of representing the social service sector, the Teamsters backed away. Rather than negotiate with workers, the city terminated its contract with Morrisania in early July 1978 and reassigned the women to two Manhattan agencies.[133]

The problem was both structural and cultural. The vendor shell game inhibited social movements from winning a seat at the table and obtaining accountability. In addition, the Teamsters lacked the social movement culture, civil rights heritage, community connections, and familiarity with human services that would prove essential for organizing women still generally described as domestic workers. Shaped by private sector bargaining, they lacked experience negotiating with public agencies; neither did they understand public employment nor care work. But they had shown New York's municipal and health care unions that poor women of color doing household labor were organizable. Other unions began listening to these workers. As an AFSCME official told the *Daily News*, "It's not if they can organize, it is how they should do it."[134]

Contracting Out in California

What happened at the San Francisco Home Health Service suggests an alternative scenario: unionization and vendorization could work together. Founded in 1957 by Junior Leaguers and social planners to provide homemaker service to the elderly, this private service agency followed the shift of other nonprofits to home health amid the Great Society. Its workforce also consisted of older African American women who had labored as domestics and in nursing homes, with three-quarters of them drawn from the welfare rolls.[135] When the AIDS epidemic hit, it recruited men. This high-minded group instigated SEIU's first home care organizing as part of the politics of vendorization in the City by the Bay, which like New York sought to meet increased demand through contracting out homemaker/chore positions rather than augmenting its civil service workforce.[136]

Informed by an enlightened maternalism, the founders recognized the value of women's work, paying as much as the agency could and providing uniforms, health and disability insurance, Social Security, and other benefits. Through education and training, they sought to counter the maid association. Executive director Hadley D. Hall, a social work professional, defended the labor as not "just housework," but rather the necessary creation of "a hygienic environment" by trained and supervised providers whose labor would keep people out of expensive and dehumanizing institutions. The agency initiated career ladders, moving those with aptitude to white-collar jobs, and paid some employees to attend school. A homemaker representative served on the Board of Directors.[137] The WPA could have written its manual of dos and don'ts when it came to instructions on tasks, behavior, and appearance.[138] Indeed, the agency claimed to have transformed those on public assistance into "taxpayers" while "prevent[ing] abuses in the homes of the disabled and homebound."[139]

The San Francisco agency, however, lacked the political influence to wrestle higher reimbursement rates from the city. In the late 1960s, Hall asked Timothy Twomey, leader of SEIU 250, the Hospital and Allied Workers Union, to organize his employees as a way to make headway with elected officials in this union town. Hall facilitated the campaign by leaving the employment roster ("the list") on his desk for a union representative to take. The women—suspicious of the union from its mixed record with other low-wage health care workers and questioning the need for one in the first place—rejected affiliation. Eight months later, after Hall personally explained to them the situation with the city, SEIU won the revote "hands down."[140]

The presence of a well-organized and vocal independent living movement distinguished the process of privatization in California from that in New York. This movement gained legislative authorization for consumer choice of attendants through an independent provider organization of home care. That family members could become attendants further differentiated California from most states; it enabled families to use the service as a form of income support during a period when the federal establishment of SSI ideologically and administratively separated AFDC from disability and elder assistance. Like New York, California counties also contracted out housekeeping and aide services to private agencies, with similar problems of lack of regulation, charges of corruption, and inefficiency. Unionization would follow from, rather than spark, California's welfare wars.

By the late 1970s, the job of homemaker–home health aide remained on the lowest rungs of health care and service labor. Yet it had become essential to the privatizing welfare state. The legal determination that home care would be low-paid, low-cost, casual labor somehow reassured governments that herein lay the answer to several public welfare budget problems. Working conditions never deterred policy makers who sought to end women's "dependency" on public assistance. At the very same moment that investigations reported extensive labor violations in New York City's Home Attendant Program, public officials celebrated these jobs as "excellent employment opportunities for thousands of public assistance recipients who are able to work and thereby break their public assistance dependency with gainful employment."[141] Independence for the elderly continued to rest on the domestic labor and impoverishment of other poor women. But such government contracts eventually landed home care back in the public realm, setting off a new wave of struggle in the shifting boundaries of the welfare state, when home care workers themselves demanded, "Take us out of slavery," and Ronald Reagan moved into the White House.

Figure 5.1 "Take Us Out of Slavery," August 1979, "Union Seeks Collective Bargaining Rights for 20,000 Home Attendants," *SEIU 32B-32J*, 47 (August-September 1979), 1. Photographer: Unknown. SEIU Collection, Wayne State University; Permission from SEIU International, Washington, DC.

5

"Take Us Out of Slavery"

In September 1979, nearly 1,000 New York home attendants gathered in front of City Hall Park to demand their rights as workers and as black women. With many dressed in the white uniforms of nurses or maids, they wore caps emblazoned with "Local 32B-32J." Working on their own, they had been caring for the clients of New York's Division of Home Attendant Service. Funded through federal, state, and city money, the workers still were denied the basic labor rights extended to other workers. Chanting "We want SEIU now," they marched with signs that announced, "Home Attendants Are People Too," and urged, "Stop Denying Our Right to Vote." The placard "Take Us Out of Slavery" most powerfully situated their campaign for union recognition in the long history of the African American freedom struggle and its demand for human rights.[1]

Within a few years, New York home attendants built a new union local, although they were not granted the status of city employee. Their union therefore had to take shape at the interstices of a range of jobs associated with care work: cleaning, hospital support and housekeeping, nursing home and institutional care. Their union tapped the organizing experience, staff, resources, and government relationships of unions in building services, nursing homes, and public-sector hospitals.

Organizing among home care workers drew on an additional wellspring during the 1970s: a new movement among domestic workers. Emerging from different institutional, ideological, and geographical bases, this movement blended the self-help and self-improvement orientation long present in women's reform organizations with a professionalizing impulse also characteristic of earlier efforts to transform private household labor. It combined political organizing to win legal rights, especially inclusion under the nation's primary wage and hour law, the Fair Labor Standards Act (FLSA); and collective organizing to win some means of leverage vis-à-vis the household employer or over the isolated workplace. Initially, most of these organizations never intended to be trade unions. Yet some of the rising leaders of the 1970s, such as Edith Barksdale-Sloan, saw the limits of professionalism and a voluntary code of standards. These strategies could not tip the larger scales of inequality, particularly if the household remained unrecognized and devalued as a work site. Household workers needed a larger strategy that could link home-based labor with the growing service and care work economy.

The decline of manufacturing, job loss, and an enervated industrial unionism dominate the story of labor in the 1970s. These narratives define the working class as male, white, and industrial. Yet to understand transformations in the American economy, and the labor movement, we must consider the service sector, where jobs were expanding.[2] While stagnation characterized the manufacturing economy, jobs classified as "medical and other health services" steadily grew through the sluggish years of 1970–1971, and the recession years of 1974–1976. The robust service sector unions of SEIU, American Federation of State, County, and Municipal Employees (AFSCME), 1199 hospital employees, and American Federation of Teachers sought to organize the vast new multiracial and female working class. The 1970s were a decade of privatization, when the states increasingly contracted their responsibility for social welfare to private agencies. Organizing home care under such circumstances was difficult, but gained momentum from the sixties-style community unionism of farm workers and other low-waged laborers, as well as the militant spirit of the public sector.

As invisible as home care workers appeared, they proved more traceable than domestics employed by individual families. So when unions went to organize domestics, they found home attendants instead. Women of color and immigrants predominated in the home care workforce, as they did the personnel in public or nonprofit service sectors, particularly hospitals, nursing homes, welfare agencies, and other city bureaucracies. New York and other states deployed the title of "home attendant" to emphasize personal assistance given to adults but also to distinguish Medicaid-funded positions from similar jobs administrated differently. The state location of payment for the labor generated a trail for organizing, once unions untangled the bureaucratic maze that developed during the Johnson and Nixon years.

In the late 1970s, SEIU launched an organizing campaign for household workers in New York City; at about the same time, community organizers in San Diego, inspired by the United Farm Workers, began a union for domestics. Both groups found their constituency among home care workers. Hospital unions further discovered housekeeping and health aides doing the same tasks as their members during weekends or evenings, but in the private setting of the home, and they too began to organize such workers. Whether defined as a domestic, aide, or attendant, whether laboring for a hospital, family, nonprofit agency, or a government department, women were becoming fed up with their wages and working conditions in the emerging care work economy. The militancy of African American, Caribbean, and Latina women proved central for the transformation of household workers into unionized home attendants.

This powerful self-organization and movement transformation would become ensnared within a national labor law unwilling to recognize the overlapping tasks of caring labor for the body and the home, for strangers and family members. After 1975, home care workers found themselves excluded again from the FLSA, and thus every subsequent organizing campaign had to prove not only majority support among employees but also the very legitimacy of the job as one worthy of worker rights.

Transformations in Household Labor

Home care emerged as a distinct occupation not only from the expansion of health care and social welfare services, as we have seen, but also from the restructuring of the market for domestic labor. By the 1960s, a combination of demographic, economic, and political forces led to a reorganization of household employment. Domestics not only "lived out," as they had since the 1920s, but increasingly had to patch together a series of day jobs because of the shifts taking place in middle-class life. The rising labor force participation of married women, along with the jump in elders living longer and alone, ratcheted up the demand for paid household labor, while the overall time spent by women on their own housework declined. Even if some cleaning and cooking left private residences for laundries, restaurants, and other commercial venues, the home remained the preferred location for care of dependents, whether infants or frail elderly.[3] Additionally, more specialized jobs—like child or elder care aide, party caterer, and apartment cleaner—emerged. New temporary work services supplied both maids and home aides. In time, some of these evolved into home care agencies.[4]

The demand for household services may have expanded, but women still left paid housework whenever they could because of the exploitative wages, irregular hours, and servile status found there. Between 1960 and 1970, at least a million women "threw down their scrub brushes, took off their aprons and quit," claimed Edith Barksdale-Sloan, executive director of the National Committee on Household Employment, before a 1971 convention of over 500 household workers. The "official count" of domestics stood at 1.5 million workers, with estimates suggesting double that number actually earned their keep through household labor. Their profile matched that of the home aide: over 90 percent of these were women; a majority, African American. Most women were middle-aged with less than a high school education; a quarter of a million headed families. They earned only three-quarters as much as the $2,400 a year guaranteed income proposed by President Richard Nixon to replace Aid to Families with Dependent Children (AFDC), which welfare rights activists protested as too meager.[5] In subsequent decades, as civil rights initiatives opened new employment to

African Americans, renewed immigration meant that women from Latin America, Asia, and Eastern Europe would undertake housework, especially outside the South.[6]

Attempting to shape these changes were labor feminists, notably the current and former Women's Bureau directors Esther Peterson and Frieda Miller; prominent women's organizations, like the national councils of Negro, Jewish, and Catholic women; and national public welfare, home economics, and nursing associations. Like their counterparts in the 1930s, these groups sought "to reconstitute household service as a dignified and responsible occupation." In 1963, the President's Commission on the Status of Women, under Peterson and her allies, asked employers of domestics to abide by labor standards and employees to improve skills and display "responsible work attitudes." True to its roots in the old social welfare network, the Commission also recommended more widespread provision of homemaker services.[7]

In the mid-1960s, with the support of Dorothy Height and the National Council of Negro Women, the Women's Bureau sparked the revival of the 1930s National Committee on Household Employment (NCHE) as a nonprofit corporation to coordinate the efforts of all groups concerned with domestic service. NCHE's first activities reflected the liberal and laborite women in government and the professions, who were mostly white and employers of household labor. In the long tradition of women's reform, NCHE gathered information, publicized conditions, and educated the public.[8] It promoted a voluntary code of standards with provisions for minimum wages, overtime, Social Security, sick leave, vacations, paid holidays, and a "professional" working relationship.[9] Changing the name of the occupation to "household technician" further appeared as a way to dignify the labor, as did more specialized jobs, like that of the home attendant.[10]

Through government and private grants, prominently from the Ford Foundation, NCHE developed demonstration projects, training programs, handbooks, and experimental minority-owned businesses and cooperatives. Under a multiyear federal Manpower training contract awarded in 1966, it ran eight pilot projects, each of which offered a road toward "modernization." NCHE partnered with local groups, including the YWCA in Chicago, the Urban League in Northern Virginia, a business firm in New York, a nonprofit household association in Philadelphia, and the Women's Service Club in Boston.[11] No self-sustaining businesses emerged from these projects, though most met their training and educational goals and improved wages and conditions for participants.[12] Some workers gained individual empowerment. "For the first time in my life," one Philadelphia woman admitted, "I feel like a first-class American citizen. I am paying my Social Security and I am trained for my job. I am making a living wage and I am treated like a human being on my job." As NCHE leaders put it, "self-dependency" was replacing public assistance—a goal that labor feminists shared with the War on Poverty.[13]

As NCHE sought to position itself as the gatekeeper for household labor, it saw these jobs begin to move from the margins into the growing web of the service economy. Promoting home care as an alternative to day work, it offered to help local welfare and health departments and state employment services to certify assistants for elder care.[14] Along with the National Council for Homemaker–Home Health Aide Services, the Public Health Service, and the Children's Bureau, it prepared training curriculums that included sections on the care of children, the elderly, and ill people.[15] NCHE took particular pride in "minority" businesses like Capitol Hill Homemaker and Health Aid Services, Inc., a Washington, D.C., service rescued from bankruptcy in 1976 by trained medical technician and Howard University graduate Loretta Hurley. With a contract for over $600,000 from the District's Department of Human Resources and a staff of 150, Hurley provided skilled nursing, home health aid, nutrition counseling, and various forms of therapy, child care, live-in, home management, and cleaning services to hundreds of the District's elderly and disabled residents.[16] Hurley's business represented the spectrum of the burgeoning care work economy.

One Manpower-funded homemaker project further illuminates the use of home care to upgrade domestic labor. Run by the Department of Family Economics at Kansas State University between 1968 and 1970, the Homemaker Service Demonstration Project consisted of a series of month-long courses in a residential setting that combined classroom and laboratory work with a week-long field placement. During the two years of the program, homemaker service grew in Kansas from 13 to 64 providers, consisting of state and county departments, welfare offices, volunteer agencies, model cities programs, and a housing project.[17]

Despite rural origins, the Kansas recruits resembled participants in other projects and in the overall domestic labor force, except that nearly three-quarters were white. Some trainees were on welfare; others were under- or unemployed; about half were married and over half had completed high school.[18] Reporting on its outcome, the Project showcased responses of training program graduates. "I'm having the time of my life," one woman reflected, ". . . Of course, I do more housework than what I realize I should, but it is really satisfying to help people." Another white graduate remarked, "I'm proud to be a paraprofessional now."[19] Like other training programs, the goal was as much to transform the worker as to improve their role as housewives.

By the time its original pilot projects ended, NCHE had emerged as a black feminist organization. Its new leader, Edith Barksdale-Sloan, recognized the political gains for poor women from a multiracial organization under black women's leadership. A graduate of Hunter College and a former Peace Corps volunteer,

Barksdale-Sloan previously worked for the U.S. Commission on Civil Rights and would finish a law degree during her NCHE tenure. Hired in 1969, she once narrated the NCHE trajectory as a move from "employers (who wanted 'better' maids)" and a "program . . . to train welfare mothers and make them economically independent" to a membership of domestics dedicated to "winning good wages and benefits, raising consciousness and educating consumers of domestic services." While the national women's organizations remained on the Board of Directors, NCHE local affiliates consisted of women who intersected with the more militant National Welfare Rights Organization. Both groups shared similar black feminist and class perspectives, and faced internal divisions from their mixture of middle-class and poor staffers and board members.[20] A fierce champion of the dignity and rights of household laborers, Barksdale-Sloan insisted on equal treatment for black women in politics, no less than the workplace. When a White House meeting of national women's organizations in 1974 only included the middle-class National Council of Negro Women, she lectured President Ford: "We who are poor, poor Black and Spanish surnamed and Native and Asian American and female deserve to have our representatives consulted and our views heard also. Upper and Middle Class white women do not speak for us."[21]

Consequently, Barksdale-Sloan moved beyond the tactics of the earlier era, pointing toward self-organization that looked more like union organizing. In 1972, the NCHE helped create the Household Technicians of America. It assisted local worker associations, pushed for coverage of domestics under the FLSA and enforcement of labor laws, and fought for more aggressive responses to the worsening economic conditions of the 1970s. In 1974, the year that Congress included domestics in the wage and hour law, local worker associations reached a high point of 37, with 25,000 members.[22] Moreover, NCHE aimed at organizing the proliferating care work economy. Its 1977 "Practical Workers' Congress: Strategies for Greater Opportunity and Respect" attempted to bring together those who toiled in homes, hospitals, restaurants, hotels, and buildings with unions, women's groups, and civil rights organizations.[23]

Ultimately, since they were not embraced as workers or allies by the mainstream labor movement, NCHE had to rely on the unpredictable generosity of foundations and government grants. Nor did NCHE have many feminist allies. Unable to change the traditional expectations of deference and the arbitrariness of informal household jobs, Barksdale-Sloan could not sustain NCHE as an independent organization. Nor could she or her coworkers maintain the fledgling domestic worker associations and unions that NCHE had helped foster in an attempt to alter the nature of the employment relationship. In 1977, NCHE became a minor project of the National Urban League, at a time when such mainstream civil rights groups were faltering.[24] NCHE did have a measurable long-term impact by leading the campaign to amend the FLSA. Through coalition politics, it overturned a major injustice: the exclusion of domestics from the nation's bedrock labor law. Yet accompanying that victory was a new exclusion that applied to the most rapidly growing field of household labor: home health care.

(Un)Defined by the Law

The conflation of homemakers, housekeepers, and home attendants with family labor long reinforced a subordinate legal status. Courts judged such work as impossible to regulate because of its location in the private realm of the home. Despite European precedents, the formulators of Social Security in 1935 believed that administrative problems precluded coverage of domestics. Even more forcefully, the lack of powerful advocates, the racialism of New Dealers, and Roosevelt's dependence on Southern Congressional votes kept domestic workers outside the new labor laws. Professional women also had a vested interest in a cheap supply of servants. Most housewives never viewed themselves as employers; middle-class activists among them thwarted any inspection of their homes for violations of labor standards.[25] Moreover, Congress disassociated home labor with employment; those with "full-time housekeeping responsibilities," that is, housewives, gained no right to a job, for example, under the proposed Full Employment Act of 1946.[26]

Over the next decade, some liberal officials began to argue for Social Security coverage of domestics, if only to keep them off the welfare rolls. In 1949, Social Security Commissioner Arthur Altmeyer saw inclusion of domestics under Old Age Social Insurance as relieving dependency, thus reducing the cost of public assistance when they could no longer labor.[27] Extrapolating from the numbers of domestics on relief during the Depression, the Women's Bureau also warned of future welfare needs, while Secretary of Labor Lewis B. Schwellenbach noted that domestics, when working at other jobs, often paid into the system yet were unable to fully access benefits for technical reasons. Fairness required their inclusion.[28]

Unions and liberal allies, including many national women's organizations, strongly argued for extending Social Security to household employees based on social rights.[29] The U.S. Women's Bureau directly connected the worth of such labor to the provision of "socially worth-while services" for homes, families, and communities, such as "[y]oung mothers who need help to give proper care to little children, old folks who can continue to maintain their homes if some of the heavy work is done for them, and homes where sickness creates a serious problem."[30] Linking welfare services and domestic labor, Bureau Chief Frieda Miller attempted to revalue both public assistance, the second fiddle to old age insurance under Social Security, and home labor, presumably an outmoded form of production further degraded through racial stigma. In 1950 and 1954, some domestic workers gained Social Security eligibility.[31]

Obtaining coverage under the FLSA proved more difficult. During the 1960s, agricultural, nursing home, and many retail workers came under the federal wage and hour law; yet, by 1972, only Wisconsin, Massachusetts, and New York included domestics in state minimum wage laws.[32] At a time when welfare rolls were rising, supporters still insisted that rewarding those who worked full-time with a floor under their wages would reduce reliance on public assistance. Congress resisted these arguments for ideological and political reasons. Most in Congress could not accept such labor as work, on par with other paid employment, and thus prolonged the political work of inclusion.[33] Moreover, with a stalled economy and rising inflation in the early 1970s, Congress could easily be convinced that raising wages—especially in sectors where there was little organized pressure to do so—would just fuel the fire of inflation.

Claiming housework as real work and struggling against discrimination in the employment of women, feminists cleared the way for finally placing domestic work in the labor law. Middle-class professional women allied with civil rights and trade unionists to fight for expanding the law's coverage.[34] Citing rising demand for such labor, including homemakers for the elderly, Barksdale-Sloan testified that decent wages would bring more skilled, self-respecting workers to "a demanding occupation requiring a variety of skills," human no less than technical.[35]

In 1974, two years after professional women came under the FLSA, Congress finally included private household workers in the wage and hour law in one of the largest legislative expansions of FLSA. New York City representatives and leading feminists Shirley Chisholm and Bella Abzug called for the valuing of household labor, and they were not alone. Senator Harrison Williams (D-NJ) noted, "The lack of respect accorded domestics is in many ways an unfortunate reflection of the value we placd [*sic*] on the traditional role of women in our society." Williams headed the Labor and Education Committee, and he skillfully steered the amendments through the Senate in order to end the persistent treatment of domestics as "slaves."[36] Workers in nursing homes also became eligible for overtime pay. But at this moment of triumph—a critical civil rights gain for women of color—those doing the same care work in individual homes were left out.[37]

We know how home care came to be excluded from the FLSA, but no direct evidence exists to answer why. We surmise that the answer is partly ideological, partly what social scientists have called "path dependence," and partly organized opposition by business to push back labor's gains. Policy choices made in earlier eras can channel how legislators acted in subsequent reform moments. It might be that senators thought of home care as belonging to the policy realms of welfare, poverty, health, and aging. Consequently, they were used to thinking about the recipients, rather than the providers, of care. Senator Williams, long a champion of worker rights, was well aware of the need for home aides. In the early 1970s, he supported the extension of Medicare coverage for non-medical home care. Disability militant Judy Heumann joined his staff a few years later. While stressing the plight of "frail individuals" and monetary savings from shorter hospital stays, he ignored the home care aide, however, who appeared as a means for the betterment of others rather than as a subject in her own right.[38]

A definitional ruse ultimately reduced the home aide to an elder companion, but again this took place in the context of existing policies. Other social programs helped generate the perception that a home care worker was merely a friendly visitor. Responding to activism around the 1971 White House Conference on Aging, Nixon initiated the Senior Companion Program, which offered opportunities for those age 60 and older to assist the "homebound."[39] Some social welfare groups sponsored elder companion programs to supplement homemaker–home health aide services, especially given the agencies' often meager funding. Undertaking tasks associated with the home care worker, but under the rubric of volunteering, these initiatives obscured the distinction between friendship and work that further devalued the skill involved, as had happened within Berkeley's independent living milieu.[40] There was no denying that, at its best, companionship was part of the job. A home aide interviewed in the 1980s explained, "You're not just their worker, you're their friend. And if they didn't have you for a friend, they would just give up all together."[41]

The initial attempt to amend FLSA in 1971 exempted babysitters, a group of domestic employees with whom home attendants would become linked through analogy as elder sitters. In reporting on the bill, the Senate Committee on Labor and Public Welfare explicitly refused "to include within the terms 'domestic service' such activities as babysitting and acting as a companion." Williams linked the two by analogizing that "a babysitter is there . . . to watch the youngsters" and a "'companion,' as we mean it, is in the same role—to be there and to watch an older person."[42] The passive term "watch" implied that no real work was going on. The babysitter was the teenage girl next door, not a family breadwinner who needed higher wages to support others; so, too, the elder sitter was a friend or neighbor whom senators assumed would not be employed otherwise. Some child minders, though, were workers, and so the managers of the bill added "casual" to clarify the distinction between a teenage babysitter and a family breadwinner.[43] At precisely the time that federal funding was fanning the growth of home care, Congress either had not caught up to these developments or chose to ignore them.[44] Even the old excuse against coverage—difficulty of recordkeeping—persisted for "casual" babysitters and companions, including among those arguing for extension of the law to domestic servants.[45]

Some of the most vocal opponents of paying companions the minimum wage were well-organized trade associations and business interests who had long rejected the entire idea of the minimum wage and the New Deal welfare state. They couched their opposition in a mixture of sympathy for women and families and the racialized rhetoric of welfare fraud, but their vigilant stance here was part of a broader new offensive by conservative business interests across the board to push back any gains for labor. The Southern States Industrial Council, one of the most conservative and segregationist business associations, recruited members to testify. To counter the arguments for minimum wage, they projected inevitable family hardship for employees struggling to care for aging parents.[46] The National Restaurant Association presented its concern for their female employees, who would become responsible for paying minimum wages for child care.[47] Mothers could not afford to hire sitters, they noted, and thus they would be forced to leave the labor force, causing shortages in teaching, clerical work, and other female dominated fields.[48] At no time did employers of women workers suggest raising wages as a solution. As Barksdale-Sloan countered such arguments, "The relatively marginal wage of one group of workers is not a sound or just reason to legally allow them to pay less than the minimum set by law to persons whom they employ in their homes."[49] Although political economic power was shifting the other way, women like Barksdale-Sloan tried to resist the neoliberal project of ratcheting down workers' compensation and security.

Congress had begun amending the FLSA with the intent to expand its coverage, but when it came to home care workers, the opposite occurred. The final legislative language opened the way for administrative rule-making that removed this type of household labor from the law. Whether from outdated notions of the companion or downright ignorance about the maintenance of impaired individuals, Congress classified household chores such as "making lunch or throwing a diaper into the washing machine" as "incidental" rather than integral to the labor.[50] It was then up to the Department of Labor's Wage and Hour Division to draft the new regulations that would implement the FLSA amendments. After an open comment period, Wage and Hour issued its final ruling in February 1975, exempting elder companions from the newly extended FLSA coverage. What distinguished the companion from the domestic now was the amount of time spent in housework not directly related to care. If housework was incidental to the job, less than 20 percent of the workday, then the worker was a companion rather than a domestic and therefore outside the law. This formulation ignored the actual work of home care, which involved a range of household tasks that allowed the family or individual to function in a domestic environment.[51] The final rule excluded not only aides hired directly by a household but also those employed by hospitals and private health and social welfare agencies (referred to as "third parties") previously covered under the law.[52] Wage and Hour offered no explanation for changing the status of home care workers.

But were home care workers even employees? For over a decade, they had faced classification as independent contractors. Public agencies not only acted as though the job was casual; they constantly sought to obscure their own role as employers. Despite footing the bill, organizing the service, and even determining appropriate hours of care, governments designated workers as "independent contractors" to obscure their own responsibility as employers. In Washington, D.C., under federal oversight, home chore aides in one section of the Department of Human Services became employees, while personal care aides, who were moved to another section in 1975, became independent contractors, even though they performed similar work.[53] New York, California, and other states increasingly contracted out home care services to private agencies, thus denying their responsibility for labor standards, collective bargaining, or certain Medicaid requirements. Different payment mechanisms, modes of service, and contradictory interpretations of the FLSA created a continuously uncertain legal situation, with courts sometimes ruling that the consumer employed the caregiver and other times seeing her as a government worker or an employee of a private agency.[54] The resulting tangle of job titles and work definitions generated a confusing maze that home care users and providers would try to navigate for the rest of the century.

Not all workers accepted treatment as independent contractors. In 1980, Mary McClendon was a 59-year-old black widow on public assistance. During the early 1970s, she headed Detroit's Household Workers Organization, Inc., an affiliate of the NCHE.[55] Later in the decade, she worked for the Motor City's Neighborhood Services Department as a homemaker aide. "Lifting the seniors up off the floor, the sidewalk, in and out of the bathtub," she claimed, left her ill. She sued the city for workers' compensation and challenged the city's claim that she was not an employee. In her deposition, McClendon said she had assumed that she would receive "the same type of benefits any other citizen receive [*sic*]"—even if her job was limited to a year. The behavior of supervisors gave her reason to believe that she was an employee. "I don't think that they would check on us as often as they did if we'd have been contractors," she argued. Supervisors told them what to wear to weekly meetings or while performing tasks. The city provided orientation, a book of guidelines, and her client list. Finally, "you wouldn't tell a contractor what to discuss and what not to discuss with the senior citizens." The city countered that she had no rights to benefits from a workfare job. McClendon lost her case. And so, despite its role in direct supervision, Detroit, like other cities, continued to classify the aides as contractors rather than employees.[56]

McClendon fought nearly alone, but where a leftist feminist movement had emerged, home care workers found allies at the intersection of the new service sector unionism and feminist groups. In California, a legal fight took place between SEIU Local 250 and Homemakers, Inc., of Los Angeles. Homemakers, a subsidiary of the Upjohn Pharmaceutical Company, had gone into the business of supplying housekeeping/chore services to individuals and cities, including San Francisco, and did not want to have to pay these women for overtime. So Homemakers filed a suit to overturn the state's Progressive Era protective legislation that required overtime pay only for female workers, arguing that it discriminated against men.[57] Feminist groups that both supported equal rights and labor rights joined the suit as *amicae curiae*. These supporters included the socialist Union Women's Alliance to Gain Equality (Union WAGE), the San Francisco chapter of the National Organization for Women, and the NCHE. They argued that women instead needed "premium pay" to meet their own family responsibilities, including the cost of substitute caregivers for their overtime hours. WAGE organized pickets at Homemakers' offices and before city budget hearings. These activists declared that "many household workers here feel that unionization is the answer." Concluded Ruth Fagan Ginger of the National Lawyer's Guild, "No low-paying employer . . . that pays minimum wages for domestic workers should be able to wipe out overtime pay protections for all workers by posing as a friend to men workers and to Women's Liberation. . . ." Ironically, with discrimination on the basis of sex prohibited under the federal law, Homemakers, Inc., ultimately won in court.[58] The company would not have to pay any home health worker overtime.

Feminist involvement in this case was an exception. The new feminism rarely tackled the concerns of either the recipients or providers of home care. Given members' own life cycle concerns, most of the women's movement focused on child rather than elder care and on the renegotiation of domestic labor within the household between the sexes rather than the upgrading of paid domestic labor. Indeed, cheap household help was making it possible for professional women to go out to work.[59]

In the mid-1970s, when older women themselves turned up the pressure, more feminists took notice. Home care offered a double remedy for aging women. The elderly wanted assistance. The middle-aged, especially "displaced homemakers" who had to fend for themselves following the loss of a male breadwinner from death or divorce, sought jobs. Long removed from the labor market, they faced age discrimination and the need to upgrade skills. But they had experience for home care—a job that potentially could provide them with independence, claimed feminist Tish Sommers, a displaced homemaker herself who founded the Older Women's League. In 1975, she joined with Bay Area groups to create the Jobs for Older Women Action Project, lobbying county governments for higher wages. "Please compare what your city pays street cleaners and plumbers to what you are willing to pay for the vital service of keeping your older citizens independent and happy, and consider carefully which is the more important service being rendered," she pleaded. Quality care would not come from the forced labor of welfare recipients but from "adequate paid jobs for older women as a most positive and practical form of preventive aging,"[60] she noted, echoing the previous generation of social welfare advocates. In 1977, the National Women's Conference in Houston called for the passage of the Displaced Homemakers Act as well as offered support for home health care. During the following decades, state commissions on the status of women would advocate for home care and other senior services.[61] Still, they mostly focused on the needs of recipients rather than on the working conditions of providers.

"Proud as We Are, We Work for a Living, Too": From Mutual Aid to Unionization

Even though Congress separated home companions from domestic servants, home aides became the major beneficiaries of the movement to extend labor rights to household workers.[62] Ever since the late nineteenth century, sporadic efforts to improve working conditions emerged; it was not that domestic workers were unorganizable, but that their isolated location and intimate relation with their employers placed additional barriers in the way.[63] The civil rights movement and a revived feminism unleashed a new phase of domestic worker rights. For Eleanor Holmes Norton, chair of the New York City Commission on Human Rights in 1975, "of all occupations that might make the point about the black women's stake in the movement for freedom, none seemed to me, could better dramatize the point than household workers."[64] In 1977, organized domestics generally agreed that "a union must come, but clearly it is a long way off."[65] Those who cared for the elderly and disabled under services paid for by public monies, however, already were beginning to act collectively.

Organization among domestics hardly resembled traditional unionism. Although the AFL-CIO fought for labor standards coverage, it could not imagine adapting organizing, collective bargaining, and grievance machinery to a situation in which workers had several different employers in the course of a week. The Household Technicians of America organized to seek better working conditions and higher pay, but it was an association, not a union. Some affiliates were hostile to trade unions, even while its mission included gaining rights at work through "the strength of their numbers." Chapters in New York, Ohio, and the Carolinas, like McClendon's group in Detroit, focused on "pay, protection, and professionalism." As one organizer announced, "The garbage men have been upgraded to sanitation workers, with all the benefits, and that is just what we have to do. If you are tough enough to talk back to your big man on Sunday, don't tell me you're afraid of Miss Suzy on Monday." Given the stigma of service, they sought "recognition that household workers are among 'the cleanest, most respectable women in the world,'" declared the head of the 600-member Domestics United from Charlotte, North Carolina.[66] Some in these groups viewed themselves as part of the feminist movement.[67]

Domestics followed generations of black Americans in forming mutual aid organizations. The Atlanta-based National Domestic Workers Union, founded by Dorothy Bolden in 1968, provided solidarity for those engaged in individual negotiations.[68] With help from NCHE, Washington, D.C., home aides established the Organization of Personal Care and Chore Services in 1979, referred to by the *Washington Post* as both a lobby and a bargaining group. They not only pressured the City Council for inclusion under the District's minimum wage law but requested Congress to instruct the District that they were "eligible to form a labor union" since they were not independent contractors. The local government insisted that they were contractors, despite assigning "where they work and the hours designated and the clients," and refused to recognize them.[69] It would take 15 years for the personal care attendants, aided by SEIU Local 722, to be reclassified as employees and thus become eligible for health benefits, social security, and workers' compensation.[70]

The California Homemakers Association (CHA) called itself a "mutual benefits association." Though it targeted all kinds of household occupations, it emerged not from the domestic worker movement but as a practical application of "New Communist" theories and as an offshoot of farm worker organizing.[71] Through a cadre of volunteer professionals, CHA provided members with health care, legal advice, welfare advocacy, and general support in navigating the bureaucracy of public assistance. It advocated "strata organizing" of low-paid workers unrecognized by the labor law—service and migrant field workers, general assistance and AFDC recipients, and the unemployed. Moreover, it brought the providers and receivers of home care into one organization. CHA argued for common interests among these groups in the face of welfare policies that sought to have women on AFDC work off benefits in community service jobs, like home care, without gaining the status of worker, displacing those who earned wages for the same tasks. The labels of domestic, household, and attendant care worker were interchangeable for this group of idealistic poor black women, radical social workers, white students, and self-styled "revolutionaries."

These radical activists sought to organize the most oppressed and casualized laborers and found their chance in the struggle to gain collective bargaining for home attendants in Sacramento, Santa Cruz, Yolo, and other counties. CHA had its largest impact in Sacramento, where it claimed 4,000 members by 1975. It relied on bucket drives at shopping centers, benefit dinners, rummage sales, and volunteer labor. The Campaign for Human Development, the Catholic Church's mechanism to support grassroots groups, funded expansion to other cities.[72] Poor black, older, Southern migrants, household laborers since childhood—like President Viola Mitchell, Della Mae Tribbitts, and "Queen" Esther Johnson—sustained the group. These women knew how to make do; they stretched food, housed organizers, involved churches, and bore witness before resistant county supervisors. They told what it was like to live on under $1,000 a year, sometimes earning less than 30 cents an hour for live-in care work, and warned the Sacramento supervisors, as did Pearlie Alexander, that "we'll stay with you until we get what we need, just like a yellowjacket on a hound!"[73] Persist they did, crowding meetings and convincing county supervisors to allow CHA as their representative. With the law against them, however, CHA could win neither a contract nor a hiring hall.[74]

Unionization finally took off when the role of the state changed, enabling civil rights organizing to come together with rising service sector unionism. In the 1970s, labor rights for domestics stood as one of the most prominent civil rights issues in New York, where union activists and progressive legislators long had turned to the state for remedies. Eleanor Holmes Norton used her position as chair of the Commission on Human Rights to speak out for their labor rights, chiding the women's movement to take up the campaign. "[B]lack women should note that the issue of exploitation of women in low paid and undignified work makes us who are black as much a part of the women's rights struggle as any women in America," she exhorted. Domestic labor was something other than "a cast-off profession for cast-off women." In 1971, Holmes Norton brought together some 100 experts from government, employer, women's, labor, and civil rights organizations to discuss raising wages, more comprehensive legal protections, unionization, and work restructuring. Of those present, Bronx State Assemblyman Seymour Posner would provide the crucial legislation for organizing the city's home care workers.[75]

Posner, the social worker and unionist turned legislator, led the struggle to pass a collective bargaining law for household workers.[76] He previously had sponsored successful legislation bringing domestic workers under the state's minimum wage. Beginning in 1974, he introduced a bill designating the term "employee" to cover domestic workers.[77] The bill was meant to apply to contract cleaning firms and employment agencies. "Sometimes the same people clean business establishments or schools and also clean homes for the same contracting firm," Posner explained. "When they clean the former, they have collective bargaining rights; when they clean homes, they do not." Thus, as he argued, this bill "will give household workers the same status and dignity before the law enjoyed by other American workers."[78] The bill's sponsors subsequently amended it to exclude "babysitters and companion[s] to sick, convalescing, and elderly people," paralleling the Wage and Hour rule at the federal level.[79]

The newly emerging powerhouse, SEIU, united with civil rights advocates—such as the A. Philip Randolph Institute (led by Bayard Rustin), the Urban League, the NAACP, the American Jewish Congress, and NCHE—to support Posner's bill. SEIU originated in 1921 when seven small janitorial locals formed the Building Service Employees International Union; over the next decades, its reach extended to hospitals, public employment, security, and even household workers. Changing its name to the Service Employees International Union in 1968 reflected this larger sectoral domain.[80] While many of the old AFL craft unions dug in their heels against integrating women and minorities, SEIU saw this legislation as a springboard for new organizing. During the 1975 hearings, Posner specifically asked the union whether it would commit to organizing household workers. He lamented that the majority leader of the State Senate "says no unions are going to go in there . . . too much effort, too much money, too much everything to organize household workers." To which the SEIU representative responded emphatically: "Twenty-five years ago the same thing was said about organizing building employees, cleaners, the very employees that now enjoy the benefits of unionization. It will be a difficult task, but by no means impossible and the outlook is very positive." They would go in and organize.[81]

With the backing of the civil rights community, SEIU's flagship and largest local, New York City's 32B-32J, led by its new president John Sweeney, initiated a Household Workers Organizing Committee. Representing building supers, elevator operators, building maintenance crews, and office and store cleaners, including women who labored at night, 32B-32J had grown to almost 40,000 members by organizing small groups, building by building. It conceived of its household workers organizing campaign as an extension of its representation of cleaners. Unlike some older industrial unions, it understood that workers in non-industrial settings were "organizable." The institutional culture of this old AFL union, rooted in scattered small work sites, allowed it to seek out the "invisible workforce" of home care.[82]

Vice President Cecil Ward, a Trinidadian-born ally of Sweeney, took charge. Within a year, Ward had a staff of four women organizers working solely on the "household workers" effort, a significant dedication of resources, according to white activist Barbara Shulman, who became his assistant. Laura Hopkins and Josephine Bond, both African American former service workers, were among the lead organizers. Because the new collective bargaining law did not apply to individuals hired directly by someone in the home, the Household Workers' Organizing Committee had to decode the business structure that daily sent tens of thousands of workers into domestic spaces. Their attention was soon drawn to the so-called housekeeping programs of private charitable agencies. At the end of 1977, at the same time that the Morrisania workers were demanding justice, 32B-32J filed its first NLRB petition to represent 400 workers employed by the

Federation of the Handicapped, who earned an average wage below the federal minimum.[83]

The organizing committee struggled over how to define the job, as well as the structure of the industry. "It was never clear to me what a domestic worker was, whether she was a cleaner, nanny, child care worker," admitted Shulman. Ward acknowledged that the ambiguity of household labor itself made it difficult to determine what constituted fair working conditions: "Since their jobs are not clearly defined, they can be asked to perform duties ranging from those of a practical nurse in the care of the elderly or handicapped to those of cook, cleaner, and window washer."[84] The continual use of the term "domestic" reflected such confusion, but it also served symbolic purposes. It marked the workers as black women, with a history of laboring in the homes of others for little pay.

Metaphors of slavery and *ancien regime* pervaded the organizing campaign. Associating low-paid household work with a corrupt bygone era, SEIU's organizers cast the union drive as a liberation struggle that would carry women of color across time. "It is most amazing in this modern day and age," said Ward, "that these dedicated workers are still in the dark ages." In meetings with workers, he told them "we are on the march . . . to organize and to free you good people from slavery."[85] Home care workers themselves took this rhetoric to City Hall during their September 1979 rally. The union printed signs pleading, "Take Us Out of Slavery" and spread that iconic image throughout its publications, flyers, and other publicity, particularly on the eve of any election for union representation.[86] Posner, who became active in the organizing campaign, later wrote in the *Household Workers News*, "Even though people are now paid for working, the attitude of the masters toward the servant in their home remains the same. The City administration is now the 'lady of the house.' The 'girl' or the 'maid' or 'servant' who is treated like a slave still exists." Yet he promised, "History is on your side. The Constitution of the United States says that slavery ended more than 100 years ago. With . . . SEIU you will make it come true in the 1980s."[87]

In the summer of 1978, the union won its first major organizing victory when 150 housekeepers, homemakers, and home attendants, many of them Chinese (employed by the First Chinese Presbyterian Church), voted to join. Eager to present itself as a pioneering and dynamic union and perhaps to justify the long struggle ahead, 32B-32J and SEIU ignored the intermittent history of domestic worker organizing when boasting that this victory "marks the first time that household employees have joined a union to achieve a better way of life through collective bargaining. . . . This is a great moment for all of organized labor."[88]

Initially, the strategy had been to seek out each identified agency throughout the city. The organizing committee soon figured out that wherever the workers might have been sent from, most were servicing clients who received their benefits through a public welfare program or a hospital overseen by larger city institutions.

The source, it appeared, was New York City's troubled Division of Home Attendant Service. Yet the Division did not employ attendants directly; instead, it referred them to clients and paid for the service through a dual-party check issued to the client, as we have seen. Consequently, 32B-32J decided to confront the city over recognizing home attendants as city employees who should have the same collective bargaining rights as other city employees. The union filed a certification petition with the city's Office of Collective Bargaining (OCB) to represent over 11,000 home attendants working for the Division.

SEIU 32B-32J was not alone in seeking to organize the city's home care workforce. Two other unions also petitioned to represent these workers in 1978, claiming jurisdiction by defining the work from different angles. Each union simultaneously considered these workers as domestics, health care workers, or municipal employees, and would come to see them as all three. Whether their target was commercial cleaning contractors, hospitals, or city agencies, service sector unions now sought to ensure that such employers could not use the privacy and insularity of the home as a spatial location of labor free from labor standards—or as "off-site production" that could drop the bottom out of labor standards for those working in more formal institutional settings.

Local 144, the Hotel, Hospital, Nursing Home and Allied Health Services Union—the second largest local in SEIU—regarded home care workers as belonging to the same health care workforce that labored in nursing homes and hospitals. Coordinating its campaign were African American women, Alma Robinson, director of its Civil Service Division, and Florence Gibson, once a home attendant, who leaders thought could best reach the African American and Caribbean, middle-aged workforce.[89] AFSCME also filed a petition for certification, asserting that housekeepers and home attendants who worked for Harlem Hospital and other city hospitals were employees of the New York City Health and Hospitals Corporation. Hence, home attendants were like any other municipal employee of the Human Resources Administration.

At about the same time that 32B-32J won its first drive, 3,000 workers for the vendor Self Help, Inc., mostly women from the Caribbean, voted to join AFSCME District Council 1707. AFSCME also viewed these workers as domestics. "We are all proud of the work we do, glad that we are able to relieve the suffering of the aged and sick clients," a rank-and-file leader proclaimed at what was described as a revival meeting mixed with militant trade unionism. These women cheered speakers who recognized their double oppression as minorities and women. The new executive director of the NCHE declared, "We may have to get on our knees to clean a floor but no one said we have to live on our knees." Creating solidarity and affirming dignity as black and Latina women, however, proved easier than gaining a contract with the city, as the Morrisania battle already had shown.[90]

The OCB reviewed certification petitions from the three unions in the Fall of 1978. The city, not surprisingly, rejected all of the unions' demands, insisting that these workers were "independent contractors and not employees as contemplated by the New York City Collective Bargaining Law." The New York City Health and Hospitals Corporations responded by pointing to their casualization of the labor as evidence that that these workers were not employees: "documents pertaining to standards and eligibility requirements: there are none; Job specifications. There are none." At the end of November 1978, the OCB dismissed the petitions on a technicality, refusing to rule on the status of employment.[91]

While awaiting the outcome, 32B-32J and 144 decided to merge their campaigns into a united drive. With their efforts now combined, the building and cleaning employees local and the nursing home local resubmitted their certification petition the following month, with a sufficient number of signed authorization cards. This time, the OCB initiated hearings in the summer of 1979 to determine the actual employment status of home attendants. The city maintained that Home Attendant Service was an "individual provider system," and the attendant, an independent contractor. Moreover, it insisted that in more than half of the cases, the client recruited the home attendant. Local 32B-32J and Local 144, in turn, submitted evidence meant to demonstrate that an employment relationship existed between the home attendants and the city: training requirements and training courses, home attendant information records and personnel forms, manual of duties, evaluation of client forms, payment instructions, and reimbursement and grievance forms filed with the Human Resources Administration. The unions showed that agencies, such as the Federation of the Handicapped, held contracts with the city for the provision of services.[92]

Just as the OCB was about to rule on the employment and bargaining status of home attendants, the city found its escape hatch: after January 1, 1980, it would contract all service through vendor agencies. Vendors would assume all responsibilities for recruitment, employment, payment, supervision, grievances, everything. With the announcement of vendorization, OCB dismissed the unions' case. There was no longer any matter to settle.[93] Privatization of social services functioned as a key tactic to avoid unions.

From that point on, SEIU in New York would have to organize home care workers—whatever their title—private agency by private agency. Every new organizing drive would need yet another NLRB petition and election. This effort required fighting the same battle over and over again. Thus when the union attempted to organize vendors such as the Home Attendant Program of Central Harlem Meals on Wheels, the agencies tried to take advantage of the murky definitional milieu to claim that the workers were domestics and therefore not legally entitled to union representation. The union had to prove that their employees came under New York's collective bargaining law. When the NLRB and federal district court agreed with the union, the organizing committee announced not a mere victory but a transformation: "'Domestic Workers Become Home Attendants.' Only then could they move forward with a representation election.[94]

Despite the labor-intensive nature of the organizing, the all-female organizing staff steadily built the union. By mid-1981, there were about 6,400 members and contracts with 16 vendor agencies. Union ballots appeared in eight different languages, including Spanish, French, Polish, Russian, Hebrew, and Chinese. A year later, the union could claim 14,000 home care members, nearly three-quarters of whom were under contract as of September 1982.[95]

In the early 1980s, SEIU itself formally acknowledged that the workers being organized were indeed caregivers more than cleaners. The organizing committee changed its name to the Home Care Workers Committee at the end of 1980 and then, in 1981, took on the name of Home Care Division of Local 32B-32J and Local 144 SEIU. Partly out of the changing nature of the work and partly out of increasing competition with rival union Local 1199, organizers began representing their local as a health sector union. The SEIU local reinvented its identity, naming itself in the early 1980s as "the home attendant union" and more broadly as "part of America's largest health care workers' union."[96] It considered housekeepers, home attendants, and nursing home aides as workers who were waging a battle together.

SEIU also began to emphasize the welfare state location of the labor to link the rights of workers and clients. First, organizers articulated a broader set of rights claims as an organizing tactic: "Protect your rights and the rights of your patient by joining Locals 32b-32J and 144, SEIU." Second, as budget cuts hit both workers and clients, the union sought to activate clients to pressure the welfare state over cuts in hours, announcing that it would assist clients in obtaining a fair hearing from Social Services and would represent the client at the hearing at no charge. Thus when CABS Home Attendant Services, a program of one of the city's community development agencies, cut the hours for Naomi Branker-Harrington, SEIU got her a fair hearing, won an increase in hours, and secured about $800 in back pay for her attendant, Mae Bradford. "We were successful because we worked as a team," proclaimed the union.[97] The union learned to link decent benefits to decent care, an association that would dominate future drives.

The Home Care Division had become so successful that on Labor Day of 1982, SEIU granted it a charter as the somewhat unwieldy named Local 32B-32J-144. The new local was a tribute to the achievement of the black and female organizers—Florence Gibson, Alma Robinson, Veronica Gaston, Josephine Bond, Laura Hopkins, and organizing coordinator Barbara Shulman. It came about because of tremendous grassroots unionizing and the commitment of

Cecil Ward. Yet the chartering also marked a turning point, an initial step in the undemocratic takeover of this mostly female, women of color union by 32B-32J's overweening new president, Gus Bevona—the successor to Sweeney, who became president of the International. Bevona installed himself as head of the Home Attendants local. Ward soon retired and Bevona named two men, neither involved with the women's struggle, as vice president and secretary-treasurer. Within a couple of years, Bevona succeeded in forcing out those who built the local. Suppressing internal democracy, organizing, and rank-and-file participation, the self-aggrandizing Bevona let the union coast.[98] Meanwhile, SEIU elsewhere, notably in Chicago, focused on this expanding workforce.

As household workers became home attendants in New York, another union came to the same discovery in San Diego. According to the founding narrative of the United Domestic Workers of America (UDWA), United Farm Workers of America (UFWA) President Cesar Chavez long had envisioned a union for domestic workers and searched for someone whom he could convince to embrace this dream. Chavez found that someone in Ken Seaton-Msemaji, president of the San Diego-based Black Power NIA Cultural Organization, who participated in a coalitional effort in the mid-1970s to defend the California Agricultural Labor Relations Board against agribusiness interests. Msemaji, along with cofounders Fahari Jeffers—his wife—and Greg Akili—later an SEIU organizer—had been community activists since the 1960s; they soon would join Tom Hayden's Campaign for Economic Democracy. As Msemaji remembered, "We were looking for a more direct and meaningful way to focus our social activism."[99] The task made sense: Jeffers had "lived in" as a home attendant to pay for college. Like other black women, her mother and Msemaji's grandmother also had performed domestic labor. Jeffers later confessed that "years of political activism set the framework for her dedication to labor."[100] Msemaji further explained, "Labor has such a tremendous potential, to work with a truly mass constituency. . . . It's very hard work organizing a union, but it's a lot more solid than much of our earlier work."[101]

In Msemaji's account, Chavez planted the seeds for the union, taught the value of nonviolence to this militant from Watts, and returned him to his religious roots in Catholicism. "My life and the lives of many of my associates were changed forever," Msemaji recalled. "We went on and founded the Domestic Workers Organizing Committee on August 14, 1977 in Cesar's backyard." They received financial aid from the UFWA, sessions in organizing by the legendary Fred Ross, who had trained Chavez, and negotiating lessons under the UFWA's Dolores Huerta. The new group sought to form "a poor people's union in an urban setting," a black and Latino union for and by domestic workers, laborers who fared even worse than those who toiled in the fields.[102] They gained additional financial and moral support from the Catholic Church.[103]

Civil rights unionism shaped UDWA from the start. It claimed to be "the third successful and enduring union in American labor history to be founded by blacks or Latinos." Whether converted by Chavez's example or merely a pragmatist, Msemaji left his earlier politics behind and embraced humanism over racial nationalism. Middle-aged white women constituted 30 percent of the rank and file and composed the key local leadership in some of the rural counties, such as Tulare, where UDWA would come to have most of its contracts. Like Latinas and Asian Americans, they sat on the executive board under black officers.[104]

Organizers more than railed against injustices of misuse and exploitation; they sought to defend the worth of domestic labor. They understood that black women historically have known that their labor was crucial for the running of other people's homes, but they faced the dilemma, as one domestic put it, that "My work isn't recognized as work. It's taken for granted and most people think any woman can do it and ought to love doing it."[105] While UDWA shared the multiracial perspective of the National Welfare Rights Organization and NCHE, tropes of slavery pervaded its discussion of domestic labor, much as they had for Cecil Ward and SEIU's New York organizers. "Our immediate goal must be to relieve a situation that is tantamount to plantation slavery," Msemaji declared in 1980.[106] The preamble to its constitution rejected "the notion that domestic work is slave work." In expressing faith "in the dignity of caring for those who need help, of preparing the food that nourishes our bodies and of caring for the children, the sick, the elderly and their homes," the union embraced the designation "domestic worker." It combined a revaluing of domestic labor with rights talk, bolstered by the authority of Pope Leo XIII's chastisement against those who "make one's profit out of the need of another." Indeed, Jeffers and Msemaji credited the support of the Church as crucial to sustaining their union. Religiosity took a popular form in upholding the right to unionize, as the preamble declared, "Cleanliness is Godliness, God bless those who clean."[107]

The UDWA did not start with a plan to organize home care attendants, but those were the only home-based workers they could find in any numbers.[108] Early on, it envisioned a membership that would include private household workers, hotel maids and nursing home workers. Its first election was a losing one at a nursing home. Reaching a scattered constituency proved daunting, even though the five organizers chatted with women waiting for early morning buses, set up house meetings, established neighborhood committees, and planned a service center for advocacy and assisting home care workers with problems like housing and hunger. They worked in Tijuana, where some household workers lived, as well as San Diego, in an attempt "to build locally" before expanding throughout California and joining with others to form a national union.[109] In April 1979, 150 delegates attended a founding convention at a time when San Diego County had about 15,000 domestics.

Union staff soon realized that this kind of unionism hinged on the state. Given the primary mode of service in its area of southern California, the union targeted the county welfare department and private homemaker corporations that subcontracted through the county. These included companies such as Remedy and Upjohn. Msemaji understood that organizing home care workers required political clout. He explained, "The county gives out contracts to . . . companies in a bidding process and sets the wage scale and benefits in their bid instruction package. So you really end up negotiating with the [Board of] supervisors on the wages."[110]

Over the next 18 months, the union's staff, then grown to 10, put into high gear the UFWA model of worker-to-worker organizing through house meetings, training 80 homemakers, who then organized their coworkers. As Msemaji explained their strategy, "We're trying to stay away from the public because this kind of organizing is different—the union's strength will be the workers themselves and our task is to work among them and if we can defeat their fears, then the union can succeed."[111] One breakthrough occurred in March 1980, when organizers found three women leaving a training session held by the contractor, Remedy Home and Health Care, Inc.—a Southern California–based temporary worker company that had expanded into the home care field. Claudia Bowens was a 59-year-old black woman; Margaret Insko, a Chicana domestic for over a decade; and Carol Leonard, a twenty-something white woman. Like other home care workers, these women had suffered from underpayment and delayed checks, minimal deductions that made it difficult to pay taxes at year's end, and lack of sick days. Or, as Bowen put it, "We get sick from clients and don't get a doggone thing." The 59-year-old announced: "We do care about people and, in return, we think someone should care about us. . . . We are not just objects."[112]

These women became central to the organizing effort. The Domestic Workers Service Center generated local community support and participation of the homemakers at Board of Supervisors hearings. Union members Bowens and Leonard testified in April how "another year of $3.10 [the minimum wage] an hour without benefits would not be acceptable." The county had had some kind of home care since 1951, with the Welfare Department from 1968 to 1976 running a homemaker program with county employees, when it responded to complaints about poorly trained workers, high turnover, and poor attendance by contracting out the service to Remedy. Four years later, San Diego County decided to open the home attendant contract to competitive bidding. With consultation from SEIU 250, which was organizing Bay Area health care workers, UDWA used this process as its point of leverage.[113] Through lobbying and testifying, the UDWA helped block the award to another company that had a pattern of wage violations and other problems.[114]

The following November, UDWA signed its first agreement with Remedy, which employed 2,100 homemakers under a $7.2 million contract to run the bulk of San Diego's In-Home Supportive Services (IHSS) program. The Remedy contract covered most of the union, since it had only another 300 members, half of whom were "private domestics," and the rest, independent providers of IHSS services. These minimum-wage workers gained a raise of 30 cents, five sick days, a week's vacation, health plan, seniority, training, and a grievance procedure. Wages and benefits were set by the bid guidelines that the union in essence obtained through political struggle at the county level and in the state legislature. Rosa Perez, one of the core members from San Ysidro, expressed the general satisfaction at the time: "It's not a whole lot," she explained, "but it's a start. . . . I've been working for eight years and I've never had any vacation, and if I had to take sick leave it was the same thing—I wouldn't be paid."[115] Members began to learn the lesson of unionization: "In unity we have *strength*," roared Claudia Bowens. Msemaji emphasized, "The biggest thing in their [union members'] lives is that they've learned . . . they don't have to settle for working conditions if they're not fair, that they can change things. . . . The contract is secondary to that."[116]

But the contract was primary for the maintenance of the union; the easiest way to sign up members and have an employer to bargain with was for counties to subcontract the management of IHSS. Otherwise, the union was left trying to reach the independent contractors who never went to any central agency. In 1981, UDWA founded the California In-Home Care Council as an industry-wide body with contractor representatives. Necessity led UDWA to join with employers to lobby government on all levels for increased appropriations, which would pay for raises and benefits and ease county fears that they would have to fund such increases from their already strained revenues. UDWA adopted a nonpartisan stance and attracted supporters from both political parties as it turned to the California legislature for enabling legislation. As one Democratic assemblyman observed, "They have a constituency base that is naturally Democratic, yet they're in a special circumstance in terms of supporting privatization, which historically has been identified with Republican policy."[117]

Once they focused on the private companies that served as contractors, UDWA experienced a burst of organizing. The union won victories in seven counties during the next two years that brought in over 3,000 workers. It formally affiliated with SEIU in 1982, again demonstrating SEIU's dynamism in recognizing the changing demographics of the American working class. UDWA's strategy, however, put it on a collision course with the independent living movement. Disability activists favored independent providers and fought aggressively against contracting services through private companies. Defining workers' and clients' interests separately, these movements did not become easy allies. In the future, these differences would constrain UDWA's growth.

More immediately, union organizing ran up against the new constraints of Reagan era political economy. Budget cuts and block grants of federal monies for social services necessitated state reductions. Despite initial success, membership declined in the early 1980s, and the union constantly fought attempts by Boards of Supervisors to drop more costly contractors for minimum-waged independent providers or to lower the wage itself. To bring some stability to the system, UDWA won legislation that permitted counties to subcontract for two years, rather than yearly, but more counties, under pressure from disability rights activists, shifted toward independent providers.[118] Thus cultural and political notions of care, especially where the caretaker was a relative, justified county cost-cutting. In 1982, San Diego, for example, used a threat to halve contract hours in order to reduce the starting wage by ten cents an hour; five years later, San Bernardino saved $4 million by reverting entirely to independent providers.[119]

Worker conditions hardly improved. Few gained health or vacation benefits because these required laboring 30 hours a week, and the county assigned cases needing fewer hours to the contractor. Remedy in San Diego did become the site of a Ford Foundation demonstration project on improving the conditions of home care workers. Guaranteed hours, subsidized health insurance, and increased training, this project revealed, facilitate worker retention. But soon afterward, the county moved its contract to a cheaper bidder, National Homecare Systems.[120] The number of union members in San Diego dropped from over 2,000 in 1980 to less than 600 in 1989.[121]

By then, UDWA was acting alone after being expelled from SEIU in 1984, charged with financial improprieties.[122] Over the years it successfully advanced legislation to provide cost of living raises; increases in the national minimum wage aided this effort. It pushed the state to pay for more of the service in the face of spiraling costs to the counties.[123] UDWA constantly lobbied for various adjustments to the IHSS program, particularly for instructions to counties to adopt some form of managed care, which would concentrate workers in agencies and presumably ease organization.[124]

Blocked from generating substantial raises by constant fiscal crisis in California and the political mobilization of disability activists, UDWA had to find other ways to deliver to its members. It developed nonprofit service centers, including food banks, work training, and assistance with obtaining welfare. Like Local 32B-32J-144, it defended the hours of clients at administrative hearings. One member noted in 1985, "The union has helped us a lot. . . . A lot of unions are bad, but our union is for the people and for us, too." Within a decade of its first contract, UDWA was in 15 counties. It would affiliate with AFSCME in 1994, "in order to protect our ability to carry out this mission."[125] It was now competing against SEIU, which elsewhere in the state chose to support the disability movement's preference for independent contractors as the primary IHSS workforce.

During a period when domestic work underwent significant reorganization, unions discovered home care workers. Despite similarity of tasks and shared location in private residences, the legal status of the two jobs diverged during these years. Classified as elder companions and so excluded from FLSA, home care workers faced an additional barrier to obtaining higher wages. But as part of the civil rights surge among black women workers, they refused the legacy of slavery and demanded rights and recognition.

Unions in the service sector took notice. Their responses reflected the prior organization of home care by the state. UDWA linked its organizing and bargaining strategy to one particular and contested structure for long-term care—vendorization. Other forms of delivering home care in California and across the nation posed their own challenges. As SEIU expanded its home care organizing beyond New York, it faced the task of matching unionizing strategies to local conditions and state programs. Led by a talented cadre of community organizers and political tacticians, militant home care workers themselves ignited a new period of creative innovation to meet the exigencies of a neoliberal age.

6

"The Union Is Us"

On Halloween 1988, 75 Chicago home care workers shouted in front of the Evanston residence of Janet Otwell, director of the Illinois Department of Aging (IDOA): "No more tricks, treat us with dignity and respect!" For weeks Otwell had rebuffed their requests for a meeting, so these black women, members of SEIU Local 880, finally took dramatic action. Seeking to draw attention to "poverty wages and the union busting activity of vendors in the state's home health care program," they marched on her lawn, posted notices on her door and those of her neighbors, and caused a commotion reminiscent of the heyday of the welfare rights movement. Declared 880 President Irma Sherman: "The vendors are making a tidy profit and we are left living from paycheck to paycheck, with no health coverage and no benefits to speak of—we're tired of their bag of tricks. . . ."[1] Since IDOA set the framework for elder home care, the union demanded a voice in policy making, along with advocates for the aged. Local 880 got the attention of the state and soon became a player in home care politics.

Community organizing and political unionism, Local 880 found, could together improve the lives of home health care workers. On the one hand, SEIU had discovered an alternative route to unionization through grassroots action. Rather than an offshoot of a preexisting local, Local 880 began as part of the United Labor Unions (ULU), a project of the Association for Community Organizations for Reform Now (ACORN). ULU represented a workforce counterpart to the neighborhood organizing of ACORN. On the other hand, given the structure of home care, as New York unions knew well, it was never enough just to win collective bargaining rights with individual agencies. To make economic gains, the union had to go to government. But with Reagan era assaults on public benefits and government employees, turning to the state for economic rights was no easy matter. Reagan shifted the fiscal, ideological, and political ground within American federalism away from national programs and state funding of social services, so political unionism would require innovative tactics and new allies.

Ronald Reagan had spent eight years as governor locking horns with social justice advocates. As president, his agenda for restructuring and downsizing the federal non-defense budget was not just aimed at defunding hard-won social assistance programs; it also sought to undercut the power bases of urban minorities and liberals. Within months, he pushed through cuts in Aid to Families with Dependent Children (AFDC) and anti-poverty agencies, new and more restrictive payment methods for Medicare and Medicaid, massive tax cuts for businesses and individuals, and the substitution of block grants to the states for separate funding of social services and welfare.

The Democratically controlled Congress initially did little to stand in Reagan's way. Both parties linked the economic difficulties of the 1970s to excessive public spending, government regulation, and waste, fraud, and abuse within social programs. They agreed that more market competition was the solution to health care inflation; the disciplining effects of the market would solve the problems of allocation and lack of access. Reagan expanded the project of deregulation already under way from the Carter years. "Removing government's smothering hand" not only meant liberating private industry but also downsizing the state. In one of his first acts in office, Reagan froze all civilian federal hiring, which he promised as a step toward cutting the federal payroll by a projected 75,000. On a crest of cultural and social resentment, Reagan announced confidently, the era of governmental expansion was over.[2]

Reagan's policies not only targeted the public budget but also aimed to discipline labor costs across the economy. Firing the striking air traffic controllers in August 1981, Reagan sent a message to corporations that they too could now resist workers' demands. After that, companies began to openly use permanent replacement workers with impunity; strikes became a losing proposition in the 1980s. The combination of Reagan's high interest rate Federal Reserve policy, toleration of steep unemployment, refusal to create a jobs program, and anti-unionism drove down wages across the nation. Americans found themselves struggling in what at the time was the worst recession since World War II, with fewer resources to fight back.[3]

Thus home care organizing seemed poised to take off at an inauspicious moment. Having blamed their workers for inflation, governments at all levels sought to restrain the growth of the public workforce. In the private sector, a new anti-union consulting industry provided firms with a host of resources to fight off unions, subvert the National Labor Relations Board (NLRB), and eliminate militant employees. In the early 1980s, home care organizers faced formidable obstacles.

Not the least of these hurdles came from Reagan's embrace of home care as compatible with private solutions for public responsibilities. Issuing yearly proclamations for National Home Care Week, Reagan praised certified agencies as well as individual caregivers for maintaining the independence and dignity of elderly people and reducing medical costs.[4] He celebrated such private solutions even while eliminating the very public funds that social welfare agencies depended upon. Home care organizers had to counter such ideological appeals to independence and redeploy this rhetoric to obtain state funding.

Chicago's Local 880 would develop successful models to win real gains from private agencies as well as government. The union learned to pressure state and local officials for pay increases and higher contractor reimbursements. What began as a militant community organizing movement generated adaptive strategies for union growth in an increasingly hostile anti-labor, neoliberal climate. The rights of poor women as both clients of and workers for the welfare state defined this struggle.

Launching the Reagan Revolution

Unions in the 1980s faced the challenge of figuring out the structures of an ever-evolving welfare state upon which their success depended. Their task became daunting because the president and Congress pushed through policy changes in so many major areas. Within the political economy of human services, workers and managers, administrators and consumers seemingly all at once confronted policy transformations in health care, welfare, tax, trade, and employment. States tried to capitalize on and at times dodge the imperatives of the New Federalism. These changes also opened social provision to profit-seeking players.

Congress permitted for-profit agencies to provide Medicare-funded home care services for the first time in 1980. It eliminated the three-day hospital stay prerequisite for home care and loosened some of the regulatory requirements for home health agencies. Claiming that nonprofit providers had impeded the growth of a home care market, some Medicare administrators argued that the use of for-profit enterprises would lead to competition, efficiency, wider access, and cost savings. Traditional agencies would have to imitate for-profit innovators or lose out.[5]

This particular policy change affected the entire market for home care, even though Medicare, with its requirements for medical certification, was not at this point a major payer. (Less than 1 percent of Medicare's budget went to home care services.)[6] To participate in Medicare, proprietary agencies had to offer "skilled nursing care." Given consumer demand, however, they added homemakers and health aides, expanding the paraprofessional end of the labor market. While public funding assured a steady income, the same companies also served private-pay clients. The proprietary agencies were more likely to rely on part-time employees and temps. Growth in demand for subsidized services drew women into this field, and yet limited hours of employment forced them to pick up more than one job to make ends meet.[7]

This Medicare precedent spread to other social programs. Soon Medicaid and various services for the elderly allowed for-profit contractors, who from then on became central players. By mid-decade, new proprietary chains dominated the field of home health.[8] Beginning with a 1981 executive order, President Reagan had enshrined a general model for social policy that intensified reliance on the private sector to solve public problems and thereby decrease dependence on government. During the next several years, the Reagan administration transferred numerous areas of social and urban policy to "private sector action."[9] Allowing for-profit contractors seemed a small step, in keeping with developments of the 1970s, but the Reaganite restructuring of the American welfare state magnified its consequences and more fully placed its private-public contours into a neoliberal mold.

To gain greater control over social spending, Reagan used the budget reconciliation process to bypass congressional committees and convert large chunks of the social budget into block grants. Block grants represented both a fiscal and a political strategy originating in the Nixon years. As fiscal strategy, each block grant would consolidate myriad federal programs under one general category, but with a budget ceiling, so that states would have to make tough decisions about how to divvy up limited money for health care, education, and community development. Politically, the block grants approach would loosen congressional control over specific social programs by shifting political decision-making to the states.[10]

The Reagan administration sped up block grants with the Omnibus Budget Reconciliation Act of 1981 (OBRA), probably the most significant piece of social legislation since the Great Society. Instead of matching state expenditures, the new law capped federal outlay for almost all programs, with a 22 percent cut in federal funds across the board. Federal aid to state and local governments declined in absolute dollars for the first time in two decades. Simultaneous individual and corporate tax cuts assured a lack of additional revenue flow, even if Congress had second thoughts.[11]

OBRA 1981 aimed to up-end the War on Poverty—permanently. Its transformative impact lay not just in the reduced level of federal funds. It blindsided the big cities and rebuffed their recently mobilized constituencies of African Americans, Latinos, poor people, feminists, and public employees. With block grants, state governments could displace economic and social welfare programs run by big cities, especially those under Community Action Agencies (CAA) that had served as the institutional vehicle for the urban poor to challenge state and local governments. Now Reagan finally gave state officials the political relief they sought by placing the funding of community services directly under state governments. This law further undermined Community Development Corporations, the vehicle New York City had turned to in the 1970s for home care, by prohibiting funding from the federal block grant. But many CAAs had mutated into vital deliverers of social services, with some becoming Area Agencies on Aging. Never much invested in them, states responded to federal cuts by spending less of their own money and exerting more control over agency budgets and activities. The result was a slow choke.[12]

Under the new block grants, states had to select which social services to reduce or eliminate. Some of them ended day care, counseling, and child protection. Administrators shifted costs to users through increased fees and eligibility restrictions until programs served only the poorest households. Through the 1982 Tax Equity and Fiscal Responsibility Act, which set stricter limits on hospital reimbursement, states also could impose deductibles, co-insurance, co-payments, or other user charges on services for the needy.[13] As officials in California, New York, and Oregon—states heavily reliant on these monies—recognized, funding cuts undermined whatever benefits came with the increased flexibility of the New Federalism.[14]

States turned to Medicaid to make up the loss. Medicaid increasingly became their long-term care program, with a heavy emphasis on institutionalization. Elderly and disabled persons represented a small proportion of recipients, yet their expenditures consumed a substantial chunk of the Medicaid budget. At the beginning of the 1980s, 42 percent of Medicaid outlays went to nursing homes.[15] Not only had Medicaid come to dominate state and local health budgeting, amounting sometimes to one-third of expenditures, it was often the largest program in the whole state budget, accounting for 20 percent of annual outlays, with the fastest-growing rate of spending.[16] Under these stresses, state Medicaid directors claimed that they had to make trade-offs between the elderly and primary care for women and children.[17] In turn, these pressures drove Medicaid reform onto the federal agenda.

Responding to legislators' alarm that Medicaid spending had reached critical levels, the Congressional Budget Office proposed remedies premised on reducing costs in an era of tax cuts. While it recommended restricted eligibility, co-payments for physicians' services and hospital stays, and individual curtailment of use, it hoped to gain the biggest savings from interjecting the state into a whole range of family decisions. Law could force relatives to take financial responsibility to "reduce federal and state expenditures for institutionalized people." But questions of care and obligation were not so easily sorted out and the cost-benefit calculation not so clear-cut. The Congressional Budget Office wondered, for example, "Are only biologically related children responsible for their parents? . . . Should children be required to support their biological parents, even in instances in which these parents provided little or no support to their children?"[18] Could the state really determine, let alone enforce, who owes what to whom within families?

Resolving the ambiguities of care could not rest strictly on budget analysis. The route forward represented an opportunistic convergence between liberal advocates for the elderly and the Reagan administration. Medicaid "reform" became an early test case of Reagan's promise to restore "the 10th Article of the Bill of Rights"—to hand back to the states anything that was not explicitly given to the federal government in the Constitution.[19] At the same time, the perpetual limitations that Medicare and Medicaid placed on home care support frustrated liberals on the House Select Committee on Aging, especially Claude Pepper and Henry Waxman, who advocated that state Medicaid programs develop their own alternatives to institutionalization. As a result, the 1981 budget bill included changes to Medicaid that allowed states to redirect funds away from institutionalization into home- and community-based long-term care by applying for a waiver from federal requirements. The Department of Health and Human Services (HHS) would grant a state a three-year waiver that could be renewed for another three years. The state could provide Medicaid reimbursable home care to those who would otherwise require institutionalization, if such services cost less. Waivers could restrict recipients to "only efficient and cost-effective providers"—a new specification that dovetailed nicely with opening up government-funded services to private industry.[20] Such compromise by Republicans and Democrats ended up furthering a neoliberal agenda.

Welfare Redux

Cutting labor costs proved to be the primary method for expanding the home care system. Once again, welfare policy seemed in sync with these demands. Relying on advisers from his years as governor, Reagan won two such reforms in OBRA 1981: states would be permitted to initiate Community Work Experience Programs for AFDC recipients, and they could apply for broadened waivers from AFDC rules to encourage "welfare to work." The Reaganites failed at requiring workfare, but states steadily applied for these waivers, some 38 of them within the next six years. The Reagan administration boasted of creating "new-style workfare" that would not merely "deter loafers" but would "rehabilitate the dependent poor."[21] Reaganites and conservative governors revived *rehabilitation* to meet the imperatives of the privatizing welfare state.[22]

To reduce both welfare dependency and elder institutionalization, OBRA authorized demonstration projects to deploy AFDC recipients as homemaker–home health aides. Seven states—Arkansas, Kentucky, New Jersey, New York, Ohio, South Carolina, and Texas—with different welfare philosophies, administrative centralization, and capacity for delivery of social services participated in the project.[23] As in earlier eras, program evaluators insisted that everyone gained: trainees increased their earnings and labor market skills; clients benefited from improved mental and physical functioning; and taxpayers found their money well spent.[24] The upshot was that home care more firmly became integrated into workfare. Looking back at this evolving relationship in 1992, social work scholar Davida Unterbach described it as "a public works program" where "two 'client' groups are united, one to help the other, both impoverished."[25]

How AFDC recipients felt about these jobs varied. Activists, we have seen, dismissed them as just another form of low-paying domestic service. Other women interviewed during these demonstration projects reinforced evaluator findings. As one San Diego woman admitted, "You can work a schedule so you can be with your children. It helped me a lot. I'll tell you, because I was so glad to get off of welfare." Many women lived in households where various welfare benefits—Supplemental Security Income, AFDC, Medicare, and housing subsidies—enhanced their incomes. Some found in home care greater freedom than a job in an institutional setting, whether a hospital or an office. What disappointed these workers were not only the low wages but also the paucity of hours, which were often less than necessary to qualify for medical insurance or other available benefits.[26]

In the 1980s, government channeled work-based "rehabilitation" through private-sector jobs. Previously, the Comprehensive Employment and Training Act (CETA) had aimed at job training and job creation through public service employment; the ACORN unions initially set their sights on these workers.[27] In contrast, Reagan's Job Training Partnership Act gave federal funds to the private sector. At a time when 14 million Americans were unemployed, this program, senators insisted, would lead welfare recipients to "economic independence." Rather than aiding these poor women to find good jobs, it helped private employers locate temporary, low-wage workers.[28]

An exception to this general trend developed in New York, where in 1985 a cooperative home care agency in the South Bronx began training women on welfare as home health aides, offering them an opportunity to have a stake in the enterprise. Rick Surpin of the Community Service Society established Cooperative Home Care Associates (CHCA) as an experiment in worker ownership with funding from religious organizations, the United Hospital Fund, and the National Co-op Bank. CHCA would cater to a new niche for medically related home care, such as taking blood pressure, which more rapid release of sicker people from hospitals had created.[29] Through upgrading opportunities, some workers became paraprofessionals, allowing the cooperative to expand its range of services. Its future became secure after winning sub-contracts from the Visiting Nurse Association and Montefiore Hospital. By 1989, its 100 members could vote themselves an equivalent to a shareholder dividend.[30]

CHCA transformed lives through training, education, and the labor itself. "There's little techniques that they show you," one woman explained. Popular education methods reached women with limited schooling but who had lifetime experience caring for relatives and neighbors. Ana Cuevas expressed the feeling of many members when she told interviewers in the mid-1990s, "Cooperative is an open door for a woman to become independent . . . to feel that she is somebody." Nonetheless, workers and managers realized the fiscal constraints under which they labored. "I know we need a raise," one woman admitted, "but if you can't get it, you can't get it, that's all. Because Medicaid is cutting out and this is cutting out and that is cutting out. So what can you do?" This worker-owner displayed a kind of fatalism that union organizers would counter by directing member ire toward employers and by fighting for greater state funding.[31]

Grey Power and the New Federalism in Oregon

Not sure whether home care was cheaper, or whether the federal government would back up its new policy priorities beyond the short term, few states rushed to implement such programs. Oregon was the exception. The first state to apply for a Medicaid Home and Community-based Services Waiver, it had used federal and state funds to develop alternatives to institutionalization since 1981. Eventually, 73 percent of its Medicaid long-term care budget went to home care. Policy discussions of long-term care usually begin with the Oregon wavier, but this seemingly trail-blazing action was possible because a decade-long social struggle had won seniors the right to independence through home care.[32]

Oregon's home- and community-based programs originated in homemaker and chore services, which, like almost all public health efforts, were located at the county level.[33] Populous counties drew upon federal monies for social services, especially after the 1965 Older Americans Act; so did private organizations, such as the Portland-area Kaiser Permanente Health Plan.[34] With Older Americans Act support, Oregonians formed viable Area Agencies on Aging (AAAs) at the county level to deliver home and community center meals to a wide range of citizens, including elderly Japanese, Jews, Latinos, and Native Americans. Senior centers provided legal counseling, shopping assistance, and chore and homemaker services.[35] Nonetheless, as the decade wore on, an extraordinarily high percentage of older people remained institutionalized.

Frustrated elders began organizing through publicly funded senior centers, demanding that policy makers curb nursing home admissions, which had grown at twice the rate of population growth for those over 75. In 1973, a legislative Special Committee on Aging toured the state listening to them. To its surprise, the Committee found seniors incredibly well mobilized, with bills in hand and prepared to lobby. Seniors urged the Committee to recognize in-home services as a viable alternative to institutionalization.[36] Out of this initiative came Oregon Project Independence, enacted in 1975 as federal Social Service block funds became available, which provided people over 60 with some housekeeping, meal preparation, and personal care. It covered low-income seniors not on Medicaid through a sliding fee schedule, an important universalizing component.

Two years later, activists kept their movement going by forming the United Seniors Cooperative. They brought together the Gray Panthers, Retired Teachers' Association, NOW's Older Women's Task Force, Salem's National Council of Senior Citizens, AAAs volunteers, union retirees, and retired government staffers. In the midst of an economic recession, United Seniors' political demands for remaining in the community, what began to be called aging in place, started to look fiscally attractive. Certainly, Oregon Project Independence was cheaper than nursing home confinement, since it depended on both low-paid workers and volunteers subsidized by the Older Americans Act.[37]

Lacking the institutional and financial capacity to develop these services more systematically, the state obtained two demonstration project grants from the federal government to run short-term, community-based care in four counties. While this project failed to lessen poverty, either among elderly women or workers, it apparently proved that community-based care offered tremendous savings over nursing homes.[38] When the Oregon Department of Human Resources tried to limit the autonomy and activity of the AAAs and exclude United Seniors from the planning of a new state-level division, irate seniors went straight to the governor, who quickly handed the proposal over to them for revision.[39]

The social service infrastructure of the welfare state became a site of mobilization. Because they were organized at the county level, seniors were well situated to influence the new home care policy, even as the state transferred its caseload mostly to Medicaid. United Seniors initiated a series of open, participatory meetings at senior centers and AAAs, continuously lobbied legislators, and established conferences with state welfare administrators. During 1981, senior activists led the lobbying effort and, by the end of the summer, the legislature passed two landmark bills that together constituted the Oregon Plan. One established a new agency, the Oregon Senior Services Division, and the other announced a State Policy on Aging. The state would support elders in the least restrictive setting possible, maximizing in-home, community-based, and independent living to promote "independence, dignity, privacy, and appreciation of individuality." The state would relocate nursing home residents capable of living elsewhere, with cost savings reinvested into community-based care.[40] The organized seniors had won.

Only then did Oregon apply to Health and Human Services for its pioneering waiver in order to fund alternatives to nursing homes. Home care became a right: anyone who met the criteria would be enrolled.[41] The majority of relocated clients, however, had no home to return to and could not live alone, so the adult foster home emerged to meet this need. Proprietors could develop a supervised living situation for up to five elderly persons in a private home. In the 1980s, these homes proliferated rapidly and became a more widely used option for those who could purchase care on their own through the market. Later in the decade, the *Salem Statesman-Journal* observed, the "Senior Services [Division] is such a large buyer of elderly care services that its actions help shape the entire long-term care industry."[42]

For those who could stay home, the state offered two possibilities, both transferring responsibility to the private sector. AAAs could contract with service providers, such as state-licensed home care agencies. Oregon also established an independent provider system, wherein individuals hired and supervised an attendant. Despite receiving wages from the state, here, too, attendants became independent contractors, not state employees. Further, the state wage and hour code, following the FLSA, exempted companionship services and household work related to the care of an elderly or infirm person, removing precisely those services—"fellowship, care, and protection" and "meal preparation, bed making, washing of clothes"—that the state had agreed to compensate through its long-term care policy. Also excluded were resident managers and caregivers in adult foster homes.[43]

By the end of the 1980s, the state and the AAAs faced troubling labor shortages and high turnover rates. Demand for services had risen dramatically, but the number of workers stagnated because the pay was so low. In 1989, Oregon secured a demonstration grant, proudly billed as "Who Will Care?," to focus on recruiting and retaining long-term care workers, increasing their "self-esteem," and standardizing training.[44] Counties generated public relations remedies, including an "in-home care workbook," "Careers in Caring" public service announcements, and employee recognition rituals. They did nothing about wages, health insurance, or immigrant support services—remedies that may have enabled low-wage workers to become more economically secure. All the emphasis was on the caring nature of the job—none on its employment aspect. As if to devalue the labor further, the Central Oregon Council on Aging established a volunteer program with unpaid students performing in-home care.[45] Nonetheless, Oregon showed that the state could organize long-term care to meet the desires as well as the needs of senior citizens. Whether those who did the labor of care also could obtain recognition and dignity still remained an open question.

The New Political Economy of Home Care

Nearly all other states eventually joined Oregon in acquiring Medicaid waivers for home health care during the 1980s. But the waivers were a limited policy solution, since they were not meant to open the door to higher levels of social spending. States had little choice but to make sure that home care was much cheaper than nursing homes. The number of people requiring the service grew rapidly, partly owing to demographic trends. In the 1980s, the elderly population increased at twice the rate of the population under age 65, reaching 28 million at mid-decade, with a historic rise in the number of persons living beyond age 75, and even 85.[46] Longer life expectancy meant more people with chronic illness. Yet, during the Reagan years, states had to prove that per capita spending under a waiver would not exceed what spending would have been without it and, further, that aggregate program costs would not be higher than previously. In the name of state flexibility, federal regulations imposed tight control on the net cost of new home- and community-based services.[47] In 1987, Congress placed a cap on a state's total Medicaid long-term care expenditures.[48]

Fiscal imperatives of the 1980s exposed the contradictions of relying on the acute care model as an overarching framework for long-term care.[49] The government no longer wanted to pay for indefinite hospital care. Before 1983, Medicare paid hospitals retroactively, after the patient had received treatment, for however long. Under the new mechanism of prospective payment, Medicare announced in advance what it would pay based on medical diagnosis. If a hospital offered treatment costing more, it would have to absorb the difference. The new approach reduced payments to providers, leading hospitals to discharge patients with greater needs earlier. The demands on home care soared.[50]

With entry into the home health market deregulated, the home health sector became the home health industry. Medicare-certified agencies proliferated rapidly after 1980, especially proprietary firms. For-profit agencies jumped tenfold in the first half of the decade, capturing 30 percent of the market by 1986. Their growth introduced intensified competitive pressures into home care. After the beginning of Medicare prospective payment, hospitals moved to recoup lost revenue by expanding more aggressively into home health care, opening their own agencies, subsidiaries, or joint ventures. These joint ventures might be with nonprofit charities, for-profit agencies, or even pharmaceutical companies. Large chains also emerged from two different ends of the market: health care and domestic labor. More attuned to the workings of the market than traditional visiting nurse associations, these new providers created an industrial infrastructure, including professional journals and trade associations, such as the National Association for Home Care and the American Federation of Home Health Agencies. In the mid-1980s, home health care products and services grossed an estimated $9 billion.[51] Despite their private nature, these proprietaries relied heavily on public spending.

Congress began to wonder what the government was getting for its money, which amounted to nearly $3 billion dollars by 1986.[52] Under the leadership of Democratic liberals, the House Select Committee on Aging announced aggressive action to address the many grievances it had received from elderly Americans. A decade had passed since Claude Pepper and his colleagues had tried to enact home care entitlement and protection. Now once again the Committee tried to push forward a bill. A commissioned report and hearings bore a title that captured the liberal conundrum: "The Black Box of Home Care Quality." Recognizing a new booming industry, fueled by government funds, Committee members acknowledged a government obligation to protect and regulate. The obstacle, as they saw it, arose out of "the in-home location of the services . . . [which] makes their actual delivery essentially invisible and therefore largely beyond the easy reach of public or professional scrutiny." Following revelations of nursing home abuses, representatives feared the worst. They could only declare, "the quality of care in the home is a 'black box'—a virtual unknown."[53]

The Black Box hearings highlighted "exploitation" as a key problem within the home. With great urgency, Chair Edward Roybal (D-CA) framed the challenge of long-term care in the 1980s as one of consumer protection against "unreliable and poorly trained aides" and "questionable care techniques." This consumer protection stance led to a definition of exploitation that positioned workers as perpetrators and consumers as victims. On the list of exploitations were "failure of workers to appear on time and sitting down on the job"; "inadequate or improper performance of duties," physical harm to and abuse of clients, "tardiness or failure to spend the specified amount of time," and "theft and financial exploitation." Legislators perpetuated long-standing racialized stigmas attached to black women workers when they pointed to "attitudinal problems, insensitivity, disrespect, [and] intimidation" of clients. It never occurred to them that home attendants faced exploitation or that restrictive policies and lower funding had anything to do with deteriorating care.[54]

At the height of the Reagan era, these legislators relied on the market models infiltrating all realms of social policy, rather than asking whether budget cuts compromised quality. Committee member John McCain (R-AZ) was an exception in wondering, "Why is the reimbursement rate so low?"[55] But the Committee was unwilling to debate the relationship between strategies of cost containment and quality of care. Instead, it weighed the consequences of policy intervention within restricted ideological parameters. Committee members wanted to increase consumer "choices" in the marketplace, alleging that it would improve accountability, yet discourage consumer "over-utilization." Assuring quality required new standards, but accreditation, it was claimed, burdened proprietary agencies with an additional cost barrier. Well-intentioned regulations, the Committee insisted, would create a greater administrative burden and narrow the range of providers willing to enter the market.[56]

For San Franciscan Hadley Hall, who represented the social welfare community at the hearings, the inability to move past a medical model of care was also deeply connected to the gendered nature of the labor. He urged legislators to see the labor question as central to improving quality. "[T]he reason this problem exists is because most of the work . . . is a mothering function activity," he asserted. Comparing the home aide's tasks with those of hospital and nursing home workers, Hall explained, "When we perform exactly the same functions in the home, those euphemisms become cleaning, shopping, cooking, laundry, help with personal care and transportation, and that's women's work and by God, we shouldn't have to pay very much for it because that is done with love and affection."[57] Until Congress repaired the policy that "split the social from the health," long-term care would remain an insoluble dilemma.[58]

In the end, Roybal's Home Care Quality Assurance bill took the form of a "bill of rights for home care consumers" without reforming the structure of the industry or the labor conditions generated by earlier politics and policy. Thus, it included grievance mechanisms, consumer input in program evaluation, quality assurance monitoring, training certification, and a home care ombudsman to investigate consumer complaints.[59] Although not passed on its own, various pieces of this bill made their way into law through the budget act of 1987. Health and Human Services followed up with new consumer protection requirements, ignoring labor protections.[60]

Ultimately, Congress was caught in a contradiction of its own making. Advocates wanted to help the worthy recipients of the welfare state, America's elderly population, and even recognized that the problem lay not solely in the home but in the realm of policy. They grasped that "the limited Medicare definition of home health services no longer serves as a useful benchmark for home care. It is out of step with the changing marketplace which has recognized a broader, evolving range of needs and services essential to maintain people . . . in the community."[61] That limited definition, of course, came from the medical model imported directly into Medicare at its inception in 1965. It reflected not the reality of home care needs, but rather the political balance of power and professional authority at the time. Within 20 years, it clearly had become anachronistic. The question for Congress was how to bring about change. What structural, fiscal, or social arguments could be made to push aside the medical model and have government pay for assistance with daily tasks of living, services historically defined as welfare support? In the Reagan era, this challenge became ideologically insurmountable. Not only had Reagan's assault specifically discredited welfare and social services; Democrats and Republicans alike thoroughly imbibed market discourse and the idea that too much regulation hurts the market. Although long-term care persisted on the national agenda, expanding the actual availability of home care to mass numbers of Americans remained on the cutting room floor. It did not even make it into the ultimately ill-fated Medicare Catastrophic Coverage Act, the first major amendment to Medicare, passed in 1988 and revoked one year later.[62]

Consequently, Claude Pepper also introduced a separate bill that year to cover home care through Medicare, but congressional Democrats were in no mood to fight for a "big government solution." When the powerful chair of House Ways and Means, Dan Rostenkowski (D-IL), moved to block it for reasons of personal turf, Democrats professed their love and respect for the venerable 89-year-old Pepper but brought the bill down to defeat. House leaders assured Pepper that his chance would come again. Soon afterward, America lost its fighting champion for the elderly when Pepper died in May 1989.[63]

Community Organizing in the Welfare State

On the ground, the Reagan revolution looked more like trench warfare. While the president fought against entitlements from the top down, women claimed rights as both clients of and workers for an embattled welfare state. They brought the home into the center of the welfare state and the union movement into the home.

In the mid-1970s, Illinois took advantage of federal monies to develop community care for the elderly. It intended to meet basic needs but did not count on the numbers of widowed, older women who soon applied for home care. A long waiting list quickly developed. When Mrs. Annie Benson, an African American in her seventies with multiple chronic conditions, found herself on that waiting list, Legal Aid—Reagan's old nemesis—sued the state. A federal court ruled that the waiting list violated equal protection; persons on it were as entitled to services as those already receiving them. With the mandated dissolution of the waiting list, Benson's case classified home care as a new entitlement.[64] In an environment of tax cuts and budget ceilings, that entitlement could become a reality only by creating an arena of struggle in which workers refused to play their role—providing care on the cheap.

Like New York and California, Illinois initially ran its home care program out of public welfare, assisted, like Oregon, by Area Agencies on Aging.[65] Home care served not only as an alternative to institutionalization, but clearly, union organizers charged, "as a way to implement a 'workfare' program to get people off of public aid"—although it paid so little that "some are forced back on Public Aid in their struggle to keep their families fed and clothed." As one activist worker explained, "The State thinks they can get away with this because we are black, brown, and female."[66]

In 1979 Illinois established two programs to pay for home care through its general revenues. The Illinois Department of Aging (IDOA) started the Community Care Program, which contracted with a wide range of nonprofit and proprietary agencies to offer homemaker and housekeeping services to those over age 60. As in New York, workers became employees of vendors rather than the state. Disabled people under 60 would receive similar assistance from the Department of Rehabilitative Services (DORS). In keeping with the ethos of independence, DORS relied on a different mode: clients hired their own providers, who could be family or friends, with the state claiming to be a co-employer. Once again, government created distinctive job categories with unequal reimbursement rates for similar work. Home care remained a welfare program, open only to the needy.

Despite an apparent expansion of the welfare state, Illinois seriously underfunded home care.[67] Even after Benson's suit forced the IDOA to expand the service, the state still appropriated only $23 million in 1983, one-third of what Massachusetts, for example, spent. Reimbursements to provider agencies lagged months behind.[68] Under pressure to enroll all those who applied but unwilling to raise state revenue, Illinois chose two strategies. IDOA added an income ceiling and required user fees for the first time. It also looked around for other sources of funding, applying in 1983 for a waiver to cover personal care service for those eligible for Medicaid. From 3,600 clients in 1979, the caseload grew to 17,500 with the waiver; five years later, it expanded to 27,000 elderly recipients per month.[69] By 1993, IDOA vendors employed over 10,000 workers, with some 2,500 in the union. In granting such waivers, though, the federal government demanded that states keep the cost of home care measurably below that of institutional care.[70]

DORS operated statewide and was equally desperate for funding. It received a federal Medicaid waiver in 1984, covering 50 percent of the cost per person. The client hired, fired, and supervised the worker but DORS set the wage. For homemakers and housekeepers, DORS kept wages at the federal minimum of $3.35 through most of the decade. In the mid-1980s, an estimated 2,500 workers serviced DORS clients statewide, about half of whom worked in Chicago and Cook County. They had no hospital or medical insurance, paid vacation, compensated sick days, life insurance, or compensation for time spent traveling to and from clients' homes, often on long bus and subway rides.[71]

ACORN came to town to change all of this. It started community organizing among Chicago home care workers in 1983. Key ACORN leaders and rank-and-filers came out of the welfare rights movement. Along with other radicals of the period, they had developed a sectoral analysis that linked low-wage workers with those on public assistance, including poor single mothers. ACORN formed the United Labor Unions (ULU) to organize low-wage workers outside traditional workplaces. Like the United Farmworkers, ULU sought to enhance participation, mobilization, and militancy among low-wage workers. It would "*build an organization* first" that could maintain itself during workplace campaigns that could take years. Members paid dues from the moment they signed up, well before the union had certification or a contract; for people who made little, handing over that few dollars a month cemented organizational loyalty.[72]

Head organizer Keith Kelleher arrived from a successful campaign among fast-food workers in Detroit. A graduate of Fordham University, he came out of the Catholic social justice tradition. During his childhood, his grandmother, who had labored as a domestic, took him along while caring for "shut-ins." Kelleher left his native New York after college and headed to Detroit with the Jesuit Volunteer Corp. Through the local Catholic Worker House, he met radical priests who connected young peace and anti-nuclear activists to labor politics, from the UFW boycott to striking newspaper workers. There he also joined ACORN, which trained him as an organizer in the late 1970s.[73] When ACORN reassigned him to Chicago, Kelleher set about cultivating Catholic Church support for organizing the poor. Putting together proposals, he jokingly considered himself a "Catholic grant writer," substituting his own lyrics to the Beatles' "Paperback Writer." Indeed, he succeeded in recruiting support from various Catholic social action funds, along with the Discount Foundation and others in the ACORN network. Members themselves also engaged in perpetual fund-raisers to keep the union going, including canvass collections, bake sales, raffles, dollar parties, and event fees—the money gathering techniques of grassroots politics and African American community support. Selling dinners and tickets at senior homes proved doubly advantageous: organizers could meet aides and educate recipients on the issues while raising funds.[74]

Kelleher not only drew upon his own organizing experiences, but he also tapped those of an already successful ULU local in Boston. Organizers there discovered hundreds of disgruntled and militant African American, Latina, and Caribbean women working below the minimum wage for agencies with contracts from the state. ULU learned where to find these workers; how to follow the money trail; and how to take advantage of the structure of home care—its ties to the welfare state and the bonds between workers and clients generated through the labor process itself.[75]

The Chicago organizers perfected the practice of grassroots activism. They went to the places where the workers were, rather than spending all their time trying to obtain a list of workers from reluctant government offices or contractors. They stood at bus and subway stops and roamed the hallways of housing projects and the streets of neighborhoods. As Kelleher explained: "You have to *build your own list*. You do this by hitting the check pickups, in services [training], and company events on a regular basis and passing the cards and making the contacts." Building the list often meant "dumpster diving"—scavenging through the garbage dumpsters for monthly employment rosters tossed out by the agency. Member-organizers held thousands of house visits, established organizing committees, and cultivated leadership among the local women. Turnover and isolation meant that the employer did not have much daily control over the workforce. Thus, according to Kelleher, "If you do the work and get to enough workers fast enough, you have as much access and influence . . . as the company does and that is the key!"[76]

Early on, Kelleher concluded that "the political reality is that the clients are too infirm and the companies too competitive to get together to raise the necessary hell with the government agencies, executive and legislative bodies to make the programs work the way they should." Thus, he asked, "Who better than the homemakers themselves, acting in their own self interest and out of genuine love and concern for the clients they see every day, can carry the fight for decent, adequately funded home care programs?" The union had to organize the clients, going to where they lived. Kelleher shrewdly noted, "It is obvious that there [*sic*] issues are real and life and death and could help us immensely because if we don't organize them, then the state will organize their leaders against us." Increased state funding would allow clients more hours as well as improve worker paychecks. "The clients could also give us a tremendous boost in the public's mind and lend us even more legitimacy and moral superiority over the state." In short, home care organizing required an effective citizens' organization of workers and client/consumers with churches, other unions, and community organizations as allies.[77] ACORN, churches, and the AFL-CIO initially constituted its organized allies, but by 1993, the union also worked with various local disability rights and independent living groups and organized seniors, including the feminist Older Women's League.[78]

In the face of home care's tangle of public/private authority, SEIU 880 combined community organizing, legal suits, direct action, and political lobbying with agency-by-agency bargaining. It built loyalty and trust through participation in local campaigns against redlining in African American neighborhoods and for affordable housing, cheaper banking fees, and a citywide living wage ordinance. Often, monthly union meetings were as much about these community issues as about specific organizing drives or contract negotiations. ULU got members involved in political work right away. Starting with the 1984 campaign season, its members registered 1,500 new voters and did extensive phone banking for Senator Paul Simon, who won a narrow victory. From then on, 880 brought out volunteers for political campaigns, especially for the offices of mayor and governor. They helped with the reelection of Chicago's reform African American mayor, Harold Washington.

The union remained rooted in the ACORN culture. Personal ties undoubtedly helped: Kelleher's spouse Madeline Talbott headed ACORN in the city. But these key activists stayed behind the scenes. The union consistently cultivated rank-and-file leaders from among home attendant members, like local presidents Irma Sherman and Helen Miller. The women created a social world around the union, with regular meetings, parties, barbeques, recognition ceremonies, letter-writing campaigns, marches, and neighborhood alliances. Monthly meetings seemed like "almost religious experiences" filled with "emotion and spirituality." Reports described how "workers will rise and testify about how they have to work three jobs caring for others to make ends meet but no one cares for them. . . ." They held "speakouts" and "honk-ins," stopping traffic. They linked low wages, misuse of public funds (spent on union-busting lawyers rather than going to clients and providers), and institutional racism, deploying tropes of slavery, dignity, justice, and rights. Like home care workers elsewhere, Mary Jones, who worked for a vendor that refused to settle with the union, pronounced, "It's just not fair! This isn't a job—this is Slavery!"[79]

An involved workforce remained essential to 880's vision of unionism. Without member participation "in all aspects of the organizing committee and the Local then you are beat before you start," Kelleher argued, "because the economics of the industry are such that members have to be involved in every step or they will think the 'union' has sold them out or didn't fight hard enough, and if they aren't involved in the negotiations, and the march on the capitol and the meetings with the legislators, they will never understand it or believe you." Only an active membership could hold the staff more accountable.[80]

Still, Local 880 and ACORN ran up against the public-private conundrum that shaped home care employment. Vendors claimed that the state was the employer or co-employer, and the state argued that the vendors were the responsible party. As one worker at a 1985 public hearing complained, "We are volunteering ourselves, but there is no consideration (to us) as employees. The clients think they are our boss, and in a way they are. We have no guidelines." Another testified, "They say we are not state workers. We don't know who we are. We go to work, but we have no one to complain to. We are unidentified." The state considered itself merely the agent of the client who received vouchers to pay attendants, who came under the Domestic Workers Law. But the state determined from the outset "that (the) federal minimum wage would be used."[81] Once again, workers felt they were treated like maids or servants.[82] Yet, when the union tried to gain redress for wage and hour violations, it found itself stymied by the 1975 FLSA companionship restrictions. The union had to prove that the worker spent most of her time on domestic tasks. It had to deny the emotional labor involved in home care.[83]

ULU 880 won its first victory at National Homecare Systems (NHS). While the union grew in members throughout the 1980s, NHS remained the only shop under contract, anchoring the union during its formative period. It produced the first generation of leadership, women such as Irma Sherman and Doris Gould. Here they honed their tactics: recognition actions, member bargaining, direct action, political pressure, and strategic use of consumer "choice." The NHS contract established standards—not only for wages and benefits but also through a

"Dignity and Respect" clause, grievance procedure, and even a union shop. The union and company formed a workable partnership in fighting for increased funding from the state. NHS became the model, as Local 880's workers at other agencies fought for years to win recognition and contracts.

NHS began as McMaid, Inc., typical of the new "temp labor" companies emerging in the mid-1970s to dispatch cleaners to homes and offices. When entrepreneur Andrew Wright purchased McMaid in 1979, the company already offered in-home services to elderly public aid recipients in Chicago. Over the next few years, this segment of the business expanded rapidly, especially with state contracts for "chore housekeepers." McMaid combined flexible low-wage employment with a rigid, authoritarian, and paternalistic management.[84] Supervisors called middle-aged, black female employees "girls" and required the wearing of special uniforms. In the fall of 1983, the company formed a new division, National Home Care Systems (soon National Homecare Systems), to service contracts with the Illinois Community Care Program.[85]

With a cadre of just 15 to 20 paid members, out of a total workforce of 225, the union dramatically made its presence known soon afterward. In October 1983, an organizing committee, led by employees Sherman, Gould, and Juanita Hill, showed up at the McMaid/NHS office on payday, and gathered workers willing to listen to their testimonials of mistreatment and disrespect. "We're fired up," as they put it. Sherman, Gould, Hill, and others marched into the offices chanting, singing, and demanding a meeting with the boss. When the executive director came out, Sherman announced that their union was ULU 880, and asked him to sign a "Recognition Agreement." He declined, called the police, and retreated to his office amid louder chants. Their union had become public; the workers had made their point. This event was the first of many "recognition actions." Local 880's collective self-assertion of the union served as an adaptive strategy to deal with the limitations of the NLRB, which by the 1980s had become essentially dysfunctional as management perfected ways to contest every aspect of the organizing process, undermine union elections, and stall bargaining. As lead organizer Kelleher explained, "We didn't wait for the employer to formally recognize us, but forced the employer to deal with us without official recognition." The members made it a union, not the state.[86]

In this case, the union won a formal NLRB election fairly quickly in December 1983; after mild legal protest by the company, the NLRB certified the union two months later and ordered negotiations to commence. Members chose co-workers to serve on the bargaining committee, and soon after elected Sherman their president. Once a nurses' aide, Sherman formerly was a steward for the early hospital workers' union in Chicago, the Health Employees Labor Program. Forced to retire from hospital work for medical reasons, Sherman now became a militant, eloquent leader for home care.[87]

The trench warfare, it turned out, would be fought over settlement of a contract. Management evaded, vacillated, and subverted for another year and a half; 880 filed charges with the NLRB against the company for refusing to bargain, only to be sent back into another round of irresolution. Members continued to sign up, pay dues, attend meetings, and serve on organizing and bargaining committees. Being part of the bargaining committee not only enabled these women, most of whom were black, to articulate their specific demands; it also gave them the opportunity to face their white male bosses as equals. Their newsletter, *The Homemakers' Voice*, reported: "[Director] Olson knows now that we're not illiterate, we read our demands to him one by one. . . . He knows we mean business and we're just as smart as he is!"[88] This was an empowering experience, even as the company stonewalled.

Still without a contract a year later, union members realized they had to ratchet up the pressure. Drawing upon the welfare rights tradition, 880 creatively deployed tactics that crossed public and private domains. When negotiations broke down in June 1985, NHS employees picketed Andrew Wright's posh Barrington Hills estate. Seeing his swimming pool, multiple garages, and horse stables, Lillie Mae Thomas wondered whether "that's our money he's spending on that house and all those cars!"[89] Workers also threatened to ask clients to transfer to another agency. In the care work sector, moving consumers from one agency to another had a similar impact to a strike, without leaving those cared for stranded. The Local then gambled on a strike vote, agreeing to walk out on July 1. Notice of the impending stoppage went out not only to the company but also to IDOA. Wright now faced the prospect that the state would drop him as a problematic contractor. A week after paying a visit to his home, the combination of direct action and appeal to the state forced NHS to sign a contract.[90]

When Local 880 announced victory, it put the union shop at the top of its list of achievements. Everyone who worked 21 hours or more would be required to join the union and pay dues. Well aware that raises were linked to the state budget, 880 astutely included a particular contract reopener: any time the state raised the rate paid to the company, then the contract automatically reopened and the union could negotiate a wage increase.[91]

They had won a big victory—their first contract—but given the political economy of home care, it was just step one. While negotiating the "private" contract and organizing other shops, 880 put a "raise the rate" public budget campaign in motion, explaining to members, "ULU Members from all over the city have been meeting with the politicians who control the MONEY that the Company you work for gets from the government."[92] Even before the contract settlement, workers voted to take busloads of union members to Springfield to meet with legislators, IDOA staff, and Republican Governor Jim Thompson.

Member Mary Jones explained, "We have to take it to the top! . . . Big Jim is the man in charge of this, and he has to hear us!"[93]

For such battles, ULU locals learned that they needed greater political clout and a larger support network. Wade Rathke, who founded ACORN and ran the New Orleans chapter, negotiated their merger into SEIU. After a member vote, Chicago's unit became SEIU 880 during the summer of 1985. SEIU affiliation meant, as Kelleher admitted, that "you didn't have to suck up to foundations. These people just wanted to know, how many are you organizing. They spoke our language."[94] ULU saw SEIU as kindred: it had shown a commitment to organize those left behind by the increasingly sclerotic AFL-CIO and, at the time, allowed autonomy for its locals. Kelleher turned to Gene Moats, president of Joint Council #1 in Chicago, to pressure state and local politicians, obtain lawyers and legal advice, and run interference with other unions. Well into the next decade, the ULU/ACORN network—Rathke, Kelleher, and others—remained intact within SEIU, allied with its director of organizing, Andy Stern, who would become the International's president in 1995.[95]

Armed with SEIU resources, Local 880 cut its own political path. It continued with direct action tactics more familiar to welfare rights than to the late-twentieth-century labor movement. Toward the end of 1985, 70 members picketed the governor's office and won a new state Home Care Task Force, which would enable all players to develop policy guidelines and to coordinate demands for increased reimbursement rates.[96] Such political remedies institutionalized the potential of provider agencies and the union to work together in the arena of the welfare state.

One other key factor helped the union win its first contract. A new NHS executive director, Mark Heaney, came on board in May 1985, and he, too, understood the political economy of home care. Where Wright and the previous executive took an ideological hard line against the union, Heaney approached the situation as a pragmatist. He grasped both the potential threat from the union's appeal to the state and the strategic advantages of "partnership." Heaney realized that the union's political organizing and disruption could cost NHS its state contract. After the June 1985 settlement, Heaney developed a respectful, personal rapport with Kelleher; he kept communication open, worked with the union to implement a health insurance plan, and sought out the points where NHS could use the union to increase its client base.[97] Heaney was not an unequivocal friend of the union, but he recognized that they had a common interest in protecting the state's social welfare budget, fighting tax cuts, and disciplining the market.

Where those interests overlapped, the partnership worked. Heaney served on the Governor's Task Force, too, where he joined the union in pushing to increase the state reimbursement rate. Described by the union as the first substantial raise in four years, this 1986 boost helped secure an even better second contract from NHS and affected thousands of other home care workers around Illinois.[98] Amid Reagan's open warfare on the welfare state, the for-profit, corporate NHS distributed postcards to all staff employees to write to the legislature and the governor to support proposed tax *increases*. "The Aging network is indeed a network and we must all work together to support increased funding," Heaney wrote.[99] By the early 1990s, NHS top management even appropriated the language of justice and comparable worth. Pointing out that Illinois paid more to "a janitor to clean floors and toilets" than to homemakers and aides, NHS owner Andrew Wright asserted "that a gross injustice exists in the reimbursement rates paid for homecare services and that a rate *adjustment* is due. . . ."[100] To coordinate collective bargaining with the state budget process, NHS shared information with the union on hours billed to the state for chore housekeepers and homemakers, and both union and company cooperated to force shady agencies out of the market. In that sense, the union helped to stabilize its industry by setting best practices, rewarding firms that met its labor standards, and policing non-union employers, much as unions like the United Mine Workers and Amalgamated Clothing Workers did earlier in the century.

Cooperation, though, remained circumscribed, especially concerning the balance of power between company and union. NHS and Local 880 did not exactly lobby together. The union sent its people to Springfield, while the company or Association of Home Care Providers worked their own channels of influence. When it came down to dividing up the rate increase between wages and profits, they became adversaries again.[101] Meanwhile, the union continually filed grievances against the company on minimum wage violations.

One of the most important changes the union won through the Governor's Task Force was the end of competitive bidding. In the early years of the Community Care Program, IDOA proceeded like any other state agency: it chose the lowest bids. But underbidding the state's top reimbursement rate meant suppressing wages to the bare minimum. Since for-profit and nonprofit providers competed in the same market, they equally drove wages down to the poverty level. Elder care, though, was not quite like other state work. With reimbursement rates so low, agencies came and went rather quickly.[102] By ending this process, the union put a floor under wages across the industry and gave consumers more stability.

Winning better compensation also meant working the politics of federalism at all levels. In 1986, Local 880 members traveled to Washington, D.C., for a national joint meeting of SEIU with ACORN. They heard Jesse Jackson applaud their efforts to unionize low wage workers, pressured the American Bankers Association to negotiate credit for poor people, and protested against apartheid at the South African embassy—all actions in keeping with embedding union politics in a larger poor people's movement. Most significantly, they met with Congress. Lobbying their local representative, Charles Hayes, paid off in terms of political access if not immediate policy change. Hayes became an advocate for increased Medicaid reimbursement rates, the first step toward higher wages. In Congress, he promoted Local 880's proposals: greater funding for adequate client hours and living wages, but also prohibitions against vendor discretion "to hire anti-union consultants—(union busters)—denying low income people their right to organize." The union announced, "Now that we've won commitments at the national level, we must, as Local 880 President Irma Sherman says, 'bring it home, and make our local politicians respect People Power!'" So the local turned out members for public meetings of the Governor's Task Force on Home Care to push for contracts that put less downward pressure on wages and created incentives for choosing vendors that accepted collective bargaining.[103]

Through Heaney and Kelleher, NHS and the union leveraged the four-way relations of state-consumer-worker-company to mutual advantage. When NHS sought to provide homemaker services to families in Chicago public housing, Heaney asked Local 880 and ACORN to write letters of endorsement to the Department of Children and Family Services. Kelleher agreed, since it meant more union jobs.[104] After new Medicaid rules clarified home care clients' right to choose a provider agency or switch to a new one, Local 880 mobilized consumers to switch away from union-busting agencies to companies like NHS.[105]

Nonetheless, maintaining a union shop was difficult. NHS could rely on the structural pitfalls of the job to keep turnover high and union membership in flux. The company did not keep the check-off list current, evaded sending names of new employees to the union, and often failed to deduct union dues from paychecks. The company further devised a new position, the "permanent temporary," to keep workers out of the bargaining unit. It required perpetual vigilance on the part of 880 staff and workers to sustain the union.[106]

The staff worked hard as well to cultivate a rank-and-file steward system. Genuinely invested in participatory unionism, 880 sought to adapt the traditional shop steward to service labor in a sector where there was no common shop. They recruited stewards from all agencies and DORS, even if there was no union contract, and offered regular steward training sessions. Stewards helped workers with grievances and moved petitions. They kept up with members by phone. They also planned the agenda of the monthly membership meetings, which were impressively well attended, drawing between 75 and 150 people. But given all that it took to sustain the union and its political work, staff lamented that they could never find enough stewards to take over from them, at least until the end of the twentieth century.[107]

Expansion outside Chicago generated new conflicts. When NHS sought contracts for other Illinois towns and counties, it sometimes openly fought the union. In places like East St. Louis, the workforce in surrounding towns, trailer parks, and rural areas predominantly consisted of poor whites. These workers had their own, if different, traditions of resistance. Where ACORN had a strong presence, it lent significant support and resources to 880 organizing drives in the late 1980s. Elsewhere, the company would be successful in drumming up racialized fears about outside agitators from Chicago.[108]

The state budget cast a long shadow, yet prompted innovation. When fiscal crisis deepened in 1991, NHS pushed for concessions, insisting that it was at the mercy of state budget cuts. Local 880 tried to turn the pressures of budget politics into a tool to build the organization for the next round of collective bargaining. Unable to win immediate wage increases for current members, 880 experimented with new tactics to leverage the power it had in Chicago. Kelleher suggested to Heaney, "Since the company is asking for concessions and asking for fairness and cooperation in negotiations, we believe it is only fair that National allow workers across the state to freely decide for or against the union." By the 1980s, labor law allowed employers extraordinarily wide latitude to interfere with union organizing campaigns and to discourage workers from voting to join. Thus locals sought ways to extend the base where they were organized without having to run that mostly losing gauntlet, a strategy that came to be known as "bargaining to organize." SEIU attorneys proposed a "legal recognition agreement" in which the company consented to neutrality during organizing. Once a majority of workers had signed union cards (card check), the employer either accepted the union or agreed to an accelerated NLRB election.[109] The use of neutrality agreements and card check turned into a national strategy within home care organizing, which made sense, given NHS's presence in California as well. With hostile employers hijacking the NLRB process, the neutrality agreement would become the quintessential tactic for labor organizing in a conservative age, eventually becoming one of SEIU's hallmark approaches.

The union sought to influence the entire regional labor market for home care, but still required one substantial group of workers to realize this "density" strategy. Illinois's Department of Rehabilitative Services (DORS) delivered home care not through contractors, but rather through individual personal care attendants or PCAs. With thousands of clients, the number of DORS attendants equaled those of all the IDOA vendors combined. Without them on board, the state had an enormous reserve pool of labor.

In 1985, the State Labor Relations Board determined that the department and individual client were co-employers, which left the PCAs in limbo, like the independent providers in California. The state set the terms of employment, including salaries, service plan, and assessment. It processed the payroll, withholding FICA, unemployment, and worker compensation. Clients, however, had "the sole responsibility to hire, dismiss, train, supervise and discipline workers," even if state counselors advised them in this process. Without jurisdiction over both joint employers, the State Board refused to treat attendants as public employees, undermining SEIU's claim for a Chicago and Cook County bargaining unit.[110]

The local proceeded with its organizing project anyway. The state comptroller's office maintained records of checks issued to the attendants, available for public viewing. Local 880 organizers combed through these and painstakingly built their list. As luck would have it, Kelleher's father had been a pioneer at Publishers' Clearing House and coached him on how to set up computerized direct mail. Through such means, organizers reached middle-aged women like future president Helen Miller, a transplanted rural Mississippian who had labored in laundries and factories. Her husband was a union man, and she was among those women whose efforts sustained the black church. Soon she was going along on house visits and, like other DORS workers, participating in the life of the local through membership meetings, fund-raising events, canvassing, and lobbying days. These members led a legislative campaign for a Homecare Workers' Bill of Rights, collecting pledges from legislators.[111]

Demonstrations became public performances, complete with props like a burial casket, live turkey, and giant penny. They bore witness to the refusal of administrators and elected officials to meet with or take seriously the demands of workers and clients. When Secretary of Labor Lynn Martin visited Chicago in

Figure 6.1 Workers and consumers march on Illinois State Capitol, Springfield, 1992. WHI-85573, SEIU 880 Manuscript Collection, Wisconsin Historical Society.

Figure 6.2 Giant penny demonstration at the State Capitol, Springfield, 1992. WHI-85567, SEIU 880 Manuscript Collection, Wisconsin Historical Society.

May 1991, for example, 880 greeted her with the sign, "We Do Our Job. You Do Yours. Enforce Minimum Wage Laws!"[112] Chants and songs took center stage at protests that brought together workers and clients already mobilized through various networks (community, ethnic, disability, and age). These performances strengthened the identity of the home care provider and consumer, as well as serving as spaces to launch lobbying and push elected officials. Workers and consumers confronted state officials with the expectation that labor laws had to be extended to the growing care work economy. Public action made visible this "invisible" constituency, warning politicians to take notice of potential voters. It also exposed the vagaries of the social welfare budget.[113]

The union organized members through electoral districts, so accountability was no idle threat. It mobilized a wide network of friends to pressure the agency, including the Catholic Campaign for Human Development and Carol Moseley Braun, then Assistant Majority Leader of the State House and later the first black woman elected to the U.S. Senate.[114] Between 1985 and 1990, through member lobbying and political friends, the union managed to win pay hikes to just above minimum wage.[115] Kelleher later reflected, "Legislators recognized us as a union even if the state did not."[116]

DORS actively discouraged workers from joining the union. So Helen Miller and the others persisted "just like people did before the NLRA," Kelleher noted.[117] With the help of SEIU lawyers, the local compiled a list of potentially serious and embarrassing labor standards violations, and with the political clout of SEIU's Gene Moats, gained dues check-off and a "Meet and Confer" agreement in October 1990 at the end of Governor Thompson's term. The state, in theory, had to discuss with the union wages, hours, and working conditions, and provide lists of workers monthly.[118] The "Meet and Confer" was a breakthrough, but it was no union contract. DORS administrators would only deal with grievances and the issuance of checks.[119] The "Meet and Confer" gave the union an institutional foothold within the state, but as a limited resolution, it required perpetual renewal.

When fiscal crisis hit the state in 1991, the union's "Raise the Rate" turned into a "Stop the Cuts" campaign. The union had won a major rate increase in 1989, which translated into better contracts from agencies, yet now it was caught in a double squeeze. A federally mandated increase in the minimum wage went into effect that year, but the state refused to raise its own reimbursement rate to accommodate the higher minimum wage, leaving agencies in a crunch. NHS thus sought concessions and suspended the health insurance plan. Just as workers would finally win a boost from a higher wage, NHS adapted to the state's intransigence by cutting hours.[120]

Waiting lists for homemakers and attendants soared, creating a political crisis. In 1991, a thousand elderly clients lost home care. DORS's director feared that militant disability groups and gay activists, the latter turning to home care to cope with the AIDS epidemic, would target the state after it refused new applicants early the next year. ADAPT fulfilled that fear by launching confrontational protests in Chicago. Disability rights activists brought suit, with the result that a federal court prohibited the state from denying eligible Medicaid recipients in-home services, thus forcing the department to accept applications six months later.[121] In 1992, the union could only express relief at stopping future cuts.

By then, SEIU Local 880 had about 3,600 dues-paying members and five contracts. While the total may seem small, it won an award from SEIU, two years in a row, for the highest percentage of increase in membership in the central states' region. Still, Kelleher acknowledged that Local 880's modest success fundamentally reflected the "difficulties of labor organizing in the 1980s." Members as well as staff were aware of the constraints of unionism tied to the welfare state. They talked about organizing consumers to switch to union companies but noted that the tactic could also "break the bank by straining the already tight state home care budget."[122]

Budget battles pitted the legislature against the governor, exposing the precariousness of political unionism without collective bargaining. In 1992, home care workers and clients could celebrate the legislature's passage of a cost of living adjustment and back pay for DORS personal attendants, over Governor Jim Edgar's veto. Subsequently, in 1994, SEIU backed the Republican Edgar for reelection as the lesser evil; he delivered by approving a "fair share" agreement that guaranteed that all workers in the DORS unit either would join the union or pay for its services. Local 880 suddenly surged to 10,000 workers, breaking new ground through direct recognition from a state government. Less than four years later, however, the political winds turned; the same governor negated the fair share agreement, and DORS membership plummeted by nearly half. A militant 880 repeatedly secured wage gains and other benefits, but it required a new, massive fight almost every year.[123]

Soul Power, Union Power, and Political Power in New York

The effectiveness of a metro-level alliance between unions and agencies was realized not in Chicago but in New York. In early 1988, the New York Home Care Union Coalition, led by the National Union of Hospital and Health Care Employees Local 1199, and the Home Care Council of New York City, composed of 60 nonprofit vendor agencies, won a pattern-setting agreement by securing increased state and city funding. Along with the American Federation of State, County, and Municipal Employees (AFSCME), the hospital worker union undertook a two-pronged strategy: press agencies to raise wages and add health benefits and together get the state to increase Medicaid reimbursement so that the agencies could fulfill the terms of the contract. Also essential was having the city, which awarded agency contracts, approve rate hikes.[124] New York unionists, like SEIU in Chicago, found a winning strategy that at its best kept members mobilized, maintained coalitions with elder and disability groups, promoted collective bargaining, and enhanced the provision of necessary services.

Since 1958, when a group of left-wing pharmacists and drug clerks set out to organize the city's hospital workers, 1199 was as much a political as a union movement. It fully identified with the civil rights struggle. In just over a decade, its overwhelmingly poor, female, black, and Latina/o workers built a union that swept through a sector once entirely ignored by the labor movement and excluded by the labor law. In organizing hospital dietary, housekeeping, maintenance staff, orderlies, aides, and clerks, 1199 relied upon "union power, soul power"—a symbiotic relationship with community civil rights activists.[125] From 1963 throughout the 1970s, it turned workplace organizing drives into political campaigns that won bargaining rights from the same state that funded and oversaw hospitals. Whether organizing public or "private" employers, 1199 knew that the state mattered. Like AFSCME before it, 1199 learned how to pressure politicians.[126]

Figure 6.3 Cover, *HealthPac Bulletin*, Fall 1988. Photo by George Cohen, with his permission. Courtesy of Robb Burlage.

In some key respects, 1199 was still very much an industrial union, used to organizing many workers in one place. Though recognizing a group other than the traditional white and male constituency of industrial unions, leaders did not sufficiently acknowledge that the work itself also differed. Despite the intimate and interactive nature of care work, 1199 initially paid little attention to consumers and rarely deployed a strategy based on quality of care. Perhaps because management long had exploited the humanitarian mission of hospitals, 1199 concentrated heavily on living wage demands. "Organizing," leader Moe Foner said, "is key and everything else is peripheral";[127] but lack of attention to the particular dimensions of this labor reflected a traditional adversarial understanding of the employment relation that initially impeded home care organizing.

Provision of home care in New York remained fragmented, and the city still was incapable of meeting the need—despite obtaining a disproportionate share of federal spending. With the quickening discharge of patients from hospitals under the new Medicare reimbursement system and with growing Medicaid rolls, the number of persons receiving home care rose to nearly double those in nursing homes. Medicaid paid 83 percent of home care for New York City; home attendants accounted for nearly 90 percent of that cost in 1984 alone. The workforce continued to resemble the city's laboring poor: nearly all women, with 70 percent black or Latina and an increasing number, nearly half, immigrant and Caribbean. These mostly middle-aged women, many without high school degrees, were often eligible for, but did not necessarily receive, AFDC and Medicaid. "Many workers struggle with the persistent threat of homelessness and hunger," reported social work professor Rebecca Donovan, the first to systematically survey 1199 members. They traveled from one borough to another to care for other poor women.[128]

After a failed attempt to merge with SEIU in 1982, 1199 became SEIU's chief rival in New York City. Home care was a logical extension of its efforts: in the continuum of care work, hospital aides and dietary workers often became home attendants or homemakers on weekends or at night.[129] By the mid-1980s, 1199 represented a third of unionized home care workers, some 20,000 women in 22 agencies. AFSCME had another 6,000, with most of the remaining 24,000 workers in SEIU. Yet, after several years of collective bargaining, wages had risen only 80 cents above the minimum. Paid vacation, sick leave, pensions, and job security were nearly nonexistent. When 1199's 1987 contract ended, most earned less than $7,000 a year, well below the poverty line for a family of four.[130]

Collective bargaining stalled as "the invisible hand at the bargaining table belong[ed] to the city and state."[131] As was the case in Illinois, the terms of vendor contracts with the city and state ultimately curtailed private agencies from negotiating much of a wage increase. If a hospital strike was a bitter pill to swallow, a strike by home care workers would be even more so. With around 50,000 separate, uncoordinated work sites and tens of thousands of frail and disabled clients dependent on attendants, workers could not easily walk out on their own.[132]

Factionalism and racial polarization within 1199 in the mid-1980s certainly did not help matters. The retirement of the founding generation of Jewish Communists generated a succession crisis. With home care workers folded into the hospital division, the union was ill equipped to confront vendorization. After a nasty struggle, the multicultural and militant "Save Our Union" faction took over in 1985 and soon gained a majority vote to establish a separate home care division.[133]

Unionized home care workers in New York City steadily grew in the 1980s, but the social movement begun by SEIU's Cecil Ward and his corps of women organizers that sought to revalue the gendered labor of care, empower women of color, and increase the quality of public benefits stumbled. Both 1199 and AFSCME saw that substantive gains would come only if they stepped outside the NLRB bargaining structure; they launched a political campaign, mobilizing the grassroots in the process. When these unions approached the SEIU local to join them, Gus Bevona—its corrupt president—refused.[134] Here SEIU could not carry the movement forward, partly because the International allowed an autocratic leader unchecked reign over this local. The Bevona leadership did not recognize the essential elements that made unionizing different in home care: the service needs of clients, the community networks that linked these women, and the welfare state location of the labor.

AFSCME and 1199 would move on without this once pioneering union. These New Yorkers were less confrontational than SEIU 880, but they too appealed to public opinion and garnered political support. Beginning with rallies outside City Hall in 1987, they enlisted presidential candidate Jesse Jackson and Cardinal John O'Connor for their cause.[135] The unions had Manhattan Borough President David Dinkins hold a public hearing on the plight of the home care worker. Under the banner of the Campaign for Justice for Home Care Workers, they launched an educational drive to garner public support, with the slogan, "We Care for the Most Important People in Your Life." The nonprofit vendors and nearly every liberal politician joined them. Together, the unions pressured the governor and the mayor. After receiving no response the first time, they doubled mobilizing efforts, brought in more politicians, religious leaders, and bigwigs, and set off a full-scale press blitz.[136]

This coalition of workers and their employers claimed that they were not asking to compensate home attendants "for the patience, the persistence, the loving concern it takes to do their jobs." Instead, they requested "just a living wage." In a series of advertisements run in the *New York Times* in March 1988, they appealed to the ethical sense of the public. The advertisements gave voice to previously silent caregivers, although they also invoked the tropes of pity that disability activists fought against. Readers learned of women like Cynthia Dilligard, who looked after AIDS patients "with a measure of compassion fueled by her strong faith," and Francella Beavers, whose 90-year-old, wheelchair-bound client says, "She anticipates my every need." Such portraits reinscribed the home care worker as a saint rather than welfare cheat, a servant to a higher calling, who soothed the poor, helpless, sick, and friendless, and thus deserved respect, dignity, and just compensation. The active testimony of workers, infused with religious idioms, asked the city to act like Moses leading his people to the promised land and away from poverty.[137] The campaign intersected with

Reagan's rhetoric of service to the needy but redirected such tropes toward state intervention.

On March 31, 1988, after unprecedented negotiations between Governor Mario Cuomo's office and the unions, the state allocated the highest level of new funds for home care ever obtained. The agreement granted both unions a 53 percent wage increase, health insurance, guaranteed days off, and prescription drug coverage. Workers would begin receiving $5.00 an hour, although wages remained 35 percent less than their nursing home and hospital counterparts.[138] 1199 predicted a tremendous impact, with an additional $315 million annually into poor neighborhoods; improved quality of life for 145,000 people; a new minimum wage standard; and real implementation of "welfare to work" for higher wages and health benefits. Moreover, the settlement affirmed the significance of home care for the city's health system and reestablished the position of 1199 as "once again an important force in the city and state."[139]

Worker mobilization had returned as part of the repertoire and radicalism of the union, with 1199 activating some 15 percent of its membership in this home care campaign, a high participation rate for such an atomized workforce.[140] Then, in 1989, Dennis Rivera emerged as the face of the union, elected with newly empowered home care votes. Less than a decade before, Rivera had arrived on the mainland from Puerto Rico already as a committed union organizer. He became a prominent spokesman for working families by building a revitalized 1199 into a political powerhouse during the last decade of the twentieth century.[141]

Adopting the political philosophy of AFSCME, New York's home care unions learned that protecting and expanding the public budget was essential to enhancing the lives of workers. With all parties coming together in 1988, the New York campaign offered a model for other home care organizing, which sociologist Immanuel Ness has named "political action as labor market action."[142] Coalition with nonprofits rested on mutual dependence on state and city monies and a shared interest in the fiscal structure of the service. The campaign both turned home care workers into the deserving poor and directly referenced middle-class anxiety about the fate of their own elderly relatives and their own old age. Finally, it utilized the moral authority of the Catholic Church and the mantle of social justice through the presence of Jesse Jackson and other clergy and civil rights leaders. The strength of unions in New York distinguished this resolution from the long battle that SEIU would begin that very year in the less labor-friendly environment of Los Angeles, where former United Labor Union organizers sought to replicate the model that Kelleher and his members forged in Chicago.

Reflecting in 1993 on the previous decade of struggle during the Reagan era, Kelleher questioned: "Many people would say, is this really worth it—All that work and all that time and all that money to organize these folks and get bad contracts?" They were building a union movement amid the most open assault on the welfare state, the right to organize, and labor standards since the Progressive Era. Still, he answered confidently, "I, of course, would say yes. . . . When you look at all those projections for future employment put out by the Bureau of Labor Statistics, home care workers, security guards and janitors are always the top three. Welcome to the future."[143]

Figure 7.1 Los Angeles 434 Homeworkers United demonstration, c. 1988. Photographer: unknown. Courtesy of SEIU United Long Term Care Workers.

7

"We Were the Invisible Workforce"

Commemorating the death of Martin Luther King Jr., a hundred Los Angeles home care workers marched to demand union recognition on April 4, 1988. "This is Memphis all over again," civil rights leaders addressed the mostly female and minority crowd. "We are saying again today, 'We are somebody.' We're men and women who deserve to be treated with dignity."[1] Grassroots leader Esperanza De Anda remembered: "We were the invisible workforce."[2] Eleven years later, building upon lessons learned in Chicago and New York, the Service Employees International Union (SEIU) "took another step for quality care for Californians and quality jobs for workers," boasted International President Andrew L. Stern, when women like De Anda and 74,000 others voted to join the country's most dynamic union. "I believe the history books will show that their triumph today will play as important a role in American history as the mass organizing drives of the 1930s," declared the AFL-CIO's John Sweeney. Berkeley professor Harley Shaiken captured the ebullient mood of the time when he exclaimed, "It represents the new face of labor—women workers, minority workers, low-paid workers, people who have often been so hard to organize."[3] The Los Angeles home care victory renewed hope that unionization indeed was possible in late-twentieth-century America.

Setback after setback had swept over the union movement since the 1970s. Membership declined from 29 percent of the entire workforce in 1973 to 16 percent in 1991; the number of strikes and other signs of union power sunk with it. Once solidly unionized industries—garments, trucking, steel, meatpacking, and construction—were no longer so. The AFL-CIO had banked heavily on labor law reform in 1978, even seeking a Wagner Act for public employees, but an increasingly business-friendly Democratic Party in control of Congress and the White House failed to push for its passage. After that, the National Labor Relations Board (NLRB) became ever more susceptible to corporate subversion. As the norms and structures of labor law, collective bargaining, and union organization remained rooted in the economy and society of a different time, labor also seemed caught off guard by the new logistics revolution that swept through retail, grocery, warehousing, and distribution. Firms such as Wal-Mart and Home Depot altered the terrain of American employment, with jobs that started to look a lot more like home health care: low wages, floating hours, and non-standard work weeks. Despite this landscape of insecurity, journalists, social theorists, and politicians from across the political spectrum asserted that unions were irrelevant in a "post-industrial" global economy.[4]

The adaptive and purely defensive strategies of the once dominant unions within the AFL-CIO had clearly run dry. Yet the organizing and energy among women, immigrants, Latina/os, and African Americans, combined with surviving union dissident movements, finally pushed the AFL-CIO in a new direction with the first contested election in its history. In 1995, delegates elected John Sweeney's "New Voice Slate" to streamline the federation bureaucracy; to invest more in organizing; to support immigrant, women, and ethnic minority workers in service labors; and to promote equal rights, work-family balance, and other issues pushed by these new constituencies. The challenges of unionizing the service sector moved to the forefront of the labor movement.

In this context, California, the seventh-largest economy in the world, would serve as the bellwether for a revitalized union movement, as it did for so much of the nation's political, economic, and cultural trends. With its extensive public parks, beaches, and highways, housing subdivisions, irrigated deserts, top-ranked research universities, and relatively generous social benefits, California had reaped the fruits of post–World War II public investment. It also became one of the crucibles of modern conservatism, especially the strand that embraced uninhibited free enterprise, anti-unionism, tax revolt, intensive incarceration, and privatization. Hit by a deep recession in the early 1990s, the Golden State encountered the challenges that soon would mark the new political economy: declining manufacturing; growing service, financial, and technological sectors; an eroding tax base; and a deadlocked polity. California embodied the two poles of the new age of inequality: well-educated, high-paid professionals in banking, high tech, and entertainment; and the low-paid strata of restaurant, hotel, cleaning, health and child care, and agricultural workers.

Despite the rise in crime, unaffordable housing, and job flight in the late 1980s and early 1990s, California's population continued to surge. About half of all immigrants made their way there, and these migrants from Latin America and from across the Pacific were turning California into a "majority minority" state. With many benefiting from the 1986 federal immigration amnesty law, they became more visible and vocal members of a newly unionizing workforce. Even those with precarious legal and economic standing injected a new militancy into the labor movement, fighting for a broader citizenship along with rights on the job. Their battleground became the expanding care work economy.

Care work organizing was never easy, but it seemed more promising than unionizing any of the declining sectors. It became prominent as neoliberal elites sought to restructure and privatize government, deregulate business and finance, and expand free trade. Capital flight and offshore production reshaped manufacturing and business services, like data processing and sales, but care work was among those jobs—health care, distribution and transport, janitorial and hotel, retail and restaurant, security, and personal services—that, we have noted, were harder to export. So were social services, despite active downsizing by governments.

In the face of the most hostile anti-union climate in nearly a century, SEIU figured out how to draw new workers and new industries into its orbit. By the late 1980s, it was on its way toward becoming the most innovative and influential union in the nation. In 1979, John Sweeney initiated Local 32 B-32J's home care effort in New York before moving onto the presidency of the International. Just over a decade later, the Justice for Janitors campaign in Los Angeles showed that immigrant workers could spark labor movement revitalization in what had been an anti-union town.[5] Sweeney would bring similar commitments to capturing low-wage workforces for the AFL-CIO when he took its helm and diversified its leadership. His successor, Andy Stern, linked a new focus on organizing with a turn to electoral politics and a shrewd marketing of the union through signature purple shirts and cultivation of journalists and intellectuals. A middle-class son of a New Jersey lawyer and a graduate of the University of Pennsylvania, Stern got his start as a union dissident in a social worker local. He then became Sweeney's organizing director. Growth in home care helped solidify and reorganize union power as SEIU expanded from 625,000 members in 1980 to 1.4 million members two decades later.[6] Rooted in immigrant workforces, SEIU represented a multiracial and increasingly female membership. Under Stern, it sought to adapt to the neoliberal global order in which employers "under intense pressure to lower costs, were simply doing what they thought they had to do to survive, and if you wanted them to behave better you had to make good behavior viable for them," Stern once explained.[7]

In California, SEIU finally assembled all the components necessary for victory when it embraced the users of home care as active partners in its campaign. While the long battle in Los Angeles embodied the hallmarks of a new social movement unionism—constant membership meetings, numerous demonstrations, community and faith-based partners, and political education—legislative mandates and increased funding were necessary to improve conditions and, for that, workers had to join with consumers to lobby the state. Having closely watched the development of home care, health care, and long-term care on both coasts since the 1970s, SEIU leaders now argued for the "expansion of homecare as a progressive and compassionate health care delivery model."[8]

They directed such arguments to consumers, captured through logos like "There's No Place Like Home."[9] The union adopted a cooperative stance because home care fostered a "unique relationship between the homecare workers and their 'boss', the homecare consumer."[10] Taking on home care meant organizing a social service for poor people who relied on minimum-wage workers.

The new care work economy generated a rethinking of unionism and labor's relation to the state, families, and markets. In California, competing unions emerged to capture the different forms of home care, negotiate with the prominent disability rights movement, and confront the development of for-profit hospital and health care chains. As in Illinois, home care unionism in Los Angeles was really welfare state unionism beholden to the location of home-based, long-term care in government welfare programs. But in northern California, SEIU simultaneously promoted a health care unionism that incorporated home-based workers into the medical sector.

By the late twentieth century, the International confronted head-on a fundamental strategic question: how to build a labor movement of poor people in a service so completely dependent on the welfare state. What did it take or what did it mean to have power within this type of structure? Did it require ground-level organization—stewards and monthly participatory membership meetings? Did it require mass numbers and political clout at the top—where the state budget is hammered out? What are the goals of such unionism, where many think of themselves as caregivers rather than employees? These sorts of questions and strategies fermented in California and SEIU International circles, with increasingly higher stakes as the nation confronted the inadequacy of its social welfare, long-term care, and health care systems.

Moreover, as workers and unions reformulated who constituted their movement, they had to build concepts and strategies reflective of the increasingly complex interpersonal relations essential to care work. What could they do when potential coalition partners such as disability activists (who called themselves consumers) had different ideas about "care"? How could they build a care worker unionism when the idea of care was so bound up with multiple negative connotations of dependency, which all involved struggled to reject? Home care workers not only had to overcome representations of helplessness to build political coalitions; they had to challenge such stigmatization within the labor movement and find local unions willing to forge new solidarities. They had to change the exclusion of care workers from the labor law (especially confusion over their employment status) and wrestle from state legislatures and governors the funding on which the entire system depended.

Disability Rights, Health Care, and Welfare Reform

The ideology of independence and individual achievement over adversity central to the new conservatism of the late twentieth century dovetailed with disability rights claims, enabling activists to win political recognition and legislative gains amid an overall delegitimization of social assistance. Independent living activists particularly valorized self-sufficiency. Contesting their portrayal as objects of pity, they sought to counter images of dependency long associated with the "handicapped" and to eliminate barriers to full participation in society. Radical activists embraced an identity politics that promoted a distinctive, pride-oriented "crip" culture.[11] Politicians across the political spectrum supported the worthiness of the disability cause.[12]

Disability rights emphasized the positive, empowering side of deinstitutionalization of aged, ill, and disabled people. The leaders of disability groups were mostly white, educated, and middle class. Portrayed as strivers, who took advantage of public support to overcome adversity, disabled people represented the opposite of mothers on welfare, who were seen as feeding off government largess. (Disabled people actually could be found throughout the society, among both wealthy and poor.) The political affirmation of disability rights in the 1990s emerged in tandem with intensified punishment of poor women, whom states continued to compel to work as a condition for receiving welfare. With a stingy state that refused to raise benefits to meet either market demand or the cost of living, recruiting those on Aid to Families with Dependent Children (AFDC) for home care jobs persisted as an attractive solution for independent living. The more coercive and callous aspects of "self-sufficiency" as part of the neoliberal restructuring of the welfare state and its privatization of social services remained. Disability rights and welfare reform retained a structural connection.

Thus, while rights for poor single mothers became frayed, those for the disabled expanded. The Americans with Disability Act (ADA), signed by George H.W. Bush in 1990, barred discrimination in employment, public accommodation, and transport and required "reasonable accommodation" and accessibility from business and government. It contained a generous definition of disability as "a physical or mental impairment that substantially limits one or more of the major life activities of an individual." Upon passage, the militant direct action group ADAPT changed the meaning of its acronym from American Disabled for Accessible Public Transit to American Disabled for Attendant Programs Today and shifted the target of protest from the U.S. Department of Transportation to Health and Human Services. In lobbying for the ADA, proponents tapped into dominant ideas of worthy citizenship: personal attendants enabled access to employment that would eliminate welfare dependency.[13]

Other activists were less sanguine about the ADA. Edward Roberts, then co-director of the Oakland-based World Institute on Disability (WID), remarked that "[t]he intent of the law will make a major difference, but it will take years."[14] It took until 1999 for the Supreme Court to rule in *Olmstead v. L.C.* that the ADA required states to provide community-based treatment as a right; undue institutionalization qualified as discrimination "by reason of . . . disability." The editor of the movement journal *Ragged Edge* understood that the political struggle was by no means over: "Getting states to implement the Supreme Court's integration ruling means fighting for dollars that nursing home operators see as rightfully theirs."[15]

Disability activists sought further systemic changes through Bill Clinton's health care reform. For nearly 20 years, they had called for comprehensive national health insurance that would include coverage for people with "preexisting conditions," home care, and long-term care.[16] They conducted investigations and offered expert advice, with advocates from WID testifying before Congress and serving on the Clinton Health Care Reform Task Force. WID's other co-chair, Judy Heumann, joined the Clinton administration as an Undersecretary of Education.[17]

During the presidential campaign, Clinton pledged to promote consumer-driven personal assistance services and to expand home health care for the elderly as part of comprehensive reform.[18] As Arkansas governor, he oversaw Elder Choices, a program that entitled recipients to spend money previously targeted for nursing homes on home health care, personal care, adult day centers, or other services; one of his first acts as president was to allow states greater flexibility in this regard. The Presidential Task Force on National Health Care Reform recommended transferring spending from institutions to community-based care. His health plan, announced in September 1993, would have made long-term care and help with daily activities in the home available, regardless of age or income, through an additional monthly premium under Medicare. Employed people with disabilities could qualify for a federal tax credit to offset the cost of personal care or equipment, while the government would set minimum standards for long-term insurance.[19]

The implosion of Clinton's grand effort became a generational defeat for broad health care reform and social welfare. The debacle so completely discredited government social support that it quickly fueled "welfare reform." Enacted two years later in 1996, welfare reform further eroded health care access. The Personal Responsibility and Work Opportunity Act not only forced single mothers to toil for benefits and restricted eligibility for AFDC, and thus Medicaid, but eliminated any right to public assistance.[20] It initially barred thousands of disabled and elderly immigrants from Supplemental Security Income (SSI). In California and many other states, this disqualification then blocked eligibility for home care and medical assistance.[21]

When it came to the providers of care, the old rehabilitation narrative justified a new push for workfare, despite the paucity of training monies. The Personal Responsibility Act limited lifetime public assistance to five years and encouraged the states to place recipients into employment as soon as possible, even if they had infants. States designated home care, like home-based child care, an appropriate workfare placement only if performed for individuals other than family.[22] For over five decades, politicians and welfare administrators had insisted that home care jobs would end women's dependency and poverty. Despite a lack of evidence, they once again acted on this steadfast assumption.

With the demise of Clinton's plan, corporate-driven managed care rapidly became the dominant form of health coverage in America. Although HMOs had been around for decades, and even had cooperative, progressive roots, now for-profit conglomerates devised financial incentives and administrative controls to reduce utilization, restrain doctor decisions about treatments, and push providers to make cost-efficient choices.[23] Managers pursued cost containment through deskilling of nursing, including the use of floaters and other temporary employees. Insurance gatekeepers policed reimbursable procedures, trumping medical diagnosis.[24] Managed care threatened to reduce services and individual control over treatment, changes that the disability movement found abhorrent. Managed care's stringent policies also served to reshape public programs, since the number of HMO-enrolled Medicaid recipients soared during the 1990s.[25]

The Challenges of IHSS

In many ways, California helped drive managed care, and yet it also became a recognized leader in consumer-directed home care services. What happened there offered an exemplar for other states. Winning a consumer-friendly system took a protracted political struggle that brought SEIU into coalition with retiree and disability groups to obtain higher wages and more funding from the state. Some California counties contracted out services to private agencies, as in New York and Chicago, but the California Foundation for Independent Living Centers mobilized to push the independent provider system instead, especially to combat managed care.[26] In the 1990s, independent providers made up most of the labor force. Consequently, the union had to organize these workers to gain the political momentum necessary for improving the wages and working conditions of home care.[27]

There was no way that the old NLRB factory-based model could work here; labor had to devise a creative offensive. As the presence of the United Domestic Workers of America (UDWA) underscores, multiple paths to unionization existed in California. During these years, SEIU came to dominate home care organizing, but union locals in northern and southern California developed out of their own contexts as much as from the overall structure of the occupation. Their various adaptations inadvertently helped to sow ideological and strategic conflicts that subsequently would disrupt the American labor movement in the twenty-first century.

Home care advocates in California were constantly embattled. Forced to ride the crests and troughs of state politics, In-Home Supportive Services (IHSS) suffered from uneven administration, financial shortfalls, and bureaucratic red tape. From its beginning in 1972, the program grew rapidly: its $70 million budget in 1976 rose to some $623.4 million in 1989. Still, underfunding was ever present, whether from faulty estimates of utilization or shifts in federal ceilings on matching funds. Without standardized procedures designating allowable costs, the yearly process of contracting out the service generated intense lobbying, political pressures, and rock-bottom bids that only could be fulfilled by cutting workers' wages.[28] Some critics saw the fragmentation of responsibility between levels of government, families, and recipients as a deliberate attempt at cost cutting.[29] Concluded one former home care agency executive, "The present homemaker/chore program in California is a system of statutory and administrative neglect which has led to a fairly racist, sexist program which victimizes the poor, the uneducated, the disadvantaged . . . most of whom are minority women."[30]

The numbers served by IHSS nearly tripled from 1974 to 1990, from some 60,000 to 170,000 recipients.[31] These clients also differed in age and status from the profile of the most vocal disability rights activists. As in other states, nearly 70 percent were elderly women and, in contrast to older men, about 90 percent had no family or relative available to provide care. They had a monthly income of less than $600 and usually were receiving SSI. Recipients mostly needed housekeeping, with some personal care, like help with bathing. Others required accompaniment to doctors. The significantly disabled, defined as receivers of personal care for up to 285 hours a month, accounted for only 20 percent of the caseload.[32]

Recipients who required around-the-clock care relied on undocumented immigrants. IHSS colluded by issuing "pseudo" Social Security numbers for payroll purposes, until the federal government ended the practice in 1988. Consumers responded with frustration and anger. One woman confessed a few years later: "[T]hey want you to have attendants with social security numbers. . . . Let them work if there [*sic*] willing to work, if I run an add and somebody is not an American and cant show me a SS # you think I care!!! I want to get out of bed in the morning. . . ."[33]

Others wanted to hire a family member, though counties only reimbursed relatives for tasks beyond expected routines. Family caregivers resented the attitude of authorities who felt that "we should volunteer . . . that we should be willing to sacrifice our health, well-being and lives . . . and that we should be grateful for any dime our government generously hands out to us to do this care providing."[34] Their numbers grew only after union victories raised wages and provided health benefits; by 2003 they constituted 70 percent of providers in some counties.[35]

Tales of elder abuse haunted public discussions.[36] In 1991, California's Little Hoover Commission, established to improve government performance, fed into such fears by concluding, "The State's efforts to help this vulnerable population may instead leave the frail elderly at the mercy of untrained, unreliable and even abusive care givers who are largely unmonitored by either the State or the counties." Even when silent on race, such comments reinforced racialist stereotypes because most workers were African American, Latina, or immigrant.[37] At the same time, state and county officials often ignored abuse of workers, as when clients accused them of stealing, accosted them in foul language, threatened them sexually, and burdened them with extra household tasks. As one worker complained, "You don't take advantage of elderly people, they take advantage of you."[38]

If these problems were not enough, IHSS's major growth spurts occurred just when California's robust economy and political confidence faltered. The Reagan recession of the early 1980s hit the state hard, followed by another in the early 1990s when Cold War defense spending wound down. The state budget declined for the first time in a half century.[39] The radical tax reductions and budget restrictions of Proposition 13, passed in 1978, were making it increasingly difficult to adapt the state budget to economic changes and population growth. Inequality intensified as California became a laboratory of the new global economic order, containing innovative and well-compensated high-tech industries and expanding agribusiness, retail, and service sectors. Low-paid jobs replaced unionized ones. California politics remained unsettled, combining strong support for civil, women's, and worker rights with passage of propositions against affirmative action and for mandatory sentencing and immigrant restriction. Enough citizens embraced a "law and order" political ethos to give power to a conservative Republican Party, which spent billions on mass incarceration. Proposition 13 and subsequent ballot initiatives laid the groundwork for permanent financial instability: the legislature could pass spending increases with a simple majority, but revenue increases required two-thirds votes.[40]

Whether under Democrat Jerry Brown or subsequent Republican governors, IHSS served as a convenient target for budget slashing—even after the legislature in 1988 deemed home care an entitlement for those who met income and needs requirements.[41] Legislators introduced various proposals to reduce state funding, cap worker wages, eliminate family providers, restrict the service to the most impaired, and limit client hours. The governor would propose less funding, newspapers would run horror stories about worthy recipients and their caregivers who faced dire consequences from the state's uncaring budget axe, workers and consumer advocates would demonstrate at the capitol, local officials would lament ill treatment of the vulnerable, and the courts would compel payment of withheld wages during the time that the state operated without a budget. After all this, the legislature would force the governor to withdraw most, if not always all, of the cuts. A political game unfolded in which governors could appear tough and avoid asking for new revenues, but also look compassionate because, after all the commotion, they would restore what amounted to a small percentage of the state's budget to avert "human tragedy."[42]

Exasperated IHSS workers and disability advocates perceived such brinksmanship as a double insult, disrespecting vital needs and labor. A mother attending to two developmentally disabled adult sons, only partially compensated with minimum wage for her around-the-clock on-call work, fumed, "If they [state officials] can be so capricious about paying us, obviously they do not respect the level of effort involved."[43] Such workers became assertive, demanding their rights because, as one live-in attendant declared, "We earned this money."[44]

In the late 1980s, SEIU had to devise ways to reach this workforce of women caregivers, most of them poor and tending to family.[45] Following the money trail, it initially argued that home care workers, including independent contractors, were public employees. With Los Angeles containing half the state's IHSS caseload, its public sector union local took the lead.

SEIU's presence in southern California dated back to the late 1940s, when it organized janitors and building service workers throughout the sprawling metropolis. A decade later, over a third of its Los Angeles members were in public sector jobs. After merging with a radical local of the United Public Workers, SEIU had 20,000 Los Angeles members in 1960, over half of them African American and Mexican American. With a strong base among blue-collar men in sanitation and janitorial jobs, as well as men and women in public hospitals, the union early on promoted African American leadership and equal rights. Unionized public employees played prominent roles in civil rights struggles in California. By the 1970s, SEIU had established itself as an important and widely recognized institution in black Los Angeles.[46] Local 434 represented about 7,000 Los Angeles county-employed health care workers in the mid 1980s, when it started looking at home care.

The International took a gamble and dispatched top staff from around the country to initiate a plan for organizing the Homecare Workers Union 434B. Lead organizers came from the ACORN unions absorbed into SEIU a few years before. The International sent veterans Kirk Adams and Mike Gallagher, who understood the significant distinctions between the medical and social service organization of home care. Certified home health agencies, spawned by Reagan's budget reforms, they left to SEIU health care locals. They concluded that "private pay agencies are in the same category as temp or pool outfits and therefore not easily targetable for organizing." Instead, state-funded programs, with workers and clients traceable through welfare departments, formed their objective: these employed more people and had poorer wages and working conditions. In the late 1980s, the SEIU International deliberately settled on Los Angeles as "a big city with a large program, good access to workers, plenty of issues, a contracting and rate reimbursement system which could be pressured, political allies at hand, an existing SEIU local with an interest in homecare, and a chicken in every pot."[47]

Following the Chicago model, SEIU drew on a repertoire of tactics that blurred the lines between community organizing and political unionism. Organizers built a city-wide organizing committee through home visits and direct mail, trying to reach 40,000 attendants, whose numbers kept growing. Instead of industrial unionism's focus on the shop, they divided the local into district membership chapters based on political canvassing and grounded the campaign in issues of public concern, like minimum wages and quality care.[48] Gallagher and Adams launched a massive campaign in October 1987, spending $285,000 during nine months in 1988 alone and hiring over 20 full-time organizers.[49] Taking a cue from both New York and Chicago, they put forward a "Homecare Workers Bill of Rights" that called for fair wages, a referral system, health insurance, adequate training, and reimbursement for work expenses—planks reflective of typical union demands.[50] For the final drive, the International brought in David Rolf, a young organizer from Georgia, who oversaw a victory that took a decade to achieve.[51]

Bay Area locals followed other paths. Local 616 in Alameda County, representing white-collar public workers in Berkeley and Oakland, established a home care division that cultivated worker organizers and developed leadership from within. Health care Local 250 added a home care division to its nursing home and hospital units. After a triumphant but draining strike in 1986 against Kaiser Permanente and a short period of trusteeship (International control of the local's affairs), Local 250 flourished under new leadership from rank-and-file activists Sal Rosselli and Shirley Ware. Promoting union democracy, the local valued a vigorous participatory culture and built an active shop steward organization. Home care members were fully incorporated into the new union structure.[52] What became a tradition of member involvement ironically would prove troublesome for SEIU International two decades later, when Rosselli and his allies fought a top-down order that home care and nursing home workers be transferred from their jurisdiction into a separate California long-term care local.

Local 250 began organizing agency-employed workers, winning an agreement with San Francisco's major vendor, Remedy, the same company that UDWA faced in San Diego. When National Homecare Systems (NHS) replaced Remedy in 1989, the company planned to gut the soon-to-expire union contract. The elected bargaining committee, comprised of NHS workers such as Mabel Davis and Rosie Byers, showed the Chicago interloper otherwise. When the company stonewalled, home care workers turned to their political allies among city officials and the San Francisco Board of Supervisors that Local 250 had built through its hospital organizing. "Our political clout nailed down this contract and avoided a strike," reported President Rosselli. Workers won ten paid holidays and up to four weeks of paid vacations a year.[53] As in Chicago, NHS remained Local 250's only shop under contract in the early 1990s, but well aware of SEIU organizing elsewhere, the union launched its independent provider drive in 1991. Worker leaders like Ella Raiford, who not only labored full-time at a nursing home but also cared for a family friend part-time, jumped on board.[54]

Locating the workers was not the only hurdle that home care organizing committees faced. Even as they signed up thousands of independent providers, it was not clear who could legally negotiate with the union. As more counties moved toward using independent providers, SEIU strategists thought the law would tip their way. Between 1983 and 1985, California's courts and its attorney general ruled at least three times that the state was the employer of home-based caregivers. In 1983, the federal Ninth Circuit held the state and counties liable for the wages and hours of workers for the purpose of enforcing the Fair Labor Standards Act (FLSA), since the Department of Social Services and county welfare agencies "controlled the rate and method payment, and . . . maintained employment records." Particularly important was their assignment of hours, even though consumers supervised aides on a daily basis.[55] Two years later, the California Court of Appeals asserted that the county's "*sufficient control* over the IHSS provider" made the state an employer for the purpose of workers' compensation.[56] California's attorney general therefore determined that IHSS attendants would be treated like employees for Social Security deductions and tax withholding as well as workers' compensation. Yet, he made clear, they were not civil service employees.[57]

SEIU assumed that California's courts soon would resolve the larger question of employment status in its favor. But the Court of Appeals ultimately ruled against the union by claiming that previous decisions were inapplicable because they never considered whether IHSS workers could be considered public employees. Instead, it argued that since counties did not supervise activities on the job, IHSS workers were "independent contractors" and thus were not subject to California's public employee bargaining law. Like the state of Illinois, Los Angeles County consequently refused to negotiate with the union. It was not the employer. Yet neither were the state Department of Social Services, the IHSS program, MediCal, or individual clients.[58]

Blocked in the courts, the union turned to a political solution. SEIU legal strategists proposed the creation of a public authority to serve as an employer for collective bargaining purposes.[59] By the fall of 1990, a task force within the union, led by its chief representative in Sacramento, Maury Kealey, and UCLA law professor Craig Becker, began sketching the power of such an authority, its legal basis, and political saliency. In crafting the legislation, SEIU aimed to provide IHSS workers with the benefits of public employees, without classifying them as civil servants, both to maximize flexibility for bargaining and ease enactment.[60] In the 1980s, SEIU had made big organizing breakthroughs by moving outside individual firms and confronting national chains, or attacking on all fronts of a local industry to raise wages.[61] The public authority was an attempt to create a public sector analog that could overcome the fragmentation of home care by the state.

Consumers agreed to try the authority idea. A coalition already existed in Sacramento that worked closely on legislative issues. It flourished through the efforts of dedicated organizers, like SEIU's Janet Heinritz-Canterbury (previously executive director of the Congress of California Seniors), who spent hours meeting in elder centers and with disability activists to build the trust necessary to carry forward the project.[62] Some of these men and women represented both disability organizations and the union—to the chagrin of diehard consumer advocates who smelled a conspiracy to place the union in control of their lives.[63]

Seniors, represented by such groups as the Older Women's League and California Senior Legislature (CSL), had lobbied effectively to shift state priorities from nursing homes to home care. They worried more about reduced hours and competent aides than about power relations with attendants.[64] Starting in 1992, key activists from the CSL agreed to cooperate with SEIU on legislation to meet standards that seniors wanted, like criminal background checks, and to improve worker pay as well. Because of the Older Americans Act and its Area Agencies on Aging, California seniors, like their counterparts in Oregon, were well organized at the county level; they in turn elected statewide delegates to represent them and intervene on legislative issues in Sacramento.[65] For the home care cause, they could be mobilized for both the provision of services and the shaping of legislation.

Deep internal tensions and lack of understanding, however, needed to be overcome before the union and the independent living movement could work together. When SEIU began its Los Angeles campaign, disability activists had spent nearly two decades fighting to choose, train, and control the attendants who made independent living possible. They demanded a full range of services, not just personal maintenance, but also mobility and household assistance. They also objected to restrictive income limits that placed recipients in a bind similar to the catch-22 that had hampered Connie Panzarino in New York.[66] Militants opposed agency contracts, or vendorization. Shrewdly, they saw it as "privatizing government services" and opening the door to profit-driven managed care. They considered such efforts a way both to limit consumer choice and relocate funding from services to supervision and company profits. Activists, such as ADAPT's Marta Russell, charged that contractors, like public officials before them, risked the well-being of consumers by neglecting "certain authorized services under the *assumption* that family members and neighbors would do them."[67]

Moreover, the independent living movement and their attendants had a fundamental disagreement about the nature of the job. The World Institute on Disability rejected the designation "care work" and instead spoke about "attendant services."[68] Organized seniors also preferred to call the IHSS worker a "service provider."[69] Politicized workers refused this characterization. The term "personal assistant," insisted Sacramento union activist Lola Young, "implies a gopher." But, "I'm nobody's gopher," declared Young, a white woman who entered the field attending to her former husband. "I'm a careworker."[70]

To its credit, SEIU recognized that its real adversaries were not the consumers but government bureaucrats and elected officials.[71] To secure funding from the state, SEIU was ready to concede labor control to organized consumers in return for their collaboration. By the summer of 1992, independent living centers agreed to support collective bargaining if disabled people would retain consumer control over the authorities and retain the right to hire, fire, and direct their attendants.[72] That fall, African American Assemblywoman Gwen Moore (D-L.A.), elected with SEIU support, successfully introduced a bill that enabled counties to develop local public authorities. This new law created an employer to bargain with—as well as a central registry to locate the home care workforce. It mandated that at least half of the members of the authorities would be current or past IHSS recipients.[73] To organize home care, the union had to break through narrow and rigid definitions of public employment. It thus not only had to innovate on the ground but create a new state structure in order to accommodate the complex employment relations of home care.

SEIU's Bay Area locals first realized the potential gains of the public authority. San Mateo County created the first one in September 1993, with Alameda County following a month later.[74] For Berkeley disability activist Hale Zukas, who would sit on the public authority, this board would "improve referral so that when attendants do quit it will at least be somewhat easier to find someone to replace them." With formation of these public authorities and a more definite handle on who and where the workers were, SEIU 616 began enrolling members. As part of the legislative compromise to proceed with public authorities, IHSS applied for a federal Medicaid waiver to pay for personal care services not automatically covered by Medicaid.[75] But funding was not fungible. The federal waiver would not cover household tasks or family providers, which meant that these components of IHSS remained hostage to the politics of the state budget.[76] Alameda County Supervisor Gail Steele boasted of helping "the neediest," but Zukas offered a more reserved perspective. "The biggest problem is the low pay," he explained, "but the money is not there to do much about that."[77]

Reflecting its particular mixture of progressive politics, community involvement, and history of working relations between the union, advocates, and officials, San Francisco developed the best conditions for home care workers in the country. With an on-the-ground presence in hospitals and nursing homes, Local 250 had earned the city's respect. For years it had supported both local and statewide issues, participated in health care coalitions, and promoted big ideas, like the single payer alternative to Clinton's plan for managed care. Local 250 also had been politically active in Sacramento since the 1950s.[78] In May 1995, San Francisco voted for a public authority that would be independent of the supervisors and accountable to consumer groups like Planning for Elders in the Central City, which, with the union, crafted the ordinance through a series of strategy meetings and community forums.[79]

The new wave of home care organizing began with multilingual teams canvassing the city, reaching those who spoke Spanish, Cantonese, Mandarin, Tagalog, and Russian.[80] As in Chicago, organizers targeted neighborhoods with lots of low-income buildings and senior housing subsidized by the city and the U.S. Department of Housing and Urban Development. In an effort to educate the consumers and reach workers, Karen Sherr, a social worker turned lead organizer, enlisted other social workers to leave union flyers in the washrooms at the senior buildings and to invite union speakers to tenant meetings. Meanwhile, the union trained a remarkable group of worker leaders, who over the next few years made thousands of home visits.[81] Aides like Mabel Davis, Rosie Byers, and Ethel Richardson, all of them African American, defended the rights of workers and consumers before county supervisors; at one point activists brought a bag of groceries before one commission to dramatize "what the raise meant." The cross-sector strength of the union, even in the mid-1990s, was apparent. Home care workers walked hospital worker picket lines and expected solidarity from others in return. Said home care member-organizer Myra Howard, "We supported our fellow union members to unite with them and strengthen the union for all of us. When it comes time to get the public authority and . . . get a contract we will need the help of our brothers and sisters in the other divisions."[82]

Ties cultivated by the hospital workers with Mayor Willie Brown and supervisors paid off. In San Francisco's largest union election in decades, 5,600 independent providers voted to join Local 250 in the spring of 1996, bringing the union's overall membership to over 40,000.[83] The county board passed $1.3 million for higher wages, the first raise in 20 years.[84] Then, in 1997, San Francisco became the first county in California to sign a union agreement covering independent providers.[85]

Government and workers were not the only ones at the bargaining table. Also present were the consumers, many of whom feared the influence of the union. Yet the trust that advocates in San Francisco had earned allowed them to organize with the consumers in ways that never happened in the more fragmented environment of Los Angeles. They recognized the need to give consumers "voice."[86] What resulted, Sherr explained, "was more of a social contract—about living together in society—it was about the further organization of society, about political aims and alliances" that would enhance the "vested interest in a continuous and well-qualified care program" by the workers, clients, community, and state social services.[87] Within a decade, with continuous improvement in wages and health benefits, economist Candace Howes found, turnover among San Francisco's IHSS workers decreased by nearly a quarter. Along with Santa Clara, its home care wages became the highest in the state, topping $10 an hour.[88]

Local 250 also used campaigns for a public authority as a unionizing tool. In the mid-1990s, it had organizing committees in Contra Costa, Marin, Sacramento, Fresno, and Sonoma counties. In each place, Local 250 approached disability and senior groups and built coalitions that educated the county Board of Supervisors on home care issues and the benefits of a public authority. Through these meetings, union organizers would sign up more workers. By 1994, Local 250 had a regional strategy in play, though in each case, the union was built around local issues and politics. It encouraged new members in these other counties to participate in the union's Homecare Steward Council, well before they had an authority, recognition or contract. In this way, Local 250 resembled SEIU 880, which early on had pioneered in going "metro."[89]

In creating its home care division, Local 250 developed a participatory and democratic union culture that persisted into the next century. To be sure, there were internal disputes and power struggles, but it prided itself on member involvement. Its elected bargaining committees shaped contracts after surveying the workforce; bargaining sessions were transparent and open to members. It trained a strong steward's council, representative of its multicultural workforce. The Homecare Leadership Committee went over flyers and handbooks to ensure the accuracy of information and appropriateness of style. Finally, Local 250 joined with locals from Los Angeles, San Mateo, and Alameda counties to create a statewide movement, but understood that the county organization of the service necessitated a county-based union.[90]

Unionists in Los Angeles faced greater obstacles. SEIU established a Los Angeles County IHSS Coalition that reassured the disability community that public authorities would adhere to consumer rights. Heinritz-Canterbury shuttled from group to group. She finally got the widely admired Ed Roberts to mediate between factions.[91] Roberts felt more threatened by managed care companies, which would end consumer control, than by the union. In September 1993, he backed SEIU because it "has gone a long way on this issue—no strikes, people with disabilities have the right to hire and fire—this is unusual."[92]

A group of outspoken activists nonetheless remained convinced that the interests between the two groups conflicted. Marta Russell charged that unions opportunistically saw "attendant services as a lucrative area in which to organize previously unorganized workers."[93] Another ADAPT activist fretted, "With a union fighting for 'terms and conditions' of their attendants and no one fighting for our basic right . . . to move, go to bed, have a shower, a bowel movement[,] a meal, it will be more of a David and Goliath situation than it already is."[94] Fearing strikes and union interference in employment and supervision of attendants, these militants formed an opposing coalition. Mostly they worried about a power imbalance, that they "would be steamrolled."[95] To allay such concerns, the Homecare Workers Union, Local 434B, joined with the independent living centers and seniors groups to protest any move toward managed care.[96] This protest allowed Local 434B to distinguish itself from UDWA, which by then held contracts with National Homecare Systems in 13 counties.[97]

The SEIU-consumer alliance appeared unusual if we only consider the disability groups dominated by younger white activists. As one Local 616 organizer underscored the larger situation: "The recipients are low income and are not even in the coalition," that is, most consumers resembled their providers more than they did the disability rights organizations.[98] Chinese immigrants, for example, worked for "elders, not consumers," older members of their ethnic community who were "to be honored, respected, cared for," as SEIU member LaiXiao Jiang explained in 2008.[99] The representative recipient of state-subsidized home care—a poor elderly woman of color—herself would gain from unionization: increased hours of service, perhaps additional household income paid to her caregiver, and better overall care. Not only did savvy militants obscure the race of home care consumers by offering themselves as the body and face of disability, but their opposition to the establishment of the Los Angeles public authority helped delay higher wages and better conditions to a poor women of color workforce. It was as if the focus on one identity blinded some independent living activists to the compound harms of race, gender, class, nationality, and ability.

Noisy consumer opposition allowed Los Angeles County to drag its feet on the public authority. Even to have the Board of Supervisors commission a feasibility study, SEIU 434B had to mobilize hundreds to demand action. Only continual political pressure led the supervisors to cave in 1997. Together, the union and consumer activists drafted a public authority ordinance with the county that not only created an employer for workers, but also a consumer-led board. They prohibited strikes. That disability activists divided on features of the authority inadvertently shows the importance of strong coalitions, as in San Francisco, for home care unionism.[100] Yet the primary reason for delay came from the reluctance of supervisors, consultants, and the county Department of Public Social Services to implement legislation that they deemed just too expensive without more state monies.[101]

Massive mobilization proved crucial for additional public action. Faced with the necessity of obtaining increased funding from the state to win over local officials, SEIU activated the grassroots again and again. Through letter writing, picketing, sit-ins, and other demonstrations, the coalition made it politically feasible and necessary for Sacramento to pass additional bills. In 1999, after Democrat Gray Davis's election to the governorship, the SEIU coalition won greater pay. The public authorities joined the unions and their coalition partners to win an additional provision compelling all counties to establish some type of central employer for collective bargaining purposes by 2003.[102]

The union, of course, still had to gain representation. Although SEIU had signed up workers for years, Los Angeles County claimed that it would not recognize a union until SEIU held a majority among the total number of independent providers. The campaign kicked into high gear. Other SEIU locals helped with phone banking in the final months of a long struggle, while Los Angeles home care workers hit "the laundromats, check-cashing outlets, bus stops—anywhere workers might be reached." At the first meeting of the Public Authority in November 1998, the union showed up with enough representation cards to request an election. A decade of organizing and political creativity finally paid off in February 1999, when 74,000 workers in Los Angeles voted ten to one to join the union in one of the largest mail-in elections ever. With the decline in large-scale manufacturing, American labor had seen few victories on such a scale in the late twentieth century. SEIU showed that a combination of card check, political solutions, and active mobilization could bring in the huge numbers reminiscent of a CIO victory from an earlier era.[103]

Soon after the big election, Andy Stern sent his new protégé, Tyrone Freeman, to run this enormous local—one of the largest in the country. A dynamic young African American leader, Freeman was fresh from major victories in the South.[104] In the ensuing years, however, the Los Angeles union grew through accretion and mergers, rather than active organizing, and Freeman consolidated power at the top. It became a massive, stand-alone, long-term care local of low-paid nursing home and home care workers, where internal opposition dried up as the union moved further out of the hands of the rank-and-file leadership. This trajectory also put SEIU 434B on a different path from Local 250, which linked its smaller home care division with hospital and nursing home workers to form a multi-sited health care union that maintained a commitment to internal democracy and rank-and-file development.

The Culture of Organizing

If home care unionization depended on political victories, what kind of organizing sustained the effort, and what kind of union culture emerged after the establishment of public authorities? Unionists had to work on multiple fronts: building organizations, developing leadership, forging bonds with communities, and bridging the multiple constituencies that constituted home care. By asking workers about their interests and concerns, SEIU attempted to meet local needs. Joining with community-based organizations on campaigns to raise the minimum wage or fight welfare reform, it cultivated long-term relationships that would facilitate the organizing of immigrant and poor communities.[105] Meanwhile, forging community substituted for a shared workplace. Moldovan immigrant "L. C." underscored the importance of creating a social world. "The union would celebrate our birthdays, invite people to get together once a month to talk, share our experiences," she remembered in 2008. "There are New Year's parties, holiday parties. We learn about each other's cultures, as well as celebrate." Said family care worker Rosario Arias, an immigrant from Mexico, the union "gave me the ability to get together with others, to have fun, to talk about our lives."[106]

SEIU favored a "neighborhood/political model." Neither traditional servicing nor social service forms of organizing addressed the particularities of home care. It had to "do the organizing against poverty that will keep this membership connected to the Locals," but not let services for individuals substitute for "collective creation of an organization." The union might attract people by providing membership in discount retailer Price Club and credit unions, offering dental clinics, and running interference with public bureaucracies. The task was to deploy multiple strategies to gain new members and develop leadership.[107]

Worker Centers represented one fresh approach to the growth of low-waged jobs that some locals tried. Emerging in areas with concentrations of immigrants and African Americans, like San Francisco's Chinatown and Los Angeles's Garment District, centers often substituted for traditional unions. They offered support services, a legal clinic, training, a gathering place, and advice with taxes, housing, and immigrant status. With their scattered workplaces, home care and garments were the most prominent industries that lent themselves to this enterprise, and unions turned to this model in cooperation with community groups, like churches and ethnic societies.[108] They also did not require the paralyzing hurdle of state recognition. Local 616 established a worker center in the same building as its downtown Oakland headquarters in early 1998. Labor educator Karen Orlando, a former organizer with Local 616, commented that centers were a "way to create a home for home care workers."[109]

Local 250 chose a different mechanism to connect workers. Leon Chow, a former hotel worker and HERE activist who went on staff at SEIU 250 in 1998, judged the worker center approach inadequate "because it still requires the worker going to a central location—having time and ability to leave their consumer/client and take a couple of hours to be somewhere else." So his local "made the tactical decision instead to go out to the workers. To have an individual in the neighborhood who visits the member." Local 250 in this way approached the steward system differently. It renamed stewards "member action gathering leaders," or MAGs, a cumbersome but quite descriptive phrase. Since aides caring for severely disabled people often could not leave the house, MAGs used the telephone to maintain contact with their group of workers. They circulated information and attempted to service members by informing them about benefits, like the registry and unemployment compensation; helping them with late checks and unruly clients; and generally providing advice. When possible, they organized house meetings with a small group of workers living or working close to each other. Thus, while the setting and means had changed, MAGs served as the connective tissue of the union on a day-to-day basis, the traditional role of a steward system.[110] Just because their workplaces were isolated, then, did not mean that home care providers were unresponsive to unionization. "People who do this work are looking for collective support and engagement. They get that people should improve their conditions together," explained Paul Kumar, the former political director of United Healthcare Workers West (UHW), the successor to Local 250. "They're very susceptible to SEIU unionism."[111] Claudia Johnson, who became a vice president of Local 434B, remembered: "It was phenomenal . . . once they saw a flyer or heard about the union, they would call in to the union for more information. . . ."[112]

Immigrant workers were revitalizing unions throughout the nation, and home care locals were no exception.[113] With their own traditions of struggle, worker leaders had strong ties to immigrant communities. A Hmong organizer brought into the union 24-year-old Xiong Yang, one of less than 10 percent of men in this labor force. For over five years he had fulfilled his duty as the elder son by caring for both his disabled mother and ailing grandmother, women who came to the United States as political refugees from Laos and Thailand.[114] Local 616 also relied on immigrant members to recruit others. Separate ethnic and language committees met, much like the ladies' garment union (ILGWU) of old; these came together at the monthly meeting of the local, which attracted as many as a hundred people when the office was near major transportation lines.[115]

The personal narratives of worker leaders reveal what participatory unionism meant to them. We had the opportunity to talk with several Bay Area union members in September 2008.[116] Their stories illuminate the ways that the union at its best transformed caregivers into workers and workers into trade unionists. Amanda Carles, an Anglo woman who cared for an adult daughter with Down syndrome, explained that she had "become much more aware of all the things you do [for the person you're taking care of.] Once you actually have to document your hours to get paid by IHSS, you see how much work you do." Fifty-one-year-old Mexican American Danny Villasenor learned through his participation in the union that "I was always a health care worker but I never realized it." Formerly a small businessman, he had supported his schizophrenic cousin for 28 years, but only in 2005 did he find out about IHSS. "When you get paid for something," he noted, "you look at it differently." African American Rosie Byers, an executive board member, recalled, "In the 1970s, we didn't see ourselves as health care workers because back then we didn't do that kind of 'sick care taking.' It was more chore work." But with the entry of sicker people into the home in need of medical assistance, "we began to see ourselves as health care workers."[117]

For Villasenor, the union reinforced his self-image as someone who spoke up for those "who can't fight for themselves." He took pride in being able to show others how to maneuver around the IHSS system. But the union was no charity; it was a vehicle through which to work for social justice—and an arena to display leadership qualities. With gusto, he described being on the bargaining committee for Contra Costa County. "I learned so much—learned about the insurance, the pension, all the benefits—and I thought, wow, I really want to be part of that and really fight for this. I saw I could make a difference in people's lives." He saw the effectiveness of "standing as a whole group."[118]

The union provided opportunity for other men. In 1979, Juan Antonio Molina fled El Salvador, where he had taught high school social studies and was politically active. Since 2002, he has worked under IHSS caring for his mother, who has dementia. When the social worker gave his mother more hours, he left his night job at the airport, work he found to be abusive and exploitative. Becoming a full-time "professional" care worker led to union involvement and a new outlook. At the airport, he was a low-wage worker. Now he gets to work with other people, doing "public service." He takes great pride in his union work, especially in providing his group of workers with concrete services. Being a union steward has enabled him to continue as a teacher and community leader.[119]

We also spoke with African American women who built Local 250's home care division. A recent entrant to the job called Hollice Hollman, Mabel Davis, and Rosie Byers "the pioneers." She exclaimed, "I didn't get to meet Rosa Parks but now I'm sitting in the room with a lot of them." Hollman lost her job at an insurance company that moved its work elsewhere in response to a union drive. Byers, a single mother in 1977, turned to home care as a way to leave welfare. Davis had labored as a short-order cook; working for Remedy, she looked after as many as five people a day in 1979.[120] In the early 1980s, these women became shop stewards. After Rosselli and Ware took control of the union, Davis joined the election committee and Byers became a vice president. The union trained them to speak, read contracts, and organize others. "We started telling people . . . you'll be able to speak up and speak out about the contract. You can even have a say on the contract," Byers said. "That really had a big impact." Indeed, getting worker investment in the union depended on having them belong to the contract fight. Thus the local always had worker

Figure 7.2 Authors with former United Healthcare Workers West Activists. Seated: Mabel Davis, Hollice Hollman, Rosie Byers; Standing: Jennifer Klein, Blondell Rice, and Eileen Boris, San Francisco, September 2008.

leaders at the table. Public demonstrations and other participatory actions took place so that "the workers own the process and the contract," a former director of the home care division explained.[121]

Concern for others, so apparent with the everyday labors of these workers, spilled over into their political activities. "Being in the union, it's always a struggle and always a fight," Davis claimed. It was also "fun going to Sacramento to lobby. We feel it's where we really make the elected people accountable. You're there for the consumers, not just for yourself." For these black women, lobbying signified their attainment of civil rights. Byers confessed, "It was very exciting . . . talking to these senators and legislators. . . . I'm from Alabama. I would never, ever get a chance to stand in front of any of them and tell them who I am and what my story is."[122]

Immigrant workers also found citizenship rights through the union. "In the U.S.," exclaimed an Armenian who tended mostly to Russian clients, "you can step forward, have a voice, you can have free speech." A Chinese worker, who cares for her disabled son who gained IHSS benefits after becoming a citizen in 2002, not only viewed the union as a "justice organization" where she could "fight for human rights and disabled rights." It also was a place that made her feel "really part of American society."[123]

Popular education became a key to worker empowerment. Training sessions taught workers about power: who has it and how to get it.[124] Storytelling and essay writing allowed both consumers and providers to appreciate each other. As former organizer Sherr reflected, this technique "helped bridge different literacy levels, multicultural and multilingual issues among workers." It also enabled them to create their own forms of knowledge. At conscious-raising groups, workers started to look for collective ways to solve their issues. An artist as well as social worker, Sherr conducted workshops that used drawings based on the experiences of workers to deal with emotional aspects of care labor, such as loss and grief.[125] With each loss of a client, workers had to begin again—building the relationship, the trust, the ways of interacting that made the job possible.

Union culture also involved teaching new workers cumulative knowledge won from the years of struggle and cooperation. Every time you bring in new workers, explained Leon Chow, "you have to give them a background of disability rights and independent living. . . . The theory of patients' rights and independent living always has to be up front." Consumers have rights, and workers have rights. The relationship between the individuals will be a personal and intimate one, and the union does not get involved directly in that relationship. The union is the public advocate for a living wage, higher benefits, and more government expenditures. The fight, however, is everyone's. Chow emphasized, "We tell workers that the tradition is we fight together"—consumers and providers.[126]

Adapting the Organizing Model

Buoyed by momentum in California, SEIU in 1997 formally launched a campaign among home care workers in Oregon. Here, too, political creativity, movement building, and attention to regional political structures generated union success in a general era of labor decline. During the 1990s, demand for the service had continued to rise, and while some counties tried various schemes to improve wages, the state held a lid on compensation.[127] SEIU organizers from Local 503, Oregon Public Employees Union, convinced the governor to hand over lists of providers and, as in other places, made thousands of house visits. Rather than lobbying each county for recognition, SEIU 503 developed a shrewd innovation. It pushed for a statewide referendum that would establish a Home Care Commission, one public authority for all of Oregon.[128]

In the fall of 2000, Measure 99 appeared on the state ballot. This constitutional amendment formally recognized care work as employment. It called not only for the establishment of a commission, with members appointed by the governor, but also included the right of workers to join a union and engage in collective bargaining with the commission. They would have rights just like public employees, including "mediation and interest arbitration." And while not classified as state employees, they still qualified for unemployment insurance.[129] The amendment passed in November with 63 percent of the vote, creating a distinct innovation in labor policy. Private in-home care businesses opposed it, as well as Oregon's AARP, yet it passed in all counties. "It was the first time that collective bargaining rights were extended through a ballot measure," said Steven Ward, then Local 503's organizing director.[130]

The voters may have expressed their will, but the money still had to come from the state. That meant yet another political campaign—to convince the Republican legislature to appropriate funds for the new commission. This time, home care workers teamed up with disability activists and those well-organized seniors to lobby legislators, district by district. Thousands sent letters. "It was so exciting," said Karen Thompson, a worker who became president of the home care sub-local. "We got to pour out our stories. We weren't isolated any more." The vote to approve funding was really to recognize new employment rights for care workers; it was overwhelmingly in favor.[131]

At the end of 2001, workers got their union as well. Through a state labor board election, they won what *Northwest Labor Press* called the "largest public sector union victory in Oregon history." Twelve thousand new members joined SEIU Local 503, forming Home Care Workers 99. The union organized mainly the state-paid independent providers who served Medicaid and Oregon Project Independence clients.[132] Initial bargaining in 2002 centered on designating the work as formal employment. So, in a state that helped launch anti-tax revolts, home care workers held a huge Tax Day Rally on April 15 to demand that state and federal taxes be withheld from their paychecks. In its first year, the union won members' inclusion in the workers' compensation system, with the Home Care Commission paying the premium. It also obtained paid leave, a small pay raise, and some of the things "employees" take for granted, like tax withholding and direct deposit. The state would furnish health and safety equipment as well. In 2004, the union further gained health insurance for those who worked 80 hours a month for two consecutive months.[133]

As in California, the tropes of invisibility and "coming out of the shadows" held tremendous power. Union staffers coined the slogan "invisible no more," but home care workers embraced it to reshape their own consciousness and social reality. "Twenty years of being unrecognized, underpaid, with no benefits, essentially an invisible workforce, has many frustrated and searching for solutions," said Herk Mertens from Waldport, Oregon. "I honestly feel the union is the only way home care workers and our clients have the ability to be visible." The phrase, "invisible no more," captured the sense of dignity and the social recognition normally accorded wage work in American society that home care workers sought.[134]

Figure 7.3 Home care workers strike in New York City, June 7, 2004. DWF15-755524. © Viviane Moos/Corbis.

Home care workers entered the twenty-first century with a dynamic union movement—one of the few success stories of recent decades. Like public sector workers in the 1960s and 1970s, care workers for the welfare state repoliticized American labor relations. Mobilization to pass laws helped to organize workers; in turn, political victories provided institutional spaces for union organizing. Paid out of public funds, IHSS workers pushed collective bargaining into the political arena.[135] It took 30 years of experimenting, but by the mid-1990s, drawing on tactics developed by various locals in different places, SEIU finally put together a winning formula. The California campaigns built alliances, stepped outside the NLRB framework, organized tens of thousands of workers, and created new institutional state structures that enabled union representation on a sectoral, rather than work site, basis. The union put aside the "straight adversarial approach to bargaining" that would "alienate the Consumer community," with the result that each group saw the public authority as their victory and together could demand broader social goals.[136] UDWA and SEIU resolved their jurisdictional disputes to create first a joint lobbying and organizing effort in

2000 and subsequently to work together to bring rural counties under union representation.[137]

During their formative phase, all of SEIU's California locals used the same repertoire for organizing and movement building. They lobbied the state and pressured governors in various ways. They pursued the public authority not only as a platform for collective bargaining but also as a foothold within the state. Indeed, the public authority offered an institutional base within the government at the county level, where the hours of service and wage rate were actually set. It made home care visible.

The public authorities, however, were ultimately creatures of local politics—and California's counties run the spectrum from progressive to reactionary. The authorities had varying degrees of independence from county supervisors; many overlapped directly with the Board of Supervisors, especially in smaller counties. Labor negotiations that occurred through the public authority still had to pass through the budget process of the Board of Supervisors. That meant that unions negotiated contracts with an entity that really did not have the fiscal authority to fund them. For consumers, the public authority gave them a say in IHSS, as well as some very practical services, like attendant registries, emergency on-call systems, peer education, and training for workers. Advisory boards mostly fulfilled the function of a public stage on which consumers could dramatize rights claims and standards of just and decent care. Workers also could articulate publicly their claims for justice. For them, the authorities enabled wages to rise above the minimum, albeit in some places only barely. Where the union developed political power, community support, and community mobilization, wages increased significantly more. For the union, the public authority served a political, perhaps even more than an economic, role. It helped solidify and facilitate the relationship between home care providers and the county. UHW's Chow explained. "Without it, we'd have to start over every time a new Board of Supervisors gets elected."[138] According to Donna Calame of San Francisco's public authority, at their best, the authorities show "that a consumer directed form of home care provides a viable way to deliver long-term care."[139]

The victories of the 1990s suggested that the unionization of low-wage workers was more than possible; it could galvanize the union idea again and politicize other unionized workers. The very dependency of home care on the state and the interdependence of the care relation itself led unionists to devise a strategic model that seemed perfect for the era. Precisely because the work of care rests on trust and attentiveness, home care offered the possibility of a unionism that could define the employment relationship as non-adversarial; consumers and caregivers would act together on shared interests and respect the needs of each for dignity, autonomy, and security. In the process, such coalition politics opened up a space for the self-activity and politicization of tens of thousands of low-wage women.

The results would vary. By the end of the twentieth century, two different care worker movements had emerged: a welfare state unionism, with a core political strategy reliant on creating density within the long-term care sector; and a health care unionism, which viewed medical institutions as part of an aggressive for-profit industry that perpetually sought to reduce costs by off-loading more care work to the home, or similarly marginalized spaces. This dual structure replicated the hybridity that has characterized home care in its historical development: an occupational mixture of both nursing and maid work, formed by social workers and hospital administrators, and located in public welfare departments and state health divisions. Its double association with welfare—relying on African Americans and other poor women of color to provide for other dependent people—tarred home care, subjected the service to politicized charges of fraud and abuse, and relegated it to the second tier of the Social Security system with uncertain, and all too meager, state support. Only by moving home care from the arena of welfare to that of health and tapping health care financing, advocates came to believe, might its prestige improve.

But home care workers inhabited the lowest rung of the medical hierarchy. For hospital workers, organizing them was essential to counter the outsourcing of labor to the privacy of the home, the "black box" feared by Congress, a space beyond regulation and outside of the labor law. The only way to fight for dignity and recognition was to morph homemakers and personal attendants into health care workers. That risked further splitting of hand, heart, and head—the professional from the emotional and social and both from the hands-on physical component of intimate labor. Despite feminist insistence on its worth, care would remain undervalued as long as we thought we could get it through love or exploitation and as long as families had to face an inequitable health care system. This reliance on the unpaid and underpaid labor of women persisted into the twenty-first century, when a heightened economic crisis threatened to unravel the home care formula that dedicated SEIU members had fought so hard to achieve.

Senator Obama participates in "Walk a Day in My Shoes" Program, August 8, 2007.
42-18768131 © Lea Suzuki/San Francisco Chronicle/Corbis.

Epilogue

Challenging Care

During the 2008 presidential primary, Barack Obama spent a day on the job with a prototypical American worker and union member. He followed around not an auto or steelworker but a home care worker, Pauline Beck, an African American SEIU member from Alameda County, California. While on the job with Beck, Obama cooked breakfast and lunch, made the bed, cleaned the house, and did laundry. Beck talked to him about her economic concerns, like wages, sick leave, and benefits, and described her union, SEIU, as "my voice." Obama confirmed that "it makes all the difference to have a union representing somebody like Pauline." Yet, as a provider of care, Beck viewed her job as having an even deeper meaning, affirming, "This is my calling." Obama agreed that the value of care work lies as much in its intangibles as in beds made and meals cooked. Home care workers indeed had become the new face of American labor.[1]

The history that we tell in this book has no neat ending. In the years immediately after SEIU's triumph in Los Angeles, the story line seemed clear: we would explain how women like Beck—and all the others we have encountered in this book—turned upside down conventional understandings of who is a worker, what is work, and who can be organized. And our narrative does that, through a reconstruction of the ideas and interests behind public policies that organized home care into a low-wage job for women of color, especially African Americans. We have connected the realms of social work, health, labor, and welfare and have traced the changing national and local political economy against which unionization occurred and care receivers demanded their own rights. Now our assessment is more sober. The intervening years suggest an ongoing struggle, the outcome of which is in doubt.

None of the locals that pioneered home care organizing exist in the form in which they won their initial successes. In 1999, SEIU International kicked out the notorious Gus Bevona, who had subverted union democracy and organizing, and soon folded his workers into 1199, which had affiliated the year before to emerge as New York City's largest and most powerful union.[2] AFSCME placed UDWA into receivership in 2005, also removing Ken Seaton-Msemaji and Fahari Jeffers from leadership.[3] SEIU International merged home care locals in the Northeast, Midwest, and California to create "dense" concentrations in the health care industry in order to generate greater political and economic clout. Local 250 joined the Southern California Hospital Workers Local 399 to become United Healthcare Workers West (UHW). The International put together a number of public sector locals with Local 434B to form the new Long Term Care Local 6434.[4] In 2008, Tyrone Freeman, then president of 6434, went the way of Bevona, charged with misuse of members' dues for personal gain.[5]

Meanwhile, a fierce battle over organizing strategy wracked SEIU in California. Behind personal animosities and organizational conflict lay different visions of how the union should grow. Should home care workers be joined with nursing home counterparts to form long-term care locals, as happened in southern California? Or did they belong with other hospital and health care workers, as in New York? Or perhaps they should be linked with social service labor, like home child care workers, as they were in Illinois under SEIU 880 and after 880's merger with other Midwestern locals?

Internal SEIU conflicts further encouraged skeptics to question the basis of care worker unionism as a whole. Some continued to ask whether "parents and children who got government money for taking care of family members or close friends" really were workers, charging that "Stern cannily used political contributions and organizing to reroute welfare dollars into his union and create a whole new class of members." Others wondered whether a union dependent on state funding for and of poor people could ever be democratic, with leaders accountable to members.[6] Political scandals swirling around Illinois Governor Rob Blagojevich after Obama's election threatened the very foundation of home care unionization: anti-union opponents sought to criminalize union involvement in politics by suggesting a quid quo pro between Blagojevich and SEIU.[7]

To rethink home care requires both a hard look at the promises of care work unionism and an assessment of its welfare state funding. SEIU extended its organizing model across the country, but its success depended on convincing legislatures and governors to cover workers compensated through state and federal social programs. Its record with private sector contractors remained mixed. To make a real dent, it would have to change the classification of home care workers as elder companions. While it was busy challenging home care's exclusion from the labor law, the foundations it had built through political efficacy and grassroots mobilization began to crumble, especially after the deepest economic crisis since the Great Depression destabilized union strategy, state budgets for social assistance, and public sector unionism more generally.

Revisiting Legal Exclusion

Although home care workers had become visible, they still labored outside the law. Their earlier removal from the FLSA hindered organizing efforts. The growth of the home health industry since the late 1970s exposed the elder companion classification as out of touch with the occupation—a fictitious and opportunistic distinction. Thus, in the 1990s, SEIU pressed the Clinton administration to revisit this exclusion, but the Department of Labor could not reconcile union demands with consumer anxieties over a presumed trade-off between higher wages and fewer hours of care.[8] When it finally issued new proposals on the day before the inauguration of George W. Bush, the political moment to change the companionship rule had passed. Bush's Department of Labor withdrew the proposals.[9]

Stymied in the executive branch, SEIU turned to the courts, which often served as an essential arena of struggle against other branches of government. It found a willing plaintiff in Jamaican immigrant Evelyn Coke, whose story began this book. Coke had worked for years for a Long Island agency without being paid overtime. She now demanded back pay. Lawyer Craig Becker, a major architect of California's public authorities and then an associate general counsel with SEIU, shepherded her case through the federal courts.[10] The Second Circuit found for Coke, determining that the 1975 rule undermined the intended expansion of the FLSA, lacked a stated rationale for removing workers previously covered by the law, and went against the procedures of administrative rule making by never subjecting this provision to public comments.[11] The Bush administration objected, issuing a post hoc "Advisory Memorandum" claiming that the rule served the public good by making home care more affordable to those "with modest means." On appeal, *Long Island Care at Home v. Evelyn Coke* landed at the Supreme Court.[12]

In April 2007, the Supreme Court considered whether the Department of Labor had overstepped its rule-making authority three decades before. Lawyers, jurists, and various *amici* reiterated all the fears and rationales that Americans had expressed about home care over the years. Exemption supporters upheld the power of the department to interpret legislation. They warned, as did New York's Corporation Counsel, that any other outcome threatened the financial basis of the service, limiting consumer access.[13] Opponents of the rule, like the American Association of Retired Persons and the American Association of

People with Disabilities, contended that decent pay was necessary to maintain "a sufficient and qualified labor pool." The Urban Justice Center, representing civil, women's, and immigrant rights groups, highlighted the intent of the 1974 amendments to correct prior discrimination and revalue domestic labor.[14]

During oral testimony, the Justices stressed the needs of consumers, much as had congressional committees in the past. In foregrounding the anxieties of receivers of domestic and personal services, they erased the very presence of the low-wage women workers for whom the case was brought. The terms of the juridical contest, revolving around administrative rule-making authority and congressional intent, obscured the presence of women like plaintiff Coke, for whom companionship, rather than housework and personal care, was "incidental" to their labors.[15] There was no contest; the Court unanimously ruled in favor of the government's right to make the rule.[16]

Only a political solution could readdress the classification: either Congress could legislate or the Department of Labor could promulgate new rules. A few months after the Court's decision, Senator Tom Harkin (D-IA), a long-time advocate for disabled people, and Congresswoman Lynn Woolsey (D-CA), the only former welfare mother in Congress, introduced the Fair Home Health Care Act. They proposed to limit the definition of "casual" to those who worked fewer than 20 hours a week; all other home care workers would come under minimum wage and overtime guidelines.[17] Becker reframed the claims of consumer advocates by arguing that "the greatest threat to their ability to secure such services lies in homecare workers *not* gaining that right and continuing to labor in the shadows of our economy."[18] Consumers remained integral to the home care political coalition. Yet as long as state actors could justify care on the cheap in their name, an internal tension persisted.[19] The measure stalled. It became too late for Evelyn Coke, who died on July 9, 2009.[20] Obama finally proposed ending the companionship exemption in late 2011. But another administration or Congress could overturn any new rule.

SEIU's Strategic Vision for Unionism in a Neoliberal Age

Even without legal resolution, SEIU pushed to replicate its California and Oregon victories elsewhere, relying upon referendums, legislation, executive orders, and subsequent large-scale union elections.[21] Washington followed Oregon in creating a statewide union in coalition with disability and senior rights activists. In 2003, Illinois's Democratic Governor Blagojevich, newly elected with SEIU support, granted collective bargaining rights to home-based health attendants previously classified as independent contractors. Within months, the state legislature responded to massive lobbying and codified his executive order into law.[22]

In 2006, the Massachusetts legislature, over Republican Governor Mitt Romney's veto, created the Quality Home Care Workforce Council, with a joint employment relation between the state and consumers.[23] By then, SEIU had agreements with 100 companies in 20 states.

Some SEIU locals extended the organizing model to other parts of the care work spectrum. With the security of state recognition, SEIU 880 applied lessons learned from two decades of grassroots efforts to another group of home-based workers, those who became child care providers in the wake of welfare reform. These women, some of them former home health care workers, gained collective bargaining rights in December 2005, and over 13,000 subsequently voted for SEIU 880 as their union. The resulting three-year contract included an average 35 percent increase in daily rates, health-care coverage in the third year, and training incentives. Similarly, in Michigan, child care workers voted for an AFSCME-UAW partnership in 2006.[24] In New Jersey, ACORN started organizing among child care providers, and soon gained the Communications Workers of America as a partner; building on ACORN's strong organizing culture, the union won a contract with the state in 2008, shared with AFSCME.[25]

Creative forms of alliances continued. SEIU partnered with independent living centers and the American Association of Retired Persons to create the Virginia Association of Personal Care Attendants. Campaigns persisted in uncovered states. In 2009, SEIU joined disability and senior allies to pass Measure B in Missouri, which established the Quality Home Care Council, and in May 2010, organized 12,000 home attendants into a joint local with AFSCME. Days later, following a gubernatorial executive order, some 5,500 Wisconsin workers voted to affiliate with SEIU.[26]

Even at its most robust, however, home care unionism lacked the routinized stability characteristic of collective bargaining during its industrial heyday. Although home aides and attendants in New York had gained much during their initial unionization, momentum stalled at the turn of the twenty-first century. Local 1199 had become an important player in state politics, despite spending the 1990s reeling from the impact of managed care on its hospital core. In early 2002, Republican Governor George Pataki, whom the union would soon endorse for reelection, increased funding for the personal care aides represented by 1199. The deal left out home health aides employed by non-union contractors.[27] The ability to hold sway over the labor market or supply of labor always remained well beyond the union's grasp. A home-care strike two years later could not force the state to contract only with unionized vendors.[28] By the end of the decade, wages remained between $7.50 and $9.50 an hour, despite increased reimbursements for contractors.[29]

Throughout this mass organization of home care, SEIU had honed a series of tactics for unionizing the service and care work economy. Its approach rested on an analysis that if huge multistate or multinational corporations were not bound by central work sites or state lines, then labor had to organize on a similar scale. The union therefore committed itself to creating mega-locals to match the reorganization of capital, which had extended its reach across industries and regions. As articulated by International leader Steven Lerner, the architect of the successful Justice for Janitors campaign, the fate of unions rested on "consolidation, rationalization, and reorganization." These "dense" units would have the resources to crack the resistance of private employers to collective bargaining and hold politicians accountable. Unions then would be able to raise labor standards because their reach would inhibit the pitting of one region or firm against another.[30] Labor's revitalization required a federation committed to this "density" organizing strategy. To act on this belief, SEIU led several other major service-sector unions out of the AFL-CIO in 2005, forming Change to Win.[31]

The density model sparked a debate within SEIU and, ultimately, among other Change to Win unions. Could such large unions be democratic? SEIU President Stern claimed that "true worker democracy cannot exist until the 90 percent of workers in America who have no union gain a voice."[32] Member resource centers, available around the clock, would provide "quality of service to members, ease of access, multiple language capability, support available to member leaders and staff, and quality of data to support SEIU programs and strategies." These member centers adapted a practice of the old Local 880, which used its office as a place for stewards to make phone calls and for workers to call in and connect with someone to address their issues. But what made sense for the isolated world of home care was not necessarily the best practice for more traditional forms of public employment in hospitals and city halls.[33] To Stern's union critics, the union had created glorified call centers designed to replace local steward systems.[34] An internal SEIU review discovered in 2010 that a number of locals found their experience with the call centers frustrating and alienating. These locals encountered phone reps who didn't know the local contract or conditions, delayed in filing grievances, and gave inaccurate advice, without providing stewards extra support to engage with the membership.[35] The servicing apparatus became severed from the organizing culture that had been so dynamic.

SEIU also pushed for neutrality agreements with employers, a defensive adaptation to neoliberalism. Under neutrality agreements, a union accepts modest wages and benefits, a limited bargaining unit, or other restrictive terms as the price of having management restrain from active opposition to union representation. These efforts seemed to pay off when Local 880 in 2006 won the neutrality agreement that it long had sought from National Homecare Systems, which had become the major national chain, Addus HealthCare. National officers would handle work rules and grievances, rather than local stewards. The agreement allowed for paying workers for lobbying days—nodding to the need to win higher reimbursement rates from the legislature.[36] This achievement implemented SEIU's larger strategy to leverage an existing relationship with an employer in order to reach non-unionized workers in another location—even if it meant trading gains of the already unionized for the right to organize.

But would the workers be better off? At the signing ceremony for this first national organizing agreement for home care, Stern noted: "In the twenty-first century, we don't need labor relations to be about confrontation. We need it to be about cooperation and partnership and quality." In one sense, this statement captured the different aspirations that care workers and other service workers may have for unionism.[37] At the same time, it elided or erased the history of how 880 workers got there: two decades of militant confrontation and direct action in which workers constantly put themselves on the line, facing harassment, firing, and arrest. These workers saw themselves certainly as having a cooperative relationship with their clients, but they were always clear that to hold on to what they had won and make bigger gains required an ongoing collective struggle with "the boss"—either the agency or the state. Whether this national agreement would strengthen their ability to do so, or would extend that kind of power to the new, incoming members, remained to be seen. This pragmatic adaptation to the structural conditions of home care—880 had mixed success sustaining a steward system—threatened to undermine workers' personal connection to the union as a social institution made up of people who build a common experience when they lack a common workplace.

Once the most marginal workers imaginable, home care workers became central to the ideological, political, and institutional earthquake that subsequently rocked SEIU when its third-largest unit, the 150,000 strong United Healthcare Workers West, protested the maneuvers of the International. The strength of the old SEIU 250 was with its Kaiser Hospital division, but it also had some 65,000 long-term care workers. Their fate became entangled in a bitter battle between UHW and the International over national versus local bargaining, health care reform, and, ultimately, union democracy. By the spring of 2008, Stern not only sought to transfer home care and nursing home members to the jurisdiction of the Southern California Long Term Care Local 6434, but he also attempted to remove the elected leadership of UHW—even after being forced to place 6434 into trusteeship owing to public exposure of financial irregularities and abuse of member trust. UHW leaders were not against big locals; they supported one local for all health care workers, no matter where they labored. UHW under Sal Rosselli saw itself as that one big local.[38]

Strategic differences for the labor movement were at the center of this struggle. Both SEIU International and UHW promoted organizing and empowerment of those previously excluded from unions: immigrants, women, and men of color. They disagreed about where and how union power could be leveraged. UHW argued that home care and nursing home workers could only reach wage parity with their hospital counterparts if they belonged to the same union; otherwise, the job would remain low-wage and dead-end.[39] In contrast, the International contended that only a statewide unit would have the resources to organize private agency workers and address disparities between counties.[40] There was a danger, to be sure, that statewide bargaining would curtail advances by the better-situated UWH home care workers who lived in the more prosperous and liberal areas of the state and thus bargained with friendlier county governments, but, the International reasoned, all long-term care workers—no matter their region—would benefit. A statewide unit, however, went against the structure of IHSS administration on the county level.

Statewide consolidation further risked stymieing dissent.[41] Unilaterally moving members out of their union, because of a decision made by the International, denied these women the voice, autonomy, community, and self-empowerment they had finally found through unionism. Moreover, by separating home care and nursing home workers from those in hospitals, the International risked the very benefits that it had embraced when locating home care as part of the dynamic health care industry. It reinforced the association of home care with unskilled and unpaid servile labor, maintaining the service as a second-class component of the welfare state.

The die, however, was cast. On January 9, 2009, the International Executive Board voted to remove the home and nursing care workers from UHW and to place them in a mega local of long-term care workers. SEIU then put UHW in trusteeship, after which the former officers and most of its staff left to form a new union, the National Union of Hospital Workers—setting the stage for years of decertification battles and contested elections between rival unions just as it appeared possible that labor might gain new rights through the Obama administration. In April 2010, in the midst of conflicts with other unions, Andy Stern himself retired from SEIU.[42] An emphasis on scope seemed to have replaced that of density: the union could be thin, as long as its scope was wide because what counted was the aggregate number of "members." Size alone, International leaders came to believe, provided political clout. The actual engagement of members or strong contracts became decidedly less important.

The Achilles' Heel of Political Unionism

The dream of a new liberal era with the election of Barack Obama collapsed quickly. The severe recession beginning in late 2008 put fiscal pressures on cities and states. Despite overwhelming majorities, the Democratic Party failed either to shift the balance of power away from corporations or to counter the stranglehold that financial interests had over public budgets. Obama bailed out Wall Street rather than create public jobs or end the foreclosure crisis. The Employee Free Choice Act, labor's legislative priority to make it easier to unionize, died while Democrats concentrated on health care reform. The stimulus package provided some relief to states and cities, but the relief was too little to more than forestall furloughs and layoffs of public employees or cuts in programs in the face of intransigent Republican opposition to raising taxes. Local and state governments remained trapped by debt servicing to the very banks whose overreach had sunk the economy. The banks recovered, but unemployment continued to rise and state revenues still plunged.

Despite opposition within his own party, Obama managed to pass the first major health reform in 45 years. The Patient Protection and Affordable Care Act of March 2010 did not overhaul the American for-profit medical or the inadequate long-term care systems but it promised to place constraints on the market players and control costs. Though the Act was to take effect in stages, and faced intense political and legal challenges, it immediately began to bring health coverage to more Americans through regulating the rates and exclusionary practices of the private insurance market. A subsequent phase would expand Medicaid to cover everyone in households earning up to 133% of the federal poverty level, including childless adults. Increased federal matching funds would enable states to expand access to home care through a Medicaid option for personal attendant services; additional funding incentives would encourage states to move a larger proportion of long-term care away from nursing homes to community and home-based settings. States' proposals for federal support would have to show how they would recruit and retain a stable home care workforce and enhance workers' wages and benefits as part of the package. The political goal of a "wage pass through," long sought by unions like 880 at the state level, had made its way into federal policy.

Without the spectacle that surrounded so much of the health care debate, Congress included in the measure a federal long-term care insurance program, the Community Living Assistance and Services Support Act, or CLASS. At the center was a government-run, voluntary public insurance plan, funded entirely by premiums, with no exclusions for preexisting conditions. Working-age adults could purchase public long-term care insurance by paying premiums from their wages (if their employer would participate). In the event of disability, this self-financing plan would cover home-based services, especially activities of daily living usually ignored in medical models of care. But Health and Human Services administrators could not figure out how to make this provision affordable for participants, who were likely to have "particularly serious" medical problems, and abandoned it in October 2011.[43] Whether the Patient Care and Affordability

Act could truly advance the right to care would depend on the political will to realize its potential and that increasingly looked bleak.

Meanwhile, with sustained, widespread unemployment, Americans already had turned to Medicaid. Long the largest program in state budgets, its enrollments soared between 2008 and 2010. In some states, the growth rate was double, or even triple, what it had been a year earlier. Though much of the increase came from families with young children, this surge threatened access to long-term care when states considered imposing an overall cap on Medicaid spending. Medicaid, after all, remained the largest payer of services for elders and people with disabilities.[44] The end of Obama's federal stimulus and the Republican takeover of statehouses and governorships in the 2010 elections, fueled by the anti-government Tea Party, further jeopardized Medicaid spending.

With the recession, home care eventually came under the budget axe. Some 25 states cut housekeeping and personal aides. In Oregon, with its long-time preference for home over institutional care, the head of the Department of Human Services admitted, "Long-term care is a cobbled-together system with many holes, and they just got deeper." One local program director saw "in a matter of months 30 years of work go down the drain." Illinois reduced health funding, $25 million from its Community Care Program alone. In California's political stalemate over taxation, the legislature again turned to balancing the state budget disproportionately through reductions in welfare. Republican Governor Arnold Schwarzenegger charged fraud and abuse and then Democrat Jerry Brown, elected in 2010, further sought to lessen home care wages, eliminate housekeeping services, and tighten eligibility. Faced with the most expensive Medicaid bill in the nation, New York under Democratic Governor Andrew Cuomo in 2011 sought savings from restricting long-term care. Fewer home-care visits meant "an even greater burden on families," the *New York Times* recognized.[45]

The economic crisis provided an opportunity for conservatives to undermine the welfare state and the union movement that had become intertwined with it. Even before the 2010 Republican sweep, conservatives challenged the legal basis for home-care collective bargaining. The National Right to Work Legal Defense Foundation filed suits claiming that gubernatorial executive orders were illegal. By opening the door to unionization through political means, it argued, states interfered with the right to choose one's political representative—an alleged violation of the First Amendment. It resurrected the old saw that there is no employer-employee relationship between home care workers and any employer. Therefore, the state had no right to authorize unions as the representatives of care workers in negotiations with its own oversight authorities. Nor did opponents stop there. The suit denied, once again, that home care aides perform real work: "Providers," asserted the brief, "are simply a group of citizens who receive monies from a government program." Instead of being workers who can organize, care workers had been recast as poor individuals without rights.

These lawsuits represented the opening salvo of what became an all-out attack on home care and all public sector unionism. Republican capture of state governments underscored the fragility of compacts that SEIU previously had won. Despite mass protests, Wisconsin's Governor Scott Walker eliminated most collective bargaining of public employees and ended recognition of any labor rights for home care workers, disproportionately impacting women as the providers and receivers of care. Other states followed this lead. Walker and New Jersey's Governor Chris Christie drew not only from deep wells of anti-unionism but also on disdain for the work itself and those who do it—the taint of dependency laid upon something feminized and racialized. They targeted all public workers performing vital, human services for the rest of us—services that knit together a social fabric that is not strictly within the household or the market. These public workers have served people who produce no immediate surplus value; in organized form, they opened more pressure points within the political process for public claims upon the state. For conservatives, that expansion of economic and political citizenship was untenable.

The parallel assault against "big government," public employees, and the union idea itself highlighted both the precariousness and the effectiveness of political unionism. These attacks have identified the Achilles' heel of the organizing model established by SEIU and copied by other unions. Deals at the top are vulnerable. Workers themselves have to be able to build the union; top leadership cannot take shortcuts, despite the turnover of the workforce. Unions must have a social depth and culture that enable them to live on when workers (or leaders and staff) move in and out and that sustain political activism at the state house where the budget and wages take shape. Those who do the work have to be at the table and part of the process. And when political deals fall through, there has to be power on the ground—the type of power that Locals 250, UHW, and 880 originally built through rank-and-file leadership, member-to-member organizing, social bonds, mobilized political action, elected shop stewards and bargaining committee members, and strong contracts.

Are there other models for organizing besides that put forth by SEIU? The new domestic worker movement recognizes the fluidity between home care and household labor, connecting care workers and care users, especially those located in the grey market, through community- and ethnically-based organizations. Like the earlier National Committee on Household Employment, these groups establish worker cooperatives, provide training, and offer model contracts and guidelines for private employers.[46] The most prominent is Domestic Workers United (DWU), a multi-ethnic coalition of Caribbean, Latina, African, and South Asian organizations, founded in New York City in 2000.[47]

Through multiple tactics, DWU has improved working conditions. Through street theater and public shaming, it has exposed exploitative employers to win back pay and gain decent treatment. It worked with Jews for Racial and Economic Justice to organize employers. DWU, along with its allies, pushed the New York legislature to pass the Domestic Workers Bill of Rights in 2010, which guarantees a living wage, paid sick and vacation days, and health benefits, but not collective bargaining. It gained a framework for greater security—physical, legal, and economic—for all household workers and, then, sought both to monitor enforcement and use the resulting recognition for further organizing.[48] In essence, workers in the private market, hired individually by families, deployed the state to transform private labors into public work. They demanded that we recognize how the tending to individuals, homes, and families requires that care workers, too, be cared for. Then in June 2011, the International Labor Organization approved a convention insisting that governments provide domestic workers the same rights as other workers. Simultaneously, the National Domestic Workers Alliance was instrumental in launching a national campaign, "Caring Across the Generations," to improve the working conditions of long-term care and reaffirm the right of seniors and disabled people to receive care. It recognized the manifold ways that care is tied to immigration and embedded within communities by calling for a "new visa category and path to citizenship for care workers."[49]

A Right to Care?

The organizing of care workers underscores questions of collective social responsibility that haunt our present as much as they confounded our past. As with other issues of care, our society has not confronted matters of chronic illness or the end of life very well. Anything less than complete self-reliance has generated social opprobrium, marginalization, loss of citizenship rights, and punitive public policies. Unions alone cannot resolve these fundamental issues, no matter how creative their tactics. That task we had hoped welfare states would accomplish.

Care stands at the heart of the demographic challenges faced by all modern welfare states. Its organization follows existing configurations. Nordic states offer the most generous funding and most options. Central European states, like Austria, encourage family care through various payment mechanisms, and southern European states rely on private purchasing. Germany has incorporated long-term care into its social insurance system. In contrast, the grey market has flourished in Italy, where families employ immigrants from the Philippines, Peru, and Poland. Elsewhere, as in Taiwan, migrant domestic workers—taking on the duties of wives—tend to elder mothers-in-law. Facing its own challenges to traditional family structures and demographic pressures, Japan introduced long-term care insurance in 1997 as a social right, funded through a mix of compulsory contributions and general revenues.[50]

Throughout Europe, cash for care schemes have encouraged home care; some nations, notably Germany and France, provide monies to care users, who then purchase services, while others, such as Britain and Finland, pay caregivers through social security contributions. Even universal programs, as in France and the Netherlands, now depend on larger co-payments, cap benefit levels, and restrict eligibility to people with greater need for help. In Britain, private agencies increasingly receive public funds for services that government once provided.[51] "It is the irony of the 1980s and 1990s," concluded Dutch scholars Trudie Knijn and Stijn Verhagen, "that pleas for individual autonomy, community-based self-help, and clients' own choice and responsibility, which are actively voiced by clients', patients', and women's movements all over Europe and the United States, got mixed up with neoliberalism and its belief in the market."[52] Users may have more choice, but workers face more precarious conditions of employment, and family members take up the slack. With the worldwide recession that started in 2008, European conservatives began slashing social welfare and cutting government services. They claimed that austerity was the only path to economic recovery, making the United States appear as a model rather than a laggard in this twenty-first-century trajectory of social provision.

How states incorporate care, then, has paradoxical results. That old distinction between paid and unpaid labor dissolves, as many nations seek to buttress the use of family members for the primary caregiver, jeopardizing women's future income and pension levels. Meager payments to caregivers actually reinforce the distinction, originally raised by feminist scholars, between productive and reproductive labor.[53] But policy maker distaste over paying for work ideologically assumed to be the freely given obligation of wives and daughters, or other family, only partially explains the perpetual evasion of a social commitment to long-term care.

Nor is the commodification of care the essence of the problem. We have long incorporated cooking, cleaning, and caring into market exchange. Under capitalism, people must sell their labor power. And not everyone has family around to perform care, or to do it on a constant basis. Despite the objections of some feminists, there is not an inherent problem with paying for care—and decently compensating for it. The more essential question is: What sets up and perpetuates conditions of exploitation? As we have shown throughout this book, in the United States, devaluation comes not merely from the association of care with women, but from the historical creation of racialized labor markets, the location of care as welfare services, and the political and legal structures that sustain low wages and inhibit quality access.

With care labor either naturalized or stigmatized, lawmakers, nonetheless, have taken the easy way out by justifying policy decisions, especially stingy or punitive ones, on the basis of such devaluations. Politicians and legislators tap into familiar discourses of welfare—rhetorics of fraud, cheating, and undeservedness—to mask assaults on public responsibility, on the support required by the old or young. Thus, we cannot improve conditions of care merely by shifting its location from the private market to nonprofit organizations and government. Workers have had to take on the state.

Care workers themselves embraced the different arguments about the labor of care that we have encountered in these pages: that their work is of social and economic value, that it is a calling based on love and service, that their labor produces larger public goods. They also redeploy these understandings in political struggles. Collective forms of self-organization have provided a vehicle through which they have expressed and integrated the dimensions of care. Unions enabled them to act politically to counter devaluation, marginalization, and exploitation. That is why attacks on public employees are so dangerous for care workers. As we have shown, only when workers have organized through their own institutions, however defined, has the right to care been linked with economic justice.

It is time to see that the making and maintaining of people are of value in themselves and claim the worth of service labor on its own terms. The actual labor process creates interdependence. Previously our polity has denied the relational aspect of such occupations (call it emotional labor, affection, or trust) because ideology, law, and policy have defined these qualities as non-compensable. Yet such work is more than tasks completed. The quality of the relationship matters to both parties—as with a wide range of other "service" jobs throughout the economy: lawyers, teachers, nurses, doctors, financial planners, psychologists, waitresses, and personal trainers. What makes any of these professionals skilled at their job? It is the relationship they create, the trust they build, the care they take with their client, student, patient, or customer. Revaluing what is integral to the labor, establishing the legitimacy of care as productive and necessary labor, represents a recognition that would require redefining worth and remuneration across the whole economy.

This reevaluation of what care means and what it is worth is necessary not only for care as such, and for fairness for the home attendants and aides whose history we have traced, but also is more attuned to the actual workings of our economy. Without valuing care, there is no fair way we can cope with an aging population and limited natural resources. At its best, service sector unionism has emphasized respect, dignity, meaningful social relationships, citizenship rights, political power, and defense of social benefits (like education and health care). The centrality of care provides it with a more vital, urgent role than ever. Such organization, whether through unions or other political formations, can enable us to see and act on fundamental connections. The social interdependence of care, which is woven throughout the service economy, might just give solidarity a new meaning.

Afterword

State Power and the Fate of Home Care Organizing

When home care organizers gathered in Chicago in September 2013, they celebrated thirty years of struggle. Helen Miller, former president of SEIU 880 who had worked under Illinois's Department of Rehabilitative Services (DORS), declared, "If we keep fighting, if we keep caring, if we keep sharing, things will work out."[1] The efforts of such home care workers seemed to brighten when, just days later, President Obama's administration placed them under the Fair Labor Standards Act, some twenty-one months after the president first announced his intention to change the companionship rule that had for so long denied access to overtime pay—and recognition as workers.

The rights that one branch of government gave, however, another could take away. Nine months later in June 2014, the U.S. Supreme Court denied the public employee status of DORS attendants and the union's standing as an agency shop in *Harris v. Quinn*. As a consequence, the union local that Miller once headed, whose advances we charted in chapter six, found a large chunk of its membership potentially slashed and the political clout of SEIU threatened in Chicago and throughout the nation. The strategy of classifying home care workers as state employees for the purpose of collective bargaining crumbled not from the internal divisions that had loomed so large in 2010 and 2011, but rather from a coordinated assault by anti-union conservatives, who found in the characteristics of home care and its female workforce an opening to damage the legal basis for public employee unionism.

In the time since the publication of the hardcover edition of this book, the attack on government intensified. The backlash against the Obama Administration, fueled by racism and expressed through tax-cutting, voter suppression, and restrictions on women's reproductive rights, persisted with a range of conservative and right-wing political forces labeling public employees, including teachers and nurses, the new welfare queens. In this climate, as the nation headed into the

2012 presidential election, Obama dawdled over eliminating the companionship exemption—although the Department of Labor (DOL) delivered a positive cost-benefit assessment and two-thirds of 26,000 public comments supported a new rule. Meanwhile, most home care workers still earned less than $10 an hour and nearly half lived in households dependent on some form of public benefits, such as food stamps.[2]

Despite Obama's reelection, it took until September 2013 for the newly installed Secretary of Labor, Thomas Perez, to announce a final change. FLSA status, he proclaimed, represented an "important step toward guaranteeing that these professionals receive the wage protections they deserve while protecting the right of individuals to live at home." In naming home aides "professionals," Perez gave notice that the attendants are not anybody's friendly neighbor or wifely servant, but workers with designated skills, whether or not credentialed.[3] The revised rules clearly sought to define care as *work* and acknowledge the home as a place of wage labor. Care replaced household labor as the controlling term. An attendant who spends more than 20% of her time assisting with activities of daily living, including meal preparation, driving, light housework, managing finances, or household tasks, came under minimum wage and overtime regulations. Using delineated percentages sought to make legible tasks that overflow such quantifiable frameworks, but the careful designation of the rules at least attempted to acknowledge the dual nature of care as relation and labor.

In spite of vigorous last-minute lobbying, the booming $84 billion home care industry could no longer legally hide behind the opportunistic "companionship" designation. The revision explicitly prohibited third-party employers from claiming either the minimum wage or overtime exemption. Agencies cannot circumvent payment through circumstances of *joint employment* with the care recipient, family members, or private households.[4] Some 70% of the agency workforce was to benefit from FLSA inclusion.[5]

But this real victory contained loopholes derived from home care structures developed to contain costs and maintain the coalition between providers and consumers. In attempting to accommodate the independent living movement, the rule did not apply to aides directly hired by households or individuals apart from government programs or agencies. It also limited the hours of family members who are paid under Medicaid (or by programs, like California's In-Home Supportive Services) under a "plan of care" or other determination by social services, making it difficult for such workers to receive overtime.[6] In doing so, DOL sought to accommodate the concerns of both governors who fear ballooning costs and the independent living movement and other consumers. Ever politically cautious, the Obama DOL also delayed the start date of the rule until January 2015, instead of the usual 60-day wait period, so that employers, state home care services, and users could adjust. In response, employers unsuccessfully lobbied for further delays and Republicans toyed with legislation to end the rule before it ever came into effect.[7]

Less than one year later, the U.S. Supreme Court stepped in to subvert these gains—ideologically, politically, and economically. In the fall of 2013 it agreed to hear a case of eight personal assistants paid under Illinois's Department of Rehabilitation Services and Department of Disability Services. *Harris v. Quinn* originated with the National Right to Work Legal Defense Foundation, joined by a who's who of anti-union legal think tanks and funded by the Koch brothers and Wal-Mart's Walton family, notorious conservative billionaires. For decades, such groups have fought to eliminate unionism by any means necessary and have found a willing group of accomplices in the Republican appointees to the Supreme Court.

As a matter of law, *Harris* addressed whether the state of Illinois is a co-employer of home attendants. If it is, the state can require those who decline to join a union to pay a "fair share" agency fee to help support the expense of collective bargaining. But the litigants hoped to prod the Court into overturning an almost 40-year-old precedent, *Abood v. Detroit Bd. of Education* (431 U.S. 2009), which has served as a bulwark for public sector unionism more generally. Although no one can be forced to join, *Abood* determined that public sector unions must bargain for everyone. The idea of the agency fee was meant to offset the inherent "free rider" problem, since non-members would also reap the gains of negotiated higher wages and benefits. Conservatives intended to mortally wound all public sector unions by denying them the ability to collect these fees, initiating the free rider disincentive: fewer members weakens union power to deliver gains, further lessening the reason to join, reducing union resources and generating a downward spiral toward evisceration.

Plaintiffs advanced a dual argument. First, they denied an employer-employee relationship between the providers and the state. The attendants are "caregivers" who receive public benefits, thus they fail to come under labor law. Indeed, they implied that unionization rested on a corrupt deal with the disgraced former governor, Rod Blagovitch. Second, petitioners transformed the central question from employment to First Amendment rights. In obtaining increased public benefits, they contended, states have designated representatives for personal care providers (the union), thereby denying them the right to choose their own political representatives. In accepting such reasoning, the Court would create a legal fiction that elevates abstract freedoms at the expense of women's lives and pushes home care workers back into the shadows of homes, hidden from the rights of economic citizenship.[8]

The very reasoning that led the Court's conservative 5-4 majority to rule in favor of the *Harris* plaintiffs made the case inappropriate to overturn *Abood*. Thousands of home attendants represented by SEIU were not public employees, concluded Associate Justice Samuel Alito, but rather some made-up category of "partial public employee," and thus fell outside of the rationale for payment of agency fees. "Personal assistants spend all their time in private homes," Alito wrote in the majority opinion. Union organization therefore "does not further the [public] interest of labor peace."[9] The male justices of the Court's majority repeatedly displayed a discomfort with blurred lines and an ideological imperative to separate home from work and the public from the private—as if that is really possible. The *Harris* decision denied women working in the home the same rights as other employees, returning unionized personal attendants to the status of household workers still excluded from the National Labor Relations Act. Further, the Court's majority bought the conflation that these are "just moms," taking care of their children in their own homes, doing what female family members should do: providing support as unpaid labors out of love and obligation, which by definition means they are not workers.[10] The home becomes a private place that a union has no business invading.

But history, as we've seen, contradicts this view. The idea of the private, insular home, untouched by market or state, is a myth. Government has long shaped the conditions of home care and determined its workforce; it has set wages, recruited workers, conducted training, and monitored performance. The provision of home care as long-term care was based in public welfare—for both the recipients and the workers. Through home care, welfare agencies connected what went on in the home with the public interests of the state.[11]

While the plaintiffs feared a potential restriction in their motherly duties from unionization, activists like Chicagoan Flora Johnson, an African-American mother of an adult son with cerebral palsy and the chair of the SEIU Health Care local's Executive Board, faced the loss of the vehicle that won a more than 50% wage increase and health benefits over the last decade. Johnson offered a contrasting path to performing good motherhood, one that depends on unionization: "So many mothers in my position have faced an awful choice: Stay at home to care for a child with a disability, or see them forced into institutions. Many of those mothers simply couldn't afford to stay home if home care didn't pay a decent wage."[12] Rather than an invader, the union has protected her home and privacy. As with so much else, race and class interests shaped this contest over rights, recognition, and dignity.

Whereas the Court's majority deliberately evaded the nature of care work, Associate Justice Elena Kagan, in her dissent, keenly grasped the reality. "The dispersion of employees across numerous workplaces" is a compelling reason, she wrote, for Illinois "to want to 'address concerns common to all personal assistants' by negotiating with a single representative.... The individual customers are powerless to address those systemic issues; rather, the state—because of its control over work-force wide terms of employment—is the single employer that can do so."[13]

The state of Illinois, in 2003, had agreed with that assessment. It decided that collective bargaining best enabled the state to reduce labor turnover in a low-wage sector, attract and maintain good workers, provide stable and improved service, and monitor the quality of care. Given the nature of the "public interests at stake," Kagan asserted, the state determined that the workers are public employees. The state also chose to share such authority with disabled consumers to accommodate particular needs.[14] Yet, as Kagan rightly noted, there is "no warrant for holding that joint public employees are not real ones."[15] To do so is purely a function of ideology.

Having ruled that these are not public employees, however, the majority could not go so far as to overturn *Abood*. Nonetheless, Alito used his opinion to shake its foundations. In an elaborate digression, he claimed that the original *Abood* Court "seriously erred," opening the door for another case involving recognized public employees, like *Friedrichs v. California Teachers Association* which is already winding its way to the Court, to further undermine public sector unionism.[16] Still, conservatives hailed the decision as a protection of freedom of association and free speech.

If the arena of national politics is hostile to the aspirations of home care workers, a counter vision of interdependence has emerged on the local and the international levels, powered by new forms of collective organization among low-waged women of color. The success of the domestic worker movement proceeds nationally and globally. Since 2012, California, Hawaii, and other states have passed or are on the verge of approving Domestic Worker Bills of Rights. Days after the *Harris* decision Massachusetts enacted the most sweeping legislation yet. This bill requires a written contract specifying the work, maternity leave, and a month's notice for termination of live-in workers. It includes overtime and rest breaks. There are protections from retaliation from "complaining about wage violations," from being overcharged for food and lodging, and from other abuses, such as sexual harassment and trafficking, and interference with phone calls and privacy more generally. There are even mechanisms for enforcement, albeit cumbersome: the Attorney General's Office and the Massachusetts Commission Against Discrimination. In recognizing how domestic work is similar to but also different from other forms of labor, the bill promotes a broad social justice through provisions that the ILO, in its 2011 "Decent Work for Domestics" convention, relegated to an accompanying non-binding recommendation.[17]

The "bill of rights" campaigns represent one of the devices that domestic worker organizations have deployed in struggling for rights, dignity, recognition, and better conditions. They demanded state responsibility for reproductive labor, and acknowledgment that its benefits are public even if it occurs in homes, families, and intimate spaces.[18] Being excluded from collective bargaining has generated alternative forms of association and organizing that are paving the way for other workers who are being shut out of rights through the stymieing of the National Labor Relations Board (NLRB) and decades of harmful legal precedents. Rooted in ethnic associations and worker communities, domestic worker groups have displayed the social movement character that home care unions at their best expressed before being confined by formal NLRB recognition. After *Harris,* those who work for private households might have more rights, better conditions, and potentially a more viable structure than those working for the state itself.

Without the vital movement of care workers and its web of social alliances we end up with care on the cheap, pitting workers against recipients—hardly a stable solution to the mounting demand for long-term care at home. By ignoring realities on the ground we succumb to the racialized and gendered anxieties of the past, rather than meeting the needs of elderly people and those with disabilities. Collective bargaining with a union chosen by a majority of workers may have been stymied, but we can follow the creative lead of the domestic workers "caring across the generations" to build the political power necessary to nourish new forms of solidarity.

Notes

Preface

1. In the Supreme Court of the United States, *Long Island Care At Home v. Evelyn Coke*, No. 06-593, Transcript of Oral Testimony, April 16, 2007 (Washington, DC: Alderson Reporting Company, 2007), 27.

Introduction

1. E-mail Shoshana McCallum to Boris, December 5, 2003; Press Release, "Long Term Care Recipients and Providers Oppose Governor's Proposed Budget Cuts," December 2, 2003, in authors' possession.
2. H. G. Reza, "These Poor Toil Unseen to Care for Poor," *Los Angeles Times (LAT)*, March 6, 1989.
3. Erik Eckholm, "A Welfare Law Milestone Finds Many Left Behind," *New York Times (NYT)*, August 22, 2006.
4. Steven Greenhouse, "Justices to Hear Care on Wages of Home Aides," *NYT*, March 25, 2007.
5. *Long Island Care at Home v. Evelyn Coke*, 127 S.Ct. 2339 (2007).
6. William Crown, Dennis Ahlburg, and Margaret MacAdam, "The Demographic and Employment Characteristics of Home Care Aides: A Comparison with Nursing Home Aides, Hospital Aides, and Other Workers," *The Gerontologist* 35: 2 (1995), 163–169; Lyn C. Burbridge, "The Labor Market for Home Care Workers: Demand, Supply, and Institutional Barriers," *The Gerontologist* 33: 1 (1993), 41–46; Steven Dawson and Rick Surpin, *Direct Care Health Workers: The Unnecessary Crisis in Long-Term Care*, Report Submitted by the Paraprofessional Health Care Institute to Aspen Institute (January 2001), 11–12, at www.paraprofessional.org/publications/Aspen.pdf, accessed October 14, 2005.
7. Eileen Appelbaum and Carrie Leana, *Improving Job Quality: Direct Care Workers in the U.S.* (Washington, DC: Center for Economic and Policy Research, September 2011), 1, table-1.
8. U.S. Bureau of Labor Statistics, "Home Health Aides and Personal and Home Care Aides," *Occupational Outlook Handbook, 2010–2011 Edition* (U.S. Department of Labor), 4–5, at http://data.bls.gov/cgi-bin/print.pl/oco/ocos326.htm, accessed January 7, 2010; U.S. Bureau of Labor Statistics, "Personal and Home Care Aides," and "Home Health Aides, *Occupational Employment and Wages, May 2008*, http://bls.gov/oes/2008/may399021 and 311011/, accessed January 7, 2010.
9. U.S. Bureau of Labor Statistics, *Occupational Employment Statistics: May 2008 National Occupational Employment and Wage Estimates*. See "Personal Care and Service Occupations," and "Healthcare Support Occupations," at http://www.bls.gov/oes/2008/may/oes_nat.htm, accessed January 7, 2010.

10. Table D-3, National Center for Health Workforce Analyses, Bureau of Health Professions, Health Resources & Services Administration, *Nursing Aides, Home Health Aides, and Related Health Care Occupations: National and Local Workforce Shortages and Associated Data Needs*, February 2004, 92, at http://bhpr.hrsa.gov/healthworkforce/reports/nursinghomeaid/nursinghome.htm, accessed October 9, 2005; Patrick McGeehan, "For New York, Big Job Growth in Home Care," *NYT*, May 25, 2007; Appelbaum and Leana, *Improving Job Quality*, 1.
11. John Schmitt and Kris Warner, *The Changing Face of Labor, 1983–2008* (Washington, DC: Center for Economic and Policy Research, November 2009), 1.
12. Virginia Held, "Care and the Extension of Markets," *Hypatia* 17 (Spring 2002), 21–2; Susan Himmelweit, "Caring Labor," *ANNALS, AAPS* 561 (January 1999), 30, 36–37.
13. The literature on care work is growing. See, for example, Drucilla K. Barker and Susan F. Feiner, "Affect, Race, and Class: An Interpretive Reading of Caring Labor," *Frontiers* 30:1 (2009), 46–49; Paula England, "Emerging Theories of Care Work," *Annual Review of Sociology* 31 (2005), 381–399; Arlie Russell Hochschild, *The Commercialization of Intimate Life: Notes from Home and Work* (Berkeley: University of California Press, 2003); Joan C. Williams and Viviana A. Zelizer, "To Commodify or Not to Commodify: That Is Not the Question," in *Rethinking Commodification: Cases and Readings in Law and Culture*, Martha H. Ertman and Joan C. Williams, eds. (New York: NYU Press, 2005), 362–363; Nancy Folbre, *The Invisible Heart: Economics and Family Values* (New York: The New Press, 2001).
14. Phyllis Palmer, *Domesticity and Dirt: Housewives and Domestic Servants in the United States, 1920–1945* (Philadelphia: Temple University Press, 1989); Evelyn Nakano Glenn, "From Servitude to Service Work: Historical Continuities in the Racial Division of Paid Reproductive Labor," *Signs* 18 (Fall 1992), 1–43; Peggie R. Smith, "Organizing the Unorganizable: Private Paid Household Workers and Approaches to Employee Representation," 79 *North Carolina Law Review* 45 (2000); Cameron Lynne MacDonald and David A. Merrill, "'It Shouldn't Have to Be a Trade': Recognition and Redistribution in Care Work Advocacy," *Hypatia* 17 (Spring 2002), 75; Paula England, Michelle Budig, and Nancy Folbre, "Wages of Virtue: The Relative Pay of Care Work," *Social Problems*, 49 (November 2002), 455–473.
15. In the Supreme Court of the United States, *Long Island Care At Home, v. Evelyn Coke*, No. 06–593, Transcript of Oral Testimony, April 16, 2007 (Washington, DC: Alderson Reporting Company, 2007), 27.
16. Deborah Stone, "Caring by the Book," in *Care Work: Gender, Labor, and the Welfare State*, Madonna Harrington Meyer, ed. (New York: Routledge, 2003), 110.
17. The Feldman Group, Inc., "Focus Group Memo Homecare Workers," Prepared for the Homecare Workers Union, April, 1998, 2, 7, 8, Janet Heinritz-Canterbury Papers, in authors' possession.
18. Margaret Ann Baker, "The Paid Caring Relationship: Workers' Views and Public Policy Regarding Paraprofessional Home Care for the Elderly," unpublished Ph.D. dissertation, UC Berkeley, 1987, 219, 222.
19. Eva Feder Kittay, *Love's Labor: Essays on Women, Equality, and Dependency* (New York: Routledge, 1999).
20. Shelia M. Neysmith and Jane Aronson, "Home Care Workers Discuss Their Work: The Skills Required to 'Use Your Common Sense,'" *Journal of Aging Studies* 10 (1996), 1–14. For Evelyn Nakano Glenn, care work is a realm of coercion and the denial of freedom and citizenship, stemming from inequalities between husbands and wives and between mistresses and servants, reinforced by family and labor law. Glenn, *Forced to Care: Coercion and Caregiving in America* (Cambridge, MA: Harvard University Press, 2010).
21. Arlie Russell Hochschild, *The Managed Heart: The Commercialization of Human Feeling* (Berkeley: University of California Press, 1983); Clare L. Stacey, *The Caring Self: The Work Experiences of Home Care Aides* (Ithaca: Cornell University Press, 2011).

22. Viviana A. Zelizer, *The Purchase of Intimacy* (Princeton: Princeton University Press, 2005); for popular discourse, Joe Garofoli, "Recognizing Caregivers' Hard Work," *Contra Costa Times*, September 4, 1998; Carla Albano to Thomas Markey, "Comments Regarding Rule Changes to FLSA," March 19, 2001, 3, Freedom of Information Act (FIOA) Materials, SEIU, in authors' possession.
23. Dorothy Sue Cobble, "Lost Ways of Unionism: Historical Perspectives on Reinventing the Labor Movement," in *Rekindling the Movement: Labor's Quest for Relevance in the Twenty-first Century*, Lowell Turner, Harry C. Katz, and Richard W. Hurd, eds. (Ithaca: Cornell University Press, 2001), 82–96.
24. For more on inevitable dependencies and ethics of interconnectedness, Kittay, *Love's Labor*.
25. Medicaid still spent more on institutional services. Ellen O'Brien and Risa Elias, "Medicaid and Long Term Care," Report prepared for the Kaiser Commission on Medicaid and the Uninsured, (Washington, DC: Henry J. Kaiser Family Foundation, May 2004), 2–3, 6. Paying for 62% ($125 billion) of all spending on long-term services, Medicaid remains the biggest funder. PHI, "Medicaid Matters, For Long-Term Services and Supports" April 2011, at www.directcareclearinghouse.org/download/medicaidmatters-20110408.pdf, accessed June 11, 2011.
26. Robert C. Lieberman, *Shifting the Color Line: Race and the American Welfare State* (Cambridge, MA: Harvard University Press, 1998); Deborah Stone, *The Disabled State* (Philadelphia: Temple University Press, 1984).
27. *Social Welfare in New York State in 1962*, 96th Annual Report, 1963, New York State Department of Social Welfare, 2–3; "The New Public Welfare System: A Progress Report on the 1962 Amendments to the Social Security Act," in *Social Welfare in New York State in 1964*, 10, State Library of New York, Albany, New York.
28. Office of Economic Opportunity, *A Nation Aroused*, 1st Annual Report, 1965, 41, "The War on Poverty, 1964–1968," Part I: The White House Central Files, Reel 9, Box 125, microfilm edition.
29. Mary Poole, *Segregated Origins of Social Security: African Americans and the Welfare State* (Chapel Hill: University of North Carolina Press, 2006), 35–38, 90–96.
30. Jennifer Klein, *For All These Rights: Business, Labor, and the Shaping of America's Public-Private Welfare State* (Princeton: Princeton University Press, 2003); Gail Radford, "From Municipal Socialism To Public Authorities: Institutional Factors in the Shaping of American Public Enterprise," *Journal of American History* 90 (December 2003), 864, 866–867.
31. McGeehan, "For New York, Big Job Growth Is in Home Care."
32. Leon Fink and Jennifer Luff, "An Interview with SEIU President Emeritus Andy Stern," *Labor: Studies in Working-Class History of the Americas* 8 (Summer 2011), 30–31.

Chapter 1

1. "Report on the First Year's Work of WPA Project," February 15, 1937, Box 4, folder 50, Mary C. Jarrett Papers, Sophia Smith Collection, Smith College (Jarrett Papers).
2. "Excerpt from Ohio Press Release, September 8, 1936," Ohio, Toledo, 2, IS, Box 38, folder: "616-A," Records of Works Progress Administration, RG 69, NARA.
3. Catherine MacKenzie, "Aides for Homes of the Ill," *NYT*, September 4, 1938.
4. Maud Morlock, *Homemaker Services History and Bibliography* (Washington, DC: GPO, 1964), 4.
5. John Demos, *A Little Commonwealth: Family Life in Plymouth Colony* (New York: Oxford University Press, 1970); Elizabeth Fox-Genovese, *Within the Plantation Household: Black and White Women of the Old South* (Chapel Hill: University of North Carolina Press, 1988).
6. Laurel Thatcher Ulrich, *A Midwife's Tale: The Life of Martha Ballard* (New York: Knopf, 1990); Emily Abel, *Hearts of Wisdom: American Women Caring for Kin, 1850–1940* (Cambridge, MA: Harvard University Press, 2000); Sarah Deutsch, *No Separate Refuge: Culture, Class,*

and Gender on an Anglo-Hispanic Frontier in the American Southwest, 1880–1940 (New York: Oxford University Press, 1987); Jacqueline Jones, *Labor of Love, Labor of Sorrow: Black Women, Work, and the Family from Slavery to the Present* (New York: Basic Books, 1985); Susan Porter Benson, *Household Accounts: Working-Class Family Economies in the Interwar United States* (Ithaca: Cornell University Press, 2007).

7. Ellen Schell, "The Origins of Geriatric Nursing: The Chronically Ill Elderly in Almshouses and Nursing Homes, 1900–1950," *Nursing History Review* 1, no.1 (1993), 203–216; Michael B. Katz, *In the Shadow of the Poorhouse: A Social History of Welfare in America* (New York: Basic Books, 1986), 3–35; Maureen Fitzgerald, *Habits of Compassion: Irish Catholic Nuns and the Origins of New York's Welfare System, 1830–1920* (Urbana: University of Illinois Press, 2006).
8. Abel, *Hearts of Wisdom*, 168–174; Charles Rosenberg, *Care of Strangers: The Rise of America's Hospital System* (New York: Basic Books, 1987); Karen Buhler-Wilkerson, *No Place Like Home: A History of Nursing and Home Care in the United States* (Baltimore: Johns Hopkins University Press, 2001), esp. 53; Margaret Ann Baker, "The Paid Caring Relationship: Workers' Views and Public Policy Regarding Paraprofessional Home Care for the Elderly," unpublished Ph.D. dissertation, UC Berkeley, 1987, 82–83.
9. Morlock, *Homemaker Services*, 1–4; Mrs. Bessie Bishop Bothwell, "Visiting Housekeeping Work in Detroit," *The Journal of Home Economics* 6 (February 1914), 6–11; Mary K. Simkhovitch, "Consulting Housekeepers," *The Survey* 25 (December 31, 1910), 513; Marilyn Schultz Blackwell, "Keeping the 'Household Machine' Running: Attendant Nursing and Social Reform in the Progressive Era," *Bulletin of the History of Medicine* 74 (2000), 248, 250.
10. Barbara Blumberg, *The New Deal and the Unemployed: The View from New York City* (Lewisburg: Bucknell University Press, 1979).
11. Ella Baker and Marvel Cooke, "The Bronx Slave Market," *Crisis* 42 (November 1935), 330–331, 340.
12. Franklin D. Roosevelt, *Public Papers and Addresses of Franklin D. Roosevelt*, Vol. 2 (New York: Random House, 1938), 13.
13. Chad Alan Goldberg, "Contesting the Status of Relief Workers During the New Deal: The Workers Alliance of America and the WPA, 1935–1941," *Social Science History* 29 (Fall 2005), 337–371. The only evidence we have uncovered of Worker Alliance organizing on housekeeping projects comes from San Francisco, where a woman passed over for a position claimed that Alliance members chose comrades to fill fieldworker openings and lobbied for the dismissal of non-members. Mable Lockman to President Franklin D. Roosevelt, February 6, 1938, Div. of Women's and Professional Projects, Box 6, "California," RG 69.
14. Martha H. Swain, *Ellen S. Woodward: New Deal Advocate for Women* (Jackson: University Press of Mississippi, 1995), 40.
15. Federal Works Agency, WPA, Division of Community Service Programs, Washington, DC, *Housekeeping Aide Circular*, WPA Technical Series, "Welfare Circular No. 3, September 10, 1941," A3187, 1, Box 38, folder: "Visiting Housekeepers, Alabama–Louisiana, 616-A," IS, 1936–1942, RG 69; WPA, Housekeeping Aide Projects, WPA Technical Series, "Housekeeping Aide Circular No. 1, August 24, 1937," 1, in IS, Box 39, folder: "616-B, 1936–42," RG 69; Morlock, *Homemaker Services*, 4; Phyllis Palmer, *Domesticity and Dirt: Housewives and Domestic Servants in the United States, 1920–1945* (Philadelphia: Temple Univ. Press, 1989), 102.
16. Donald S. Howard, *The WPA and Federal Relief Policy* (New York: Russell Sage Foundation, 1943), 130. Wage differences persisted under the WPA, which meant that the housekeepers labored more hours to make their security wage.
17. Nancy E. Rose, *Put to Work: Relief Programs During the Great Depression* (New York: Monthly Review Press, 1999), 103; Michael K. Brown, *Race. Money, and the American Welfare State* (Ithaca: Cornell University Press, 1999), 78–79.

18. Rose, *Put to Work*, 50; Nancy E. Rose, *Workfare or Fair Work: Women, Welfare, and Government Work Programs* (New Brunswick: Rutgers University Press, 1995), 31–57; Edwin Amenta, *Bold Relief: Institutional Politics and the Origins of Modern American Social Policy* (Princeton: Princeton University Press, 1998).
19. Julia Kirk Blackwelder, *Women of the Depression: Caste and Culture in San Antonio, 1929–1939* (College Station: Texas A & M University Press, 1984), 109–110.
20. Anthony J. Badger, *The New Deal: The Depression Years, 1933–1940* (New York: Macmillan, 1989), 205.
21. So Grace Abbott argued in retrospect. Swain, *Ellen S. Woodward*, 63.
22. Rose, *Workfare or Fair Work*, 32; Palmer, *Domesticity and Dirt*, 102–103.
23. "The Story of the Housekeeping Aides Project," Dated March 7, 1938, 1–2, in Health, Production & Service Projects of the Professional & Service Division of the WPA, New York City, May 1939, Part I, PSP, Box 19, folder: "Narrative Reports NYC (1939), RG 69. See also Swain, *Ellen S. Woodward*, 94–95.
24. Jessie Thomas Moore, *A Search for Equality: The National Urban League, 1910–1964* (University Park: Pennsylvania State University Press, 1981).
25. "The Story of the Housekeeping Aides Project," 1–2; "Circular of Information on WPA Housekeeping Service in New York City," January 1, 1939, in Box 131, folder 4, Henry Street Settlement Papers, Social Welfare History Archives, Univ. of Minnesota (HSS); Brooklyn Urban League-Lincoln Settlement, Inc., "Report of the Industrial Department," 1; *Thirteen Reasons Why the Brooklyn Urban League-Lincoln Settlement, Inc . . . Warrant the Support of the People of Brooklyn*, both in Part I, Series IV, Box 28, folder: "Brooklyn, NY," National Urban League, Library of Congress (NUL); "Report of the Editing Committee on the Annual Conference of the National Urban League," May 29 to 31st, 1937, 2, Part I, Series IX, Container A, Box 12, folder: "Speeches, Statements, Reports 1937)," NUL; "A Brief Statement Concerning the Activities of the National Urban League During 1935," 1, Part I, Series I, Container A, Box 1, folder: "Activities Report 1935," NUL.
26. "Negro Women Ten Years Old and Over in General Divisions of Occupations, Boroughs of Manhattan and Brooklyn, New York City 1930," attached to Ann Tanneyhill to Robert J. Elzy, January 22, 1937, in Part 1, Series IV, Box 28, folder: "Brooklyn, NY," NUL; Blumberg, *The New Deal and the Unemployed*, 153.
27. "Conditions of Negro Domestics in Various Parts of the United States," Part I, Reel 1, 00471, National Negro Congress (NNC), microfilm edition; Esther Victoria Cooper, "The Negro Woman Domestic Worker in Relation to Trade Unionism," 7, unpublished MA thesis, Fisk University, Sociology, June, 1940, Social Science Library, Fisk University; Brenda Clegg Gray, *Black Female Domestics During the Depression in New York City, 1930–1940* (New York: Garland Publishing, 1993).
28. Rose, *Put to Work*, 107.
29. Daniel J. Walkowitz, *Working with Class: Social Workers and the Politics of Middle-Class Identity* (Chapel Hill: University of North Carolina Press, 1999), 126–128; Maud Morlock to Lillian Lebowitz, January 5, 1939, Central Files (CF) 1937–1940, Box 781, folder: "December 1937 4-11-6," Records of U.S. Children's Bureau, RG 102, NARA.
30. MacKenzie, "Aides for Homes of the Ill"; Marie De Montalvo, "When Age and Illness Meet: New York's Home Care of Dependents," *Trained Nurse and Hospital Review* (*TNAHR*) 102 (March 1939), 315; "Servant Aid Not New," *NYT*, September 17, 1935; "The Story of the Housekeeping Aides Project," 5; Driscoll to Scott, May 4, 1937; "Housekeeping Aides Project Increase Personnel to 1794," *New York Age*, August 6, 1938; *Final Report of the Work Projects Administration for the City of New York*, March 2, 1945, 212, Box 6, folder: "New York City (Final Report) 1943," SPFR, Folder II, RG 69.
31. Palmer, *Domesticity and Dirt*, 111–135; Mary Poole, *Segregated Origins of Social Security: African Americans and the Welfare State* (Chapel Hill: University of North Carolina Press, 2006).

32. Vanessa May, *Unprotected Labor: Household Workers, Politics, and Middle-Class Reform in New York City, 1870–1940* (Chapel Hill: University of North Carolina Press, 2011), 127–133.
33. Marta Fraenkel, *Housekeeping Service for Chronic Patients* (New York: Welfare Council of New York City, 1942), 87–93.
34. Fraenkel, *Housekeeping Service for Chronic Patients,* 108; De Montalvo, "When Age and Illness Meet," 321.
35. "The Story of the Home Care of Old Age Assistance Clients Project," Dated June 6, 1938, 6, Box 16, folder "Narrative Reports New York City (1939)," PSP, RG69.
36. Mary C. Jarrett, *Housekeeping Service for Home Care of Chronic Patients,* Report on Official Project No. 165-97-7002, (New York: Division of Women's and Professional Projects, Works Progress Administration, December 31, 1938), 20–22; Fraenkel, *Housekeeping Service for Chronic Patients,* 87–88, 92–94.
37. "Maids Project," [Louisiana], WPP, Box 7, folder "Consultants Reports: Housekeeping Aides," RG 69; Barbara Wright, "Housekeeping Project Prevents Broken Homes," *The Detroit News,* October 12, 1941.
38. "Housekeeping Aides—Staten Island," 3–4.
39. "For Immediate Release," August 30, 1937, 3. Officially, the housekeeping projects prohibited "discrimination as to race, creed or color. Only women with . . . knowledge of the wants and needs of all sects and nationalities are eligible for this type of work." See, "Excerpt from Ohio Press Release, September 8, 1936," Ohio, Toledo, IS, Box 38, folder: "616–A," RG 69.
40. "Investigators' Manual New York City," 8–9, Box 7, WPP, folder: "Conference—Department of Labor, November 6, 1937," RG 69.
41. "The Story of the Housekeeping Aides Project," 5.
42. "WPA Model House Opened by Ridder," *NYT,* June 6, 1936; "WPA Opens a School for Household Aides," *NYT,* October 1, 1940; Fraenkel, *Housekeeping Service for Chronic Patients,* 105–106.
43. Palmer, *Domesticity and Dirt,* 100–110, 116–118; Cooper, "The Negro Woman Domestic Worker," 78–97; "America's Number One Problem in Education: An Interview with Nannie H. Burroughs, Outstanding Negro Woman Educator, on the 'Servant Problem,'" Part I, Reel 12, 00289–94, NNC.
44. "February 8, 1937—New York City," 2–3; Palmer, *Domesticity and Dirt,* 104–110.
45. "Report on Housekeeping Service, Brooklyn and New York Urban Leagues," February 1934–July 1935, 5, 8–9, Box 3, folder 53, Jarrett Papers.
46. Gray, *Black Female Domestics,* 126.
47. Memo, Anna Marie Driscoll to Mr. March, February 8, 1937, 2, WPP, Box 8, folder: "Reports on Field Trips," RG 69.
48. Eileen Boris and Premilla Nadasen, "Domestic Workers Organize!," *WorkingUSA* 11 (December 2008), 417–420.
49. Mary C. Jarrett, *The Care of the Chronically Ill* (The United Hospital Fund of New York, 1937), Box 3, folder 47, Jarrett Papers.
50. Sandra Opdycke, *No One Was Turned Away: The Role of Public Hospitals in New York City since 1900* (New York: Oxford University Press, 1999), 14, 71–77; Buhler-Wilkerson, *No Place Like Home,* 112; "Mayor Urges Gifts to Nursing Service," *NYT,* October 10, 1934; "Nurse Fund Drive to Begin at Once," *NYT,* October 26, 1934.
51. The Council consisted of private organizations, government agencies, researchers, and philanthropic individuals. For its size, see Leonard W. Mayo to Ellen S. Woodward, August 31, 1936, WPP, Box 9, folder: "Public Welfare," RG 69; Walkowitz, *Working with Class,* 46; "Mary C. Jarrett, Health Aide, Dies," *NYT,* August 5, 1961; Charlotte Hughes, "Training Housekeepers to Help Families Burdened by Illness," *NYT,* December 10, 1939.
52. "The Committee on Chronic Illness of the Welfare Council of New York City, May 1933–November 1936," n.d., Box 3, folder 48, Jarrett Papers; Fraenkel, *Housekeeping Service for Chronic Patients,* 69–70; "New Board to Aid Chronically Sick," *NYT,* March 25, 1934; De Montalvo, "When Age and Illness Meet," 315.

53. Ellen S. Woodward to Mary C. Jarrett, August 24, 1936; Woodward to Richard Cadbury, August 27, 1936; Ruth Hill to Woodward, August 26, 1936; Hill to Woodward, September 1, 1936; Leonard W. Mayo to Woodward, August 31, 1936; Mayo to Harry L. Hopkins, August 31, 1936; see also, Cadbury to Woodward, August 25, 1936; Bailey B. Burritt to Hopkins, September 2, 1936; Emma Weil Lewi to Hopkins, August 29, 1936, all in WPP, Box 9, folder: "Public Welfare," RG 69.
54. "For Immediate Release," August 30, 1937, 4–5; "The Story of the Home Care of Old Age Assistance."
55. Dr. S. S. Goldwater, *The Hospitalization of the Chronically Ill*, A Radio Broadcast by the National Broadcasting Co., April 18, 1935 (New York: The Committee on Chronic Illness, 1935), 4, 5, 7; Dr. S. S. Goldwater, "The Aims of the Department of Hospitals," in *The Significance of Research in Prevention and Care of Chronic Illness: Summary of Proceedings of the Meeting Held by the Committee on Chronic Illness, January 22, 1936* (New York: Committee on Chronic Illness, 1936), both in Box 3, folder 48, Jarrett Papers.
56. These included representatives from Catholic Charities, the Home for Aged and Infirm Hebrews, Federation of Protestant Welfare Agencies, Russell Sage Foundation, United Hospital Fund, and New York City Committee on Mental Hygiene.
57. The Committee on Chronic Illness of the Welfare Council of New York City, "Annual Report, May 1935–May 1936," Box 3, folder 49, Jarrett Papers.
58. MacKenzie, "Aides for Homes of the Ill"; Fraenkel, *Housekeeping Service for Chronic Patients*, 70–75, 79; Jarrett, *Housekeeping Service for Home Care of Chronic Patients*, 8–9.
59. Fraenkel, *Housekeeping Service for Chronic Patients*, 122–123.
60. Mary C. Jarrett to Agnes K. Hanna, July 19, 1940, 2, in CF 1937–1940, Box 781, folder: "December 1, 1940, RG 102.
61. No organized groups seemed to protest this merger. *Final Report of the Work Projects Administration for the City of New York*, March 2, 1945, 212
62. Fraenkel, *Housekeeping Service for Chronic Patients*, 71–72; The Hospital Council of Greater New York, *Organized Home Medical Care in New York City: A Study of Nineteen Programs* (Cambridge, MA: Harvard University Press, 1956), 35–37.
63. E. H. L. Corwin, Executive Secretary, New York Academy of Medicine, to Members of the Board of Estimate, October 15, 1935, Committee on Public Health, folder: "NYC Charter Revision 1934–1936," Letters, Records of New York Academy of Medicine, New York, NY (NYAMR).
64. "Domiciliary Medical Care," June 3, 1935, 2; Special Investigating Committee on Chronic Disease of the Department of Hospital of New York City, "Report on the Care of the Chronic Sick By the Department of Hospitals, Part II: Home Medical and Nursing Care," December 1934, 2, 4, all in Committee on Public Health, folder: "NYC Charter Revision, 1934–1936," Home Care, NYAMR.
65. Secretary to Dr. John Hartwell, October 4, 1935, Committee on Public Health, folder: "NYC Charter Revision, 1934–1936," Letters, NYAMR.
66. Fraenkel, *Housekeeping Service for Chronic Patients*, 119. Among women, 35% could not "participate in the work of the household."
67. Fraenkel, *Housekeeping Service for Chronic Patients*, 71–72; The Hospital Council of Greater New York, *Organized Home Medical Care*, 35–37.
68. Fraenkel, *Housekeeping Service for Chronic Patients*, 100.
69. Fraenkel, *Housekeeping Service for Chronic Patients*, 81–82.
70. Nancy W. Walburn, "The Nurse's Place in the Sun: A Discussion of New York's Nurse Practice Bill," *TNAHR* 40 (February 1938), 146–148; Meta R. Pennock, "Just a Word for the New Year," *TNAHR* 41 (January 1939), 13.
71. Alden B. Mills, "The Need for Subsidiary Workers in Nursing Service," *American Journal of Nursing* (*AJN*), 34 (June 1934), 591–594; Susan M. Reverby, *Ordered to Care: The Dilemma of American Nursing, 1850–1945* (New York: Cambridge University Press, 1987), 164–198, 193.
72. "Subsidiary Workers," *TNAHR* 40 (June 1938), 669.
73. Reverby, *Ordered to Care*, 177, quote from 175.

74. "Minutes of Meeting of Housekeeping Aid Project," November 26, 1937, 3.
75. Ellen Woodward to Miss I. Melinda Havey, February 9, 1938, in WPP, Box 8, folder: "Nursing," RG 69.
76. Ellen S. Woodward to Mary C. Jarrett, May 5, 1938, in WPP, Box 7, folder: "Correspondence—Regional and Persons Not in WPA," RG 69.
77. Frank A. March to Ben Stephens, October 22, 1937, WPP, Box 6, folder: "Oklahoma"; Ellen S. Woodward to Mrs. Dot Deennan, May 2, 1938, WPP, Box 6, folder: "Arkansas," both in RG 69.
78. Woodward to Deennan; "Report on the Care of the Chronic Sick by the Department of Hospitals, Part II: Home Medical and Nursing Care," December 1934, 7.
79. Fraenkel, *Housekeeping Service for Chronic Patients*, 102, 99.
80. Telegram from Ella Best to Mrs. Ellen S. Woodward, June 3; Woodward to Best, July 14, 1937, in WPP, Box 8, folder: "Nursing," RG 69.
81. "Free Household Help Offered in Kenton County Through Services of WPA Setup," *Cincinnati Ohio Post* (Kentucky Edition), November 7, 1937, clipping in IS, Box 38, folder: "616-A, Alabama–Louisiana," RG 69.
82. "Investigators' Manual New York City," 6–7, 10–12.
83. "Investigators' Manual New York City," 7. See also, "Work Book for Housekeeping Aide Project Workers."
84. "Section 10. Personal Hygiene," *Housekeeping Aide Circular*, September 10, 1941.
85. "Part 2, Section 3, Uniforms and Appearance," *Work Book;* "Section 11, Uniforms," 1, *Housekeeping Aide Circular*, September 10, 1941; "Part 2, Section 2, Personal Health and Hygiene," "Section 3, Uniforms and Appearance," *Work Book.*
86. "Section 11, Uniforms," 1, *Housekeeping Aide Circular*, September 10, 1941, "Part 2, Section 2, Personal Health and Hygiene," *Work Book.*
87. We date a more general use of "rehabilitation" earlier than does Jennifer Mittelstadt, *From Welfare to Workfare: The Unintended Consequences of Liberal Reform, 1945–1965* (Chapel Hill: University of North Carolina Press, 2005), 11–13. On New Deal emphasis, see Sarah Phillips, *This Land, This Nation: Conservation, Rural America, and the New Deal* (New York: Cambridge University Press, 2007).
88. S. S. Goldwater, M.D., to Hon. Frank J. Taylor, Comptroller, City of New York, October 15, 1935, NYAM, Committee on Public Health, folder: "NYC Charter Revision, 1934–36," Letters, NYAMR.
89. Ellen S. Woodward, "WPA Housekeeping Aide Project," for *What's New in Home Economics*, August 23, 1938, 8, typescript, IS, Box 39, folder: "616-B," RG 69.
90. "House Rehabilitation Workers Act on Principle of Service," *Oklahoma City Times*, Oklahoma City, November 7, 1941.
91. Marisa Chappell, *The War on Welfare: Family, Poverty, and Politics in Modern America* (Philadelphia: University of Pennsylvania Press, 2009).
92. Jarrett, *Housekeeping Service for Home Care of Chronic Patients*, 68–70; De Montalvo, "When Age and Illness Meet," 317–318, 320; Fraenkel, *Housekeeping Service for Chronic Patients*, 97; MacKenzie, "Aides for Homes of the Ill."
93. (Mrs.) M. Lockman, San Francisco, "Visiting Housekeepers' Project," Letter to the Editor, *The Chronicle*, March 17, 1936, IS, Box 38, folder: "616-A, Alabama–Louisiana," RG 69.
94. Dorothea M. Argo, "What Housekeeping Aides Do," *AJN* 41 (July 1941), 780.
95. "Monthly News Letter," October 1936, 1.
96. "Firm Refusal," *Lincoln (Nebraska) Star*, January 1942, clipping in Box 39, folder: "616-A, Maine–Wyoming," RG 69, IS; "Visiting Nurses Defend Project," *Times Herald* (District of Columbia), Mary 14, 1941; M. E. Bennett, M.D., to Mrs. Marie Judd, Supervisor, November 19, 1936, in WPA, District No. 11, Los Angeles County, California, "A Report Covering The Visiting Housekeepers Project of Los Angeles County," December 1935–February 1937, Marie Judd-Supervisor, 44, WPP, Box 6, folder: "Reports on WPA Projects Arranged by States: California-Colorado," RG 69.

97. See a typescript draft of article in Public Information Section, WPA, NYC, "Exclusive For: "Trained Nurse & Hospital Review," 466 Fourth Ave., NYC, March 14, 1939, IS, Box 39, folder: "616–A, Maine to Wyoming," RG 69.
98. "A Report Covering the Visiting Housekeepers Project of Los Angeles County," 29–40.
99. For the perspective of the medical experts, The Hospital Council of Greater New York, *Organized Home Medical Care in New York.*
100. Fraenkel, *Housekeeping Service for Chronic Patients*, 93–94; Jarrett, *Housekeeping Service for Home Care of Chronic Patients*, 11; Vivien Hart, *Bound by Our Constitution: Women, Workers, and the Minimum Wage* (Princeton: Princeton University Press, 1994), 164–168; Suzanne Mettler, *Dividing Citizens: Gender and Federalism in New Deal Public Policy* (Ithaca: Cornell University Press, 1998), 201–205; http://www.dol.gov/esa/minwage/chart.htm, assessed August 7, 2004.
101. Fraenkel, *Housekeeping Service for Chronic Patients*, 95–97; "Women Go From WPA Into Good Jobs," *NYT*, October 3, 1937.
102. The Children's Aid Society took over the service in 1937, but this project provided a model for Junior Leagues in other cities. *Mothers on Call: The Second Report of the Housekeeper Service of the Junior League of the City of New York in Cooperation with The Children's Aid Society, 1937*, 3, 18–19, WPP, Box 7, folder: "Memos," RG 69.
103. Committee on Chronic Illness, Annual Report, May 1939–May 1940, 4, Box 3, folder 49, Jarrett Papers; Leonard W. Mayo, Assistant Executive Director, the Welfare Council of New York City, to Katherine F. Lenroot, Chief, Children's Bureau, June 30, 1937, CF 1937–40, Box 781, folder: "December 1, 1940," RG 102; "Survey of W.P.A. Housekeeping Aide Projects, For Meeting—November 6," 2, WPP, Box 7, folder: "Memos," RG 69; Memorandum to: Dr. Eliot, Miss Baker, Miss Deutsch, Miss Hanna, Miss Heseltine from: Miss Lenroot, Subject: Conference on Housekeeper Service, New York City, August 20, 1937, September 2, 1937; "Some Points for the Consideration of the Welfare Council Sub-Committee on Housekeeper Service," June 14, 1937, both in CF 1937–1940, Box 781, folder: "4-11-6," RG 102; Kriste Lindenmeyer, *"A Right to Childhood": The U.S. Children's Bureau and Child Welfare, 1912–46* (Urbana: University of Illinois Press, 1997); Walkowitz, *Working with Class.*
104. Elizabeth La Hines, "National Group Set Up to Guide 'Substitute Mother' Movement," *NYT*, November 14, 1937; "Report on Conference on Housekeeper Service Held under the Auspices of the Children's Bureau, U.S. Department of Labor (DOL), November 6, 1937, 7, with attached 'Persons Who Attended the Conference on Housekeeper Service,'" WPP, Box 6, folder: "Report on Conference on Housekeeper Service," RG 69.
105. Morlock, *Homemaker Services*, 6.
106. Andrew J. F. Morris, *The Limits of Voluntarism: Charity and Welfare from the New Deal through the Great Society* (New York: Cambridge University Press, 2009).
107. La Hines, "National Group Set Up to Guide 'Substitute Mother' Movement"; Morlock, *Homemaker Services*, 5–7; "Maud Morlock, Was Pioneer Welfare Aide," *The Washington Post*, July 25, 1980.
108. Official Release, Division of Information, WPA, Los Angeles, November 7, 1940, IS, Box 38, folder: "616-A," RG 69.
109. Gwendolyn Mink, *Wages of Motherhood: Inequality in the Welfare State, 1917–1942* (Ithaca: Cornell University Press, 1995), 162–170, quote at 169.
110. Official Release, Division of Information, WPA, Los Angeles; "Recent Trends in Homemaker Service: Report on Questionnaire, 1943–44," 1, 2; Maud Morlock to Elinor J. McCabe, June 27, 1944, both in CF 1945–48, Box 119, folder: "December 1947," RG 102.
111. Elinor McCabe to Maud Morlock, May 1, 1942; Morlock to McCabe, May 4, 1942, both in CF 1945–48, Box 119, folder: "December 1947," RG 102; "End of WPA Service Deplored by Council," *Better Times: New York City's Welfare News Weekly*, XXIV (April 2, 1943), 1, 3.
112. Karen S. Anderson, "Last Hired, First Fired: Black Women Workers During WWII," *Journal of American History* 69 (June 1982), 82–97.

113. "Minutes of the Meetings of the National Committee on Homemaker Service," February 14 and 15, 1946, New York City, 4, CF 1945–48, Box 120, folder: "January 1, 1945," RG 102.
114. Welfare Council of New York City, "A Comprehensive Housekeeper Service for New York City, A Report on Project No. 9 of the Standing Committee on Welfare and Health Services," October 8, 1945; Mary C. Jarrett to Dr. Louis Dublin, "Housekeeping Service as a Means of Home Care for the Sick," October 30, 1944, 3, both in Box 4, folder 53, Jarrett Papers.
115. "Houseworkers of the World Unite!," *The New Republic* 95 (July 6, 1938), 248–249.
116. Woodward, "WPA Housekeeping Aide Project," 4.
117. Quoted in Louise Rosenfield Noun, *Iowa Women in the WPA* (Ames: Iowa State University Press, 1999), 26–27.
118. Noun, *Iowa Women*, 24.
119. (Miss) Nellie A. Popham to Mrs. Franklin D. Roosevelt, February 18, 1938, with reply Ellen S. Woodward to Popham, WPP, Box 6, folder: "Minnesota," RG 69.
120. Quoted in Blackwelder, *Women of the Depression*, 124.

Chapter 2

1. Ellen C. Potter, M.D., "Stake in the Commission's Program of the American Public Welfare Association," Commission on Chronic Illness, *Proceedings of First Meeting*, May 20, 1949 (Chicago: Commission on Chronic Illness), 6, Box 5, folder 73, Mary C. Jarrett Papers, Sophia Smith Collection, Smith College.
2. "Interview with Frances Preston and Rika MacLennan—3/26/48—Maud Morlock," 1, CF 1945–48, Box 119, folder: "August 1–August 31, 1948," RG 102.
3. Leonard W. Mayo, "Relationships Between Public and Voluntary Health and Welfare Agencies—Philosophy and Principles," *American Journal of Public Health (AJPH)* 49 (October 1959), 1307–1312; *Homemaker Services in the United States, 1958: Twelve Statements Describing Types of Homemaker Services*, PHS Publication No.645 (Washington, DC: HEW, 1958), 56–67; Memo to Directors, Program of Study in Public Health Nursing, From Nursing Unit, CB, "Progress Report—Homemaker Service in Madison, Wisconsin," November 18, 1949, folder: "November"; Maud Morlock, "Homemaker Service to Mothers at the Time of Confinement," *Public Health Nursing* 42 (May 1950), 282–286, folder: "July 1950," both CF 1949–52, Box 413, RG 102.
4. Daniel J. Walkowitz, *Working with Class: Social Workers and the Politics of Middle-Class Identity* (Chapel Hill: University of North Carolina Press, 1999); Andrew J. F. Morris, *The Limits of Voluntarism: Charity and Welfare from the New Deal Through the Great Society* (New York: Cambridge University Press, 2009).
5. Elinor McCabe, "History of the National Committee on Homemaker Service," 1, CF 1945–48, Box 120, folder: "January 1, 1945," RG 102.
6. HEW, SSA, CB, "Homemaker Service," May 21, 1956, 8, CF 1953–57, Box 622, folder: "May 1956," RG 102.
7. Ernst Boas, "Clinical Problems," 20, 22; James R. Miller M.D., "Stake in the Commission's Program of the American Medical Association," 16–20, and Albert W. Snoke, M.D., "Stake in the Commission's Program of the American Hospital Association," 14–16, all in *Proceedings of First Meeting*.
8. Gary L. Albrecht, *The Disability Business: Rehabilitation in America* (Newbury Park: Sage Publications, 1992); Ruth O'Brien, *Crippled Justice: The History of Modern Disability Policy in the Workplace* (Chicago: University of Chicago Press, 2001), 27–87.
9. Maud Morlock, "Homemaker Service to Mothers at the Time of Confinement"; "Minutes of the Meetings of the National Committee on Homemaker Service," February 14 and 15, 1946, New York City, 2–3, CF 1945–48, Box 120, folder: "January 1, 1945," RG 102.

10. William H. Stewart, Maryland Y. Pennell, and Lucille M. Smith, *Homemaker Services in the United States, 1958: A Nationwide Study*, PHS Publication No. 644 (Washington, DC: GPO, 1958), 7, 9, 11.
11. Jean Kallenberg to Maud Morlock, December 29, 1948, CF 1945–48, Box 119, folder: "4-11-6," RG 102.
12. "Homemaker Service," For review only, 6.
13. U.S. Children's Bureau, *Supervised Homemaker Service: A Method of Child Care*, Publication 296, U.S. DOL (Washington, DC: GPO, 1943), 1–2, 5.
14. Eva VB Hansl to Mary Taylor, December 14, 1947, CF 1945–48, Box 120, "5-1948," RG 102.
15. Julia E. Robinson to Ruth McElroy, May 13, 1953, CF 1953–57, Box 619, folder: "April 1953," RG 102; HEW, *Homemaker Services in the United States: Report of the 1959 Conference*, PHS Publication 746. (Washington, DC: GPO, 1960), 4.
16. Lynn Weiner, *From Working Girl to Working Mother: The Female Labor Force in the United States, 1820–1980* (Chapel Hill: University of North Carolina Press, 1985), table 2, 6.
17. U.S. Women's Bureau, *The American Woman—Her Changing Role as Worker, Homemaker, Citizen*, Bulletin 224 (Washington, DC: GPO, 1948); *Homemaker Services in the United States: Report of the 1959 Conference*, 81.
18. NCHS, "Minutes of Meeting, November 13–14, 1947, New York," 4, CF 1949–1952, Box 119, folder: "4-11-6," RG 102.
19. Ibid.
20. "Homemaker (dom. ser.) housekeeper, visiting," 677, "Domestic Service Occupations (2.00.00 through 2–09.99)," in Division of Occupational Analysis, USES, FSA, SSA, Bureau of Employment Security, *Dictionary of Occupational Titles*, Vol. II, *Occupational Classification and Industry Index*, 2nd ed., March 1949 (Washington, DC: GPO, 1949), 59.
21. Maud Morlock to Wado C. Wright, July 5, 1947, CF 1949–52, Box 414, folder: "4-11-6," RG 102; Jewish Family Service, NY, "A Different and Economical Service to the Aged: Report on the Community Homemaker Service for the Aged Administered by the Jewish Family Service 1945–1950," 2–3, CF 1949–52, Box 413, folder: "July 1950," RG 102.
22. CB, Social Service Division, Maud Morlock, July 3–11, 1947, "Report of Field Visit, State of Illinois," 4, CF 1945–48, Box 120, folder: "5–1948," 4-11-6, RG 102.
23. Elinor McCabe to Maud Morlock, May 16, 1951, CF 1949–52, Box 412, folder: "August 1952," RG102.
24. Jewish Family Service, NY, "A Different and Economical Service to the Aged," 2–3.
25. Federal Security Agency, Social Security Admin, CB, "Recommendations for Personnel Practices for Homemakers: Committee on Homemaker Service of the Welfare Council of New York City, January, 1948," 8, CF 1949, 52, Box 413, folder: "September 1949," 4-11-6 RG 102.
26. "Homemaker Service," April 28, 1948, report, 4, CF 1945–48, Box 120, folder: "5–1948," RG 102.
27. Rose E. Drapkin to Maud Morlock, September 30, 1946, CF 1945–48, Box 120, folder: "5–1948," RG 102; "Recommendations for Personnel Practices for Homemakers."
28. "Jewish Social Service Bureau," 3, attached to "Report of Field Visit: State of Illinois."
29. *Homemaker Services in the United States, 1958: A Nationwide Study*, 12, 19–23, 39.
30. Theresa Borden to Maud Morlock, March 2, 1948, CF 1945–48, Box 119, folder: "August 1–August 31, 1948," RG 102.
31. McCabe, "History of the National Committee on Homemaker Service," 7; Memo to: Regional Directors, From Mildred Arnold, December 4, 1947, CF 1945–48, Box 120, folder: "December 1947," RG 102.
32. *Homemaker Services in the United States: Report of the 1959 Conference*, 18.
33. Joshua B. Freeman, *Working-Class New York: Life and Labor since World War II* (New York: The New Press, 2000), 99–103.
34. Ibid., 201.

35. Eleanore Lurry to Maud Morlock, April 28, 1945; Maud Morlock to John E. Grier, Ohio State Department of Public Welfare, January 6, 1948, CF 1945–48, Box 120, folder: "5-1948"; Lurry to Children's Bureau, April 11, 1945, and Gertrude Bolden to Miss Maud Morlock, May 2, 1945, CF 1945–48, Box 120, folder: "4-11-6 to 4-12-6," all in RG 102.
36. Morlock to Grier, January 6, 1948.
37. Maud Morlock to Edward E. Rhatigan, Commissioner, NYC Dept of Welfare, October 18, 1946, and Rhatigan to Morlock, November 8, 1946, CF 1945–48, Box 120, folder: "5—1948," RG 102.
38. Interview with Frances Preston and Rika MacLennan, 1; Maud Morlock, "Report of Field Visit: Ohio," November 5–9, 1951, 9, CF 1949–52, Box 412, folder: "September 1951," RG 102.
39. Jane Hoey to W. L. Mitchell, September 12, 1952, Box 412, folder: "1949–52;" Martha Wood to Regional Directors and Regional Child Welfare Consultants, February 10, 1947, CF 1945–48, Box 120, folder: "October 1946–January 1947," both in RG 102.
40. "Social Security Commissioner's Minutes," February 20, 1947; Jane M. Hoey, to Regional Director, New York, and Ms. Alice J. Weber, Public Assistance Representative, March 3, 1947; Jane M. Hoey to Regional Directors, March 19, 1947, all in CF 45–48, Box 120, folder: "October 1946–January 1947," RG 102.
41. They had up to 25 days of vacation and 18 days of sick leave. "Our Homemakers," *The Welfarer*, November 1949, 10, McMillan Library, Human Resources Administration, New York (HRA); *Homemaker Services in the United States: Report of the 1959 Conference*, 75.
42. Margret L. DeWitt, Bureau of Personnel and Training, to Maud Morlock, March 20, 1947, CF 45–48, Box 120, folder: "5–1948"; "Homemaker Service, New York City, Department of Welfare: Report of a Field Visited by Maud Morlock," April 1, 1949, CF 1949–52, Box 414, 4-11-6; Martha Wood, Social Service Division, to Regional Directors, April 21, 1947, CF 1945–48, Box 102, folder: "October 1946–January 1947," 4-11-6; Gertrude Bolden to Maud Morlock, May 20, 1949, CF 1949–52, Box 413, all in RG 102; "Our Homemakers," *The Welfarer*, 10; "Preventing Broken Homes," *The Welfarer*, August 1950, 7; *Homemaker Services in the United States, 1958: Twelve Statements*, 35–6; "New York City Department of Welfare," in Medical Care Administration Branch, Division of Community Health Services, *Directory of Homemaker Services, 1963: Homemaker Agencies in the United States with Selected Data*, Public Health Service Publication No. 928, Revised 1964 (Washington, DC: 1964), 212.
43. "Preventing Broken Homes," *The Welfarer*, August 1950, 7; *Homemaker Services in the United States, 1958: Twelve Statements*, 35–36; "New York City Department of Welfare," in *Directory of Homemaker Services, 1963*, 212.
44. "Our Homemakers," *The Welfarer*, 10.
45. "Homemaker Service, New York City, Department of Welfare: Report of a Field Visited by Maud Morlock"; Martha Wood to Regional Directors, April 21, 1947; *Homemaker Services in the United States, 1958: Twelve Statements*, 7.
46. "Homemaker Service," April 28, 1948, report, 4.
47. Morlock to Grier, January 6, 1948; Interview with Frances Preston and Rika MacLennan, 3; "State: Massachusetts, Field Report," 7–9, 11; *Homemaker Services in the United States, 1958: Twelve Statements*, 2, 7.
48. *Homemaker Services in the United States, 1958: A Nationwide Study*, 53.
49. Ibid., 53–55.
50. "Homemaker Service, New York City . . . Report of a Field Visit by Maud Morlock," April 1, 1949; "Nine- to Twenty-four-Hour Homemaker Service Project—Part II," *Child Welfare*, April 1962, 153, 155.
51. *The Welfarer*, August 1950, 7; "Homemaker Service, New York City, Department of Welfare, Report of a Field Visit by Maud Morlock," 4–5.
52. "Preserving the Home in Emergency: The Homemaking Center," *The Welfarer*, July 1954, 6; "Preventing Broken Homes."

53. Evelyn Hart, *Homemaker Services for Families and Individuals* (New York: Public Affairs Pamphlet No. 37, 1965), 8; "Jewish Social Service Bureau," 2; "Report of Field Visit: State of Illinois," 4.
54. *Homemaker Services in the United States, 1958: Twelve Statements*, 11.
55. Maud Morlock to Elinor McCabe, December 27, 1943, CF 1945–48, Box 119, folder: "4-11-6," RG 102; "Report of Field Visit: State of Illinois," 4, 7.
56. "Report of Field Visit, Ohio," 9–10. See also, Maud Morlock, "State: Massachusetts, Field Report," May 20–26, 1948, 4, CF 1945–48, Box 120, folder: "5–1948"; Morlock to Elinor McCabe, January 25, 1945, CF 1945–48, Box 120, folder: "December 1947," both in RG 102.
57. *Homemaker Services in the United States: Report of the 1959 Conference*, 77.
58. "Service Training Program," *The Welfarer*, March 1954, 4; "Preserving the Home in Emergency: The Homemaking Center," 7; "Report of a Field Visit by Maud Morlock," 1.
59. "Home Care Project for the Aged," folder: "July 1950"; Dora Goldfarb, "Homemaker Service for the Aged," esp. 3, 6, folder: "September 1949," both in CF 1949–52, Box 413, RG 102; "A Different and Economical Service to the Aged."
60. Martha Derthick, *Policymaking for Social Security* (Washington, DC: The Brookings Institution, 1979), 299–300; House Ways and Means Committee, Staff Report on the Disability Insurance Program, Part III, "A Legislative History: The Development of the Disability Program under Old-Age Survivors Insurance," July 1974, 109–110, http://www.ssa.gov/history/reports/dibhistory.html, accessed February 12, 2006.
61. Office of Vocational Rehabilitation, "Study of Programs for Homebound Physically Handicapped Individuals," January 7, 1955, Bureau of Public Assistance, Family Services Master Subject Files, Box 17, U.S. Department of Health, Education, and Welfare Records, RG 47.
62. "Submittal for Commissioner's Consideration; Subject: Homemaker Service—Illinois and New York," Bureau of Public Assistance to the Deputy Commissioner, September 12, 1952, CF 1949–52, Box 412, RG 102.
63. Jane M. Hoey to W. L. Mitchell, September 12, 1952; Alice Scott Hyatt to Miss Arnold, Miss Emery, Miss Noble, and Miss Morlock, "Decision of Commissioner of Social Security on Homemaker Service—Illinois A. and New York," September 16, 1952, all in CF 1949–52, Box 412, RG102.
64. *Homemaker Services in the United States: Report of the 1959 Conference*, 17;
65. "Mayor Announces Action Program for Aged in New York City," *The Welfarer*, January 1961, 1; "Welfare Health Aid Reported Improved," *NYT*, January 2, 1961; Robert Alan Shick, "The Contracting-Out of Local Government Services: New York City Home Health Care," unpublished Ph.D. dissertation, New York University, 1989, 48.
66. Dorothy V. Prussin, "Home Care for the Aging," *The Welfarer*, June 1957, 3; *The Welfarer*, March 1954, 4; "Home Care for the Aged," Letter to the Editor from Henry McCarthy, Chairman, Mayor's Advisory Committee for the Aged, *NYT*, August 30, 1956; Jane M. Hoey to W. L. Mitchell, September 12, 1952; Kathryn Adams to Maud Morlock, June 10, 1957, 2, CF 1953–57, Box 621, folder: "May 1957," RG 102.
67. Elinor McCabe to Maud Morlock, March 19, 1953; Morlock to McCabe, March 25, 1953, both in CF 53–57, Box 619, folder: "March 1953," RG 102.
68. *Homemaker Services in the United States, 1958: A Nationwide Study*, 9.
69. "The Bureau of Special Services," *The Welfarer*, November 1959, 6.
70. "Welfare's Homemakers Honored with Ten–Year Service Awards," *The Welfarer*, August 1959, 3; "A Decade of Service," *The Welfarer*, July 1961, 11; Shick, "The Contracting Out of Local Government Services," 48; "New York City Department of Welfare," 212, 206, 208.
71. *Homemaker Services in the United States, 1958: Twelve Statements*, 8, 98.
72. Shick, "The Contracting Out of Local Government Services," 49–50, 52; "Nine- to Twenty-four-Hour Homemaker Service Project—Part II," *Child Welfare*, April 1962, 156.
73. "The Bureau of Special Services," 7; *Homemaker Services in the United States, 1958: Twelve Statements*, 40, 91; "Keeping Families United," *NYT*, August 16, 1964. See chapter three for the consequences.

74. "Public Assistance," 8, 10, Social Security Administration, Bureau of Public Assistance (SSA, BPA), Family Services Master Subject Files, Box 17, folder: "600.05 1954," RG 47.
75. *Public Welfare News*, September 1954; *Public Welfare News*, March 1954; December 1954, March 1955, North Carolina State Library, Raleigh, North Carolina.
76. *Public Welfare News*, June 1955; *Public Welfare News*, December 1958.
77. "Review of Public Assistance Achievements in 1956," 2, SSA, BPA, Family Services Master Subject Files, Box 17, folder: "600.05 1954," RG 47.
78. Jennifer Mittelstadt, *From Welfare to Workfare: The Unintended Consequences of Liberal Reform, 1945–1965* (Chapel Hill: University of North Carolina Press, 2005), 12–13; 37, 41–42, 65–67.
79. "Review of Public Assistance Achievements in 1956."
80. Maud Morlock to Margaret R. Fitzsimmons, August 13, 1956, 4-5, CF 1953-57, Box 622, folder "October 1956;" Morlock to Claire N. Kirk, May 10, 1957, CF 1953–57, Box 621, folder: "May 1957," both in RG 102.
81. "Reports and Enquires: Home Aides Services," *International Labour Review*, 56 (July 1947), 39–46; *Home Help and the Nations*, Report of First Conference on the Home Help Service (London: Home Help Organization, 1952), 41–43, 117; Margareta Nordström, "Social Home Help Services in Sweden," *International Labour Review* 88 (1963), 366–379.
82. *Home Help and the Nations*, 18, 83–84, 106, 131–132.
83. International Labour Office, "Notes on Homemaker or Home-Help Services," 1965, D.6.1965, typescript, 7, WN8-3-1002-01, Archive of the International Labor Organization, Geneva, Switzerland.
84. Dr. E. B. Brooke, "Home Help in the Domiciliary Care of the Aged," *Home Help and the Nations*, 6–7; James Struthers, "'No Place Like Home': Gender, Family, and the Politics of Home Care in Post-World War II Ontario," *Canadian Bulletin of Medical History* 20:2 (2003), 392, 394.
85. "Notes on Homemaker or Home-Help Services," 10.
86. Leila Simonen, *Feminist Social Policy in Finland: Contradictions of Municipal Homemaking* (Brookfield: Avebury, 1991), especially 67, 82, 89; *Proceedings of the International Congress on HOME HELP Services*, English translation, WA Publication No. 10 (Washington, DC: GPO, 1962), 1–2.
87. *Study of Selected Home Care Programs: A Joint Project of the Public Health Service and the Commission on Chronic Illness, Part II: Individual Programs*, Public Health Monograph No. 35 (Washington, DC: GPO, May 1955), 17–33.
88. Helen Cole to Maud Morlock, September 5, 1945, and June 4, 1945, CF 1945-1948, Box 120, folder: "1945," RG 102; "Homemaker Service, New York City . . . Report of a Field Visited by Maud Morlock," passim.
89. "Planning for the Chronically Ill," *AJPH* 10 (October 1947), 1257–1260.
90. *Homemaker Services in the United States, 1958: 12 Statements*, 81–85.
91. Edward S. Rogers, "Stake in the Commission's Program of the American Public Health Association," *Proceedings of First Meeting of the Commission on Chronic Illness*, 13.
92. Ernst Boas, M.D., "Clinical Problems," 20, and Leonard A. Scheele, Surgeon General, Public Health Service, "The Turning Point in Care of the Chronically Ill," 42, *Proceedings of First Meeting*.
93. Rosemary Stevens, *In Sickness and Wealth: American Hospitals in the 20th Century* (New York: Basic Books, 1989), 141, 159, 209.
94. Daniel M. Fox, *Health Policies, Health Politics: The British and American Experience, 1911–1965* (Princeton: Princeton University Press, 1986).
95. Stevens, *In Sickness and Wealth*, 4–7; 230; 236; Sandra Opdycke, *No One Was Turned Away: The Role of Public Hospitals in New York City since 1900* (New York: Oxford University Press, 1999), 50; 84.
96. Stevens, *In Sickness and Wealth*, 11; Opdycke, *No One Was Turned Away*, 81–90; Edward M. Bernecker to Mayor William O'Dwyer, April 26, 1948, NYAM Health and Hospital Planning Council, Box 106, folder 2: "home medical care, 1948–1952," NYAMR.

97. "Hospital to Test Home Cancer Aid," *NYT*, December 30, 1946; Martin Cherkasky, "The Montefiore Hospital Home Program," *AJPH-Nation's Health* 39 (February, 1949), 165; Hospital Council of Greater New York, *Organized Home Medical Care in New York City: A Study of Nineteen Programs* (Cambridge, MA: Harvard University Press, 1956), 352.
98. David M. Halbfinger, "Dr. Martin Cherkasky," *NYT*, September 8, 1997.
99. Cherkasky, "The Montefiore Hospital Home Program," 164–165.
100. *Organized Home Medical Care*, 360.
101. Cherkasky, "The Montefiore Hospital Home Program," 163, 164, 165.
102. "Hospital to Test Home Cancer Aid"; Bluestone, "Home Care and the Practitioner," *Postgraduate Medicine*, 24:2 (August 1958), 139.
103. New York Department of Hospitals (DOH), *Home for Dependents Annual Report, 1948*; DOH *Annual Report*, 1950, 19, Municipal Library of New York.
104. DOH *Annual Report 1946*, 6; DOH *Annual Report 1952*, 9.
105. DOH, *Annual Report 1948*, 8, 51; DOH *Annual Report 1950*, 19; DOH, *Annual Report 1951*, 16. Russell Sage Foundation, "Extension of Medical Care and Social Service into the Home for a Selected Group of Indigent Patients at Queens General Hospital," May 19, 1948, CF 1949–52, Box 119, folder: "visiting housekeeper aide," RG 102.
106. DOH *Annual Report 1951*, 16; *DOH Annual Report 1956*, 7.
107. Special Investigating Committee on Chronic Diseases of the Department of Hospitals, NYC, "Report on the Care of the Chronic Sick by the Department of Hospitals, Part II: Home Medical and Nursing Care," December 1934, NYAM Committee on Public Health, folder: "NYC Charter Revisions, 1934–36 Home Care," NYAMR.
108. DOH *Annual Report 1948*, 51; DOH *Annual Report 1950*, 19, 26.
109. Bernecker to O'Dwyer, April 26, 1948; DOH *Annual Report 1949*, 35.
110. DOH *Annual Report 1949*, 32; Bernecker to O'Dwyer; DOH *Annual Report 1948*, 35.
111. Murray Teigh Bloom, "One Answer to Our Hospital Shortage," *Woman's Home Companion* 75 (November 1948), 188.
112. *Organized Home Medical Care*, 7.
113. Office of Vocational Rehabilitation, "Study of Programs for Homebound Physically Handicapped Individuals," 19–20.
114. Joseph H. Kinnaman, "Problems of an Aging Population: Sheltered Care of the Aged," *AJPH* 37 (February 1947), 163–169; Joseph H. Kinnaman, "The Nursing Home—A Medical Care Facility," *AJPH* 39 (September 1949), 1099–1105; Eleanor Cryan, "Foster Home Care for Older People," *AJN* 49 (August 1954), 954–955; Ellen Schell, "The Origins of Geriatric Nursing: The Chronically Ill Elderly in Almshouses and Nursing Homes, 1900–1950," *Nursing History Review* 1 (1993), 203–216.
115. Institutions included University of Vermont College of Medicine, Washington University in St. Louis, University of Colorado, Denver, the Medical College of Georgia in Augusta, and University of Tennessee in Knoxville.
116. Peter Meek, Assistant Director, Commission on Chronic Illness, to Peter Rogatz, M.D., September 11, 1953, NYAM Health and Hospital Planning Committee of Southern New York, Box 106, folder 3: "home medical care, 1953," NYAMR; Harriet Cross, "Hospital Service Can Be Extended," *AJN* 54 (September 1954), 127; "Richmond Home Medical Care Program," *Study of Selected Home Care Programs*, 17–33. Also, *Study of Selected Home Care Programs: A Joint Project of the Public Health Service and the Commission on Chronic Illness, Part I: Total Study*, Public Health Monograph No. 35, May 1955; Office of Vocational Rehabilitation, "Study of Programs for Homebound Physically Handicapped," January 7, 1955, 53.
117. Enid Bailey Callahan, "Extending Hospital Services into the Home," *AJN* 61 (June 1961), 59–62.
118. Emilie G. Sargent, "Evolution of a Home Care Plan," *AJN* 61 (July 1961), 89; *A Study of Selected Home Care Programs*, Part I, "Definition of Terms," viii; *First Proceedings Commission on Chronic Illness*, "Recommendations," 59–63; Enid Bailey Callahan, "Extending Hospital Services into the Home."

119. *Summary Information on Medical and Remedial Care Provided in Approved State and Public Assistance Plans* (Washington, DC: HEW, SSA, Bureau of Public Assistance, 1960).
120. Howard M. Rusk, "Rehabilitation: The Third Phase of Medical Care," *The Westchester Medical Bulletin* 15 (October 1947), 14; Albrecht, *The Disability Business*, 121–128.
121. Office of Vocational Rehabilitation, "Study of Programs for Homebound Physically Handicapped Individuals," 48; Jacqueline Vaughn Switzer, *Disabled Rights: American Disability Policy and the Fight for Equality* (Washington, DC: Georgetown University Press, 2003), 52.
122. "One Answer to Our Hospital Shortage."
123. Ibid.
124. Harriet Fraad, Stephen Resnick, and Richard Wolff, "For Every Knight in Shining Armor, There's a Castle Waiting to Be Cleaned: A Marxist-Feminist Analysis of the Household," *Rethinking Marxism* 2:4 (1989), 9–69.
125. *Organized Home Medical Care*, 106, 379, 23, 96.
126. Maud Morlock to Mrs. Minna Field, Montefiore Hospital, February 11, 1949, and Minna Field to Maud Morlock, February 28, 1949, CF 1949–52, Box 414, RG 102.
127. *Organized Home Medical Care*, 109.
128. See, for example, New York DOH *Annual Reports* from 1948 through mid-1950s; *Organized Home Medical Care;* Bluestone, "Home Care in the Practitioner," *Postgraduate Medicine*, 140; *First Proceedings of Commission on Chronic Illness*, 39.
129. DOH *Annual Report 1952*, 15.
130. J. F. Follmann, Jr., *Health Insurance and Nursing and Home Care* (New York: Health Insurance Association of America, May 1959), 65.
131. Ibid., 66, 60.
132. "The City Child Who Is Ill at Home," *AJN* 49 (May 1949), 282.
133. Susan Reverby, *Ordered to Care: The Dilemma of American Nursing, 1850–1945* (New York: Cambridge University Press, 1987), 99–117, 195.
134. "The Biennial," *AJN* 46 (November 1946), 728–729; "The ANA Economic Security Program," *AJN* 47 (February 1947), 70–73; "ANA Statement on the Taft-Harley Act," *AJN* 53 (June 1953), 699–700; Thelma M. Mermelstein in "Economic Facts of Life for Nurses: III," *AJN* 52 (September 1952), 1115.
135. Patricia Cayo Sexton, *The New Nightingales: Hospital Workers, Unions, New Women's Issues* (New York: Enquiry Press, 1981).
136. Etta A. Creech, "Home Nursing Experience for the Student Practical Nurse," *AJN* 52 (February 1952), 218; "Nurse Practice Acts," *AJN* 49 (April 1949), 198; Dorothy N. Kelly, "Practical Nurse Students And the Cancer Patient," *ANJ* 55 (April 1955), 454–456.
137. Quote from "Statement of Functions of the Licensed Practical Nurse," *AJN* 57 (April 1957), 459–460; "The American Nurses' Association and Nonprofessional Workers in Nursing," *AJN* 55 (January 1955), 43–45.
138. *A Study of Selected Home Care Programs*, Part I, 5; *Homemaker Services in the United States, 1958: Twelve Statements*, 25–31; Elizabeth C. Phillips, "Visiting Home Aide Program," *Nursing Outlook* 10 (May 1962), 321-24; "The Home Aide in the Visiting Nurse Association of Greater Metropolitan Detroit," 2/10/57, 1–2, CF 1953–77, Box 622, folder: "October 1956," RG 102; Emilie G. Sargent, "Evolution of a Home Care Plan," *AJN* 61 (July 1961), 88–91.
139. John D. Thompson, "Nursing Service in a Home Care Program," *AJN* 51 (April 1951), 233–234.
140. *Homemaker Service in the United States, 1958: A Nationwide Study*, 63–64.
141. DOH *Annual Report 1958*, 14; DOH *Annual Report 1961*, 14–16, 22, 36.
142. DOH *Annual Report 1963*, 49.
143. DOH, *Annual Report* 1963, 49.
144. Harry Sesan to Administrator of Member Hospitals, January 21, 1959; Associated Hospital Service of New York, "Survey of Member Hospitals on Home Care," April 2, 1959, both in Health and Hospital Council of Greater New York Collection, Box 106, folder 6: "home medical care," NYAMR.

145. Associated Hospital Service of New York, "Survey of Member Hospitals on Home Care," 5.
146. Virginia R. Doscher, *Report of the National Conference on Homemaker Services, April 29–May 1964* (New York: National Council for Homemaker Services), 50.
147. "To Maintain Family Life: Homemaker Service," 2; Lucille Smith, "Homemaker Service: Luxury or Necessity," *Homemaker Service Bulletin* 4 (January 1963), 2; Doscher, *Report of the 1964 National Conference*, 21–22.
148. Elwin A. Miller to Katherine B. Oettinger, January 5, 1959; Clark Blackburn to Gertrude Hoffman, June 8, 1962, CF 1958–62, both in Box 837, folder "November 1961," RG102.
149. *Homemaker Services in the United States: Report of the 1959 Conference*, 147–148; "Proposed Plan for a National Voluntary Agency on Homemaker Services, April 1962," including "Appendix B," CF 1958–62, Box 837, folder: "November 1961," RG102; Maud Morlock, *Homemaker Services: History and Bibliography* (Washington, DC: GPO, 1964), 8–11; Doscher, *Report of the 1964 National Conference*, 2.

Chapter 3

1. *Home Care for the Elderly: The Need for a National Policy*, 95th Congress, 2nd Sess., February 22, 1978 (Washington, DC: GPO, 1978), 12–13
2. Martin Tolchin, "Own Home Best for an Aging Parent: Foster Care or Institution Is Costly," *NYT*, August 17, 1960.
3. Lyndon B. Johnson, "Remarks at the Signing of the Older Americans Act," July 14, 1965, John T. Woolley and Gerhard Peters, *The American Presidency Project* [online], Santa Barbara, http://www.presidency.ucsb.edu/ws/index.php?pid=27079, accessed April 5, 2010; Lyndon B. Johnson, "Remarks with President Truman at the Signing in Independence of the Medicare Bill," July 30, 1965, *Public Papers of the Presidents of the United States*, Vol. II, 811–815, http://www.lbjlib.utexas.edu/johnson/archives.hom/speeches.hom/650.
4. Premilla Nadasen, *Welfare Warriors: The Welfare Rights Movement in the United States* (New York: Routledge, 2005); Jennifer Mittlestadt, *From Welfare to Work: The Unintended Consequences of Liberal Reform, 1945–1965* (Chapel Hill: University of North Carolina Press, 2005).
5. Christopher Weeks, *Job Corps: Dollars and Dropouts* (Boston: Little, Brown, 1967), 130–31.
6. Laura Curran, "Social Work's Revised Maternalism: Mothers, Workers, and Welfare In Early Cold War America, 1946–1963," *Journal of Women's History* 17 (2005), 112–136.
7. Frances Fox Piven and Richard A. Cloward, "The Politics of the Great Society," in *The Great Society and High Tide of American Liberalism*, Sidney M. Milkis and Jerome M. Mileur, eds. (Amherst and Boston: University of Massachusetts Press, 2005), 253–269; Jill Quadagno, *The Color of Welfare: How Racism Undermined the War on Poverty* (New York: Oxford University Press, 1994).
8. Charles E. Gilbert, "Policy-Making in Public Welfare: The 1962 Amendments," *Political Science Quarterly* 81 (June 1966), 205; The President's Commission on the Status of Women, *Report of the Committee on Home and Community* (Washington, DC: GPO, October 1963), 16.
9. U.S. Congress, Senate, Committee on Labor and Public Welfare, Subcommittee on Health, *Hearings: Community Health Facilities and Services*, 87th Cong., 1st Sess., May 2–5 and August 3–4, 1961 (Washington, DC: GPO, 1961), 25–26; 75–83; *Community Health Services and Facilities Act of 1961*, Public Law 87–395, October 5, 1961, 824–827; HEW, "Homemaker and Related Services: Report of a Meeting Held June 17–18, 1957," CF 1953–57, Box 621, folder: "May 1957," RG 102.
10. Jill Quadagno, *One Nation Uninsured: Why the U.S. Has No National Health Insurance* (New York: Oxford University Press, 2005), 58–59.

11. Council of the Golden Ring Clubs, "Declaration of the Senior Citizens to the Community—Assembly of Senior Citizens at Carnegie Hall, May 27, 1958," U.S. Congress, House of Representatives, Committee on Ways and Means, *Hearings: Social Security Legislation*, 85th Cong., 2nd sess., June 16–30, 1958 (Washington, DC: GPO, 1958), 706–707.
12. *Social Security Legislation*, 1958, 707; Tom Wicker, "Congress: Medical Issue," *NYT*, August 21, 1960; Henry J. Pratt, *The Gray Lobby* (Chicago: University of Chicago Press, 1976), 47–56.
13. Emma Harrison, "15,000 at Garden Rally Demand Passage of Forand Health Bill," *NYT*, May 19, 1960; "Reuther Rallies Union Pensioners: 14,000 at Picnic in Detroit Hear Forand Bill Pleas," *NYT*, August 1960; W. H. Lawrence, "Kennedy Pledges to a Drive to Widen Social Security," *NYT*, August 15, 1960; Quadagno, *One Nation Uninsured*, 64–69; Testimonies of Francis Coon and Bobbie Hooker, U.S. Congress, Senate, Special Committee on Aging, Subcommittee on Federal and State Activities, *Hearings: Problems of the Aging*, 87th Cong., 1st sess., Part 5: Eugene, OR, November 8, 1961 (Washington, DC: GPO, 1962), 677–679, 683–684.
14. "Old Folks March: California Senior Citizens Rally for Political Fight," *NYT*, June 5, 1960; "California's Vote Highlights Aged," *NYT*, June 12, 1960.
15. Quadagno, One *Nation Uninsured*, 59; W. H. Lawrence, "Kennedy Pledges to a Drive to Widen Social Security," *NYT*, August 15, 1960; Pratt, *The Gray Lobby*, 64–65.
16. John D. Morris, "House Backs Bill on Care for Aged," *NYT*, June 23, 1960; "Senate Unit Acts on New Aged Bill," *NYT*, August 14, 1960; Tom Wicker, "Conferees Agree to Plan for Aged; States to Run It," *NYT*, August 26, 1960; Wicker, "Senate Rejects Kennedy's Plan on Care of the Aged," *NYT*, August 24, 1960; "Aged Care Bonus for States Is Seen," *NYT*, September 4, 1960; Felix Belair Jr., "Eisenhower Signs Bill on Aged Care," *NYT*, September 14, 1960.
17. U.S. House of Representatives, Committee on Ways and Means, *Summary of Major Provisions of Medical Assistance for the Aged Program* (Kerr-Mills Law) Public Law 86–778, 89th Cong, 1st sess. (Washington, DC: GPO, 1965), 1–2.
18. "Governors Back Aged Care Plan," *NYT*, June 30, 1960; Wilbur J. Cohen to Clinton P. Anderson, "Kerr-Mills Program (MAA) and Its Relation to Old Age Assistance," March 9, 1962; Helen E. Martz, "Medical Care for the Aged Under Public Assistance," x, Box 219, folder: "1963, January–June," both in Records of HEW, Office of Secretary, Secretary's General Correspondence, RG 235.
19. These were New York, Massachusetts, Michigan, and California. U.S. Senate, *Performance of the States: Eighteen Months Experience with the Medical Assistance for the Aged (Kerr-Mills) Program*, A Report to the Special Committee on Aging, 87th Cong., 2nd sess., June 15, 1962 (Washington, DC: GPO, 1962), vii–x; Jonathan Oberlander, *The Political Life of Medicare* (Chicago: University of Chicago Press, 2003), 26–28.
20. H. D. Kruse to City Editors, July 8, 1964; Clarence E. de la Chapelle to Senator, May 11, 1965; "Minutes of the Subcommittee on Medical Care for the Needy Elderly, NYAM," all in NYAM, Committee on Public Health, folder: "Aged, 1961–65," Minutes and Reports; George M. Warner, "Coordinated Home Care in New York State—The Rationale and Recent Developments," Presented at Montefiore Hospital, NYC, April 18, 1963, Health and Hospital Council of Greater New York Collection, Box 106, folder 7: "home medical care, 1963–64"; Raymond Houston to H. D. Kruse, April 29, 1961, Committee on Public Health, folder: "Aged, 1961–65," Minutes and Reports, all in NYAMR.
21. Edith Evans Asbury, "4,000 Aged Attend Democrats' Rally," *NYT*, November 4, 1960; "Aged-Care Rally To Hear Kennedy," *NYT*, March 13, 1962; U.S. Senate, *Performance of the States*, vii–x; Quadagno, *One Nation Uninsured*, 64–69.
22. Howard Rusk, "Rehabilitation Needs: First White House Conference Reports on Requirements of Elderly Indigents," *NYT*, January 15, 1961.
23. Pratt, *The Gray Lobby*, 112.

24. Mittelstadt, *From Welfare to Workfare*, 114–125.
25. Abraham Ribicoff to Honorable John. J. Williams, "Revisions in Welfare Legislation," January 10, 1962, folder: "1962"; Abraham Ribicoff to Senator Byrd, December 8, 1961; John Fogarty to Abraham Ribicoff, September 26, 1961, folder "July–December 1961", all in General Records of HEW, Secretary's General Correspondence, Box 219, RG 235.
26. Abraham Ribicoff to Hon. John E. Fogarty, December 6, 1961, 2, Box 219, folder: "July–December 1961," RG 235; Gilbert, "Policy-Making in Public Welfare," 204–210.
27. Wilbur Cohen to W. L. Mitchell, November 18, 1961, 2, Box 219, folder: "July–December 1961," RG 235.
28. U.S. Congress, House of Representatives, Committee on Ways and Means, *Hearings: Public Welfare Amendments of 1962*, 87th Cong., 2nd sess. on H.R. 10032, February 7, 9, and 13, 1962 (Washington, DC: GPO, 1962), 2–3; Gilbert, "Policy-Making in Public Welfare," 205.
29. Alice O'Connor, *Poverty Knowledge: Social Science, Social Policy, and the Poor in 20th Century U.S. History* (Princeton: Princeton University Press, 2001), 141–145.
30. Margaret Weir, *Politics and Jobs: The Boundaries of Employment Policy in the United States* (Princeton: Princeton University Press, 1992), 64–69; O'Connor, *Poverty Knowledge*, 142, 232–234.
31. *Social Welfare in New York State in 1962*, 1963, 2–3; "The New Public Welfare System: A Progress Report on the 1962 Amendments to The Social Security Act," in *Social Welfare in New York State in 1964*, 10, both New York State Department of Social Welfare, New York State Library, Albany; Gilbert, "Policy-Making in Public Welfare," 223.
32. Robert M. Ball to the Secretary, November 30, 1962, Box 219, folder "1962," RG235.
33. Virginia R. Doscher, *Report of the National Conference on Homemaker Services, April May 29, 1964* (New York: National Council for Homemaker Services), 12, 24.
34. U.S. Congress, Senate, Special Committee on Aging, Subcommittee on Federal, State, and Community Services, *Hearings: Services to the Elderly on Public Assistance*, 89th Cong., 1st sess., August 18–19, 1965 (Washington, DC: GPO, 1965), 5.
35. Mittelstadt, *From Welfare to Workfare*, 118–119; 122.
36. Wilbur Cohen to Mr. John Nolan, June 5, 1963, General Records of HEW, Office of the Secretary, Secretary's Subject Correspondence, Box 219, folder: "1963, January–June," RG 235.
37. Eve Edstrom, "All Welfare Merged as HEW Unit," *Washington Post* (*WP*), December 20, 1962; "Welfare Chief Called Critic of D.C. Program," *WP*, December 20, 1962.
38. Ellen Winston, "The Future of Public Assistance," Excerpts from an Address Delivered at the National Conference on Social Welfare, May 25, 1959, *Public Welfare News*, June 1959, 3; "Biographical Sketch: Ellen Winston," Carton 2, folder 23, Elizabeth Wickenden Papers, Wisconsin Historical Society (WHS); Johanna Schoen, *Choice and Coercion: Birth Control, Sterilization, and Abortion in Public Health and Welfare* (Chapel Hill: University of North Carolina Press, 2005), 105–110.
39. Annie May Pemberton, "Returning Senile Patients to the Community," *Public Welfare News*, March 1954, 4; "State's Licensed Boarding Homes Proving Resource for Aged and Infirm," *Public Welfare News*, March 1955, 5; "500th Boarding Home for Aged Is Licensed by Public Welfare," *Public Welfare News*, June 1961, 1.
40. J. Andrew Bowler, "Race and State Services," Box 57, folder: "General Files-Clippings [1945]," Ellen Black Winston Papers Collection, University Archives and Manuscripts, University of North Carolina at Greensboro, North Carolina.
41. Summary of Commissioner's Legislative Planning Meeting, September 9, 1963, Commissioner's Action Minutes, January 1952–January 1963, Box 1, folder: "Commissioner's Minutes, 1961–1965," 3, Records of Social and Rehabilitative Services, RG 363/RG 47.
42. President Lyndon B. Johnson, "Annual Message to the Congress on the State of the Union," January 8, 1964, http://lbjlib.utexas.edu/johnson/archives.hom/speeches.hom/640. "Outskirts of hope" also from this speech.
43. O'Connor, *Poverty Knowledge*, 146–151, 158.

44. U.S. Congress, Senate, Committee on Labor and Public Welfare, Subcommittee on Employment and Manpower, *Toward Full Employment: Proposals For a Comprehensive Employment and Manpower Policy in the United States*, 88th Cong., 2nd sess. (Washington, DC: GPO, 1964), v–vii, 25.
45. Office of Economic Opportunity (OEO), *A Nation Aroused*, 1st Annual Report, 1965, 41, "The War on Poverty, 1964–1968," Part I: The White House Central Files, Reel 9, Box 125, microfilm edition.
46. OEO, *A Nation Aroused*, 41–42.
47. Testimony of Dr. Ellen Winston, U.S. Congress, Senate, Special Committee on Aging, Subcommittee on Federal, State, and Community Services, *Hearings: Services to the Elderly on Public Assistance*, 89th Cong., 1st sess., August 18–19, 1965 (Washington, DC: GPO, 1965), 10.
48. *Public Welfare Amendments of 1962*, 171.
49. Maud Morlock, *Homemaker Services: History and Bibliography* (Washington, DC: GPO, 1964).
50. Howard Rusk, "Keeping Families United: Growing Homemaker Services Will Be Major Tool in Drive to Reduce Poverty," *NYT*, August 16, 1964.
51. *Homemaker Services in Public Welfare* (Washington, DC: HEW, April 1964), 4–5.
52. Testimony of Miss Dauch, in California Assembly, Interim Committee on Public Health, Subcommittee on Professions and Occupations, *Hearing*, December 6 and 7, 1965, 88, California State Library, Government Publications.
53. Katherine B. Oettinger to Mrs. Betty Kindleberger Stone, November 8, 1966, C F 1963–66, Box 1017, folder: "4-16-2-12," RG102; Commissioner's Action Minutes, 1961–66, Box 1 and 2, folder: "Commissioner's Minutes, 1961–65," RG 363.
54. "Troup County Homemaker Project Progress Report, September 25, 1967," 1, #044; "Troup County Homemaker Project Progress Report 12-21-66," 2, both in ORDT Case Files, Box 2, folder: "Georgia 'Homemaker Project,'" both in RG 363.
55. "Progress Report on Homemaker Services in Menominee County, Wisconsin, December 1, 1966–June 1, 1967," Project #066C-3, ORDT Case Files, Box 5, folder: "Wisconsin 'Homemaker Project,'" RG 363.
56. New Mexico Department of Welfare, "Progress Report on Bernalillo County, Homemaker Demonstration Project," August 26, 1965, cover, 6–7, in ORDT Case Files, Box 5: folder: "New Mexico 'Homemaker Demonstration Project,'" RG 363.
57. Fred H. Steininger, Director BFS to Mrs. Bruce Schaefer, Director, State Department of Family and Children Services, Atlanta, June 18, 1964; Memo from Steininger to Winston, June 8, 1964, Re: Recommendation for Action on Troup County, Georgia Homemaker Demonstration Project, #044, ORDT Case Files, Box 2, folder: "Georgia 'Homemaker Project,'" all in RG 363.
58. Winifred Bell to Jules H. Berman, "Demonstration Project No. 044—Homemaker Project—Troup County, Georgia, May 7, 1964," 2, ORDT Case Files, Box 2, folder: "Georgia 'Homemaker Project,'" RG 363.
59. "Manual of Homemaker Project–Troup County, Georgia," June 1964, 3, 1, ORDT Case Files, Box 2, folder: "Georgia 'Homemaker Project,'" RG 363.
60. Sonya Michel, "Childcare and Welfare (In)Justice," *Feminist Studies* 24 (Spring 1998), 45–46, 53 note 5; Frances Fox Piven, and Richard A. Cloward, *Regulating the Poor: The Functions of Public Welfare*, 2nd ed. (New York: Vintage Books, 1993), 382–383.
61. Martha Derthick, *Uncontrollable Spending for Social Services Grants* (Washington DC: Brookings Institution, 1975), 2, 15–19, 40.
62. "Biographical Note," *Brahna Trager, A Registry of her Papers in the Library of Congress*, 2, Manuscript Division, LC, 2007; Brahna Trager, *Training Homemaker/Home Health Aides for Community Service* (Washington, DC: U.S. Department of HEW et al., 1966), 27.
63. Trager, *Training*, 30–31.

64. Felicia Kornbluh, *The Battle for Welfare Rights: Politics and Poverty in Modern America* (Philadelphia: University of Pennsylvania Press, 2007), 1, 7, 19; Mittlestadt, *From Welfare to Workfare*, 91–104; O'Connor, *Poverty Knowledge*, 159–160.
65. Joshua B. Freeman, *Working-Class New York: Life and Labors Since World War II* (New York: The New Press, 2000).
66. Kornbluh, *The Battle for Welfare Rights*, 18–26.
67. Freeman, *Working-Class New York*, 201–205; Walkowitz, *Working with Class*; Kornbluh, *The Battle for Welfare Rights*, 26–27.
68. Freeman, *Working-Class New York*, 205–206; Emanuel Perlmutter, "The Welfare Tangle," *NYT*, January 25, 1965.
69. "Two Anti-Poverty Projects Are Approved For BSS," *The Welfarer*, December 1965, 10.
70. "Training and Employment for Mothers in Part-Time Occupations," *The Welfarer*, March 1967, 1, 8–10.
71. Ibid.
72. "Housekeeping Aide Project Trains Mothers in Management and Child Care," *The Welfarer*, September 1964, 1, 6; *1964 Annual Report of the City of New York Department of Welfare*, April 1965; "Training and Employment for Mothers in Part-Time Occupations"; "Two Anti-Poverty Projects Approved"; Annie Creola Fenton, "The Housekeeping Aide and Training Project in the New York City Department of Welfare Bureau of Special Services," unpublished MSW thesis, Fordham University, 1966.
73. Francis Caro and Arthur Blank, *Home Care in New York City: The System, the Providers, the Beneficiaries* (New York: Community Service Society of New York, July 1985), 123–133; Robert Alan Shick, "The Contracting-out of Local Government Services: New York City Home Health Care," unpublished dissertation, New York University, 1989, 57–58.
74. Gertrude Goldberg, "Nonprofessional Helpers: The Visiting Homemakers," in *Community Action Against Poverty: Readings from the Mobilization Experience*, George A. Brager and Francis P. Purcell, eds. (New Haven: College & University Press, 1967), 179, 181, 187, 192; George Brager, "The Indigenous Social Work Technician: Mobilization for Youth," in *Up from Poverty: New Career Ladders for Nonprofessionals*, Frank Riessman and Hermine I. Popper, eds. (New York: Harper & Row Publishers, 1968), 82; See also Patricia Elston, "Public Welfare: The Breath of Change: New York City and Alameda County," in *Up from Poverty*, 66–79.
75. Fred Powledge, *New Careers: Real Jobs and Opportunity for the Disadvantaged*, Public Affairs Pamphlet No. 427 (New York: Public Affairs Committee, 1968), 8, 11, 4; Frank Riessman, *New Careers: A Basic Strategy Against Poverty*, with introduction by Michael Harrington (New York: A Philip Randolph Fund, 1966), 7, 9; Arthur Pearl and Frank Riessman, *New Careers for the Poor: The Nonprofessional in Human Service* (New York: The Free Press, 1965), 249–251; Nancy Naples, *Grassroots Warriors: Activist Mothering, Community Work and the War on Poverty* (New York: Routledge, 1998), 41.
76. Joseph Loftus, "Congress Passes Poverty Program with New Curbs," *NYT*, October 21, 1966; Powledge, *New Careers*, 11.
77. "Worker Reservoir," *NYT*, August 9, 1965; Stuart Lavietes, "Frank Riessman, 79, Dies," *NYT*, March 14, 2004.
78. Naples, *Grassroots Warriors*, part II; Nancy MacLean, *Freedom Is Not Enough: The Opening of the American Workplace* (Cambridge, MA: Harvard University Press, 2006), chap. 2.
79. Riessman and Popper, "The Evolutionary Revolution," in *Up from Poverty*, 4; Alan Gartner, *Paraprofessionals and Their Performance: A Survey of Education, Health, and Social Service Programs*, with foreword by Frank Riessman (New York: Praeger Publishers, 1971).
80. Testimony of Lucy Still, Subcommittee on Professions and Occupations, *Hearing*, 89.
81. Edith F. Lynton, *The Subprofessional: From Concepts to Careers* (New York: National Committee on Employment of Youth, September 30, 1967), 78–79, 85.
82. Goldberg, "Nonprofessional Helpers," 194.

83. U.S. Congress, Senate, Committee on Labor and Public Welfare, Subcommittee on Health, *Hearings: Health Manpower Act of 1968*, 90th Cong., 2nd sess., March 20–21, 1968 (Washington, DC: GPO, 1968); *Progress Report on Nurse Training 1970, Report to the Secretary, Dept. of Health, Education, and Welfare on Administration of the Nurse Training Act of 1964, Including Amendments of the Health Manpower Act of 1968, Title II, Nurse Training* (Washington, DC: U.S. Dept. of Health, Education, and Welfare, August 1970), 28–30, 50–52.
84. Jennifer Klein, *For All These Rights: Business, Labor, and the Shaping of America's Public-Private Welfare State* (Princeton: Princeton University Press, 2003), 78–115.
85. Jonathan Engel, *Poor People's Medicine: Medicaid and American Charity Care Since 1965* (Durham: Duke University Press, 2006), 34–39; Colleen M. Grogan, "A Marriage of Convenience: The Persistent and Changing Relationship Between Long-Term Care and Medicaid," in *History and Health Policy in the United States*, Rosemary A. Stevens, Charles E. Rosenberg, and Lawton R. Burns, eds. (New Brunswick: Rutgers University Press, 2006), 203–212.
86. Karen Buhler-Wilkerson, *No Place Like Home: A History of Nursing and Home Care in the United States* (Baltimore: Johns Hopkins University Press, 2001), 200–201; Evelyn Hart, *1967 Forum on Homemaker-Home Health Aide Service* (New York: NCHS, 1967), 10–12.
87. Quadagno, *One Nation Uninsured*, 74–75; Engel, *Poor People's Medicine*, 48–49.
88. Katherine Ricker-Smith, "An Historical and Critical Overview of the Development and Operation of California's In-Home Supportive Services Program," San Francisco Home Health Service, Grant HEW-100-78–0027, December 31, 1978, 31–36, California State Library, Sacramento.
89. Andrew Szasz, "The Labor Impacts of Policy Change in Health Care: How Federal Policy Transformed Home Health Organizations and Their Labor Practices," *Journal of Health Politics, Policy, and Law* 15 (Spring 1990), 194; Penny Hollander Feldman, Alice M. Sapienza, and Nancy M. Kane, *Who Cares for Them? Workers in the Home Care Industry* (Westport, CT: Greenwood Press,1990), 55; Administration on Aging, *Human Resources in the Field of Aging: Homemaker-Home Health Aide Services*, AoA Occasional Papers in Gerontology, No. 2 (Washington, DC: U.S. Department of Health, Education, and Welfare, 1977), 2–3, 7; Sharon Fay Koch, "Diagnosing Ills in Home Health Care," *LAT*, April 25, 1971; Brahna Trager, *Homemaker-Home Health Aide Services in the U.S.* (Washington, DC: GPO, June 1973), 10–12; Caro and Blank, *Home Care in New York City: The System, the Providers, the Beneficiaries*, 13.
90. Testimony of Charles Odell, *Services to the Elderly on Public Assistance*, 59; "Medicare Provides Aides Jobs," *LAT*, December 25, 1966; Rosella M. Rubel and Peggy Keidel, "Effects of Medicare Crackdown," *LAT*, February 4, 1970; Koch, "Diagnosing Ills."
91. Gladys S. Lawson to Robert Wright, January 15, 1969, CF 1969, 4-11-6, Box 1218, folder: "1969 Homemaker Service," RG102; NCHHAS, *Focus on the Future: A Ten Year Report, 1962–1972* (1973), 3, Box 86, folder: "NCHHAS," Child Welfare League of America Records, SWHA, University of Minnesota, Minneapolis, MN.
92. Paul Houston, "Medicare Move Stirs Turmoil," *LAT*, February 9, 1970; Koch, "Diagnosing Ills"; Don Smith, "Medi-Cal Cutbacks Imperil County Visiting Nurses Assn.," *LAT*, May 31, 1971.
93. Testimony of Dr. Malcolm, Subcommittee on Professions and Occupations, *Hearing*, 46–48.
94. Ibid., 52.
95. New York Department of Social Welfare, *Public Welfare in New York State 1966 Centennial Year Report*, Legislative Document No. 96 (1967), 9–11; Engel, *Poor People's Medicine*, 61.
96. Theodore Pearson to Hon. Nelson A. Rockefeller, October 27, 1965, Box 98, folder 12, Henry Street Settlement Records, SHWA, University of Minnesota, Minneapolis, MN (HSS); NYAM, Committee on Public Health "Comments on the City's Proposed Plan for the Administration of Title XIX in New York City," September 6, 1966, folder: "Aged, 1961–65, Minutes and Reports," NYAMR.

97. Clarence E. de la Chapelle to My dear Senator, "RE: H.R. 6675," May 11, 1965, 2; Howard Reid Craig, M.D., to Doctor Lee, February 4, 1966, 1, both in folder: "Aged, 1968–65"; NYAM, Confidential Discussion Memorandum, "Comments on the City's Proposed Plan for the Administration of Title XIX in New York City," September 6, 1966, folder: "Aged, 1961–65, Minutes and Reports," all in Committee on Public Health, NYAMR; Theodore Pearson, telegram to Hon. Nelson A Rockefeller et al., March 31, 1966; Robert H. Mulreany to Mr. John J. Keppler, April 7, 1966, copy of telegram sent to Hon. Anthony Travia, both in Box 98, folder 12, HSS.
98. U.S. Senate, *The Older Americans Act of 1965: A Compilation of Materials Relevant to H.R. 3708, As Amended by the Special Subcommittee on Aging, of the Committee on Labor and Public Welfare* (Washington, DC: GPO, 1965); Laura Katz Olson, *The Political Economy of Aging: The State, Private Power, and Social Welfare* (New York: Columbia University Press, 1982), 189; David K. Brown, "Administering Aging Programs in a Federal System," *Aging and Public Policy: The Politics of Growing Old in America*, William P. Browne and Laura Katz Olson, eds. (Westport, CT: Greenwood Press, 1983), 204.
99. Katz Olson, *The Political Economy of Aging*, 188; Robert Newcomer, A. E. Benjamin, and Carroll L. Estes, "The Older Americans Act," in *Fiscal Austerity and Aging: Shifting Government Responsibility for the Elderly*, Estes et al., eds. (Beverly Hills: Sage Publications, 1983), 189.
100. Community Council of Greater New York, "Report of the Home Health and Housing Program, Citizens' Committee on Aging, January 1967 to December 1969," rev. ed. (July 1970), McMillan Library, HRA, 1–2.
101. Welfare Local 371, AFSCME, "Homemakers Collective Bargaining Program, Fall 1966," Social Service Employees Union Records, Coll. 3, Box 1, file: collective bargaining program 1966, Robert Wagner Labor Archives, Tamiment Library, New York University (Wagner Archives).
102. Damon Stetson, "Union Pickets Welfare Office to Protest City Talk Impasse," *NYT*, December 22, 1966; "State Action Asked by Welfare Pickets," *NYT*, January 12, 1967; Damon Stetson, "Welfare Strike Is Ended by Union," *NYT*, January 19, 1967.
103. Kornbluh, *The Battle for Welfare Rights*, 75–85.
104. "Appendix Figure 1: Changes in the Federal and New York State Minimum Wage, 1950 to Present," *Raising the Minimum Wage in New York: Helping Working Families and Improving the State's Economy*, Fiscal Policy Institute, January 11, 2004, 19, http://www.fiscalpolicy.org/minimumwagerreport.pdf, accessed August 23, 2004.
105. Maurice Carroll, "Mediation Effort is Set by Ginsberg," *NYT*, May 7, 1967; "Officials of a Welfare Agency Discuss Union with Ginsberg," *NYT*, May 9, 1967; "Homemakers Groups to Recognize Union," *NYT*, May 16, 1967; "Mitchell Ginsberg, Social Work Dean, NYC Welfare Chief," http://www.columbia.edu/cu/record/archives/vol21/vol21_iss19/record2119.13.html, accessed May 26, 2010.
106. Emmanuel Perlmutter, "City and Welfare Unions Agree on Cut of 9,000 Jobs," *NYT*, February 10, 1969.
107. O'Connor, *Poverty Knowledge*, 192–193.
108. Eileen Boris, "Contested Rights: How the Great Society Crossed the Boundaries of Home and Work," in *The Great Society and the Rights Revolution*, 133.
109. MacLean, *Freedom Is Not Enough*, 85–87.
110. Quadagno, *The Color of Welfare*, 158–160.
111. Select Committee on Aging, *Home Care for the Elderly*.
112. Grogan, "A Marriage of Convenience," 202, 217–222.

Chapter 4

1. Ari L. Goldman, "An Activist and Her Fight," *NYT*, June 19, 1977.
2. U.S. Congress, House of Representatives, Select Committee on Aging, *Hearings: New York Home Care Abuse*, 95th Cong., 2nd sess., February 6, 1978 (Washington, DC: GPO, 1978), 2, 6–7, 8–12.

3. John L. Hess, "Care of Aged Poor a Growing Scandal," *NYT*, October 7, 1974; Frank J. Prial, "Abram Names 4 to Panel on Nursing Home Inquiry," *NYT*, January 31, 1975.
4. U.S. Congress, House of Representatives, Select Committee on Aging, *Hearing: Comprehensive Home Health Care: Recommendations for Action*, 94th Cong., 1st sess, November 19, 1975. (Washington, DC: GPO, 1976); *New York Home Care Abuse*; California Assembly, Committee on Human Resources, *Hearing on Administration of Homemaker/ Chore Services Program*, Tuesday, November 9, 1976 (Sacramento: Assembly Committee on Human Resources, 1976).
5. Judith Stein, *Pivotal Decade: How the U.S. Traded Factories for Finance in the 1970s* (New Haven: Yale University Press, 2010); Kim Phillips-Fein, *Invisible Hands: The Making of the Conservative Movement from the New Deal to Reagan* (New York: W.W. Norton, 2009), 229, chap. 9–10.
6. Timothy Conlan, *From New Federalism to Devolution: Twenty-five Years of Intergovernmental Reform* (Washington, DC: Brookings Institution Press, 1998).
7. Barry Bluestone and Bennett Harrison, *The Deindustrialization of America* (New York: Basic Books, 1982); Joseph A. McCartin, "Fire the Hell Out of Them: Sanitation Workers Struggles and the Normalization of Striker Replacement Strategy in the 1970s," *Labor: Studies in Working-Class History of the Americas* 2 (Fall 2005), 67–92; Joshua B. Freeman, *Working-Class New York: Life and Labor since World War II* (New York: The New Press, 2000); Kim Moody, *From Welfare State to Real Estate: Regime Change in New York City, 1974 to the Present* (New York: New Press, 2007).
8. Emily Layzer, *Individual Providers in Home Care: Their Practice, Problems, and Implications in the Delivery of Homemaker-Home Health Aide Services* (New York: National HomeCaring Council, 1981).
9. Katherine Ricker-Smith, "An Historical and Critical Overview of the Development and Operation of California's In-Home Supportive Services Program," Report for the San Francisco Home Health Service, December 31, 1978, 5, 15, California State Library, Sacramento [Ricker-Smith Report]; "Bill for New Aid to Needy Disabled Hit," *LAT*, May 29, 1951; News, "Hale Zukas Is a Disability Advocate and Policy Analyst," 3, The World Institute on Disability (WID), http://www.wid.org/news/?page=hale, accessed April 4, 2006.
10. Department of Social Welfare, *Annual Report*, 1959–60 (Sacramento: State of California, 1960), 3.
11. Department of Social Welfare, "More Than Money," *Annual Report*, 1958–1959 (Sacramento: State of California, 1959), 42–43; "Dr. Jacobus tenBroek: Author, Jurist, Professor, Founder of the National Federation of the Blind," biography, 1999, National Federation of the Blind, at http://www.blind.net/bw000001.htm, accessed on May 15, 2006.
12. Joseph Tussman and Jacobus tenBroek, "The Equal Protection of the Laws," *California Law Review* 37 (1949), 341; Jacobus tenBroek, "California's Dual System of Family Law: Its Origin, Development, and Present Status," *Stanford Law Review* 16 (1964), 257–284; Jacobus tenBroek and Floyd W. Matson, "The Disabled and the Law of Welfare," *California Law Review* 14 (May 1966), 816, 840.
13. *Annual Report*, 1959–60, 14–15.
14. Department of Social Welfare, *Annual Report*, 1962–63 (Sacramento: State of California, 1963), 11; Department of Social Welfare, *Social Welfare in California, Annual Report*, 1961–62 (Sacramento: State of California, 1962), 21.
15. "More Than Money," 13–14, 30–31; *Annual Report*, 1959–60, 40–41; *Annual Report*, 1961–62, 44; Ricker-Smith Report, 20–23.
16. Deborah Reidy Kelch, *Caring for Medically Indigent Adults in California: A History* (Oakland: California Healthcare Foundation, 2005).
17. tenBroek and Matson, "The Disabled and the Law of Welfare," 840; Jack Jones, "The Poor's Angry Voices—A Warning and a Therapy," *LAT*, July 24, 1966.
18. "Welfare Pickets Seek Return of Expense Money," *LAT*, October 19, 1966; Ray Zeman, "Welfare Recipients Demonstrate, Seek Jobs and Training," *LAT*, July 1, 1970.

19. Phone interview with Catherine Jermany by E. Boris, April 30, 2006; Al Stump, "Defenders of Dole," *Los Angeles Herald Examiner* reprint in *HRD News*, November 4, 1971, in Manpower Development (1966–1974), Vol. I (3), Box H43, Ronald Reagan Library (RRL), Simi Valley, CA.
20. Ellen Reese, *Backlash Against Welfare Mothers Past and Present* (Berkeley: University of California Press, 2005).
21. Premilla Nadasen, *Welfare Warriors: The Welfare Rights Movement in the United States* (New York: Routledge, 2005), 19–20.
22. "Poor Urged to Unite for 'Welfare Power,'" *LAT*, September 6, 1966; Harry Bernstein, "Union Official Calls Welfare Setup Wasteful," *LAT*, December 29, 1965; Marty Altschul, "County Board Blamed for Welfare Failures," *LAT*, February 9, 1968.
23. Harry Bernstein, "Union Pact Would End Regular Work Hours," *LAT*, July 10, 1968; David D. Crippen, "Report," *Social Services Union Newsletter Local 535* (August, 1974), 2, Box 9, folder 4-5, Timothy Sampson Papers, San Francisco State University-Labor Archives, San Francisco (SFSU-LA). By its tenth anniversary, it bargained for over 10,000 employees of welfare departments plus a range of human service employees, including probation, mental health, and nursing professionals. But after SEIU International transferred welfare assistance technicians to another Los Angeles local in 1970, union ties with welfare rights in Los Angeles weakened.
24. "Civil Service Commission OKs Pay for Suspended Employees," *LAT*, February 14, 1969.
25. Jermany Interview; "Welfare Rights Group Pickets, Renews Yule Bonus Demands," *LAT*, December 24, 1968; "Welfare Rights Unit Charges County Cuts Relief Funds," *LAT*, December 10, 1969; telephone interview with David Novogrodsky by E. Boris, June 12, 2006.
26. Governor, "Minutes of Cabinet Meeting, February 2, 1968," 3, Governor's Papers, GO 24, Cabinet Unit, Cabinet Meeting Minutes for 1968, February [1 of 2], RRL; Peter Schrag, *Paradise Lost: California's Experience, America's Future* (New York: The New Press, 1998), 43–48; Lou Cannon, *Governor Reagan: His Rise to Power* (New York: Public Affairs, 2003), 125–126.
27. Quoted in Cannon, *Governor Reagan*, 174–175.
28. Peter Schrag, *California: America's High-Stakes Experiment* (Berkeley: University of California Press, 2006), 99–101; Schrag, *Paradise Lost*, 48; Cannon, *Governor Reagan*, 196–197; Robert Kuttner, *Revolt of the Haves: Tax Rebellions and Hard Times* (New York: Simon and Schuster, 1980).
29. Office of the Governor, Message to the Legislature, "Welfare," March 21, 1968, 3, 1, GO 185, Research File Health and Welfare, Welfare, 1968, RRL.
30. Ann B. Jenkins, "Legislative-Executive Duel Ends With Signing of Social Security Pass-On Bill," *California Journal* (October 1970), 294, in GO 186, Research File, Health and Welfare, Welfare 1970 (2/5); Press Release, 9-19-70, GO 186, Research File, Health and Welfare, Welfare 1970 (5/5); Memorandum to RR, "Relative Standing of States on Aid Payments," October 17, 1968, in GO 25, Cabinet Staff Minutes, October 1968 [1/2], RRL.
31. Cabinet Meeting, August 14, 1968, GO 25, Cabinet Minutes, August 1968 [1/2], 1; Cabinet Meeting, August 14, 1968, 2, with attached "Report of the Consultants on Proposed Regulations Governing Employer-Employee Relations in County Welfare Departments," July 9, 1968, GO 25, Cabinet Minutes, August 1968 [1/2], RRL.
32. Cabinet Staff Meeting, November 22, 1968, GO 25, Cabinet Meeting Minutes, November 1968 [2/2], 2–3, RRL; Bill Boyarsky, "Reagan Proposes $100 Million Cutback for Welfare in State," *LAT*, March 20, 1970; Philip Hager, "State Offers New Plan on Welfare to Avert Fund Cutoff," *LAT*, October 30, 1970.
33. Tom Goff, "Reagan Slashes Aid to Aged and Blind by $25 Million," *LAT*, July 11, 1970; Martha Derthick, *Uncontrollable Spending for Social Service Grants* (Washington, DC: The Brookings Institution, 1975), chap. 5.
34. "White Paper on Homemaker Services," May 1968, 1, 11–12, H62, Department of Social Welfare, State Legislature, Mobley, Ernest N. Subject File, folder: "Homemakers," RRL; Assembly Office of Research and Staff of the Assembly Committee on Social Welfare, *California Welfare: A Legislative Program for Reform* (Sacramento: California Legislature, February 1969), 258.

35. Enrolled Bill Report, Department of Finance, SB 719, July 26, 1968, in Governor's File, Microfilm, 1968, California State Archives (CSA); "Position Paper for State HR 1 Enabling Legislation," Draft 11/30/72, 6, Box 1, folder 11, Hale Zukas Papers, The Bancroft Library, University of California, Berkeley.
36. Goff, "Reagan Slashes Aid to Aged and Blind by $25 Million"; State Department of Social Welfare, 1970, "The Orange Book' Welfare Reform 1970,"1, 2a, 4, RRL; "Welfare Cut Will Strike at Top, Bottom Levels," *LAT*, July 11, 1970; Earl C. Behrens, "New Reagan Cutback In Welfare," *San Francisco Chronicle* (*SFC*), July 14, 1970; "Cutback in California," *LAT*, July 12, 1970; Ted Fourkas, "The Rush to Cut Welfare," *Sacramento Bee* (*SB*), July 27, 1970.
37. Derek Pogson, "Reagan Attacks Welfare 'Thieves,' Counties' Action," *SB*, July 16, 1970.
38. "The Orange Book," 4; Mark Neal Aaronson, "Legal Advocacy and Welfare Reform: Continuity and Change in Public Policy," unpublished Ph.D. dissertation, Political Science, University of California, Berkeley, 1975, 138.
39. Ted Fourkas, "Reagan Rescinds Aid Cut to Blind, Aged, Disabled," *SB*, July 24, 1970; Ray Zeman, "Supervisors Assail Reagan for Shift on Welfare Costs," *LAT*, July 15, 1970.
40. J. N. Bouyquin, "Protests Cut," *SB*, July 26, 1970; "The Public Speaks Out: Reagan's Cutback on Aid to Aged, Blind Called Cruel, Shortsighted," *LAT*, July 15, 1970; " "Thanks the Bee," *SB*, August 1, 1970.
41. Ricker-Smith Report, 53; Emma H. Gunterman, Oral History Interview, conducted in 1989–1990 by Jacqueline S. Reinier, 367, California State University, Sacramento, for the CSA, State Government Oral History Program, CSA.
42. Joseph P. Shapiro, *No Pity: People with Disabilities Forging a New Civil Rights Movement* (New York: Times Books, 1993), 47–51.
43. Shapiro, *No Pity*, 51, 41–53.
44. Hale Zukas, "CIL History," 1, 3, folder: "Arts Grant," Box 25, Center for Independent Living Records, The Bancroft Library, University of California, Berkeley; Doris Zames Fleischer and Frieda Zames, *The Disability Rights Movement: From Charity to Confrontation* (Philadelphia: Temple University Press, 2001), 37–43; Edward Berkowitz, *Disabled Policy: America's Programs for the Handicapped* (New York: Cambridge University Press, 1987), 109–207.
45. Albert Seltzer to All County Welfare Directors, "Social Service Letter No. 73–2: Homemaker and Chore Services for Adults," September 24, 1973; "Hearing in re: H.R. 1," May 30, 1973, 46–49; "Home and Care Needs," "Our Presentation on Attendant Care Services," all in Carton 2, folder 1, Zukas Papers.
46. Herbert R. Willsmore, "Student Resident at Cowell, 1969–1970, Business Enterprises Manager at the Center for Independent Living, 1975–1977," an oral history conducted in 1996 and 1999 by Susan O'Hara in *University of California's Cowell Hospital Residence Program for Physically Disabled Students, 1962–1975: Catalyst for Berkeley's Independent Living Movement*, 174, 198, Regional Oral History Office, The Bancroft Library, University of California, Berkeley (BANC), 2000.
47. Herbert Willsmore to John Dunlap, July 20, 1970, available from the Online Archive of California; http://ark.cdlib.org/ark:/13030/hb9r29p0cj, accessed June 15, 2006.
48. Willsmore Interview, 174–175; "Fact Sheet," Folder, "Board Minutes June 11, 1971–August 28, 1972, CIL Records.
49. Richard Rooda, "Solon Will Ask Reagan to Restore Aid Cuts to Aged, Blind, Disabled," *SB*, July 21, 1970; Willsmore Interview, 199.
50. Dennis Campbell, "Court Action Is Sought to Block Welfare Cut," *SB*, July 23, 1970; Aaronson, "Legal Advocacy and Welfare Reform," 114–115; NLADLA, "History of Civil Legal Aid," http://www.atjsupport.org/About/About_HistoryCivil#oeo.
51. Email from Peter Sitkin to E. Boris, May 19, 2006.
52. Aaronson, "Legal Advocacy and Welfare Reform," 177 n.13. Email from Steve Elias to E. Boris, April 11, 2006; Campbell, "Court Action Is Sought to Block Welfare Cut."

53. "Reagan Restores Aid to Blind, Aged, Disabled," *SFC*, July 25, 1970; Elias e-mail.
54. Office of the Governor, Press Release #378, 7-24-70, Available from the Online Archive of California; http://ark.cdlib.org/ark:/13030/hb7j49n95d, accessed June 15, 2006; Fourkas, "Reagan Rescinds Aid Cut."
55. "Welfare Workers Deny Reagan 'Sabotage' Charge," *Oakland Tribune*, July 27, 1970; "Social Workers Picket Reagan," *Long Beach Independent*, July 31, 1970; "20 Signatures," "Orders Were Clear," *SB*, July 30, 1970.
56. William Endicott, "The 'Welfare Monster' Is Apparently Dead," *LAT*, December 25, 1972; "Priority Request: 2.2.1, 3.2.1, 4.2.1," *Program Budget 1971*, Research File Health and Welfare, Welfare Reform 1971, Human Relations Agency 2/2, Box, GO 186, RRL; P. Krynski, "Services: Recent Views from the Top," *Dialog* V (April 1971), 14–16.
57. Aaronson, "Legal Advocacy and Welfare Reform," 203–208, 220–221; Tom Goff and William Endicott, "Medi-Cal and Welfare Reform Bills Advance," *LAT*, August 10, 1971; Jerome Evans, "Welfare Reform Revisited," *California Journal* (December 1972), 352–355, 375–378, quote at 352, 354; From John L. Burton, Press Release, Monday, February 21, 1972, Department of Health and Welfare, Box GO 186, Research File, Welfare Reform 6/6, RRL.
58. Endicott, "The 'Welfare Monster' Is Apparently Dead"; *Dandridge v. Williams* 397 U.S. 471 (1970); Elizabeth Bussiere, *(Dis)Entitling the Poor: The Warren Court, Welfare Rights, and the American Political Tradition* (University Park: Penn State Press, 1997).
59. Aaronson, "Legal Advocacy and Welfare Reform."
60. Initially these improvements were connected to Nixon's welfare reform, but the House moved them to Social Security legislation. Jennifer L. Erkulwater, *Disability Rights and the American Social Safety Net* (Ithaca: Cornell University Press, 2006), 65–80; Robert M. Ball, "Social Security Amendments of 1972: Summary and Legislative History," accessed at www.ssa.gov/history/1972amend.html, June 12, 2006; Berkowitz, *Disabled Policy*, 85–87; Ronald Blubaugh, "State Welfare Crisis Mounts," *SB*, September 5, 1973; Richard Rodda, "Legislators Fail to Bar Cut in Benefits for Blind, Aged, Disabled," *SB*, September 6, 1973.
61. William Endicott, "500,000 Face Welfare Cuts in Reagan-Legislature Squabble," *LAT*, September 5, 1973; Endicott, "Welfare Bill Passes by Single Vote in Assembly," *LAT*, September 13, 1973.
62. "Reagan Move in Aid to Aged Dispute," *SFC*, September 7, 1973; "State Aid to Disabled 'Assured,'" *LAT*, September 8, 1973; "Welfare: Out on a Legal Limb," *LAT*, September 30, 1973.
63. Aaronson, "Legal Advocacy and Welfare Reform," 266. Hale Zukas, "National Disability Activist: Architectural and Transit Accessibility, Personal Assistance Services," an oral history conducted in 1997 by Sharon Bonney in *Builders and Sustainers of the Independent Living Movement in Berkeley*, Vol. III, 125, Regional Oral History Office, The Bancroft Library, University of California, Berkeley, 2000, Online Archive of California at http://ark.cdlib.org/ark:/13030/kt4c6003rh [Zukas Interview]. The plaintiffs were the California League of Senior Citizens, the Committee for the Rights of the Disabled, the California Legislative Council for Older Americans, Protective Council California Senior Citizens, East Bay Legislative Council of Senior Groups, California Citizens Committee Against the Double Taxation, California Welfare Rights Organization, Northern California Welfare Rights Organization, Disabled and Blind Action Committee of California, along with two receivers of services and some heads of sponsoring organizations. See, in the Supreme Court of the State of California, *California League of Senior Citizens et al. v. Earl W. Brian, Jr. et al.*, Exhibits in Support of Petition for Extraordinary Relief in the Nature of Mandamus, 99/150c, Box 1, folder: 9, Zukas Papers.
64. *California League of Senior Citizens et al. v. Earl W. Brian Jr. et al.*, 35 Cal. App. 3d 443, November 19, 1973, at 456–457; "Reagan Plan to Boost Aid for Aged, Blind, Disabled Ruled Out," *LAT*, November 19, 1973.

65. "The President Signs H.R. 1," *APWA Washington Report* 7 (November 3, 1972), 1, 5, in Box 1, folder: 4, Zukas Papers; "Legislation News," *The Independent*, 1, no. 1, April–May 1973, 2–4; Judy Taylor and Jane Friedland, "The Advocate," *The Independent*, 1, no. 2, July–August 1973, 6–7. See also, "Minutes of the CIL Board Meeting of December 18, 1972," 1, Box 13, folder: "Board Minutes 9/11/72-11/26/73," CIL Records.
66. "Summary Northern California Information Conference on Federalization of Welfare For Aged, Blind and Disabled," 2, Box 1, folder: 11; "Minutes of the Board Meeting of February 26, 1973," 2, Box 13, folder: "Board Minutes 9/11/72-11/26/73," CIL Records; Leonard Potash to Dear Conference Participant, March 8, 1973, and Workshop Resolutions, 1–3, Carton 2, folder: 1, Zukas Papers; Zukas Interview, 125; Rodda, "Legislators Fail to Bar Cut."
67. The state had delayed the shift to homemaker services to April 1974 when the counties dragged their feet. Letter from Peter Coppelman to Phillip Newlin, December 6, 1973, Box 1, folder 11; Department of Social Welfare, James M. Moose, Jr. to All County Welfare Directors, "Notice of Action—Homemaker and Chore Services Implementation," September 4, 1973, Carton 2, folder 34, both in Zukas Papers.
68. Zukas became the leader on attendant services at the state level and an authority on Social Security and mobility issues, especially transportation and architectural barriers. Zukas Interview, "Interview History," 123, 125–126.
69. "Compromise on Aid to Aged and Blind Sought," *LAT*, November 29, 1973; "Legislature Will Convene to Act on Aid for Aged, Blind," *LAT*, November 30, 1973; William Endicott, "Passage of Welfare Bill Expected Today," *LAT*, December 5, 1973; William Endicott, "Reinecke Signs Compromise on Aid to Blind, Aged, Disabled," *LAT*, December 6, 1973; Peter Weisser, "State Raises Aid for Old, Disabled," *SFC*, December 6, 1973; David Crippen, "Executive Director Report," January 26 & 27, 1974, 1, Box 9, folder 4–5, Sampson Papers.
70. Frank Del Olmo, "Confusion Expected over New Welfare Administration Plan," *LAT*, December 19, 1973.
71. "Summary Northern California Information Conference on Federalization," 7; "Hearing in re: H.R. 1," May 30, 1973.
72. "Minutes of the Board Meeting of November 20, 1972," 1; "Eric Dibner: Advocate and Specialist in Architectural Accessibility," an oral history conducted in 1998 by Kathy Cowan in *Builders and Sustainers of the Independent Living Movement in Berkeley*, Volume III, 12, Regional Oral History Office, BANC, 2004.
73. Charles A. Wedesweiler Jr. to Citizens, "Government Services for Preventive-Care of Catastrophically Disabled Persons," October 10, 1973, and Charles A. Wedesweiler Jr. to Handicapped Organizations, "Attendant Grant for Severely Disabled," October 29, 1973, Carton 2, folder: 34, Zukas Papers; Zukas Interview, 131; Kitty Cone, "Political Organizer for Disability Rights, 1970s–1990s, and Strategist for Section 504 Demonstrations, 1977," 87, 79, an oral history conducted in 1996–1998 by David Landes, Regional Oral History Office, BANC, 2000.
74. California Legislature, Joint Committee on Federal Social Security Amendments of 1972, "Joint Committee Hearing to Investigate Operation of Attendant Care and Homemaker Service Program for the Elderly, Blind and Disabled," October 16, 1974, typescript (San Francisco: Schiller & Combs Reporting Service, 1974), 3.
75. "Attendant Care YES: Institutions NO!," *California Service Worker* 3 (January 15, 1975), 4.
76. Emmanuel Perlmutter, "City and Welfare Unions Agree on Cut of 9,000 Jobs," *NYT*, February 10, 1969; Daniel Walkowitz, *Working with Class: Social Workers and the Politics of Middle Class Identity* (Chapel Hill: University of North Carolina Press, 1999), 268–274.
77. SSEU Members for a Militant Caucus, "Strike for a New Contract," December 15, 1969; "Contract Sell Out—Budget Cuts Bluster," April 7, 1969; DC 37 Members for a Militant Caucus, "Vote for Delegate: Lyndon Henry, Al Spanfelner," June 25, 1969; SSEU Militant Caucus, "Let's Fight Back," *Militant Voice*, May 2, 1969; "Black Caucus & Community Action," *Militant Voice*, June 2, 1969, all in SSEU Members for a Militant Caucus, M86–189, MAD 4/Unprocessed SC file, Wisconsin Historical Society (WHS).

78. Peter Kihss, "Welfare Budget Asks $1.4 Billion, Biggest City Item," *NYT*, June 6, 1968.
79. Francis Clines, "Elderly Protest at Parley Here."
80. SSEU Militant Caucus, "Let's Fight Back."
81. Peter Kihss, "Work-Relief Law Assailed in Brief," *NYT*, February 27, 1972; Arnold Lubasch, "2 U.S. Judges Stay Cuts in Medicaid," *NYT*, May 13, 1971; Lubasch, "Court Order Halts Medicaid Cuts Here," *NYT*, October 23, 1971.
82. *New York Home Care Abuse*, 27.
83. Selwyn Raab, "$1.5 Million in Medicaid is Found Misspent by New York Agencies," *NYT*, December 12, 1977; Selwyn Raab, "Investigation of Private Home Care Programs Urged," *NYT*, December 13, 1977; Robert Alan Shick, "The Contracting-out of Local Government Services: New York City Home Health Care," unpublished dissertation, New York University, 1989, 54–64.
84. Derthick, *Uncontrollable Spending for Social Service Grants*, 2, 15–19, 40.
85. Peter Kihss, "State Moves to Reorganize Its Welfare Set-up," *NYT*, June 20, 1972; Kihss, "Cuts Feared Here in Aid to the Poor," *NYT*, September 13, 1972; Paul E. Mott, *Meeting Human Needs: The Social and Political History of Title XX* (Columbus, OH: National Conference on Social Welfare, 1976), 23–49, 87, 68.
86. Citizens' Committee on Aging, Community Council of Great New York, "Systems Analysis of the Home Attendant Program," January–December 1977, McMillan Library, HRA; Shick, "Contracting-out," 69–70; Office of the Comptroller of New York, Bureau of Audit and Control, "Report on the Quality of Care and Operating Practices of the Home Attendant Program: Summary of Significant Observations," October 25, 1978, 11, State Library of New York, Albany; New York State Department of Social Services, Metropolitan Regional Audit Office, "Audit of Home Attendant Services, New York City, Department of Social Services, #76-835-S-029-58," August 1977, McMillan Library, HRA; Memo to File from BB, October 8, 1973; Robert Shannon to Commissioner Dumpson, January 23, 1974, both in Box 61, folder 2, Henry Street Settlement Records (HSS), SWHA, University of Minnesota, Minneapolis, MN.
87. "Systems Analysis of the Home Attendant Program," 11; Bureau of Audit and Control, "Report on the Quality of Care and Operating Practices of the Home Attendant Program," 7; Peter Kihss, "Home Care Plan for Oldsters Scored," *NYT*, July 16, 1976; Memo to David A. Grossman, from Karen M. Eisenstadt, Subject: "A Program for Improving City Services to the Aging," October 6, 1972, 19–20, Box 34, folder 606, Reel 17, Subject Files, Mayor John Lindsay Papers (JLP), Municipal Archives, New York, NY (MA).
88. *New York Home Care Abuse*, 34.
89. "Report on the Quality of Care"; "Aide Stays by Elderly Women's Side While Pay Remains in Computer," *NYT*, May 6, 1977; Kihss, "Home Care Plan for Oldsters Scored;" "Audit of Home Attendant Services," 8, 14–18; Joan Shepard, "Payroll Foul up Angers Home Health Attendants," *New York Daily News*, December 16, 1977; Peter Kihss, "Program to Aid Elderly Sick Poor Marked by Fraud, State Audit Says," *NYT*, December 15, 1977; Richard Severo, "Troubled Program for the Disabled," *NY T*, December 27, 1977.
90. *New York Home Care Abuse*, 39.
91. *New York Home Care Abuse*, 36–39; On community development agencies' dubious use of public welfare funds, see Raab, "Investigation of Private Home-Care Programs Urged," and "$1.5 Million in Medicaid Is Found Misspent by New York Agencies"; *New York Home Care Abuse*, Part 1C: Audit Findings, Item 1, 74–79, and Item 6, 122–220.
92. *New York Home Care Abuse*, 28.
93. Saul Goldzweig to The Editors, May 15, 1963, Box 58, folder 11; Citizens' Committee on Aging, *Campaign Community Awareness*, May 1965, 4, Box 93, folder 4, both HHS.
94. Bertram Beck to Commissioner Jack Goldberg, August 18, 1969; Goldberg to Beck, September 29, 1969; Memorandum from Beck, "Housekeeper Program," April 1970, folder 9; "Position Paper on Relationship and Contracts Between HRA and HRA-Funded Agencies," December 3, 1973, 2, folder 2, both in Box 61, HSS.

95. Miguel Rios, Brochure for the participants of the Housekeepers Program, 4, folder 9; Beck to Warach, July 18, 1973, with attachment, folder 2; both in Box 61, HSS.
96. Association of Housekeepers to Atkins Preston, September 11, 1973, Box 61, folder 2, HSS.
97. Jonathan Weiner to Harvey Adelsberg, January 2, 1973; Marvin Schick to Most Rev. Edward D. Headle; Schick to Father Joseph Sullivan; Schick to John J. Keppler, January 31, 1973, all Box 5, folder 56, Microfilm Roll 3, Subject File 1966-73, JLP, MA; W. Craig Bennett to Mr. Rios, January 8, 1973, Box 61, folder 7, HSS; Shannon to Dumpson, Memo to File from BB, October 8, 1973; M to Kin, February 16, 1974; Bertram Beck to Estelle Bryant February 27, 1974, folder 2; "Negotiating Committee Report," March 19, 1974; Gary Calnek to Housekeeper Vendor Negotiating Committee, Subject: Revised Letter of Agreement, February 27, 1974; HRA, "General Provisions Governing Agreements for the Purchase of Housekeeping Services," July, 1973, 6, folder 3; Allen Flesher Methods and Systems, "Henry Street Settlement House Household Aide Services Operation," October 30, 1975, folder 9; all in Box 61, HSS.
98. Preston to Leona Gold, September 12, 1973; Bertram Beck to Leona Gold at al., Subject; Housekeeper Vendor Contract-Preparation for Out Meeting, January 14, 1974, l, folder 2; Memorandum for Files, March 27, 1974, folder 3; Beck to Bernard Warrick, Jewish Federation for Services for the Aged, June 26, 1973; Beck to Warach, July 18, 1973, with attachment; Memorandum to Robert Goldfeld from Beck, Subject: Homemakers, August 22, 1973, folder 2; all Box 61, HSS.
99. Jacqueline Vaughn Switzer, *Disabled Rights: American Disability Policy and the Fight for Equality* (Washington, DC: Georgetown University Press, 2003), 80; Disabled in Action, http://www.disabledinaction.org/learnmor.html, accessed July 31, 2007.
100. Bobbi Linn, "Activist with Disabled in Action," *New York Activists and Leaders in the Disability Rights and Independent Living Movement*, Vol. III, Interview with Denise Sherer Jacobson, 2001,186, Available from the Online Archive of California; http://ark.cdlib.org/ark:/13030/hb5n39n7m6, accessed July 2, 2011.
101. Patricio Figueroa, "Early Activist with Disabled in Action," *New York Activists and Leaders in the Disability Rights and Independent Living Movement*, Vol. II, interview by Sharon Bonney and Fred Pekla, 2000, 2001, 2002, 83–84, Available from the Online Archive of California; http://ark.cdlib.org/ark:/13030/hb2q2n990w, accessed July 2, 2011.
102. Denise McQuade, "Early Activist in Disabled in Action," *New York Activists and Leaders in the Disability Rights and Independent Living Movement*, Vol. I, interview by Denise Sherer Jacobson, 2001, 143–3, Available from the Online Archive of California; http://ark.cdlib.org/ark:/13030/hb5c60042m, accessed July 2, 2011.
103. Freeman, *Working-Class New York*, 262–263.
104. Kate Klein to Hon. Abraham D. Beame, RE: Payment of Home Attendants," n.d., ABR, Exec. Assistant Eugene Price Subject Files, Box 8, folder 215, 1977, MA.
105. HRA Press Release, December 30, 1976, ABR, Executive Assistant Eugene Price Subject Files, Box 8, folder: 215; Shepard, "Payroll Foul Up Angers Home Health Attendants;" Severo, "Troubled Program for the Disabled."
106. Memorandum to Marvin Schick and Leon Pancetta, from Alice M. Brophy, Re: Agenda for Meeting with Mayor, March 18, 1971, 2," Box 5, folder 56, Microfilm Roll 3, JLP, Subject Files 1966–73, MA.
107. John L. Hess, "Care of Aged Poor a Growing Scandal," *NYT*, October 7, 1974; "Excerpts from Cuomo's Report to Carey about Nursing Homes," *NYT*, January 17, 1975; "Abram Names 4 to Panel on Nursing Home Inquiry."
108. *New York State Consolidated Public Health Law*, Home Care Services, Chap. 895, Article 36, Approved August 11, 1977, vertical file: homemaker service, 1841–1843, HRA.
109. Memorandum Accompanying Comments on Bills Before the Governor for Executive Action, New York State Department of Social Services, August 10, 1977, Introduced by Senator Lombardi, et al., Bill Jacket, 1977, State Library of New York, Albany, NY.

110. Raab, "Investigation of Private Home-Care Programs Urged"; Janice Prindle, "Poverty Workers Fight Poverty—Their Own," *Village Voice*, November 7, 1977.
111. Annotated Agenda, Management Review Meeting, HRA, September 16, 1977, Mayor's Papers, Deputy Mayor John Zuccotti Subject Files 11, 1975–77, Box 5, 17586, folder 92: "HRA Project and Financial Summary 1977," MA; Annotated Agenda, Management Review Meeting, HRA, October 14, 1977, Box 5, 17586, folder 89: "HRA Management Review, 1977," MA.
112. Michael Milton, Union Settlement, to Mayor Beame, September 8, 1976, and John Zuccotti to Mr. Milton, October 15, 1976, Office of Mayor, Deputy Mayor John Zuccotti Subject Files II, 1975–77, Box 5, folder 88: "HRA Letters 1976–77"; Management Review Meeting, HRA, November 28, 1977, Box 5, folder 89, both in MA.
113. Annotated Agenda, Management Review Meeting, October 14, 1977; Minutes, Management Review Meeting, HRA, October 14, 1977, Box 5, folder 89, MA.
114. *New York Home Care Abuse*, 5, 10–11, 20, 24.
115. *New York Home Care Abuse*, 32.
116. Louis C. Ward, "MCC Housekeepers Picket for Better Pay, Facilities," *Amsterdam News* (*AN*), October 29, 1977.
117. The Home Attendant Advisory Committee of the Citizens' Committee on Aging, "Systems Analysis of the Home Attendant Program," January–December 1977, Community Council of Greater New York, December 1977, 11, HRA.
118. Transcript, Jeffrey Kleinman and Cara DeVito, *What Could You Do with a Nickel?*, First Run/Icarus Films, 1982, transcribed by authors.
119. *What Could You Do with a Nickel?*; *New York Home Care Abuse*, 32, 34, 28–29, 30.
120. *What Could You Do with a Nickel?*; *New York Home Care Abuse*, 32, 34, 28–29, 30.
121. Carol Polsky, "Housekeepers Move to Unionize," *In These Times*, November 30, 1977; "Housekeepers Strike for Living Wages," *The Longest Revolution* (December 1977/January 1978).
122. *What Could You Do with a Nickel?*
123. "Feds Probe Morrisania Poverty Agency Head," *AN*, September 24, 1977; "Question Actions of HRA Aide in Morrisania Center Inquiry," *AN*, November 19, 1977.
124. Prindle, "Poverty Workers Fight Poverty."
125. Charles M. Payne, *I've Got the Light of Freedom: The Organizing Tradition and the Mississippi Freedom Struggle* (Berkeley: University of California Press, 1997); Christina Greene, *Our Separate Ways: Women and the Black Freedom Movement in Durham, North Carolina* (Chapel Hill: University of North Carolina Press, 2005), 189–192.
126. Polsky, "Housekeepers Move to Unionize"; "Housekeepers Strike for Living Wages"; Donna Lamb, "Working Women: Housekeepers Organize," *Guardian*, November 9, 1977.
127. Ward, "MCC Housekeepers Picket."
128. "Housekeepers Strike for Living Wages"; Prindle, "Poverty Workers Fight Poverty."
129. Prindle, "Poverty Workers Fight Poverty."
130. *New York Home Care Abuse*, 7.
131. Polsky, "Housekeepers Move to Unionize."
132. Raab, "Investigation of Private Home-Care Programs Urged"; Prindle, "Poverty Workers Fight Poverty."
133. *What Could You Do with a Nickel?*
134. Shepard, "Payroll Foul up Angers Home Health Attendants."
135. Brahna Trager to Ken Dameron, Memo, June 28, 1972, 1, Box 25, SCA Correspondence, 72, Brahna Trager Papers, Library of Congress, Washington DC (LC).
136. Phone Interview with H. D. Hall by E. Boris, December 2, 2007; "Presentation to the Social Services Commission, February 24, 1977," Draft, 6, Box 17, "SFHHS Correspondence 1977," Trager Papers.
137. "Twenty Questions," 6, attached to H. D. Hall to Edwin Sarsfield, May 23, 1977, Box 17, "SFHHS Correspondence 1977," Trager Papers.

138. S.F. Homemaker Service, "Manual for Homemakers," February 1965, Box 17, "SFHHS Miscellany, 1959–81," Trager Papers.
139. "Presentation to the Social Services Commission," 6.
140. Hall Interview.
141. "Report on the Quality of Care," VI–VII.

Chapter 5

1. "Union Seeks Collective Bargaining Rights for 20,000 Home Attendants," *SEIU 32B-32J*, 47 (August–September 1979), 1, 5, SEIU Records, Walter P. Reuther Library, Wayne State University (WPR).
2. For contrasting perspectives, Jefferson Cowie, *Stayin' Alive: The 1970s and the Last Days of the Working Class* (New York: New Press, 2010); Dorothy Sue Cobble, "A Tiger by the Toenail: The 1970s Origins of the New Working-Class Majority," *Labor: Studies in Working-Class History of the Americas* 2:3 (Fall 2005), 103–114.
3. Susan Strasser, *Never Done: A History of American Housework* (New York: Pantheon, 1982), 282–312; Judith Rollins, *Between Women: Domestics and Their Employers* (Philadelphia: Temple University Press, 1985); Mary Romero, *Maid in the U.S.A.* (New York: Routledge, 1992).
4. Alana Erickson Coble, *Cleaning Up: The Transformation of Domestic Service in Twentieth Century New York City* (New York: Routledge, 2006); "McMaid Housekeepers Win Big," *The Homemakers' Voice*, United Labor Unions Local 880, Chicago, c. 1985. Box 8, Folder 12, SEIU 880 Records, Wisconsin Historical Society (WHS), Madison, WI.
5. Mrs. Edith B. Sloan, "Keynote Address," *NCHE NEWS*, 2, no. 7, July 1971, S5, B1, "Newsletters"; NCHE, "Facts about Private Household Employment," S1, B6, "Fact Sheet, 1976"; NCHE, *A Profile of Household Workers in the U.S.A.*, c. 1965, S5, B1, "Brochures," all in NCHE Records, National Archives for Black Women's History, Bethune House, Washington, DC. Nixon abandoned the guaranteed income to defeat in 1972, see Premilla Nadasen, *Welfare Warriors: The Welfare Rights Movement in the United States* (New York: Routledge, 2005), 157–186.
6. Grace Chang, *Disposable Domestics: Immigrant Women Workers in the Global Economy* (Boston: South End Press, 2000); Pierrette Hondagneu-Sotelo, *Doméstica: Immigrant Workers Cleaning and Caring in the Shadows of Affluence* (Berkeley: University of California Press, 2001).
7. *Report of the Committee on Home and Community to the President's Commission on the Status of Women, October 1963* (Washington, DC: GPO, 1964), 17–19; Phyllis Palmer, *Domesticity and Dirt: Housewives and Domestic Servants in the United States, 1920–1945* (Philadelphia: Temple University Press, 1989), 116–118, 122–225; NCHE, *A Profile of Household Workers in the U.S.A.*
8. Speech of Elizabeth Koontz, S1, B12, "NYCCHR 1971"; Esther Peterson to Muriel Lockhart, October 6, 1966, S1, B15, "State Activities, California 1967 May-June," NCHE Records. See also, Dorothy Sue Cobble, *The Other Women's Movement: Workplace Justice and Social Rights in Modern America* (Princeton: Princeton University Press, 2004), 198–200; Phyllis Palmer, "Housework and Domestic Labor: Racial and Technological Change," in *My Troubles Are Going to Have Trouble with Me: Everyday Trials and Triumphs of Women Workers*, Karen Brodkin Sacks and Dorothy Remy, eds. (New Brunswick: Rutgers University Press, 1984), 86–87.
9. NCHE, *A Code of Standards*, S1, B5, folder: "Brochures," NCHE Records.
10. NCHE, *A Handbook for Leaders*, 6–9, folder: "Handbook"; NCHE, *Career Ladder for Household Employment*, folder: "Brochures," S5, B1, NCHE Records.
11. NCHE, *Interim Report of the Experimental and Demonstration Projects*, S5, B1, folder: "Interim Report 2"; Duncan MacDonald, "Arriving: The Household Professional," *House Beautiful* (March 1969), reprinted, S1, B4, "Correspondence 1971 December-1972 February," NCHE Records.

12. Palmer, "Housework and Domestic Labor," 86–87.
13. Proceedings, Conference on the "Status of the Occupation of Household Worker," 9a, 18, 37, S1, B8, "Heart 1968–1969, NCHE Records.
14. NCHE, *A Handbook for Leaders*, 6–9; *NCHE News* III:8 (August 1972), 1, S5, B1, "Newsletters 1969–1979"; Janice A. Booker to David E. Landholt, May 21, 1973, S1, B4, "Correspondence 1973 May–July;" Alice M. Freeman to Edith B. Sloan, September 12, 1974, S1, B5, "Correspondence 1974, August–September," all in NCHE Records. See also, "Report No. 1," Household Technicians of Western Pa., Inc., May 18, 1970–September 18, 1970, 1, 5, "HTWP 1970"; Minutes, Board of Directors Meeting, Household Technicians of America, April 12, 1972, 4, "HTA 1971–1974," both in S1, B8; Edith Lynton, *Toward Better Jobs and Better Household Work: A Report and Recommendations*, January 19, 1972, 14, 16–17, 19, S1, B12, "NYCCHR 1972," all in NCHE Records.
15. Anita Bellamy Shelton to Florence Moore, October 13, 1977; Press Release, "Practical Workers' Congress," October 20, 1977, S3, B3, "5th NCHW Conference 1977," NCHE Records.
16. Capitol Hill Homemaker and Health Aid Services, Inc., *Interim Report 1977*; "Memo from Marlo"; "Alumna Loretta Hurley Sets Up Annual $2500 Scholarship," *Howard University Alumni News*, October 1977, 1, S2, B1, "CHHAS," all in NCHE Records.
17. NCHE, *Final Report of the Experimental and Demonstration Projects*, March 15, 1968–December 31, 1970, 52–55 S5, B1, folder "Final Report"; Homemaker Service Demonstration Training Project, "Quarterly Report III, January 1, 1970 through March 31, 1970," 40–44, S5, B1, folder: "Homemaker Service Demonstration Quarterly Report, January–March 1970," NCHE Records; "Federal Minimum Wage Rates, 1955–2006," http://www.infoplease.com/ipa/A0774473.html, accessed August 16, 2006; "New Careers," MAMC075, S5, B1, folder: "November 1969," NCHE Records.
18. NCHE, *Final Report of the Experimental and Demonstration Projects*, 47, 49–50.
19. *Interim Report of the Experimental and Demonstration Projects*, 8–9; "Quarterly Report III," 72.
20. Edith Barksdale-Sloan, "Planning Meeting, Coalition of Feminist Funding," NOW LDEF, June 28 and 29, 1974, 4, B5, "Correspondence July 1974"; Sloan to Now President Wilma Scott Heide, March 1, 1973, B4, "Correspondence 1973 January–April"; Minutes, Board of Directors Meeting, Household Technicians of America, April 12, 1972, 1, B8, "HTA 1971–1974"; Resume Edith Barksdale-Sloan, B15, "1974 Vita," all S1, NCHE Records.
21. Edith Barksdale-Sloan to Gerald Ford, September 6, 1974, S1, B5, "Correspondence 1974 August–September," NCHE Records.
22. Sloan, "Planning Meeting Coalition of Feminist Funding"; "Domestics at Session Ask Gains," *NYT*, October 10, 1972.
23. Shelton to Moore, October 13, 1977; Press Release, "Practical Workers' Congress."
24. Ernest Holsendolph, "Social Action Hit by Financial Foes," *NYT*, November 8, 1974; Press Release, "Practical Workers' Congress; Strategies for Greater Opportunity and Respect," October 20, 1977," 2, S1, B3, "5th NCHW Conference 1977"; "Strategies," *NCHE News*, XI (July 1979), 1, S5, B1, "Newsletters, 1969–1979," NCHE Records.
25. Mary Poole, *The Segregated Origins of Social Security: African Americans and the Welfare State* (Chapel Hill: University of North Carolina Press, 2006), 35–38, 90–96; Palmer, *Domesticity and Dirt*, 118–135; Vanessa May, *Unprotected Labor: Household Workers, Politics, and Middle-Class Reform, in New York City, 1870–1940* (Chapel Hill: University of North Carolina Press, 2011).
26. See Sec. 2, (b), "The Full Employment Bill as Originally Introduced," reprinted as Appendix A, in Stephen Kemp Bailey, *Congress Makes a Law: The Story Behind the Employment Act of 1946* (New York: Columbia University Press, 1950), 243.
27. Statement of Arthur J. Altmeyer, in U.S. Congress, House of Representatives, Committee on Ways and Means, *Hearings: Social Security Act Amendments of 1949*, 81st Cong., 1st sess. Part 2 (Washington, DC: GPO, 1949), 1084.

28. United States Department of Labor, Women's Bureau, *Old Age Insurance for Household Workers*, Bulletin of the Women's Bureau, No.220 (Washington, DC: GPO, 1947), 10–13; Statement of Lewis B. Schwellenbach, *Amendments to Social Security Act* (1946), Part 5 (Washington, DC: GPO, 1946), 542–545.
29. Women's Bureau, *Old Age Insurance for Household Workers*, 1–2.
30. Statement of Frieda Miller in *Social Security Act Amendments of 1949*, Part 2, 1587.
31. "Extension of Old-Age and Survivors Insurance to Additional Groups of Current Workers," Report of the Consultant Group, in U.S. Congress, House of Representatives, Committee on Ways and Means, *Hearings: Social Security Amendments of 1954, H.R. 7199*, 83rd Cong., 2nd sess. (Washington, DC: GPO, 1954), 865.
32. "Employment: Farewell to Dinah," *Newsweek*, August 2, 1971, clipping, S1, B3, "Conference Publicity 1971," NCHE Records. California placed domestics under its minimum wage law in March 1974; see Harry Bernstein, "Minimum Wage Law Will Cover Men, Domestics," *LAT*, November 30, 1973.
33. Letter from Joy R. Simonson, in U.S. Congress, House of Representatives, Committee on Education and Labor, *Hearings: Fair Labor Standards Amendments of 1973, H.R. 4757 and H.R. 2831*. 93rd Cong., 1st sess., March 13, 14, 15; April 10, 1973 (Washington, DC: GPO, 1973), 348.
34. For example, "Statement on Behalf of the American Association of University Women," in U.S. Congress, Senate, Committee on Labor and Public Welfare, Subcommittee on Labor, *Hearings: Fair Labor Standards Amendments of 1971, S. 1861 and S. 2259*. 92nd Cong., 1st sess., June 23 and 24, July 15 and 16, 1971, Part 2 (Washington, DC: GPO, 1972), 745. Phyllis Palmer, "Outside the Law: Agricultural and Domestic Workers under the Fair Labor Standards Act," *Journal of Policy History* 7 (1995), 416–440.
35. Statement of Edith Sloan, *Fair Labor Standards Amendments of 1973*, 208.
36. U.S. House, *Fair Labor Standards Amendments of 1973*, 86–87, 279; Palmer, "Outside the Law," 417–418.
37. "Highlights of the Fair Labor Standards Act Amendments of 1974," S1, B11, "Minimum Wage 1974 July–September," NCHE Records.
38. Mr. Williams, "Remarks on Introducing S. 682," *Congressional Record*, February 19, 1971, vol. 117, pts. 3–4 (1971), 3287–3288.
39. Peter Shapiro, ed., *A History of National Service in America* (Center for Political Leadership and Participation, 1994), at http://www.academy.umd.edu/publications/NationalService/senior_service.html, accessed July 29, 2007.
40. For example, the Montgomery County Homemaker Home Health Aide Service, an agency on the Main Line outside of Philadelphia, "History 1981," MC77, Series 1, Folder 1, Barbara Bates Center for the Study of the History of Nursing, University of Pennsylvania School of Nursing, Philadelphia, PA (NHA).
41. Margaret Ann Baker, "The Paid Caring Relationship: Workers' Views and Public Policy Regarding Paraprofessional Home Care for the Elderly," unpublished Ph.D. dissertation, University of California, Berkeley, 1987, 228–229.
42. U.S. Congress, Senate, Committee on Labor and Public Welfare, *Fair Labor Standards Amendments of 1971*, Part 1, May 26, June 3, 8, 9, 10, 17, and 22, 1971, 30; U.S. Congress, Senate, Committee on Labor and Public Welfare, *Legislative History of the Fair Labor Standards Amendments of 1974 (Public Law 93-259)*, 94th Cong., 2nd sess. (Washington, DC: GPO, 1976), vol. I, 963.
43. *Fair Labor Standards Amendments of 1971*, Part 1, 290–291.
44. Testimony of Susan K. Kinoy, Before the Senate Special Committee on the Aging, May 16, 1977, reprinted as Appendix A to "Statement of the National Council for Homemaker-Home Health Aide Services," in U.S. Congress, House of Representatives, Committee on Ways and Means, *Hearings: Independent Contractors, H.R. 3245*, 96th Cong., 1st sess., June 30, July 16 and 17, 1979 (Washington, DC: GPO, 1979), 656.
45. See, for example, Statement of Mr. Javits, in *Legislative History of the Fair Labor Standards Amendments of 1974*, Vol. II, 1792.

46. U.S. House, *Fair Labor Standards Amendments of 1973*, 138–140.
47. Testimony of Ira H. Nunn in *Fair Labor Standards Amendments of 1971*, Part I, 578.
48. Statement of L. H. Fountain, U.S. Congress, House of Representatives, Committee on Education and Labor, General Subcommittee on Labor, *Hearing To Amend the Fair Labor Standards Act of 1974*, 93rd Cong., 2nd sess. (Washington, DC: GPO, 1975), 4–9.
49. Edith Barksdale-Sloan to Disney D. Dell, June 19, 1974, S1, B11, "Min Wage 1974 March–June," NCHE Records.
50. *Legislative History of the Fair Labor Standards Amendments of 1974*, Vol. I, 964.
51. 39 Fed. Reg. 35, 382 (October 1, 1974) compared to 40 Fed. Reg. 7, 404 (February 20, 1975).
52. Wage and Hour Division, DOL, "Opinion Letter: FLSA," WH-174, August, 20, 1972, West Law, 1972 WL 34917.
53. "Statement of Noel Grant et al.," *Independent Contractors*, 375–381.
54. Eileen Boris and Jennifer Klein, "Organizing Home Care: Low-Waged Workers in the Welfare State," *Politics and Society* 34 (March 2006), 81–107.
55. Mary McClendon to Mr. J. A. Tedesce, February 28, 1972, B4, "Correspondence 1972"; Household Workers Organization, Inc., "Pay! Protection, Professionalism: The 3 P's of Household Work," B8, "HWO 1971–1972," both in S01, NCHE Records.
56. *Mary McClendon et al. v. City of Detroit*, No. 77 704 376 CL, State of Michigan, in the Circuit Court for the County of Wayne, "Deposition," April 18, 1980, 23, 8, 33, in McClendon Collection, Box 2, folder 30, WPR.
57. Union W.A.G.E., "For Immediate Release," 1–2, S1, B4, "1973 May–July," NCHE Records; To Sisters from Noreen Mazelis, August 19, 1973, Box 18, "Brief—Homemakers, 1971, 1972, 1973," Union Wage Records, Labor Archives and Research Center, San Francisco State University (UW Records).
58. Union W.A.G.E., "For Immediate Release"; Coordinator to Sister, August 23, 1973; Ruth Fagan Ginger, "Guild Files Amicus," both in Box 18, "Brief—Homemakers, 1971, 1972, 1973," UW Records; *Cal. Dept. of Industrial Relations v. Homemakers*, 423 U.S. 1063 (1976).
59. Sara M. Evans, *Tidal Wave: How Women Changed America at Century's End* (New York: Free Press, 2003); Barbara Ehrenreich, "Maid to Order," *Harper's Magazine* 300 (April 2000), 59–70.
60. Reprint of Cynthia Gorney, "The Discarding of Mrs. Hill," *Ladies Home Journal* XCIII (February 1976); Letter to Robert E. Buckly Jr. from Tish Sommers, July 24, 1975; Jobs for Older Women Action Project, "The Displaced Homemaker and Home Health Services for the Elderly and Handicapped (Statement to Conference February 20, 1975); all in Series IV, folder 6–41, Sommers Papers, San Diego State Archives, San Diego, CA.
61. "Plank 19: Older Women," from National Commission on the Observance of International Women's Year, *The Spirit of Houston: The First National Women's Conference* (Washington, DC: GPO, 1978), 79–80; Governor's Commission on the Status of Women, "Report of the Midlife and Older Women Committee," in *Report and Recommendations to the Governor and General Assembly, February 1985* (Springfield: Illinois Commission on the Status of Women, 1985), 7, 85–93.
62. Palmer, "Outside the Law," 416–440.
63. Eileen Boris and Premilla Nadasen, "Domestic Workers Organize!," *Working USA* 11 (December 2008), 413–437.
64. "Testimony from Eleanor Holmes Norton, Chairperson, New York City Commission on Human Rights, at a Public Hearing on Legislation Affecting Household Workers," Assembly Standing Committee on Labor, April 18, 1975, Box 1, folder: "Household Workers Collective Bargaining, 1975," Seymour Posner Papers, Wagner Archives, New York, NY.
65. Kiki Levathes, "Downstairs, They're Organizing," *New York Daily News*, October 12, 1977.
66. Sloan to George Meany, January 23, 1976; Albert Zack to Sloan, February 2, 1976, both B1, "AFL-CIO"; Mary McClendon to J. A. Tedesco; Sloan to Lane Kirkland, July 8, 1971, B4, "Correspondence 1971 July," S1, NCHE Records; "Domestics Uniting for More Pay—And Respect," *NYT*, July 18, 1971.

67. Leslie Maitland, "'They Still Call Us Girl,'" *NYT*, February 15, 1976; Judy Klemesrud, "March and Rally Celebrate First International Women's Day," *NYT*, March 9, 1975.
68. Vanessa Tait, *Poor Workers' Unions: Rebuilding Labor from Below* (Boston: South End Press, 2005), 41–42; Dorothy Sue Cobble, "'A Spontaneous Loss of Enthusiasm': Workplace Feminism and the Transformation of Women's Service Jobs in the 1970s," *International Labor and Working Class History* 56 (Fall 1999), 33–39; "Domestics at Session Ask Gains"; Boris and Nadasen, "Domestic Workers Organize!".
69. "Statement of Noel Grant et al.," 382–384; Joann Stevens, "Domestics Workers Seek Increased Benefits," *Washington Post (WP)*, July 19, 1979; Donna Yee, "Home Companions Work to Lighten Life's Daily Burdens for Elderly Residents," *WP*, August 9, 1979.
70. "Setting a Precedent," *Health Care Worker Update* VIII (Winter/Spring 1994), 4.
71. Lynn Kidder, "'Here to Win, Here to Stay,'" *The Independent* 2 (Spring 1975), 7–8; "Domestic Workers Organize! . . . A Living—Not A Dying Wage!," A Pamphlet on the California Homemakers Association, c. 1976, in EPN Files, California Homemakers Association, San Francisco State University—Labor Archives (SFSU-LA); phone interview with Sue Kern by Eileen Boris, June 11, 2006; David Shapiro, *Generations of Struggle* (Georgetown, CA: Georgetown Press, 2004).
72. Father Dan Madigan, David Fariello, and Jessica Roth, "The California Homemakers Association: Consciousness Raising at the Grass-Roots Level: From Collective Consciousness to Collective Action," 3, 6–9, Spring 1975, California State Library, Sacramento, CA.
73. John L. Erlich, "California Homemakers: The Domestic Workers Rebel," *The Nation* 219 (September 28, 1974), 273–275; "Despite Loss of Legs, She Fought for Better Care of Elderly, Disabled," *SB*, July 1, 1998; "Queen Esther Johnson, 85, Fought for Workers' Rights," *SB*, February 18, 2005.
74. "Here to Win, Here to Stay"; Bill Lawrence, "Aid-Paid Domestic Workers Are Target," *SB*, September 7, 1973; "Supervisors Agree to Consider Pay Raises for Welfare Helpers," *SB*, December 3, 1973; "Welfare Homemakers Win Right to Bargain," *SB*, March 11, 1974; "Workers Angry with County Contract Office," *CSW*, 3 (January 15, 1975), 1–2; Kern interview; "Picket Line at Upjohn: Workers and Recipients United!" *CSW, Santa Cruz Edition* 1 (October 30, 1975), 1–2; "Domestic Workers Fight for Recognition," *CSW*, Bay Area Edition 14 (November 1989), 2.
75. Press Release, "Statement of Eleanor Holmes Norton, Chairman, City Commission on Human Rights, at News Conference, Wednesday, September 23, 1970," S1, B12, "NYC-CHR 1971," NCHE Records; Susan Edmiston, "Why We Are at It, What about Maid's Lib?" *New York*, June 28, 1971, 8; Lynton, *Toward Better Jobs and Better Household Work*, 2; Appendix A. Among unions attending were Brotherhood of Sleeping Car Porters, SEIU Local 144, District 37 AFSCME, Local 169 ACWA, Central Labor Council AFL-CIO. NWRO and NCHE were also there.
76. New York State Assembly 1975 Committee Bill Memorandum, Assembly Bill A-4297, by S. Posner et al., Box 1, folder: "Household Workers Collective Bargaining, 1975," Posner Papers.
77. Ibid.
78. Posner to Colleague, April 26, 1974, Box 1, folder: "Household Workers Collective Bargaining, 1974," Posner Papers.
79. Posner to Edward Bookstein, April 3, 1974; Posner to Colleague, April 26, 1974, both in Box 1, folder: "Household Workers Collective Bargaining, 1974," Posner Papers.
80. On SEIU background, Ruth Milkman, *L.A. Story: Immigrant Workers and the Future of the U.S. Labor Movement* (New York: Russell Sage Foundation, 2006).
81. Arnold Mauer, "Statement Before the Assembly Standing Committee on Labor at a Public Hearing on Legislation Affecting Household Workers," April 18, 1975; New York State Assembly 1975 Committee Bill Memorandum, Bill A-4297, 2–3, both in Box 1, folder: "Household Workers Collective Bargaining 1975," Posner Papers.
82. Telephone Interview with Barbara Shulman, Silver Spring, MD, by J. Klein, April 8, 2005.

83. *32B-32J SEIU Newsletter* (November 1977), 3, SEIU Publications, Local 32B-32J, 1977–81, vol. 45, no. 9, WPR; *32B-32J Newsletter*, December 1977, 3.
84. Shulman interview; Ward in "Union Steps Up Drive to Organize Household Workers," *32B-32J Newsletter* 46 (May 1978), 1.
85. "Union Steps Up Drive to Organize," 1; "Household Workers Choose Local 32B-32J," *32B-32J Newsletter* 46 (August–September 1978), 3.
86. Pamphlets and postcards, Barbara Shulman Papers, in authors' possession; "N.Y. Household Workers Move 'Up from Slavery,' *Service Employee* (September 1978), 2; "In Search of Security and Dignity," *Service Employee* (September 1979), 3, Wagner Archives; "Union Seeks Collective Bargaining Rights for 20,000 Home Attendants," 1; "Home Attendants Vow Tougher Effort In Drive for Union," *Local 144 News* 27 (December 1979), 4, SEIU Collection, WPR.
87. *Household Workers News*, 2 (February 1980), 1, Shulman Papers, in authors' possession.
88. *32B-32J Newsletter* (August–September 1978), 1; *Service Employee* (September 1978), 2; Boris and Nadasen, "Domestic Workers Organize!"
89. "Home Attendants Vow Tougher Effort in Drive for Union."
90. Lorraine Haber, "NYC 'Domestics' Vote Union," *Guardian*, August 30, 1978.
91. Order of Dismissal, OCB, Decision No. 61–78, Docket No. RU-669–78, New York, NY, November 30, 1978; Kevin McCullogh to John McNamara, November 16, NYC Office of Collective Bargaining, Board Of Certification, NYC, Docket: RU-669–78, Home Attendants; Peggy Spier, NYC Health and Hospitals Corporation to Alan Friess, Office of Municipal Labor Relations, November 9, 1978, ibid.
92. RU-669–78, Folder: "RU-669–78 and 1707 Home Attendants"; and RU-695–78, Folder: "RU-695–78 Hearings and Exhibits, Home Attendants," both at New York City Office of Collective Bargaining, Board of Certification.
93. L. 144, et al v. City, 20–80 (Cert), Office of Collective Bargaining, Board of Certification; L. 32B-32J, et al v. City, 61–78 (Cert.), Office of Collective Bargaining, Board of Certification.
94. "Domestic Workers Become Home Attendants," *Home Care Workers News* 3 (September 1981), 1, SEIU Publications, WPR.
95. "Contract Talks Begin for Home Attendants," ibid; *32B-32J Newsletter* (August–September 1981), 1; *32B-32J Newsletter* (August–September 1982), 1; Sample Ballot, Shulman Papers.
96. "Vote For Your Union," Local 32B-32J and Local 144, SEIU, AFL-CIO, CLC, Home Care Division, Pamphlet; "What Is Local 32B-32J & Local 144," Pamphlet; "Don't Settle for Less Than the Best," Pamphlet, 1982, Shulman Papers.
97. "Fight the Duty Free Hour," *Home Care Workers News* 3 (September 1981), 2; "City Takes Food Out of Home Attendants Mouths," *Household Workers News* 2 (February, 1980), 1; "Home Care Workers: Why We Must Demonstrate," Pamphlet, 1982, Shulman Papers.
98. *32B-32J-144 News*, from March 1983–September 1991; Gus Bevona to John J. Sweeney, January 6, 1987, and June 26, 1987, SEIU President's Office, Box 217, folder: "Local 32B-32J-144, 1987, 1986," WPR; Steven Greenhouse, "Chief of Building Workers' Union Leaves with $1.5 Million," *NYT*, February 3, 1999.
99. Indeed, Chavez was at the 1980 convention celebrating the union's first contract and the UFWA adopted a resolution of support in 1981. See, "Domestic Workers Sign Labor Union Contract," *The Voice News and Viewpoint*, December 3, 1980; letter from Cesar E. Chavez to Ken Seaton-Msemaji with attached resolution, September 18, 1981; UDWA, "Background Information on United Domestic Workers of America," June 2002, in authors' possession (UDWA Packet); Ken Seaton-Msemaji, "A Living Legacy and Testament to Cesar Chavez's Life, Leadership," *El Sol de San Diego* VII (May 13, 1993), 2–3; "Domestic Workers Union Born in San Diego," *The Economic Democrat: A Publication of the Campaign for Economic Democracy* 1 (December 1980); UDWA, "Background Information on United Domestic Workers of America," June 2002, in authors' possession (UDWA Packet); interview with Janet Heinritz-Canterbury by E. Boris, April 13, 2005.

100. Sharon D. Smith, "She Fights for Domestic Workers: South County Spotlight," *San Diego Union*, February 8, 1986.
101. "Domestic Workers Union Born in San Diego."
102. Ken Seaton-Msemaji, "'He Believed Every Human Being Was Valuable,'" *Sacramento Observer*, May 27–June 2, 1993; "Domestic Workers Union Born in San Diego"; Lynn Eldred, "United Domestic Worker: Power and Pride," *San Diego Newsline*, November 26–December 3, 1980; Greg Gross, "Homemakers Union to Sign its 1st Pact," *San Diego Union*, November 20, 1980; H.G. Reza, "Organizing Still a Labor of Love," *LAT*, August 14, 1989.
103. "Domestic Workers Sign Labor Union Contract"; Reza, "Organizing Still a Labor of Love."
104. "United Domestic Workers of America: Brief History and Background," at www.udwa.org/history.htm; "Leadership at UDWA," www.udwa.org/leaders.htm, accessed April 24, 2005. Since then, AFSCME placed UDWA in trusteeship and changed its web pages.
105. "Organizing the Unorganized: Union of Domestic Workers Starts in San Diego," *San Diego Newsline*, May 9, 1979, in UDWA packet; Reza, "Organizing Still a Labor of Love."
106. "Domestic Workers Union Born in San Diego."
107. United Domestic Workers of America, "Constitution," As amended by the Eleventh Constitutional Convention, 2003, 2, at www.udwa.org/const_05.htm, accessed April 24, 2005.
108. Msemaji, "'He Believed Every Human Being Was Valuable.'"
109. Eldred, "United Domestic Workers."
110. "Organizing the Unorganized"; Paula Parker, "Domestics' Union Makes Gains," *LAT*, November 22, 1980; Eldred, "United Domestic Workers"; Gross, "Homemakers Union To Sign Its 1st Pact."
111. Eldred, "United Domestic Workers."
112. Eldred, "United Domestic Workers"; Parker, "Domestics' Union Makes Gains."
113. The UDWA National Executive Board to John Sweeney, March 22, 1984, 2, in SEIU, President's Office Papers, John Sweeney, Box 191, folder: "Local 7—1984," SEIU Records.
114. Eldred, "United Domestic Workers"; Parker, "Domestics' Union Makes Gains"; UDWA National Executive Board to John Sweeney, March 22, 1984, 3, Appendix A, 3, SEIU Records; John McLaren, "Union Fears Plan to Trim Home Care," *San Diego Tribune*, March 17, 1989.
115. "Organizing the Unorganized"; Eldred, "United Domestic Workers"; Parker, "Domestics' Union Makes Gains."
116. Eldred, "United Domestic Workers"; Parker, "Domestics' Union Makes Gains."
117. UDWA National Executive Board to John Sweeney, March 22, 1984, Appendix A, 3, Appendix B, 3, SEIU Records; McLaren, "Union Fears Plan to Trim Home Care."
118. UDW National Executive Board to John Sweeney, March 22, 1984, Appendix B, 1; Lori Weisbert, "Pilot Project Voted for Homemaker Aid," *San Diego Union*, January 20, 1984.
119. Penny Hollander Feldman, Alice M. Sapienza and Nancy M. Kane, *Who Cares for Them? Workers in the Home Care Industry* (New York: Greenwood Press, 1990), 81.
120. Penny Hollander Feldman, "Work Life Improvements for Home Care Workers: Impact and Feasibility," *The Gerontogist* 33 (February 1993), 52; Feldman to E. Boris, e-mail, March 25, 2003.
121. McLaren, "Union Fears Plan to Trim Home Care."
122. See overall correspondence, SEIU, President's Office Papers, John Sweeney, Box 191, folder: "Local 7, 1984," SEIU Records.
123. Claude Walbert, "New Company Awarded County Pact for In-Home Care," *San Diego Tribune*, January 21, 1988.
124. Ken Seaton-Msemaji to Honorable Gwen Moore, August 12, in Edward V. Roberts Papers, Box 7, folder 36, Roberts Papers, BANC.
125. UDWA, "Brief History and Background," in packet; Ken Seaton-Msemaji to Steve Coony, April 4, 1994, in Box 348, folder: "434B, LA, 1994," September 1997 Shipment, SEIU Records; Baker, "The Paid Caring Relationship," 300.

Chapter 6

1. "For Immediate Release: Homecare Workers Give Halloween Message to Director of Aging," October 29, 1988; Gale S. Thetford to Keith Kelleher, October 31, 1988, both in Box 3, folder 2, Records of SEIU Local 880 (Chicago), Wisconsin Historical Society (WHS), Madison, WI (880 Records).
2. Ronald Reagan, "Remarks At the Conservative Political Action Conference Dinner," March 20, 1981; "Remarks at a Conservative Political Action Conference Dinner," February 26, 1982, http://reagan.utexas.edu/archives/speeches/; "Memorandum Directing a Federal Employee Hiring Freeze," January 20, 1981, in John T. Woolley and Gerhard Peters, The American Presidency Project [online]. Santa Barbara, CA: University of California (hosted), Gerhard Peters (database), at http://www.presidency.ucsb/ws, accessed June 6, 2009.
3. Judith Stein, *Pivotal Decade: How the United States Traded Factories for Finance in the Seventies* (New Haven: Yale University Press, 2010), 262–267.
4. Ronald Reagan, "Proclamation 5282-National Home Care Week, 1984, November 26, 1984," The American Presidency Project at http://www.presidency.ucsb.edu/ws/?pid=39435, accessed June 6, 2009.
5. Carol Hall Ellenbecker, "The Competitive Experience in Home Health Care: Changes in Organizational Behavior and Service Delivery Since the Omnibus Budget Reconciliation Act of 1980," unpublished Ph.D. dissertation, Brandeis University, 1988, 17–18, 24.
6. U.S. Congress, House of Representatives, Select Committee on Aging, Subcommittee on Health and Long-Term Care, *Building a Long-Term Care Policy: Home Care Data and Implications*, 98th Cong., 2nd sess. (Washington, DC: GPO, December 1984), 4.
7. Ellenbecker, "The Competitive Experience in Home Health Care," 164–165.
8. American Bar Association, *The Black Box of Home Care Quality*, A Report Presented by the Chairman of the Select Committee on Aging, House of Representatives, 99th Cong., 2nd sess., Comm. Pub. No. 99–573, August 1986 (Washington, DC: GPO, 1986), 15 (hereafter *Black Box Report*); Carroll L. Estes, "The Reagan Legacy: Privatization, the Welfare State, and Aging in the 1990s," in *States, Labor Markets, and the Future of Old-Age Policy*, John Myles and Jill Quadagno, eds. (Philadelphia: Temple University Press, 1991), 67–68.
9. Ronald Reagan, "Executive Order 12329—President's Task Force on Private Sector Initiatives," October 14, 1981, http://www.presidency.ucsb.edu/ws/index.php?pid=44377, accessed on August 20, 2008.
10. George Peterson et al., *The Reagan Block Grants: What Have We Learned?* (Washington, DC: The Urban Institute Press, 1986), 1–7.
11. Randall R. Bovbjerg and Barbara A. Davis, "States' Response to Federal Health Care Block Grants: The First Year," *Milbank Memorial Fund Quarterly* 61:4 (1983), 528; Robert Agranoff and Alex N. Patakos, "Intergovernmental Management and Federal Changes, State Responses, and New State Initiatives," *Publius* 14 (Summer 1984), 50.
12. *The Reagan Block Grants*, 70, 81–84.
13. Agranoff and Pattakos, "Intergovernmental Management," 68–71; Bovbjerg and Davies, "States Response," 551–552; *The Reagan Block Grants*, 43–59; Jonathan Oberlander, *The Political Life of Medicare* (Chicago: University of Chicago Press, 2003), 124.
14. Bovbjerg and Davies, "States Response," 536.
15. Thomas Buchberger, *Medicaid Choices for 1982 and Beyond* (Washington, DC: GPO, 1981), xii; Jonathan Engel, *Poor People's Medicine: Medicaid and American Charity Care since 1965* (Durham: Duke University Press, 2006), 114, 164.
16. Bovbjerg and Holahan, "States Response," 3, 7; Agranoff and Pattakos, "Intergovernmental Management," 71.
17. Colleen Grogan, "A Marriage of Convenience: The Persistent and Changing Relationship Between Long-Term Care and Medicaid," in *History and Health Policy in the United States*, Rosemary Stevens, Charles Rosenberg, and Lawton Burns, eds. (New Brunswick: Rutgers University Press, 2006), 215.

18. Buchberger, "Medicaid Choices," 44, 1.
19. Ronald Reagan, "Intent to Run for President: Official Announcement," November 13, 1979, http://www.reaganlibrary.com/reagan/speeches/speech.asp?spid=4, accessed December 22, 2008.
20. U.S. House, *Building a Long-Term Care Policy*, 3–4; Agranoff and Pattakos, "Intergovernmental Management," 71, 76.
21. Gareth Davies, "The Welfare State," in *The Reagan Presidency: Pragmatic Conservatism and Its Legacies*, W. Elliot Brownlee and Hugh David Graham, eds. (Lawrence: University Press of Kansas, 2003), 213–214.
22. Carol De-Ortiz, "The Politics of Home Care for the Elderly Poor: New York City's Medicaid-Funded Home Attendant Program," *Medical Anthropology Quarterly* 7 (March 1993), 15.
23. Margot Cella, *Evaluation of the AFDC Homemaker-Home Health Aide Demonstrations: Operational Costs of Demonstration Activities* (Cambridge, MA: Abt Associates Inc., December 1987), 1–2, 7–8, 19, 26; De-Ortiz, "The Politics of Home Care," 15.
24. Stephen H. Bell, Nancy L. Burstein, and Larry L. Orr, *Evaluation of the AFDC Homemaker-Home Health Aide Demonstrations: Overview of Evaluation Results*, December 1987 (Cambridge, MA: Abt Associates, December 1987), 26–28, 66, 68, xiv.
25. Davida Unterbach, "Friends of the Family: A Socio-Economic Profile of Unionized Home Care Workers," unpublished Ph.D. dissertation, Social Welfare, CUNY, 1992, 166.
26. Margaret Ann Baker, "The Paid Caring Relationship: Workers' Views and Public Policy Regarding Paraprofessional Home Care for the Elderly," unpublished Ph.D. dissertation, University of California, Berkeley, 1987, 134, 174–176, 181.
27. Keith Kelleher, "ACORN Organizing and Chicago Homecare Workers," *Labor Research Review* 80 (1985), 36.
28. Sarah F. Liebschutz, "New Federalism Modified: Jobs and Highways in New York," *The Journal of Federalism* 14 (Summer 1984), 87–88, 92; Michael B. Katz, *The Price of Citizenship: Redefining the American Welfare State* (New York: Metropolitan Books, 2001), 66.
29. Ruth Glasser and Jeremy Brecher, "'We Are the Roots': The Culture of Home Health Aides," *New England Journal of Public Policy* 13 (Fall/Winter 1997), 113.
30. Jonthan Rowe, "Up from the Bedside: a Co-Op for Home Care Workers," *The American Prospect* 2 (Summer 1990), 88–92.
31. Glasser and Brecher, "We Are the Roots," 128, 113, 122–124.
32. Robert Kane, Richard Ladd, Rosalie Kane, and Wendy J. Nielsen, *Oregon's LTC System: A Case Study by the National LTC Mentoring Program* (Minneapolis, MN: Institute for Health Services Research, University of Minnesota, 1996); Ellen O'Brien and Risa Elias, "Medicaid and Long-term Care," *Kaiser Commission on Medicaid and the Uninsured* (Washington, DC: Kaiser Family Foundation, May 2004), 12; Statement by Roger Auerbach, "Reforming the Delivery System," Oregon Department of Human Resources, Senior & Disabled Services Division Before the Senate Special Committee on Aging, March 9, 1998, http://aging.senate.gov/public/events/hr12.htm, accessed March 2003.
33. Statement of Dr. Ellen Winston in U.S. Congress, Senate, Special Committee on Aging, Subcommittee on Federal, State, and Community Services, *Hearings: Services to the Elderly on Public Assistance*, 89th Cong., 1st sess., August 18–19, 1965 (Washington, DC: GPO, 1965), 5.
34. Jean Doris Freeman, "Community Organization to Meet the Needs of Older Adults," unpublished Master's thesis, University of Oregon, 1972, 16; Arnold V. Hurtado, Merwyn R. Greenlick, and Ernest W. Saward, "The Organization and Utilization of Home-care and Extended Care Facility Services in a Prepaid Comprehensive Group Practice Plan," *Medical Care* VII:1 (1969), 30–40.
35. Statement of Laverne Moore in U.S. Congress, House of Representatives, Select Committee on Aging, *Hearings: Impact of Reagan Economics on Aging Women: Oregon*, 97th Cong., 2nd sess., September 1, 1982 (Washington, DC: GPO, 1982), 45–46.

36. *Report of the Special Committee on Aging*, 58th Assembly—Oregon State Legislature (Salem, Oregon, January 1975), 11, 13; Elizabeth Kutza, "Long-Term Care in Oregon," Institute on Aging, Portland State University, 1994, in authors' possession.
37. Interview by Paige Austin with Richard Ladd, Administrator of Seniors Services Division from 1981–1992, February 18, 2003, notes in authors' possession.
38. U.S. House, *Hearings: Impact of Reagan Economics on Aging Women*, 45; Kutza, "Long-Term Care in Oregon"; Interview by Paige Austin with Douglas Stone, SDPD, February 18, 2003, notes in authors' possession.
39. Kutza, "Long-Term Care in Oregon," 3, 16–17.
40. Interview with Ladd; Kane at al., "Oregon's LTC System."
41. Kane et al., "Oregon's LTC System"; Interview by Paige Austin with Cynthia Hannum, Administrator of SDPD's Office of Licensing and Quality Care, March 3, 2003, notes in Klein's possession; U.S. Congress, Senate, Special Committee on Aging, Joint Hearing, *Board and Care: A Failure of Public Policy*, 101st Cong., 1st sess., March 9, 1989 (Washington, DC: GPO, 1989), 2–4; Bovbjerg and Davis, "States' Response to Federal Health Care Block Grants," 545; *The Reagan Block Grants*, 43; 111.
42. "Oregon Matches Care with Needs," *Salem Statesman-Journal*, May 29, 1988.
43. Oregon Bureau of Labor and Industries, Division 20: Wages, Procedural Rules, 839-020-0004 and 839-020-0150.
44. *Who Will Care? A Model Collaborative Project* (Salem: Oregon Senior and Disabled Services Division, 1992).
45. *Who Will Care?*
46. U.S. Congress, House of Representatives, Select Committee on Aging, Subcommittee on Health and Long-Term Care, *The Attempted Dismantling of the Medicare Home Care Benefit*, 99th Cong., 2nd sess., April 1986 (Washington, DC: GPO, 1986), 10.
47. Randall R. Bovbjerg and John Holahan, *Medicaid in the Reagan Era: Federal Policy and State Choices* (Washington, DC: The Urban Institute Press, 1982), 60–61.
48. Theresa A. Coughlin, Leighton Ku, and John Holahan, *Medicaid since 1980: Costs, Coverage, and the Shifting Alliance Between the Federal Government and the States* (Washington, DC: The Urban Institute Press, 1994), 117.
49. Marty Lynch and Carroll L. Estes, "The Underdevelopment of Community-Based Services in the U.S. Long-term Care System: A Structural Analysis," 201–213, and Estes et al., "The Medicalization and Commodification of Aging and the Privatization and Rationalization of Old Age Policy," 45–59, both in Carroll Estes and Associates, *Social Policy and Aging: A Critical Perspective* (Thousand Oaks: Sage Publications, 2001).
50. About 5 million elderly Americans, and perhaps another 2–3 million under age 65, needed home care service in 1984. Oberlander, *The Political Life of Medicare*, 120–126; U.S. House, *The Attempted Dismantling of the Medicare Home Benefits*, 4–5; U.S. House, *Building a Long-Term Care Policy*, 6.
51. Andrew Sasz, "The Labor Impacts of Policy Change in Health Care: How Federal Policy Transformed Home Health Organizations and Their Labor Practices," *Journal of Health Politics, Policy, and Law* 15 (Spring 1990), 195–196. The gross revenue statistic comes from American Bar Association, *The Black Box Report*, August 1986 (Washington, DC: GPO, 1986), 2.
52. Ellenbecker, "The Competitive Experience in Home Health Care," 111; *Black Box Report*, 2.
53. U.S. House, Select Committee on Aging, *Hearing: The Black Box of Home Care Quality*, 99th Cong., 2nd sess., July 29, 1986 (Washington, DC: GPO, 1987), 3–4; 28 (hereafter *Hearings: Black Box*); *Black Box Report*, "Introduction: The Problem," 1; 7.
54. *Black Box Report*, 5; *Hearings: Black Box*, 29.
55. *Hearings: Black Box*, 20; 22.
56. *Black Box Report*, 7–9; 28–30; 41.
57. *Hearings: Black Box*, 88–89.
58. Ibid., 63.

59. Ibid., 8.
60. Katherine Lohr, *Medicare: A Strategy for Quality Assurance,* Vol. II: *Sources and Methods* (Washington, DC: National Academy Press, 1990), 241.
61. *Black Box Report,* 40.
62. Jill Quadagno, *One Nation Uninsured: Why the U.S. Has No National Health Insurance* (New York: Oxford University Press, 2005), 149–159.
63. Julie Rovner, "Pepper Bill Pits Politics Against Process," *CQWR,* June 4, 1988, 1491; Rovner, "Long-Term Care Bill Derailed—For Now," *CQWR,* June 11, 1988, 1604; Rovner, "Singing His Praises, House Says No to Pepper," *CQWR,* June 11, 1988, 1605; Quadagno, *One Nation Uninsured,* 176–179.
64. *Community Care: Annual Joint Report to the Governor and the Illinois General Assembly on Public Act 81–20,* September 1983 (Springfield: Department of Aging, 1983), 5; *Community Care,* September 1985 (Springfield: Department of Aging, 1985), 4.
65. Kelleher, "ACORN Organizing and Chicago Homecare Workers," 41.
66. "Introduction," "Discount Foundation Application Summary," n.d., c. 1986, 3, Box 2, folder 31; "Mildred Young's Testimony for Taskforce Hearing," August 17, 1988, Box 3, folder 11; Press Release, "Homecare Workers Slam State on Union Busting Vendors, Poverty Wages, and Institutional Racism," n.d., but probably August 16, 1988, Box 3, folder 11, 880 Records.
67. "Chicago and Washington, D.C., Homemakers Organizing Project, Proposal Submitted to Discount Foundation, December, 1983," 3, Box 2, folder 31, 880 Records.
68. Ibid., 3–4.
69. *Community Care,* September, 1983, 5, 8; *Community Care,* September 1984 (Springfield: Department of Aging, 1984), conveyance letter; *Community Care,* September 1988 (Springfield: Department of Aging, 1988), 3.
70. "Health Care Division Organizing Plan 1993," 2, Box 4, folder 41, 880 Records.
71. *SEIU International v. State of Illinois, Hearing Officer's Recommended Opinion and Dismissal,* State Labor Relations Board, Case No. S-RC-115, October 24, 1985, 2–4, 9–10, Box 11, folder 3; Keith Kelleher to All Staff and Leadership, July 9, 1985, Box 4, folder 35, 880 Records.
72. "Discount Foundation Application Summary," n.d., c. 1986, 1; Kelleher, "ACORN Organizing and Chicago Homecare Workers," 33–46.
73. Keith Kelleher, "A History of SEIU Local 880, 1983–2005," Unpublished Manuscript (2005), 11–21, in authors' possession.
74. "Discount Foundation Application Summary," c. 1985, 1–2; Memo to: Interested Parties From: KK with Attached Songs, Box 4, folder 35; "Client Campaign," in "Progress and Plans to Date," July 9, 1985, 3, Box 4, folder 35, 880 Records.
75. Vanessa Tait, *Poor Workers' Unions: Rebuilding Labor from Below* (Boston: South End Press, 2005), 116–119; "Discount Foundation Application Summary," n.d., c. 1986, 1.
76. "Local 880 Industry Profile/Organizing Model for Homecare Sector," February 5, 1993, in Box 4, folder 41, 880 Records; Kelleher, "A History of SEIU Local 880," 26, 49.
77. "Discount Foundation Application Summary," c. 1985, 1–2; Memo on "Progress and Plans to Date," February 27, 1985, 3; Memo on "Progress and Plans to Date," April 27, 1985, 4, Box 4, folder 35, 880 Papers.
78. To Jerry Shea From Keith Kelleher on "May 1st Long Term Care Town Hall Meeting," April 29, 1993, Box 6, folder 50; Long Term Care Workers Project, "Steering Committee Minutes," September 17, 1991, in Box 6, folder 6, 880 Records.
79. Press release, "Homecare Workers Demand End to Slave Wages!," March 28, 1985, Box 3, folder 1, 880 Records; "Local 880 Industry Profile/Organizing Model for Homecare Sector," 6.
80. "Local 880 Industry Profile/Organizing Model for Homecare Sector," 11.
81. Juanita Bratcher, "Health Workers Hit Pay Rate," *Chicago Defender,* March 12, 1985; SEIU Local 880 Grievance Form, Frankie Sparks, with attached letters, 1990–1991, Box 14, folder 52, 880 Records.

82. "Theneita Anderson's Testimony for Taskforce Hearing," August 17, 1988, Box 3, folder 11, 880 Records.
83. Affidavit Thelma Brown, April 2, 1986; William Ghesquiere to Herbert Cohen, April 4, 1986, Keith Kelleher to Nelson Keilt and Herbert Cohen, April 25, 1986, Box 4, folder 42, 880 Records.
84. Valerie Vaughan to Employees, January 5, 1982, Box 15, folder 37, 880 Records.
85. McMaid would continue to provide private paid maid and janitorial services but no longer provide home care services. George Olson to CCP Case Management Units, September 29, 1983, Box 15, folder 36, 880 Records; Edwin Darby, "McMaids Cleans Up by Cleaning Up," *Chicago Sun Times*, April 27, 1989. On issues of disrespect and mistreatment, see for example, Kelleher, "Local 880 Industry Profile/Organizing Model For Home Care Sector," February 12, 1993, 2, Box 8, folder 49, 880 Records.
86. Keller, "A History of SEIU Local 880," 27, 51; "Union Wins YMCA Election, Company Stalls," *Local 880 Voice*, November/December 1985, 880 Records.
87. Keith Kelleher to All Staff, "United Labor Unions Local 880 YE/YB Report," December 30, 1983, Box 8, folder 41; Keith Kelleher to Andrew Wright, February 20, 1984, Box 11, folder 41; "Chicago Local 880 Year End/Year Begin Report," January 1985, Box 8, folder 41, 880 Records. Background on Sherman from authors' telephone interview with Keith Kelleher, June 15, 2009, notes in authors' possession.
88. "McMaid Negotiates," *The Homemakers' Voice*, Chicago, Illinois, [c. March 1984].
89. "McMaid Workers Picket Owner's House," *The Homemakers' Voice*, Chicago Illinois, n.d.
90. Kelleher interview.
91. "N.H.S. Contract Victory. Strike Is Off," *The Homemakers' Voice*, "Special Contract Issue," n.d., 1; Mark Heaney to Keith Kelleher, June 10, 1985, Box 11, folder 41; Kelleher to Mr. Olson/Heaney, June 17, 1985, Box 11, folder 41, 880 Records.
92. "State Reps Support," *The Homemakers' Voice*, January 1985.
93. "Union Members Going to Springfield," *The Homemakers' Voice*, March 1985.
94. Tait, *Poor Workers' Unions*, 122.
95. See correspondence with Gene Moats, Box 1, folder 33; "Confidential Memorandum" To: Keith, From: Wade 3/2/93, Box 4, folder 41, 880 Papers. See also Kelleher, "A History of SEIU," 18.
96. "Union Members Going to Springfield"; "Service Employees International Union Local 880 Year End/Year Begin Report—1986," January 2, 1987, Box 8, folder 41, 880 Records.
97. See correspondence between Mark Heaney and Keith Kelleher, 1985–1993, Box 11, folders 41–46, 880 Records.
98. "Year End/Year Begin Report—1986."
99. Heaney to National Homecare Systems Staff—Office and Field, June 5, 1987, Box 11, folder 42; Heaney to SEIU Local 880 Bargaining Committee, June 3, 1991, Box 11, folder 44, 880 Records.
100. A. Wright to Mark Heaney, December 1, 1993, Box 11, folder 46, 880 Records.
101. Kelleher Interview.
102. Kelleher, "A History of SEIU Local 880," 24; "Year End/Year Begin Report—1986," 5.
103. "Convention Highlights," *Local 880 Voice*, August/September 1986; Charles Hayes to Irma Sherman, July 30, 1986; "Statement of Representative Charles A. Hayes to Chairman Edward R. Roybal," July 29, 1986, both in Box 3, Folder 8, 880 Records.
104. Heaney to Kelleher, July 2, 1987; Kelleher to Heaney July 3, 1987; Kelleher to Department of Children and Family Services, July 3, 1987; Madeline Talbott, Regional Director Illinois ACORN, to Department of Children and Family Services, July 6, 1987, Box 11, folder 42, 880 Records.
105. "Year End/Year Begin Report—1986"; Heaney to All Field Staff, October 27, 1986, Box 11, folder 41, 880 Records.
106. Myra Glassman to Mike, April 13, 1987; Myra Glassman to Mike, April 28, 1987; Kelleher to Sandra Nimtz, July 23, 1987; Corinthian Welch to Keith Kelleher, June 9, 1987, Box 11, folder 42; Myra Glassman to Detonya, November 8, 1988, Box 11, folder 43; "Local 880 SEIU Year End Year Begin Report December 28, 1988," 2, Box 8, folder 41, 880 Records.

107. "Local 880 Service Employees International Union, AFL-CIO, CLC, Year End/Year Begin Report, December 30, 1987," Box 8, folder 41, 880 Records; Kelleher Interview.
108. Kelleher to Mark Heaney, February 1, 1991; Heaney to Kelleher, February 12, 1991, Box 11, folder 44; Various Union Members to Brothers and Sisters, January 15, 1992, Box 11, folder 45; "Local 880 SEIU Year End/Year Begin Report, December 30, 1989," and "Local 880 SEIU Year End/Year Begin Report, December 29, 1990," Box 8, folder 41, 880 Records; Kelleher, "A History of SEIU Local 880," 57–60.
109. Kelleher to Heaney, April 15, 1991, Box 11, folder 46; Kelleher to Heaney, July 26, 1993, and Attached Concepts on Accretion, Box 11, folder 46, 880 Papers. On NLRB and employer latitude, see David Brody, "On the Representation Election," in *Labor Embattled: History, Power, Rights* (Urbana: University of Illinois Press, 2005), 98–109.
110. State of Illinois, Before the State Labor Relations Board, DORS vs. SEIU, Case No. S-RC-115; "Petitioner's Post-Hearing Brief," S-RC-115, 13, both in Box 11, folder 3, 880 Records.
111. Kelleher, "A History of SEIU Local 880," 39–43, 49–51.
112. Les Lester, "SEIU Urges Probe," *Chicago Defender*, May 9, 1991; "SEIU Local 880 Action on Lynn Martin—Agenda," Box 7, folder 2, 880 Records.
113. "Year End/Year Begin Report," January 1, 1986, 4; "Year End/Year Begin Report," December 31, 1991, 8–9, Box 8, folder 41, 880 Records.
114. Sharon Jacobson to Susan Suter, October 27, 1986; Carol Moseley Braun to Suter, December 1, 1986, both in Box 1, folder 2, 880 Records.
115. To: Harry Kurshenbaum from Keith Kelleher, Re: DORS Background, February 1, 1993, Box 11, folder 15, 880 Records.
116. Kelleher, "A History of SEIU Local 880," 51.
117. Ibid., 49.
118. "Year End/Year Begin Report, December 29, 1990"; Kelleher, "A History of SEIU Local 880," 75–77.
119. Memo to Kurshenbaum, Larry Engelstein to Eugene Moats, November 14, 1989, Box 11, folder 5; Memo to Gene Moats From Keith Kelleher Re: Meeting with Janice Salini, et al, March 24, 1992, Box 1, folder 32, 880 Records.
120. Heaney to Insured Field Staff, October 8, 1991, Box 11, folder 44; Sherry A. Carroll to Kelleher, February 24, 1992, Sherry A. Carroll to Kelleher, March 9, 1992, Kelleher to Carroll, March 11, 1992, box 11, folder 45; "Local 880 SEIU Year End/Year Begin Report, December 28, 1991," and "Year End/Year Begin Report, January 1, 1993," Box 8, folder 41, 880 Records.
121. Audrey McCrimon to Joan Walers, March 10, 1992; Access Living, "Major Victory for the Disability Community in Illinois," August 20, 1992, both in Box 11, folder 13, 880 Records; Ray Sons, "Elderly Poor Pinned by Budget's Brutality," *Chicago Sun Times*, August 23, 1992; Neil Steinberg, "Disabled Stage New Battle Here," *Chicago Sun Times*, May 17, 1992; "Disabled to Get Home Aid," *Chicago Sun Times*, August 20, 1992.
122. Kelleher to SEIU Health Care Department, "Organizing At Scale: Homecare Organizing Opportunities in and Around Illinois," August 21, 1992, Box 3, folder 37; "Year End/Year Begin Report 1990" and "Local 880 YE/YB Report, December 30, 1987," Box 8, folder: 41, SEIU Records.
123. Editorial, "Give Home Care Workers a Raise," *Chicago Tribune*, November 18, 1992; Kelleher, "A History of SEIU Local 880," 89–90, 110–111.
124. Barbara Caress, "Home Is Where the Patients Are: New York's Home Care Workers' Contract Victory," *Health/PAC Bulletin* 18 (Fall 1988), 4–14; Immanuel Ness, "Organizing Home Health Workers: A New York City Case Study," *WorkingUSA* 3 (November–December 1999), 59–95.
125. Leon Fink and Brian Greenberg, *Upheaval in the Quiet Zone: A History of Hospital Workers' Union Local 1199* (Urbana: University of Illinois Press, 1989), 209.
126. Fink and Greenberg, *Upheaval in the Quiet Zone*, 44–45; 74–78; 102; 114.

127. Fink and Greenberg, *Upheaval in the Quiet Zone,* 202.
128. Unterbach, "Friends of the Family," 4, 74, 161–164; Ronald Sullivan, "New York Shifts Care for Elderly to Their Homes," *NYT,* May 4, 1987; Rebecca Donovan, "Poorly Paid Home Health Care Workers Subsidize an Industry," *NYT,* June 2, 1987.
129. The UDW National Executive Board to John Sweeney, March 22, 1984, 2, SEIU, President's Office, John Sweeney, Box 191, folder: "Local 7—1984," SEIU Records.
130. Unterbach, "Friends of the Family," 6, 101; Caress, "Home Is Where the Patients Are," 4, 9; Rebecca Donovan, Paul A. Kurzman, and Carol Rotman, "Improving the Lives of Home Care Workers: A Partnership of Social Work and Labor," *Social Work,* 38 (September 1993), 582; Ness, "Organizing Home Health Workers," 72, 92, n.6; BNA, "Union Coalition Negotiates Agreement For New York City's Home Care Workers," *Daily Labor Report,* 1-13-88, A-2.
131. Sam Roberts, "For Attendants, Poverty at Home and on the Job," *NYT,* July 27, 1987.
132. Donovan et al., "Improving the Lives of Home Care Workers," 583.
133. Fink and Greenberg, *Upheaval in the Quiet Zone,* 229. Interview with Moe Foner by Dan North, Session #22, March 5, 2001, New York, New York, Oral History Research Office, Columbia University, available at www.columbia.edu/cu/lweb/indiv/oral/foner, accessed July 20, 2005.
134. Caress, "Home Is Where the Patients Are," 9.
135. Michael Oreskes, "Jackson and Cardinal Back Union Bid," *NYT,* May 29, 1987; "Home Health Workers Seek Gains," *Health/PAC Bulletin* (Summer 1987), 29.
136. Caress, "Home Is Where the Patients Are"; *Plight of the Home Care Worker,* Report of the Manhattan Borough President's Hearing on April 29, 1987 (New York: City of New York, January 1988); BNA, "Union Coalition Negotiates Agreement."
137. "The Care-Givers—Part I," March 14, 1988; "The Care-Givers—Part II," March 18, 1988; "The Care-Givers—Part III," March 21, 1988; "The Care-Givers—Part IV," March 23, 1988; "New York's Home Health Care Crisis," March 27, 1988, all in *NYT.*
138. Caress, "Home Is Where the Patients Are," 4–14; Donovan et al., "Improving the Lives of Home Care Workers," 579; Ness, "Organizing Home Health Workers," 68.
139. "The Home Care Campaign: Impact and Significance," 4/11/88, Box 1, folder 3, 880 Records.
140. Ness, "Organizing Home Health Workers," 73–74.
141. "Dennis Rivera," description at http://www.riverkeeper.org/about-us/our-board/dennis-rivera/, accessed July 11, 2009.
142. Ness, "Organizing Home Health Workers," 63.
143. Kelleher, "Local 880 Industry Profile/Organizing Model for Homecare Sector."

Chapter 7

1. Bob Pool, "Faithful Rally Across U.S. to Keep King Dream Alive," *LAT,* April 5, 1988.
2. Carol Bidwell, "Planned Cuts to In-Home Services Hit," *Daily News* (Los Angeles), April 4, 1989; Victor Merina, "Home-Care Workers Rally, Gain Support in Pay Issue," *LAT,* December 23, 1987.
3. Jess Walsh, "Creating Unions, Creating Employers: A Los Angeles Home-Care Campaign," in *Carework: The Quest for Security,* Mary Daly, ed. (Geneva: ILO, 2001), 229; "L.A. Home Care Workers Make History," *SEIU Action* (March/April 1999), 7–9, SEIU Publications, WPR; Steven Greenhouse, "In Biggest Drive since 1937, Union Gains a Victory," *NYT,* February 26, 1999; Frank Swoboda, "A Healthy Sign for Organized Labor—Vote by L.A. Caregivers Called Historic," *Washington Post,* February 26, 1999.
4. Nelson Lichtenstein, *State of the Union: A Century of American Labor* (Princeton: Princeton University Press, 2002), 213; Dan Clawson, *The Next Upsurge: Labor the New Social Movements* (Ithaca: ILR/Cornell University Press, 2003): 13–17; Judith Stein, *The Pivotal Decade: How The United States Traded Factories For Finance in the Seventies* (New Haven: Yale University Press, 2010), 184–190.

5. Ruth Milkman, *L.A. Story: Immigrant Workers and the Future of the U.S. Labor Movement* (New York: Russell Sage, 2006), 24.
6. "SEIU History," SEIU.org at http://www.seiu.org/a/ourunion/seiu-history.php, accessed July 12, 2009.
7. Matt Bai, "The New Boss," *NYT*, January 30, 2005.
8. "Program Proposals," attached to Peter Rider to Health Care Organizing Team et al. on 5/25 Meeting Assignment, 2, SEIU Organizing Department, Box 1, folder: "Healthcare Organizing, 1988," SEIU Records, WPR.
9. Stationary from Janet Heinritz-Canterbury Papers, in authors' possession; flyer, "Honor Homecare Workers," c. 1996, Box 9, folder: "SEIU, Local 616—Homecare Worker's Center Project," Sampson Papers, SFSU-LA.
10. Memo from Pat Ford to Bob Muscat, May 1, 1996, Box 9, folder: "SEIU, Local 616—Homecare Worker's Center Project," Sampson Papers.
11. Lennard J. Davis, *The Disability Studies Reader*, 2nd ed. (New York: Routledge, 2006).
12. Jennifer L. Erkulwater, *Disability Rights and the American Social Safety Net* (Ithaca: Cornell University Press, 2006), 166; see also, Samuel R. Bagenstos, "The Americans with Disabilities Act as Welfare Reform," *William and Mary Law Review* 921 (2003) at 44.
13. Erkulwater, *Disability Rights*, 167–171; Joseph P. Shapiro, *No Pity: People with Disabilities Forging a New Civil Rights Movement* (New York: Random House, 1994), 251; "For the Record," *Modern Healthcare*, October 14, 1001, 11; Simi Linton, *Claiming Disability: Knowledge and Identity* (New York: NYU Press, 1998).
14. "'Bill of Rights' for Disabled Wins Approval in Senate," *San Jose Mercury News*, September 8, 1989; Christopher H. Schmitt, "Disabled Rights Bill Endorsed," *San Jose Mercury News*, September 9, 1989.
15. 527 U.S. 581 (1999); Jacqueline Vaughn Switzer, *Disabled Rights: American Disability Policy and the Fight for Equality* (Washington, DC: Georgetown University Press, 2003), 160–164; Mary Johnson, "Bed money," *Ragged Edge Online*, May/June 2000, at www.rageededgemagazine.com/0500/a0500cov.htm, accessed on April 11, 2005.
16. California Conference on Handicapped Individuals, "Progress Report on Implementation of Recommendations," January 1979, 1, Carton 1, folder 55, Edward V. Roberts Papers, The Bancroft Library, University of California, Berkeley.
17. Flyer, "Clinton Health Care Task Force Member to Discuss the Impact on People with Disabilities"; Carol Rasco to Judy Heumann, February 25, 1993, both in Box 28, folder 26, World Institute on Disability Records (WID Records), The Bancroft Library, University of California, Berkeley; "Judy Heumann," http://bancroft.berkeley.edu/collections/drilm/collection/items/heumann.html, accessed July 4, 2008; Paul Marchand to Robyn Stone, April 27, 1993; "Consensus Approach to Long Term Services and Supports," March 1, 1993; both in Box 28, folder 26, WID Records.
18. "Statement of Governor Clinton on Personal Assistance Services," Box 28, folder 26, WID Records.
19. Robert Pear, "Health Care Policy: How Bush and Clinton Differ," *NYT*, August 12, 1992; Pear, "U.S. Considers Aid on Long-Term Care," *NYT*, February 21, 1993; Thomas Friedman, "President Allows States Flexibility on Medicaid Funds," *NYT*, February 3, 1993; Robert Pear, "Clinton Health-Proposal Included New Program for Long-Term Care," *NYT*, September 8, 1993; Tamar Lewin, "Elderly with Large Health Care Bills See Special Boon in Clinton Proposal," *NYT*, September 27, 1993.
20. Gwendolyn Mink, ed., *Whose Welfare?* (Ithaca: Cornell University Press, 1999).
21. National Senior Citizens Law Center, "Action Alert! Thousands of Elderly and Disabled Persons Face Loss of Personal Care Attendants," 1997, Box 9, folder: "SEIU, Local 616—Homecare Worker's Center et al., 1996–1997," Sampson Papers; John Jacobs, "Ground Zero," *SB*, December 24, 1996; Lynn H. Fujiwara, "Asian Immigrant Communities and the Racial Politics of Welfare Reform," in *Whose Welfare?*, Mink, ed., 121, 127–128.
22. Noah Zatz, "Welfare to What?," *Hastings Law Journal* 57 (2006) at 1162.

23. Jill Quadagno, "Physician Sovereignty and the Purchasers' Revolt," *Journal of Health Politics, Policy and Law* 29 (August–October 2004), 828.
24. Marie Gottschalk, *The Shadow Welfare State: Labor, Business, and the Politics of Health Care in the United States* (Ithaca: ILR/Cornell University Press, 2000).
25. Thomas R. Oliver, "Policy Entrepreneurship and the Social Transformation of American Medicine: The Rise of Managed Care and Managed Competition," *Journal of Health Politics, Policy and Law* 29 (August–October 2004), 712.
26. Lynn May Rivas for WID, "A Significant Alliance: The Independent Living Movement, the Service Employees International Union and the Establishment of the first Public Authorities in California," draft pamphlet, 2005, in authors' possession.
27. Patrick Hoge, "Cutbacks in Care at Homes Attacked," *SB*, February 23, 1989; Charisse Jones, "Providers of Home Care in Budget Pinch," *LAT*, March 22, 1989.
28. Testimony of Henri Habenicht, California Assembly, Committee on Human Resources, "Hearing on Administration of Homemaker/Chore Services Program," November 9, 1976 (Sacramento: Assembly Committee Office, 1976), 80.
29. Joint Committee on Federal Social Security Amendments of 1972, "Interim Report on the Immediate Funding Crisis in the Homemaker and Chore Service Program," January 20, 1975, 4–6, Box 24, folder 21, WID Records; Adult and Family Services Division, *Title XX Block Grant Post-expenditure Report*, July 1, 1989 through June 30, 1990 (Sacramento: Department of Social Services, 1990), 2.
30. Testimony of Frederick J. Keeley, "Hearing on Administration of Homemaker/Chore Services Program," 153.
31. Adult Services Unit, Services Operations Section, Social Services Program, Department of Health Report of State-County Homemaker/Chore Services Task Force, April 1975, I, California State Library, Sacramento, CA; State of California, Little Hoover Commission, "Elder Care at Home," Recommendations, November 6, 1991, at http://www.lhc.ca.gov/lhcdir/113rp.html, accessed June 24, 2008.
32. Little Hoover Commission.
33. Victor Merina, "Disabled Fear Ruling Will Mean Loss of Helpers Who Are Illegals," *LAT*, December 4, 1988; "Helen," in "Focus Group Meeting—September 14, 1994," 5, Box 24, folder 21, WID Records.
34. Patrick Hoge, "In-Home Workers Bear Heavy Load," *SB*, April 5, 1994; Little Hoover Commission.
35. Margaret Ann Baker, "The Paid Caring Relationship: Workers' Views and Public Policy Regarding Paraprofessional Home Care for the Elderly," unpublished Ph.D. dissertation, University of California, Berkeley, 1987, 140; Candace Howes, "Upgrading California's Home Care Workforce: The Impact of Political Action and Unionization," in *The State of California Labor, 2004*, Ruth Milkman, ed. (Berkeley: University of California Press, 2004), 86; interview of Karen Orlando by E. Boris, July 9, 2008.
36. Vikki, "Focus Group Meeting—September 14, 1994," 11.
37. "The Department of Social Services Could Reduce Costs and Improve Compliance with Regulations of the In-Home Supportive Services Program," Auditor General of California, March 1987, quoted in Little Hoover Commission.
38. Baker, "The Paid Caring Relationship," 294–296.
39. Virginia Ellis, "Cuts Undermine State Pledge of Help for All," *LAT*, September 3, 1992.
40. Ruth Wilson Gilmore, *Golden Gulag: Prisons, Surplus, Crisis, and Opposition in Globalizing California* (Berkeley: University of California Press, 2007), 30–86; Milkman, *LA Story*.
41. "Appendix C," 31, Box 23, folder 9, WID Records. For example, John Kendall, "State Sued to Provide Funds for Home Care," *LAT*, August 22, 1975; Keith Love and Myrna Oliver, "State Temporarily Blocked from Cutting Support Services," *LAT*, October 14, 1981.
42. William Endicott, "Emergency Aid OKd for Aged, Blind, Disabled," *LAT*, January 23, 1975; "Governor Changes Mind: Bill to Pay In-Home Attendants Signed," *LAT*, July 20, 1983; Hoge, "Cutbacks in Care at Homes Attacked."

43. Bill Billiter, "In a Stressful State Budget Deadlock, No Paycheck Put New Pressures on Mother of Disabled Sons," *LAT* (Orange County Edition), August 27, 1992; Irene Wielawski, "Judge Orders State to Pay In-Home Service Workers," *LAT*, August 26, 1992.
44. Kathy McDonald, "Budget Impasse Riles Unpaid Workers," *Daily News* (Los Angeles), July 14, 1990.
45. Linda Delp and Katie Quan, "Homecare Worker Organizing in California: An Analysis of a Successful Strategy," *Labor Studies Journal* 27, no.1 (2002), 3–4; *We Who Care: The Story of Los Angeles County's Homecare Workers* (Los Angeles: SEIU 434, January 1988), 18, 22.
46. William P. Jones, "The Infrastructure of South Central Los Angeles: Unions, Public Service, the New Black Middle Class," unpublished paper presented at the Center for the Study of Work, Labor, and Democracy, University of California Santa Barbara, January 23, 2009, 13–14; 17–19, in authors' possession.
47. Adams and Gallagher to David Snapp, November 16, 1988, 1 (underline in original), 2, 3, in SEIU Organizing Department, Organizing Files A-N, Box 1 of 3, folder: "LA Homecare Health Care 1988 (Homecare)," SEIU Records.
48. Memo, n.d., with notation, 3–7, SEIU Organizing Department, Box 1, folder "Healthcare Organizing, 1988," SEIU Records.
49. Andy Stern to Bob Welsh, "Healthcare Organizing Subsidies," February 10, 1988, in SEIU Organizing Department, Organizing Files A-N, Box 1 of 3, folder: "Healthcare Organizing 1988," SEIU Records. On number of organizers, *Service Employees International Union, Local 434 v. County of Los Angeles*, "Complaint for Declaratory Relief," Superior Court for the State of California in and for the County of Los Angeles, December 29, 1987, 4.
50. *We Who Care*, 20–26.
51. Greenhouse, "In Biggest Drive since 1937."
52. Orlando Interview; interview with Karen Sherr by Boris, May 18, 2005, and June 15, 2006; "Getting from There to Here," *UNITY* 3 (August 1991), 12–15; various documents in Box 9, folder: "SEIU, Local 616 Homecare Worker's Center Project, 1996–1997," Sampson Papers; Ruth Needleman, "Building Relationships for the Long Haul: Unions and Community-Based Groups Working Together to Organize Low-Wage Workers," in *Organizing to Win: New Research on Union Strategies*, Kate Bronfenbrenner et al., eds, (Ithaca: Cornell University Press, 1998), 71–86.
53. "New National Homecare Contract in SF Protects Excellent Pay, Benefits," *UNITY* (Spring 1990), 5, SEIU Publications, Local 250, 1984–90, SEIU Records.
54. "Local 250 Opens Home Care Campaign," *UNITY* 3 (May/June 1991), 12–13; "Blitz II," *UNITY* 5 (September./October 1993), 12; "We're Young and On the Move," *UNITY*, n.d. (circa 1994), 12; "In the Line of Duty," *UNITY* (May/June 1994), 16; "Local 250 Bulletin: National Homecare Workers," February 25, 1993; memo also printed in Spanish and Chinese, SEIU Organizing Department, General Organizing, 84–92, Box 42, folder: "Cal. Home Care," SEIU Records.
55. *Bonnette v. California Health and Welfare Agency* (1983) 704 F.2d 1465 at 13–14, 19–21.
56. *In-Home Supportive Services v. Workers' Compensation Appeals Board* (1984) 152 Ca.App.3d 720 at 731.
57. John K. Van De Kamp, "Subject: "State Employee' Status of Employee of In-Home Supportive Services Program Aid Recipient," Opinion No. 84–308—July 23, 1985, Attorney General's *Opinions*, 68 (July 1985).
58. "Rallying Homecare Workers," *Update: Healthcare Division* II:1 (1988), 10.
59. Gail Radford, "From Municipal Socialism to Public Authorities: Institutional Factors in the Shaping of American Public Enterprise," *Journal of American History* 90 (December 2003), 863–890.
60. Memo to Dan S., Ophelia M., Jennifer F., Amado D. from Wilma C., "Attached Memos Re: Authority," December 13, 1990, in SEIU Organizing Department, General Organizing, 1984–1992, Box 42, folder: "California Home Care," SEIU Records.

61. Milkman, *L.A. Story*, 155–157.
62. Interview with Janet Heinritz-Canterbury, April 13, 2005; see Janet Heinritz-Canterbury to Ed Roberts, September 20, 1993, in Carton 7, folder 36, Roberts Papers.
63. Marta Russell, "Strange Bedfellows," *The Disability Rag* 14 (November/December, 1993), 8.
64. "Seniors Fear the New Law Will Send Many to Nursing Homes," *Sacramento Union*, July 27, 1993, in Carton 7, folder 36, Roberts Papers.
65. Rivas, "A Significant Alliance," 6–8; "About the CSL," at www.4csl.org/, accessed July 2, 2005.
66. Simi Litvak et al., *Attending to America: Personal Assistance for Independent Living* (Berkeley: World Institute on Disability, 1987).
67. Marta Russell, "California Scheming," *The Disability Rag* 14 (November/December, 1993), cover, 4–5, 7–10; Patricia Yeager to Senator David G. Kelley, June 16, 1993, Carton 7, folder 36, Roberts Papers.
68. Judy Heumann to Phyllis Zlotnick, January 5, 1987, Box 21, folder 6, WID Records; "Resolution on Personal Assistance Services," World Institute on Disability Personal Assistance Services Symposium, September 29–October 1, 1991, Oakland, in Box 28, folder: "Judy Heumann," Center for Independent Living Records, The Bancroft Library, University of California, Berkeley.
69. Senate Committee on Health and Welfare, "Hearing in re: H.R. 1," Reporter's Transcript of Proceedings (Sacramento: State of California, 1973), May 30, 1973, 45–46; Emma H. Gunterman, Oral History Interview, Conducted in 1989–1990 by Jacqueline S. Reinier, California State University, Sacramento, for the California State Archives, State Government Oral History Program, 332, 336.
70. Breakfast Meeting with Home Care Workers, Interview with Lola Young by E. Boris and J. Klein, September 6, 2008, United Health Workers-West (UHW) Leadership Convention, San Jose, CA.
71. Interview with Lola Young; Memo from Jon Showalter to Homecare Council, May 13, 1996, in Box 9, folder: "SEIU, Local 616-Various 1990s," Sampson Papers.
72. Rivas, "A Significant Alliance," documents these events, 6–9.
73. On the public authorities, see Memorandum in Support of SEIU, Local 434B's Motion to Dismiss in *Hummel v. SEIU Local 434B*, Case No. 01-10826 CAS (FMOX) (C.D.Cal), 1; and Reply Memorandum, 5, both in possession of E. Boris. 5–12; Janet Heinritz-Canterbury, *Collaborating to Improve In-Home Supportive Services: Stakeholder Perspectives on Implementing California's Public Authorities* (New York: Paraprofessional Healthcare Institute, 2002), 9–13; Delp and Quan, "Homecare Worker Organizing," 9; on the seniors, Alan Toy, "L.A. County Public Authority: An Empowering Solution," *New Mobility* 7 (November 1996), 55; Rivas, "A Significant Alliance."
74. Cinde Chorness, "Care for Seniors Made Easier," *The Times* (San Mateo County), September 15, 1993.
75. At that point, the federal government picked up 60% of the overall tab, with the remaining 40% divided between the state (65%) and the counties (35%). Walsh, "Creating Unions," 225–226; Jae Kennedy and Lance Egley, "PC Option Information for California IHSS Program Reform," c. March 1993, Carton 7, folder 36, Roberts Papers.
76. Elisa Rocha, "In-Home Care Funding Will Be Restored," *Modesto Bee*, February 9, 1993; Nancy Weaver, "Battle over Funding Priorities," *SB*, March 24, 1993.
77. Frances Dinkelspiel, "Alameda County to Vote on Role in Disabled Services," *San Jose Mercury News*, October 19, 1993.
78. Sherr Interview; Sal Rosselli, "President's Perspective," *UNITY* 5 (September/October 1993), 4.
79. "Working Session #2 on the IHSS Registry"; Tricia Leetz to City and County of San Francisco, March 16, 1994; Planning for Elders in the Central City to Supervisors Hallinan & Kaufan, May 3, 1994, all in Sherr Papers.

80. "Blitz II," *UNITY* 5 (September/October 1993), 12–13.
81. Memo to Charlie, Harold, Maria, Mila from Karen Sherr, November 8, 1993, "Organizing Workers at Senior Buildings, Centers, etc.," Sherr Papers; "Californian Dreams," *Shadow Economy and Trades Unions* (Duisburg: WAZ-Druck, March 2000), 23.
82. "Historic Victory for Homecare Workers," *The HomeCare Worker* 4 (Fall 1995), 1; Myra Howard, "Local 250 Members Unite at St. Mary's," *The HomeCare Worker* 3 (June 1994), 3.
83. Peter Fimrite, "Home Helath-Care Workers Get Raise," *SFC*, December 28, 1995.
84. "SF Homecare Workers Wages Jump 57 Cents," *UNITY* (February/March 1996), 16; "Mayor Commits Funds to Keep Raise Going," *UNITY* 8 (July 1996), 9.
85. "San Francisco Homecare Contract," *News from the Home Front*, Fall 1997.
86. Julie Murray Brenman to Debra Newman, Memorandum on Wages for IHSS Providers, October 24, 1996; "Confidential: Labor Negotiations Information" to San Francisco IHSS Public Authority Governing Body Members from Staff on Collective Bargaining Team, December 10, 1996, all in Sherr Papers.
87. "Californian Dreams," 26.
88. "The Campaign to Improve the In-Home Supportive Services Program," Sherr Papers; Candace Howes quoted in Eileen Boris et al., "Workforce Needs in California's Homecare System," *CPRC Briefing Paper*, May 2004, 2. See also Howes's chart, "California IHSS Homecare Workers Wages and Benefits Negotiated with SEIU and United Domestic Workers Union," May 31, 2004, in authors' possession.
89. "We're Young and On the Move," *UNITY*, n.d. (c. 1994), 15; "Northern California Homecare Timetable," 1993, SEIU Organizing Dept., General Organizing 1989–92, box 42, folder: "Cal home care," SEIU Records. Local 250 did clash with 616 over organizing in Alameda, requiring intervention by the International and an agreement on territorial boundaries. "Proposed Home Care Campaign—Local 250 Agreement," May 6, 1993, Box 42, folder: "Cal home care," SEIU Records.
90. Rosie Byers and Ethel Richardson, "Dear Homecare Worker," flyer c. 1995; "Notes on Workers Handbook"; "The Collective Bargaining Process," both in Sherr Papers; Rosie Byers, "High Marks for Historic Homecare Steward Council Meeting," *The HomeCare Worker* 3 (April 1994), 3, Sherr Papers.
91. Fax from Steve Wilensky to Ed Roberts, with attachment, 'Los Angeles County IHSS Coalition Recommendations," 9-8-9; Janet Heinritz-Canterbury to Ed Roberts, September 20, 1993; Dan Steward to Ed Roberts, September 22, 1993, all in Carton 7, folder 36, Roberts Papers.
92. Heinritz-Canterbuty to Roberts.
93. Russell, "California Scheming," 7.
94. Russell, "At the ATTENDANT CROSSROADS"; Nancy Becker Kennedy to Stan Greenberg, August 2, 1993, both in Carton 7, folder 36, Roberts Papers.
95. "Los Angeles IHSS Consumer Alliance: Statement of Consumers," Carton 7, folder 36, Roberts Papers; Walsh, "Creating Unions," 226–227.
96. Memo from John Frank to Julie Fulkerson, July 20, 1993, 1, Carton 7, folder 37, Roberts Papers; Kevin Fagan, "Concern over Care for Disabled," *SFC*, July 5, 1993; David Kline, "Seniors Fear the New Law Will Send Many to Nursing Homes," *Sacramento Union*, July 27, 1993.
97. Local 250, which bargained with National Homecare, was with UDWA on this point. SEIU in Chicago, as we saw, first had a contract with National and it forwarded dues to the International in Washington, which in turn was financing the Los Angeles organizing drive. See, Marta Russell, "At the ATTENDANT CROSSROADS," typescript, 7–8, August 1993, Carton 7, folder 36, Roberts Papers.
98. Quoted in Ruth Needleman, "Building Relationships for the Long Haul Between Unions and Community-Based Organizations," Draft, 16, in Box 9, folder: "SEIU, Local 616—Various 1990s," Sampson Papers. The published version is missing this comment.

99. Interview with Lai Xiao Jiang through Chinese Translator by J. Klein, UHW San Francisco Office, September 8, 2008.
100. Marta Russell, "L.A. County Public Authority: A Zero-Sum Game," *New Mobility* 7 (November 1996), 40, 50–51; Alan Toy, "L.A. County Public Authority: An Empowering Solution," 41, 55. For the best account of the L.A. struggle, Walsh, "Creating Unions," 228–230.
101. David Bloom, "Union Hopes to Organize Home Care," *Daily News (LA)*, June 24, 1996.
102. Walsh, "Creating Unions," 230–231; Janet Heinritz-Canterbury, *Collaborating to Improve In-Home Supportive Services*, 13–14.
103. Walsh, "Creating Unions," 229; "L.A. Home Care Workers Make History," *SEIU Action* (March/April 1999), 7–9, SEIU Publications, SEIU Records; Greenhouse, "In Biggest Drive since 1937."
104. "Biographical Sketch," at http://www.ilaboral.org/dinner2008/tyronefreeman.html, accessed July 5, 2008.
105. Needleman, "Building Relationships for the Long Haul." For example, "Pepsico/Taco Bell Gets Creamed," *News from the Home Front*, November 1996; "Welfare Bill Disaster for IHSS Consumers and Workers," *News from the Home Front*, Fall 1996, both in Sherr Papers.
106. Interview with L.C. through Russian Translator by J. Klein and E. Boris, UHW San Francisco Office, September 8, 2008.
107. Memo from Ford to Muscat; Memo from Showalter to Homecare Council; "Notes for SEIU Homecare Council rep model/Worker Centers discussion," 5/2/96, Box 9, folder: "SEIU, Local 616, Homecare Worker Center," Sampson Papers.
108. Interview with Nesty Firestein by E. Boris, July 10, 2008; Memo from Janet Heinritz-Canterbury to Mila Thomas, March 17, 1995, in Box 9, folder: "SEIU, Local 616, Homecare Worker Center," Sampson Papers.
109. Janice Fine, *Worker Centers: Organizing Communities at the Edge of the Dream* (Ithaca: ILR Press, 2006), 7–26, esp. 14; Orlando interview; Flyer, "Attention: Benefits of a Union Member"; "Memo, "Evaluation of the Homecare Literacy Classes," April 30, 1996, Homecare Workers' Center Advisory Committee Minutes, November 14, 1995, in Box 9, "SEIU, Local 616 Homecare Worker's Center Project, 1996–1997"; Interview with Lea Grundy by E. Boris, July 22, 2008.
110. Interview with Leon Chow and with Juan Antonio Molina, both by E. Boris and J. Klein, UHW San Francisco Office, September 8, 2008.
111. Interview with Paul Kumar by J. Klein and E. Boris, UHW Leadership Convention, San Jose, California, September 5, 2008.
112. Delp and Quan, "Homecare Worker Organizing in California," 6; Orlando interview.
113. Meetings of authors with UHW worker leaders, September 8, 2008, in San Francisco.
114. Breakfast Meeting with Home Care Workers, Xiong Yang, UHW Leadership Convention, San Jose, September 6, 2008.
115. Orlando interview; Ken Margolies, "Invisible No More: The Role of Training and Education in Increasing Union Activism of Chinese Home Care Workers in Local 1199SEIU United Healthcare Workers East (UHE)," *Labor Studies Journal* 33 (March 2008), 81–92.
116. The internal struggle within SEIU made it increasingly difficult to obtain interviews with International representatives on all sides of the controversy. As signatories to an open letter to Andy Stern from educators, which questioned his tactics against UHW, we were invited to the UHW convention, where Jennifer Klein spoke. We have analyzed comments regarding what was then a raging conflict in light of the standpoint of interviewees. The worker leaders we had the opportunity to interview, however, are demographically representative of home care providers in California, even if each has his or her own story.
117. Breakfast Meeting with Home Care Workers, Amanda Carles, UHW Leadership Convention, San Jose, California, September 6, 2008; Interview with Danny Villasenor

and Interview with Rosie Byers, both by E. Boris and J. Klein, UHW San Francisco Office, September 8, 2008.

118. Interview with Danny Villasenor.
119. Interview with Juan Antonio Molina by E. Boris and J. Klein, UHW San Francisco Office, September 8, 2008.
120. Interview with Rosie Byers, Mabel Davis, Hollice Hollman, and Blondell Rice by E. Boris and J. Klein, UHW San Francisco Office, September 8, 2008.
121. Interview with Byers et al.; Interview with Mary Ruth Gross by J. Klein and E. Boris, UHW San Francisco Office, September 8, 2008.
122. Interview with Byers et al.
123. Interview with G. S. by J. Klein and E. Boris through a Russian translator, interview with Li Bao Pan by J. Klein through a Chinese translator, UHW San Francisco Office, September 8, 2008.
124. Notes attached to "Contract Campaign Planning Meeting," December 17, 1996, in Box 9, "SEIU, Local 616 Homecare Worker's Center Project, 1996–1997," Sampson Papers.
125. "My Name Is" series of statements by recipients and their attendants, c. 1995; HERO Questionnaire, "Caregivers in America"; Karen Sherr, "Making the Story Visible: Justice of Homecare Workers and Consumers," Planning for Elders in the Central City, March 1999; all in Sherr Papers. See line drawing in introduction for an example of the kind of image that Sherr would use for popular education.
126. Chow interview; Gross interview.
127. Oregon Labor Market Information Center, "OLMIS Occupational Report for Personal and Home Care Aides," Occupational Information Center, at http://www.qualityinfor-org/olmisj/OIC, accessed March 19, 2003.
128. "Home Health Care Workers to Vote on Unionization," *Northwest Labor Press*, November 16, 2001.
129. "Measure 99 Explanatory Statement," November 2000, at www. sos.state.or.us/elections/nov72000/mea/m00/99ex.htm, accessed March 19, 2003.
130. "Home Care Campaign by Local 503 Nears Completion," *Northwest Labor Press*, September 21, 2001.
131. "Home Health Care Workers to Vote on Unionization."
132. "12,000 Home Care Workers in Oregon Say 'Union Yes'" *Northwest Labor Press*, December 21, 2001; "Oregon's Recently Formed Home Care Workers' Union Struggles," *The Oregonian*, August 19, 2002.
133. Interview with Karla Spence by J. Klein, March 2003; SEIU, "Homecare Workers Rally Together As Bargaining for First Contract Begins," SEIU Local 503, May 2002, at www.seiu503.org/articles/article.cfm, accessed May 9, 2003; Homecare Bargaining: Summary of Tentative Agreement Articles, 12/02/02, at www.seiu503.org/ourlocal/bargaining/homecare, accessed on March 27, 2003; "12,000 Home Care Workers in Oregon Say 'Union Yes;'" *HUBBNEWS*, February 2005 and Spring 2005, at www.seiu503.org/hubb/newsletters/index.cfm, accessed October 14, 2005.
134. "12,000 Home Care Workers in Oregon Say Yes"; Delp and Quan, "Homecare Organizing," 17–18.
135. Delp and Quan, "Homecare Worker Organizing," 7.
136. Memo from Ford to Muscat, May 1, 1996.
137. Michael Kinsman, "Leaders of Domestic Workers Union Resign, Recruit for Rival SEIU," July 19, 2005, at www.signonsandiego.com, accessed August 8, 2005; Michael Kinsman, "Truce Brings Joint Union for Home-Care Workers in State," September 20, 1995, at www.signonsandiego.com/news/business/20050920-9999-1b20truce.html, accessed October 14, 2005.
138. Interview with Chow.
139. Interview with Donna Calame by E. Boris, July 8, 2009.

Epilogue

1. SEIU Video: "Walk a Day in My Shoes 2008 with Senator Barack Obama and Home Care Worker Pauline Beck," at www.youtube.com/watch?v=m.US7WnMgBw, accessed July 13, 2009.
2. Steven Greenhouse, "Service Unions to Merge in Bid for More Clout," *NYT*, January 7, 1998; Steven Greenhouse, "Union Official Retires under Pressure," *NYT*, February 2, 1999; Steven Greenhouse, "Growing Health Care Union Prepares to Show Its Muscle," *NYT*, September 12, 1999.
3. Michael Kinsman, "Struggling with an Imperfect Union," *San Diego Union Tribune*, July 3, 2005.
4. SEIU 880 became SEIU Healthcare Illinois-Indiana, see http://www.seiu880.org/; "Members Vote YES to New Union!" April 15, 2008, and "SEIU Local 880 leaders honored at retirement," June 12, 2008, at http://seiu880.wtf.localsonline.org/, accessed December 7, 2008; in 2006, 1199/SEIU expanded to become United Healthcare Workers East to include "300,000 members and retirees in New York, Maryland, the District of Columbia and Massachusetts," see http://www.1199seiu.org/about/, accessed December 8, 2008; for changes in California, Gerald Hudson, Memo to Long Term Care Division Steering Committee, "Evaluation of the Reorganization of California's Long Term Care Locals," January 22, 2008, Hudson Memo, in authors' possession.
5. Paul Pringle, "Union, Charity Paid Thousands to Firms Owned by Official's Relatives," *LAT*, August 9, 2008; Pringle, "Service Union Bans Former California Local President for Life," *LAT*, November 27, 2008.
6. Reply to Robert Fitch, "A More Perfect Union?" post to Portside, received as email August 6, 2005. Paul Pringle conversation with E. Boris, December 17, 2008.
7. Kris Maher and David Kesmodel, "Illinois Scandal Spotlights SEIU's Use of Political Tactics," *Wall Street Journal*, December 20, 2008.
8. Conversations with Craig Becker; "Proposed Rules, Department of Labor, Wage and Hour Division, 29 CFR Part 552," September 8, 1995; ANCOR to Maria Echaveste, February 21, 1994; UCPA to Echaveste, February 28, 1994; FOIA Materials. During the first comment period in early 1994, the Wage and Hour Division obtained only 7 comments, all opposed to the change. 29 CFR Part 552, *Federal Register* 66:13 (January 19, 2001), 5485, 5481–89.
9. 29 CFR Part 552, *Federal Register*, 67, no. 67 (April 8, 2002), 16668.
10. On Becker, "Andy Stern's Go-To Guy," *Wall Street Journal*, May 14, 2009; *Thelma L. Harris et al. v. Dorothy L. Sims Registry*, 2001 U.S. Dist. LEXIS 23263; Nahal Toosi, "Ailing NYC Woman at Center of Supreme Court Home-Care Case," *Newsday*, April 13, 2007.
11. *Evelyn Coke v. Long Island Care at Home, LTD and Maryann Osborne*, 267 F.Supp.2d 332 (2003); *Evelyn Coke v. Long Island Care at Home, LTD and Maryann Osborne*, 2004 U.S. App. LEXIS 15191 (2004).
12. Wage and Hour Advisory Memorandum No. 2005–1, From Alfred B. Robinson, Jr., "Application of Section 13(a)(15) to Third Party Employers," December 1, 2005.
13. Press Release, New York City Law Department, Office of the Corporation Counsel, "U.S. Supreme Court Takes Case Impacting City Programs Providing Long-Term Home Health Care," January 8, 2007, at nyc.gov/law, accessed April 17, 2007.
14. Brief Amicus Curiae of AARP in Support of Plaintiff-Appellant; Brief for the Urban Justice Center, Brennan Center for Justice et al. as *Amici Curiae* Supporting Respondent in *Long Island Care at Home, LTD, et al., v. Evelyn Coke*, No. 06-593 in the Supreme Court of the United States. We joined other academics in a brief written by then University of Iowa Law School professor Peggie Smith, *Brief of Historians and Law Professors as Amici Curiae in Support of the Respondent.*
15. In the Supreme Court of the United States, *Long Island Care At Home v. Evelyn Coke*, No. 06-593, Transcript of Oral Testimony, April 16, 2007 (Washington, DC: Alderson Reporting Company, 2007); Nahal Toosi, "Ailing NYC Woman at Center of Supreme Court

Home-Care Case," *Newsday.com*, April 13, 2007, at www.newsday.com/news/loca/newyork/ny-bc-ny, assessed April 17, 2007; Steven Greenhouse, "Justices to Hear Care on Wages of Home Aides," *NYT*, March 25, 2007; Draft Brief by Plaintiff, *Coke v. Long Island Care at Home*, for motion of summary judgment, in authors' possession.

16. "Congress and the Caregivers," *NYT*, June 21, 2007.
17. "Home Care Bill Would Undo DOL's 'Casual Basis' Interpretation," September 24, 2007, at http://www.ohsonline.com/articles/50525/, accessed August 6, 2008.
18. Testimony of Manuela Butler on H.R. 3582, October 25, 2007, 1–2; Testimony of Craig Becker on H.R. 3582, Subcommittee on Workplace Protections of the Committee on Education and Labor, United States House of Representatives, October 25, 2007, 8, at http://edlabor.house.gov/hearings/wp102507.shtml, accessed August 15, 2008.
19. Testimony of Henry Claypool, on H.R.3582, October 25, 2007, 1–2.
20. See web sites: http://www.directcarealliance.org/; http://phinational.org/, accessed August 3, 2009; Douglas Martin, "Evelyn Coke, 74, Dies; Home Care Aide Fought Pay Rule," *NYT*, August 10, 2009; Steven Greenhouse, "Wage Protection for Home Care Workers," *NYT*, December 15, 2011.
21. Catherine Sullivan, "Organizing Home Care Questions," e-mail Exchange, October 18, 2007, in authors' possession.
22. See Fred P. Brooks, "New Turf for Organizing: Family Child Care," *Labor Studies Journal* 29 (January 2005), 53.
23. John Buntin "ADA's Independence Days," *Congressional Quarterly DBA Governing Magazine*, March 2002, 38; "Victory for PCAs and Consumers!" at http://pcavoice.org/, accessed December 8, 2008.
24. Stephen Franklin, "Illinois Agrees to Labor Pact on Child Care," *Chicago Tribune*, December 13, 2005; Brooks, "New Turf for Organizing,"45–47; for child care organizing, see Deborah Chalfie, Helen Blank, and Joan Entmacher, *Getting Organized: Unionizing Home-Based Child Care Providers* (Washington, DC: National Women's Law Center, February 2007), 7, available at http://www.nwlc.org/pdf/GettingOrganized2007.pdf, accessed January 12, 2008.
25. Ellis Boal, "A New Contract and a New Kind of Steward," *Labor Notes*, January 29, 2008, at www.labornotes.org, accessed on June 10, 2011.
26. "12,000 Unite in Missouri Home Care Union," Press Release, May 5, 2010, at http://www.seiu.org/2010/05/12000-unite-in-missouri-home-care-union.php; "5,500 Wisconsin Home Care Providers Unite in Wisconsin's Largest Healthcare Union," at http://www.seiu.org/2010/05/5500-wisconsin-home-care-providers-unite-in-wisconsins-largest-healthcare-union.php, both accessed July 9, 2010.
27. Steven Greenhouse, "Union Boss Says Even Democrats Can Err," *NYT*, January 20, 2002; Shaila K. Dewan, "Health Bill Leaves Out Many Home Care Aides," *NYT*, April 21, 2002; Steven Greenhouse, "For Home-Care Workers, A Fight for Pay, and Respect," *NYT*, May 28, 2002.
28. Steven Greenhouse, "Thousands of Home Aides Begin a Strike," *NYT*, June 8, 2004; Jennifer Steinhauer, "Labor Demands Cast a Rich Major in a Miserly Light," *NYT*, June 10, 2004.
29. Patrick McGeehan, "For New York, Big Job Growth in Home Care," *NYT*, May 25, 2007.
30. Steven Lerner, "An Immodest Proposal: A New Architecture for the House of Labor," *New Labor Forum* 12 (Summer 2003), 12.
31. Steven Greenhouse, "Breakaway Unions Start New Federation," *NYT*, September 28, 2005.
32. Andy Stern, "'Just Us' or 'Justice for All'?," 2, position paper, April 2008, in authors' possession.
33. Phone Interview with K. Kelleher by E. Boris and J. Klein, June 15, 2009.
34. Justice for All, Pass It On, "Recommendations to the SEIU 2008 Convention," 13, in authors' possession.
35. Steve Early, "SEIU's Dial 1-800-Solution Runs into Trouble," *Labor Notes*, June 2011, 5, 13.

36. "Union Contract Called Good Deal for Both Sides," *Chicago Sun-Times*, January 30, 2006; "Members to Vote on New Help At Home Contract," at http://www.seiu880.org/Members_to_vote_on_new_Help_At_Home_contract.aspx; "Health care, child care workers rally to protect quality care," at http://www.seiu880.org/Health_care__child_care_workers_rally_to_protect_quality_care.aspx; all accessed December 7, 2008.
37. Dorothy Sue Cobble and Michael Merrill, "The Promise of Service Unionism," in *Service Work: Critical Perspectives*, Cameron MacDonald and Marek Korczynski, eds. (New York: Routledge, 2009), 153–174.
38. Zachary Coile, "Mortal Battle Unfolding Atop Big Labor Union," *SFC*, March 27, 2008; George Raine, "Labor Groups' Dispute Turns Ugly," *SFC*, December 7, 2008; Executive Summary, "SEIU-UHW's Submission to SEIU's California Long-Term Care Jurisdiction Hearings," July 29, 2008, copy in authors' possession.
39. Interview with Leon Chow by J. Klein and E. Boris, September 8, 2008, UHW San Francisco Office.
40. Hudson Memo, 2–3.
41. Paul Krehbiel, "Members Decry Loyalty Oaths, Cozy Deals: Reform Movement Forms in SEIU," *Labor Notes*, April 28, 2008, no. 349 at http://labornotes.org/node/1583, accessed December 15, 2008.
42. Steve Early, *The Civil Wars in U.S. Labor: Birth of a New Workers Movement or Death Throws of the Old?* (Chicago: Haymarket Books, 2011).
43. "CLASS Act and Workforce Issues Subject of Report," PHI Blog, Policy Works, at http://phinational.org/archives, accessed 6/12/2011; Brett Norman, "End of CLASS Act marks rapid change for White House," Politico, October 14, 2011, at http://www.politico.com/news/stories/1011/66015.html, accessed November 5, 2011.
44. Kevin Sack and Katie Zezima, "Growing Need For Medicaid Puts Added Financial Burden on States," *NYT*, January 22, 2009; Iris Lav, "State Budgets under Stress: Impacts on Unemployment Insurance and Medicaid," Paper Presented at National Academy of Social Insurance, January 21, 2010, Washington, DC; PHI, "Medicaid Matters," April 2011, at www.PHInational.org, accessed June 10, 2011.
45. John Leland, "Cuts in Home Care Put Elderly and Disabled at Risk," *NYT*, July 16, 2010; Marty Omoto, "40,000 People on IHSS Could Face Elimination or Reduction of Services by October," June 18, 2009, at http://www.californiaprogressreport.com/2009/06/40000_people_on.html, accessed August 3, 2009; Anthony York et al., "Brown's Budget Plan," *LAT*, January 11, 2007; "Within Our Means," *NYT*, January 30, 2011.
46. Eileen Boris and Premilla Nadasen, "Domestic Workers Organize!," *WorkingUSA* 11 (December 2008), 413–437; http://www.mujeresunidas.net/english/caring.html; "Caring Hands" flyer, at http://www.caringhandsbayarea.org/index.php?option=com_content&view=article&id=11&Itemid=6, both accessed August 13, 2009; Anna Guevarra, "I am only a caregiver" Redefining the Meaning of 'Skill' among Low Wage and Highly Educated/Skilled Filipino Home Care Workers," unpublished paper presented at the 7th Carework Conference, San Francisco, August 7, 2009.
47. http://www.jfrej.org, accessed August 13, 2009.
48. www.domesticworkersunited.org/programs.php; www.domesticworkersunited.org/campaigns.php, both accessed August 12, 2009.
49. ILO News, "ILO Adopts Rules for Domestic Workers," June 16, 2011, at http://www.capitalfm.co.ke/news/Kenyanews/ILO-adopts-rules-for-domestic-workers-13228.html#ixzz1PlnSU6bY, accessed June 19, 2011; "Caring across Generations Background," May 4, 2011, in E. Boris possession.
50. Claire Ungerson and Suen Yeandle, *Cash for Care in Developed Welfare States* (New York: Palgrave, 2007); Pei-Chia Lan, *Global Cinderellas: Migrant Domestics and Newly Rich Employers in Taiwan* (Durham: Duke University Press, 2006); Ito Peng, "Social Care in Crisis: Gender, Demography, and Welfare State Restructuring in Japan," *Social Politics* 9 (Fall 2002), 411–413.

51. Ungerson and Yeandle, *Cash for Care in Developed Welfare States*; Mary Daly, "Care as a Good for Social Policy," in *Care Work: The Quest for Security*, Mary Daly, ed. (Geneva: ILO, 2002), 42–43.
52. Trudie Knijn and Stijn Verhagen, "Contested Professionalism: Payments for Care and the Quality of Home Care," *Administration & Society* 39 (July 2007), 465–466.
53. Drucilla K. Barker and Susan F. Feiner, "Affect, Race, and Class: An Interpretive Reading of Caring Labor," *Frontiers: A Journal of Women's Studies* 30: 1 (2009), 41–54.

Afterword

1. Miller speaking in "Celebrating 30," at http://www.seiuhcilin.org, accessed July 26, 2014.
2. Direct Care Alliance, Inc., "Home Care Workers Win Minimum Wage and Overtime Protections," Sept. 17, 2013, http://www.directcarealliance.org/document/docWindow.cfm?fuseaction=document.viewDocument&documentid=89&documentFormatId=95, accessed July 21, 2014.
3. Melanie Trottman and Kris Maher, "Labor Department Adds Protections for Home-Health-Care Workers," *Wall Street Journal*, September 17, 2013; WHD News Release, "Minimum wage, overtime protections extended to direct care workers by US Labor Department," September 17, 2013, at http://www.dol.gov/opa/media/press/whd/WHD20131922.htm, accessed July 29, 2014.
4. WHD, "Fact Sheet #79E: Joint Appointment in Domestic Service Under the Fair Labor Standards Act," at http://www.dol.gov/whd/regs/compliance/whdfs79e.htm, accessed July 29, 2014.
5. National Employment Law Project, "Federal Minimum Wage and Hour Protections For Home Care Workers," Oct. 2013, www.nelp.org/page/-justice/2013/NELP-Fact-Sheet-Companionship-Rules-Reform.pdf, accessed July 21, 2014.
6. Wage and Hour Division, U.S. DOL, "Fact Sheet #79F: Paid Family or Household Members in Certain Medicaid-Funded and Certain Other Publicly Funded Programs," at http://www.dol.gov/whd/regs/compliance/whdfs79f.htm, accessed July 29, 2014.
7. "No Reason to Delay Fair Wages," *New York Times*, May 17, 2014; U.S. House of Representatives, Subcommittee on Workforce Protections, Committee on Education and the Workforce, "Redefining Companion Care: Jeopardizing Access to Affordable Care for Seniors and Individuals with Disabilities," 113th Congress, First Sess., November 20, 2013, Serial No. 113–39, at http://www.gpo.gov/fdsys/pkg/CHRG-113hhrg85586/pdf/CHRG-113hhrg85586.pdf, accessed July 29, 2014.
8. Supreme Court of the United States, *Pamela Harris et al. v. Pat Quinn et al.*, typescript of oral argument, January 21, 2014, at http://www.supremecourt.gov/oral_arguments/argument_transcripts/11-681_8mj8.pdf, accessed January 21, 2014.
9. *Pamela Harris et al. v. Pat Quinn et al.*, 573 U.S. _____ (2014), at 30, 32, 38, http://www.supremecourt.gov/opinions/13pdf/11-681_j426.pdf, accessed June 30, 2014.
10. Ben Yount, "Illinois mom takes fight against forced unionization to the Supreme Court," Illinois Watchdog, January 21, 2014, at http://watchdog.org/124523/one-brave-mom-pam-harris-fight-il-unions-nears-end/ accessed February 14, 2014.
11. For our argument, see Brief for *Amicus Curiae* Homecare Historians in Support of Respondents, *Harris v. Quinn*, December 2013, at http://onlabor.files.wordpress.com/2013/12/amicus-brief-homecare-historians.pdf, accessed July 30, 2014.
12. "Statement of Flora Johnson," January 22, 2014, at http://www.seiuhcilin.org/2014/01/22/harris-vs-quinn-case-before-u-s-supreme-court-statement-of-flora-johnson-illinois-home-care-provider-and-chairperson-of-seiu-healthcare-illinois/, accessed February 14, 2014; on Johnson, Eileen Boris and Jennifer Klein, "Front Line Careworkers Still Struggling," *Dissent* (Winter 2012), 46–50.

13. Harris v. Quinn, 573 U.S. ___ (2014), dissent at 6–7.
14. Ibid., dissent at 4.
15. Ibid., at 8.
16. Benjamin Sachs and Catherine Fisk, "Why Should Unions Negotiate for Workers Who Do Not Pay Their Fair Share," *Los Angeles Times*, July 9, 2014, at http://www.latimes.com/opinion/op-ed/la-oe-sachs-unions-supreme-court-20140710-story.html, accessed July 29, 2014.
17. Michelle Chen, "Massachusetts Nannies and Housekeepers Now Protected from Long Days, Abuse, Sexual Harassment," *The Nation*, June 23, 2014, reprinted at http://www.domesticworkers.org/news/2014/massachusetts-nannies-and-housekeepers-now-protected-from-long-days-abuse-sexual, accessed July 29, 2014; ILO C189 at http://www.ilo.org/dyn/normlex/en/f?p=NORMLEXPUB:12100:0::NO::P12100_ILO_CODE:C189; ILO R201 at http://www.ilo.org/dyn/normlex/en/f?p=NORMLEXPUB:12100:0::NO:12100:P12100_INSTRUMENT_ID:2551502:NO, accessed July 29, 2014.
18. See Premilla Nadasen, "Sista' Friends and Other Allies: Domestic Workers United and Coalition Politics," in *New Social Movements in the African Diaspora: Challenging Global Apartheid*, ed. Leith Mullings (New York: Palgrave, 2009), 285–298.

Index